ON THE FRONT LINE

'Marie Colvin was the most courageous journalist I ever knew, and a wonderful reporter and writer.'

JON SNOW, presenter of Channel 4 News

'Marie was an extraordinary figure in the life of *The Sunday Times*, driven by a passion to cover wars in the conviction that what she did mattered. She believed profoundly that reporting could curtail the excesses of brutal regimes and make the international community take notice.' JOHN WITHEROW, Editor of *The Sunday Times*

'To the many who read her dispatches, Marie was one of the great foreign correspondents of her age, known to plunge to the point of deepest conflict and remain there for longer than anyone else. Her byline picture would gaze seriously out of the pages of this paper. But although she was, of course, serious, brave, clever and phenomenally daring, those weren't the qualities that made her such a great friend. Marie was the most feminine of women, the girliest of girls.' ALEX SHULMAN, Editor of British *Vogue*

'She was a brave and tireless reporter and an inspiration to women in her profession.' DAVID CAMERON, Prime Minister

'It was such fun and such a privilege being Marie's friend because she was at once the fearless, committed, globally distinguished war correspondent, and at the same time a total girl's girl. She really cared about her friends. She was kind. She made time for us, she listened, she cheered us up and let us cheer her up. And she would always laugh – especially at herself.' HELEN FIELDING, author

'She was brave, magnificent, tenacious.'
ANDREW NEIL, presenter and former Editor of *The Sunday Times*

'Marie Colvin embodied the highest values of journalism through-out her long and distinguished career as a foreign correspondent for *The Sunday Times*. For years she shone a light on stories that others could not and placed herself in the most dangerous environments to do so.'   WILLIAM HAGUE, Foreign Secretary

'She was passionate, funny and deeply caring. Marie was a lioness – she seemed to be indestructible, she was indomitable.'
   CHRISTIANE AMANPOUR, journalist for ABC News

'The journalistic community have lost one of their finest and their most fearless. Marie Colvin was not only a brave and tireless reporter across many continents and in many difficult situations, she was also an inspiration to women in her profession.'
   ED MILIBAND, Labour leader

'She was a wonderful combination of combat fatigues and elegance. She used to get very cross with me because I said when we first met her she was wearing camouflage, and she absolutely denied this. Her dress sense was incredible. I bet Marie was wearing the most wonderful underwear when she died.'
   JANE BONHAM CARTER, Liberal Democrat politician

'She was not interested in the politics, strategy or weaponry; only the effects on the people she regarded as innocents. "These are people who have no voice," she said.'
   ROY GREENSLADE, *Guardian* journalist

'Exceptionally warm, intelligent, enthusiastic and funny, a person instantly likeable, who made friends wherever she went. She had great physical presence with her good looks and animated features, so when I recall her features now, five days after her death, it is her smiles and laughter that come first to mind.'
   PATRICK COCKBURN, *Independent* journalist

'She was generous and funny and knew precisely the risks she was running. For decades, she has been a ubiquitous presence in the war zones of the world and her reports in *The Times* were admired in the close-knit world of foreign correspondents for their scrupulous and straightforward eloquence.'

DAVID REMNICK, *New Yorker* journalist

'We were all, as a people, better for her. At a time when journalists are being examined as never before, it's time to acknowledge someone who made a difference, a moral difference, to our country and our lives. That was Marie.'

BILL NEELY, International Editor of ITV News

'She was a real nuts and bolts journalist who would get down and work hard to get the story. She'll be sadly missed and this is a great tragedy.' JEREMY BOWEN, BBC Middle East Editor

'She often wrote about the quiet bravery of the civilians. Telling the story wasn't her job. It was the life she lived. She had guts and glamour, brave and beautiful. She had a wicked laugh, she had a great sense of camaraderie in the field.'

LYSE DOUCET, BBC journalist and presenter

On the Front Line

The Collected Journalism
of Marie Colvin

Harper
Press

HarperPress
An imprint of HarperCollins*Publishers*
77–85 Fulham Palace Road
Hammersmith, London W6 8JB
www.harpercollins.co.uk

Published by Harper*Press* in 2012

A catalogue record for this book
is available from the British Library

ISBN 978-0-00-748796-7

Typeset in Minion and Photina by
G&M Designs Limited, Raunds, Northamptonshire
Printed in Great Britain by
Clays Ltd, St Ives plc

MIX
Paper from
responsible sources
FSC™   **FSC™ C007454**
www.fsc.org

A portion of the proceeds from the sale of this book
goes to the Marie Colvin Memorial Fund

The Colvin family has established a memorial fund in honour
of Marie. The fund will direct donations to charitable and
educational organisations that reflect Marie's lifelong dedication
to humanitarian aid, human rights, journalism and education.

We thank you for sharing this information with others
who may be interested.

Donations may be made payable to:

The Marie Colvin Fund at LICF
1864 Muttontown Road
Syosset, N.Y. 11791

More information on the Marie Colvin Memorial Fund,
and online payment options are available at:
www.mariecolvin.org

Marie at a university party during her time at Yale, New Haven, CT.

Marie on the beach, Cyprus, 1987.

Marie with her mother Rosemarie Colvin, at her wedding
to Juan Carlos Gumucio in London.

Marie with nieces Michelle Colvin, right, and Justine Colvin,
Oyster Bay, 2004.

Marie sailing near Zakynthos, 2007.
Photograph by Richard Flaye.

Simply: there's no way to cover war properly without risk. Covering a war means going into places torn by chaos, destruction, death and pain, and trying to bear witness to that. I care about the experience of those most directly affected by war, those asked to fight and those who are just trying to survive.

Going to these places, finding out what is happening, is the only way to get at the truth. Despite all the videos you see on television, what's on the ground has remained remarkably the same for the past 100 years. Craters. Burnt houses. Women weeping for sons and daughters. Suffering. In my profession, there is no chance of unemployment. The real difficulty is having enough faith in humanity to believe that someone will care.

MARIE COLVIN

The Sunday Times, 21 October 2001,
'Bravery is not being afraid to be afraid'

CONTENTS

PART TWO

IRAQ

MIDDLE EAST

IRAN

PART THREE

FOREWORD

To me, a world without Marie is unimaginable. I am just now beginning to experience this shadow of a place, and for the first time there is no Marie to give me comfort or guide me through. Marie had so many friends and colleagues who loved her so deeply, and countless admirers who were awed by her courage as a journalist. While I mourn together with those who loved her and take enormous pride in Marie's accomplishments, my tribute is to my big sister and lost soulmate.

I try to force thoughts of her broken body out of my mind with memories of our time together – the wild adventures and late-night talks, her offbeat advice and unique view of the world. Most of all, I try to recapture the love with which she so totally and constantly enveloped me for as long as I can remember. She was my greatest admirer, my unwavering ally, my fiercest defender. To have someone as brilliant and amazing as Marie offer such love, support and admiration to me is a gift I will always treasure and desperately miss.

Marie was always my hero and to her I was perfection. She claimed me as her own when I was just a toddler, and in her eyes, I could do no wrong. She opened a big, beautiful world to me, full of laughter, excitement and adventure. My earliest memories of Marie are the bedtime stories she used to tell me, like 'postage stamp kisses' – my favourite. Marie would lie in my bed and tell me about some faraway place, with vivid descriptions of the sprawling cities, dusty back roads, flowering countrysides or lush jungles. She told me of the customs, languages and dress of the people who lived there, and what they like to do for fun. She told elaborate stories of queens and medicine women, and the beautiful clothes they wore. I learned from her how people danced in the streets of Rio at Carnival and ran with the bulls in Spain. She opened a world of adventure to me, and we explored it together. Each night, when the story was over, she would plaster me with postage stamp kisses to send me off to explore some new place in my dreams.

As we got older, Marie included me in her life in ways that were extraordinary, in retrospect. She took me with her everywhere, and dressed me to her (not my mother's) liking. We sailed all over Long Island as kids, and later in the Chesapeake Bay and the Florida Keys. We went on protest marches and hung out in the park singing to guitar music during her high school years. I tagged along with her to long classroom lectures and wild parties at Yale. She taught me the lyrics to her favourite songs by Joni Mitchell, Bonnie Raitt and Patsy Cline, and often had me sing them for her friends at parties (Marie could never carry a tune). Marie inspired me to explore the world with an open heart and mind, from backpacking through Europe at seventeen (with a luxurious stop in Paris to visit Marie) through the birth of my daughter in Santiago, Chile, nearly twenty years later.

On my last trip to London, my daughter, now 13, was still young enough to appreciate bedtime stories, and I told her that Aunt Marie was the greatest master storyteller of all time. I remembered the beautiful, exciting world she had created for me as a girl, and was thrilled for Justine to share my experience. Not long after Marie went up to Justine's bedroom, I began to hear loud bangs, crashes and shouts. I went upstairs to find Marie throwing her hands in the air and leaping around the room delivering a full warzone soundtrack for her story, as Justine listened wide-eyed and intent from her bed, resplendent in the gorgeous new pyjamas Aunt Marie had given her. The stories had changed, but in Justine's eyes I saw the same fascination I had felt as a girl basking in Marie's attention.

Marie really was the greatest master storyteller of all time, there is no doubt. She could have written novels, poems or plays and enraptured the world with the gift of her written and spoken words. But Marie chose to devote her gift to bringing the attention of the world to the innocent victims of war. Even as her reporting grew so much more dangerous and intense, and the damage to her body and soul became manifest, she never forgot how to capture the imagination of a young girl, and she never stopped believing in the importance of a little girl's dream. I hope and believe that Marie will continue to inspire young women everywhere, not only as they read about her dedication and talent, but as they dream of the difference just one little girl can make in this world.

Cat Colvin
March 2012

PART ONE

Marie in Amman, Jordan, 1991.
Photograph by Simon Townsley.

Iran–Iraq War

Basra – blitzed and battered, but not beaten

25 January 1987

Marie Colvin sends the first front-line report from inside Basra, Iraq's besieged city.

In Basra, they say the day belongs to Iraq; the night to Iran. Iraq's second city is under siege, and Iranian shells slammed into houses for the seventeenth successive day yesterday.

Two missiles hit residential areas on Friday. Long bursts of automatic fire and the sound of close fighting intermittently carry across the Shatt al-Arab waterway that flows past Basra's corniche to the Gulf.

During the day the Iranian shells fall only about once an hour. But at nightfall the shelling begins in earnest, perhaps because the Iranians are using it to cover troop movements.

The streets remain deserted and only military cars and trucks dare venture out. The shells seem to fall at random throughout the city, crashing into homes, businesses and shops. People here believe that if the Iranians cannot take Basra, they will at least make it uninhabitable.

Although thousands have fled, many remain cowering in homes behind sandbags, piled high to window tops, leaving only cracks to let in daylight and air. Basra has taken on the semblance of a giant military camp, but it has not emptied.

The train I arrived in from Baghdad consisted of 20 coaches filled with soldiers heading to the front. The few women aboard wore the black of mourning.

I took a bus which arrived at 8.30am at Saad Square in the heart of Basra. The shelling began at 8.45am. The few pedestrians on the street started hurrying for cover.

One man stopped and gave me sound advice. 'It's not a good idea to walk around Basra when they are shelling,' he said. 'You're very exposed here.'

The Ashrar neighbourhood is one of the heaviest hit in the city. A nearby hotel had its windows blown out and an air conditioner hung from one screw in a window. Branches from trees and masonry littered the streets. On a road leading into the square there was a large crater with a dead horse lying next to it.

In front of the Sheraton Hotel on the Corniche burned-out cars are scattered along the street. All the windows in the building have been shattered and the empty swimming pool is filled with shrapnel from a shell that blew apart a taverna.

While I was there, another shell slammed into the hotel, but did not explode. The building shuddered. An hour later a shell landed nearby on Al-Watani Street, the main street through the city centre which is lined with stores and night clubs which were thriving only three weeks ago.

I took refuge in a basement with a businessman who had been sleeping behind his desk for 16 hours. He gave a depressing view of the city's chances. 'I think this is how Germany must have felt in the last days of the Second World War,' he said. 'People are just waiting. It's not that they think the Iranians will take Basra, but maybe they will make it impossible for us to live here.'

The western part of the city has escaped heavy shelling, and there shops are still open and people are on the streets. Even at night soldiers stand outside at corner restaurants eating kebabs.

But everywhere there are tales of tragedy. One soldier was crying as he described how three friends had gone out to telephone home when the bombardment appeared to ease on Wednesday. All three were killed by a shell.

The hospitals are overwhelmed. Members of the Popular Army, the militia that handles logistics for the regular army, make daily rounds asking for blood donations and the sick are being moved out of hospitals to make room for soldiers.

Last week, with doctors exhausted by the influx of wounded soldiers, engineers were called to the hospital to help with amputations.

At about 9 on the evening of my arrival the incoming fire became more frequent. The Iraqis sent up huge pink flares that hung suspended over the Shatt for 10 minutes. It was night time, and night time in Basra belongs to Iran.

Black banners of death fly over Baghdad

25 January 1987

After more than two weeks of fighting, the Iranian offensive which began on 9 January appears to have established a bridgehead of about 40 square miles, according to military analysts here. The Iranian front lines are about six miles east of Basra, writes Marie Colvin in Baghdad.

Iranian troops have infiltrated at night, adding incrementally to their occupied ground. But they have not been able to breach the first main defence line between them and their target of Basra, on the east side of the Shatt al Arab waterway which, farther south, forms the border between the two countries.

Iraq has not launched a counter-offensive on the ground, the only way it could drive the Iranians out of the marshes. Iraqi officials insist this is a deliberate strategy. Iraq's acting prime minister,

Taha Yassin Ramadan, in an interview with *The Sunday Times*, said: 'We could easily repulse the Iranians but such an operation would be at the expense of losing the opportunity to kill as many of them as possible. Oddly enough they keep up their influx into this killing zone.'

Both states have about 1 million men under arms. But Iran, with its population of 45m, can afford more casualties. It relies on 'human waves' of young volunteers, who have been promised heaven if they are killed, to overwhelm the enemy's initial defences, before sending in the revolutionary guards.

Iraq, with its smaller population of 14 million, cannot afford the huge casualties such tactics entail.

As the Americans realised in Vietnam, a ground counter-offensive would prove costly in Iraqi lives and would be politically unacceptable at home. So the Iraqis in this battle, as before, have stood back and used their superiority in arms to shell the Iranian positions.

The Iranian show of muscle is potentially frightening because of Ayatollah Khomeini's vow that he will spread his brand of Shi'ite fundamentalism to the Gulf, beyond Iraq. Kuwait is the next state in line and the sound of the fighting in southern Iraq can be heard late at night in its capital, where the summit will be held. But Iraq goes into the summit holding a strong hand. Other Islamic states are known to resent the fact that Iran has completely ignored Iraq's peace initiatives. Iran has said it will not end the war until the regime of President Saddam Hussein is ousted, while Iraq would settle for peace and a return to international borders. Iran has also lost its claim to be a pure revolutionary state because of the recent revelations that it bought arms from 'Great Satan' America and 'Little Satan' Israel.

Wine and lipstick lay Iran's ghost to rest

29 October 1989

It might have been Manhattan. Guests sipped Scotch or wine and grumbled about the government. The last visitors dined on pot luck from the fridge and took a late-night tour of the wine cellar.

But this was Tehran. The host bought his Scotch on the black market for about 600,000 rials a bottle, or £372. The 'cellar' was a backyard shed hiding huge bottles of wine brewed from a Boots kit. Tame peacocks preened on the lawn and someone quietly smoked opium.

Iran has changed under its new president, Hojatolisalam Hashemi Rafsanjani. Most well-to-do Iranians have made their peace with the regime, and the mullahs need their skills. Their lifestyle is tolerated so long as it stays behind the villa walls in wealthy, tree-shaded northern Tehran.

Although women must still cover their heads in public, a new Tehran 'look' has replaced the voluminous chador. Trendy women wear stove-pipe jeans and high heels under three-quarter-length black raincoats and cover their heads with flowered scarves. Lipstick and black eyeliner have returned.

The feeling of relaxation can be deceptive. A group of West Germans had to be rescued by their ambassador a few weeks ago after a local revolutionary committee broke up their late-night party. Three other foreigners sentenced to 90 lashes for having affairs with local women had to be spirited out of the country.

But among Iranians, even former royalists have come round to Rafsanjani as the alternative to radical clerics and renewed revolutionary turmoil. 'He's a mullah but he's the only hope for Iran,' said a wealthy doctor.

Having squared the rich, Rafsanjani faces a new and much more serious threat. Tehran's poor southern suburbs, home to the 'oppressed' in whose name Ayatollah Khomeini proclaimed revolution in 1979, are seething.

Wages are low, prices mount daily, and housing is hard to find. Hopes raised by Rafsanjani's election in August are fading fast. The discontent is dangerous. The poor feel they have as much claim to the revolution as the mullahs. Their street protests drove out the shah, and they could do it again.

Anger is openly expressed. Ismail, 34, a shoemaker in the Shahpur bazaar in southern Tehran, was one of Khomeini's foot soldiers.

'Everyone around here went out in the streets,' he recalls. 'Even the six-year-olds. They promised us everything. They said it was Allah's land and we would get some of it.'

Ten years later, Ismail pays 40,000 of his 60,000-rial monthly wage (£37) to rent one ground-floor room in which he, his wife and three children eat, sleep and receive visitors. The home is meticulously clean but shabby and cramped.

The family's energy goes into finding food. Subsidies should make staples such as sugar, rice and cooking oil cheap. But Ismail's wife cannot remember the last time the government distributed rice in their neighbourhood.

A black market mafia controls food distribution and locals say government officials take bribes. Corruption goes beyond the bazaar. A surgeon said middle-men received state money for drugs but provided cheaper, often toxic, substitutes and pocketed the difference.

Despite the privations, Rafsanjani still enjoys tremendous goodwill among the poor as well as the rich. But Iran's future will be determined by whether he can overcome radicals in the regime who oppose both his desire to open Iran to the West and to give more freedom to private businessmen at home.

To secure his position he has been quietly dismantling revolutionary committees, set up to enforce Khomeini's line, and sending their members back to their own jobs.

He also seems to get support from an unexpected source. Khomeini's daughter, Fatima, said last week she was considering running for parliament in elections due in December. She is intelligent and more astute than her ambitious brother, Ahmed.

She said Rafsanjani's policies 'followed the Imam's mind', and she can cite Khomeini's name with more authority than any radical.

Rumours abound of struggles in the leadership. The strangest concerns a mysterious shipment of gold allegedly linked to radicals trying to finance their own projects.

One night earlier this month national television showed film of two lorries loaded with 10 tonnes of gold ingots, worth $120 million, allegedly captured near the border with Pakistan. Three days later the government announced the bars were in base metal painted gold. Nevertheless the entire smuggled shipment went to the central bank. Ominous graffiti reads: Khar Khodefi 'You can't fool us here'.

The unsettled climate comes at a time when Rafsanjani is trying to find an accommodation with the United States so that he can convince foreign investors their money will be secure in Iran. But the situation is stalemated. President George Bush wants Rafsanjani to show good faith by securing the release of hostages in Lebanon. Rafsanjani told western correspondents last week that Iran needed a western gesture of good faith first.

There is so little contact between them that a friendly embassy sends facsimiles of the *Tehran Times*'s leaders to Washington every day because Americans for a while believed the regime was planting messages for the administration in the newspaper's editorial page.

Middle East

Soviet settlers jolted by the promised land

ARIEL, WEST BANK

11 February 1990

Dmitri Rafalovsky had just arrived off a flight from the flatlands of the Ukraine. Now he stood in Ariel, a small town in the occupied West Bank of Israel, and stared at the starkly beautiful view.

In the distance he could see picturesque villages with stone houses wedged among unfamiliar hills. Everything looked peaceful in the promised land.

But what he and his wife, Elizabeth, did not know when they arrived here last week was that they had abandoned the Soviet Union with its anti-Semitism and threat of pogroms for a land where the villages they were now looking at housed Palestinian Arabs in revolt against their Israeli masters.

The shock was considerable. 'What do you mean, this is the West Bank? Oh my God, don't tell my wife!' he said. Rafalovsky, 55, knew only too well the dangers; Soviet television had been full of the violence for over a year, although all seemed quiet now. 'It doesn't look that dangerous,' he muttered, doubtfully.

The Rafalovskys are a tiny part of a mass emigration of Jews from the Soviet Union which is changing the demographic map of Israel. Fearful of the changes at home, and witnessing growing signs of hostility and violence, they are flooding into Israel.

The surge has been relentless. Last year 13,000 entered; in January this year 4,500 arrived; in the first week of February no fewer than 1,300 came in.

Because there are no direct flights from the Soviet Union, charter planes are arriving almost daily from East European capitals carrying the latest victims of the diaspora.

The numbers coming in are now so great that the predictions last year of 100,000 look inadequate. Some observers expect between 500,000 and 1m will enter Israel over the next few years, changing for ever a country of just 4m inhabitants.

Rafalovsky, like many of the Soviet Jews who disembarked last week, has only a vague notion of Israel. All he knew was that he wanted to leave the Soviet Union and, with the door to the United States closed, an Israeli visa was the only quick way out.

He was still vague about how he had arrived in Ariel. 'We were at Ben Gurion airport in the reception office, and the man from Ariel told me it was a small town in the mountains with not many people. He showed me on the map and said, "See, it is in the middle of Israel." I said it sounded like the place for me.'

It was only dawning on him now that he had arrived in the midst of a controversy equal to anything in the Soviet Union.

Soviet Jews are meant to be able to settle where they like, and there are clear Israeli government denials that they are being encouraged into the occupied territories.

Everyone knows, especially the United States, Israel's most generous benefactor, that immigration into these lands could jeopardise the already delicate Middle East peace process.

Despite the risks, it became evident last week that the government is concealing how many Soviet Jews are settling there. Figures released on Friday said only 63 had settled in the West Bank. In Ariel alone, however, an estimated 150 people have arrived in the past four months.

It has been a difficult choice for the Rafalovskys. Despite the intifada, they saw advantages in their new West Bank home. Their two-bedroom house is larger than their Kiev apartment, and they have brought their 17-year-old son, Vadim, and Elizabeth's elderly mother.

They have also been overwhelmed by their welcome. Neighbours have taken them shopping and have invited them to dinner. They have received a government grant for monthly rent, food and Hebrew lessons. Their first days are spent in a daze at the amount of food in the shops and the fact they are in a Jewish state.

Above all, they have escaped anti-Semitism. 'I have lived with anti-Semitism all my life. I am accustomed to it. But my son is very intelligent and he should have a chance,' said Rafalovsky.

Nobody underestimates how tough it is for these immigrants to start afresh. Few speak Hebrew. They arrive with only their luggage and $140, the maximum they are allowed to take out of the Soviet Union.

In turn they have triggered euphoria among the normally cynical Israelis, who have agonised about criticism over their treatment of Palestinians. 'This has made us feel special again. Israelis suddenly feel desired. It's the same feeling we had after the 1967 war,' said Gad Benari, a spokesman for the Jewish Agency, which handles the immigration.

But the immigrants do face a problem over their Jewishness. Under Israeli law, all Jews have a right to return to their homeland. This influx, however, is very different from the rush of Soviet 'refuseniks' in the 1970s.

They were committed Zionists who had waited in virtual internal exile for exit visas, spending the years studying Hebrew. Few of the new arrivals are religious. Many have never been to a synagogue and are the children of mixed marriages, which will raise problems with the orthodox Jews.

But for now, the benefits outweigh the problems. Most Soviet Jews feel satisfied because they have enough money to live, an apartment and work, however menial.

For most it is enough to escape the Soviet Union. There, Jews are being blamed for the failures of the economy and the uncertainty of the political situation. 'What I can't believe is that any of my Jewish friends stayed behind,' says Victor Savitsky, an engineer who arrived with his wife and their tiny daughter.

Others talk of being barred from universities by anti-Semitism and of the virulently anti-Semitic organisation, Pamyat, which has been holding rallies in cities.

The desire to leave the Soviet Union is now so great that an estimated 12,000 Soviet Jews cannot get seats on planes. The Israelis are trying to persuade the Moscow authorities to allow direct flights to Israel, but for now most immigrants come through Bucharest or Budapest. The Savitskys waited four months before they could buy a plane ticket.

Desperation has bred daring. One couple, Mark and Louisa Puzis, drove their Lada from the Ukraine with their two-month-old baby in the back, trading vodka in exchange for petrol.

Israel is just coming to terms with the magnitude of the problem. The system of absorption is showing signs of falling apart. Reception centres are full and the government budget is overspent.

Critics say the government has been slow to deal with an emerging crisis. Resources in Israel are scarce. There is high unemployment and 20% inflation. 'We should be treating this like a war situation,' said Michael Kleiner, head of the Absorption Committee at the Knesset, Israel's parliament.

He is trying to convince the government to cut red tape and provide money. He has proposed that Israel should stop all development for two years and put that money towards absorbing the new immigrants.

'Responsible people won't even make estimates on how many will arrive or how much money we will need,' said Kleiner. 'Teddy Kollech [mayor of Jerusalem] has been waiting for 20 years to finish a soccer stadium for Jerusalem. He can certainly wait another two years.'

Love sours for Romeo and Juliet of the West Bank: Avi Marek and Abir Mattar

JERUSALEM

1 April 1990

The script would probably have been rejected by even the most schmaltzy Hollywood producer. Abir, a 19-year-old Palestinian beauty who has gone home to her West Bank village to stay with her mother, meets Avi, a dashingly handsome Israeli officer who spots her when he careers by in his jeep. They go together like humous and pitta bread and talk of marriage.

If the film were ever made, love would no doubt conquer the differences of race, politics and religion. But in the harsh world of the occupied territories, life is more complicated.

Last week, the star-crossed lovers were both outcasts from their communities. Avi was suspended pending the outcome of a military investigation into his breach of the regulations forbidding fraternisation with Palestinians. Abir was hiding in a Palestinian hotel.

The story of Avi Marek and Abir Mattar is a rare glimpse of the human dramas hidden beneath the conventional rocks and riots image of the intifada. Marek is a 30-year-old Israeli captain whose infantry unit is stationed in Beit Jalla, a mostly Christian village that has virtually closed down during the three years of the Palestinian uprising.

Home life held few joys. He had married a much older woman, Rivka, less than a year ago and lived in her flat in a sterile apartment block in the settlement of Gilo outside Jerusalem. But it was better than his own neighbourhood, Shmuel Hanavi, a poor suburb of Jerusalem populated mostly by Sephardic Jews, immigrants from Arab countries.

Marek, who speaks Arabic, by all accounts fell at first sight for Mattar, who was educated in a convent school in Bethlehem and used to babysit for tourist families.

Mattar says it was mutual. In her hotel room last week, she looked at herself in the mirror and smiled when she said: 'Yes, I love him. We met for the first time eight months ago; we have been happy ever since.'

Sitting looking out on a view of a west Jerusalem street, the Jewish side of the divided city, she reflects on how circumscribed her life has become. She cooks meals on a gas burner in the room and feels out of place among package-trip tourists who fill the lobby. She is also three months pregnant with Marek's baby.

But Mattar says her life has always been difficult. Her father drank and gambled until her mother kicked him out, and she married at 16 to a man who already had a wife and five children. When he was imprisoned she returned home to Beit Jalla with a child.

Marek began his courtship by calling to her from his army jeep as she walked to a friend's house. Soon her mother, Nina, noticed she was out all night every night.

'When I asked,' she said, 'Abir replied that it was none of my business. Then I noticed an army jeep would stop outside and beep. The jeep seemed to be around all the time.'

Nina worried that her daughter's relationship would bring unwanted attention. The Mattar family was already ostracised. Nina's lifestyle is hardly suited to a traditional Arab village. Last week she dressed to greet visitors in leopard-print stretch pants and a black lace top.

Nina went out to work when her husband left, something that is not done in traditional Arab culture, and had a series of boyfriends before remarrying. 'I'm not a virgin,' she said, chain-smoking as she looked out at the village of sun-splashed stone homes. 'I've always had a boyfriend. That doesn't make me a whore like everyone in this town says. Look at my apartment, if I was a whore I would have made some money. I've only one bed and not even a proper bathroom.'

She also collaborated with the Israeli occupying forces. Left with seven children and spurned by her neighbours, she says she felt few loyalties. The police gave her 200 shekels (about £70) every time she passed them information. She stopped when the intifada began.

Before that, such activities meant ostracism. Now, with young teenagers controlling the streets and talking of purifying the Palestinian community, they are life-threatening. About 200 Palestinians have been killed for collaboration or prostitution.

But although Nina warned her daughter she was endangering the family, there was little a mother could do. 'Their love was burning. Avi was crazy about her and she lost her head.' The young couple would return together in broad daylight after nights of passion in Marek's jeep and Mattar would bring him coffee before he returned to his unit.

The family began to receive threats and Marek made things worse. He and his unit began picking up local teenagers and beating them. Nina says she thinks he was trying to show off to her daughter.

Desperate, Nina complained to the police and sent word to Marek's Israeli wife. The police ignored her but his wife came down and staked out the house in the Arab village. When Marek and Mattar returned, she ran out into the street with a kitchen knife. Mattar made off in his jeep but the story was too public to be kept quiet.

The military suspended Marek. Mattar found a mongrel dog hanging in the family toilet, dead, its head in the water. She quickly left town. Publicity about the case has made it the gossip of Israelis as well as Palestinians.

Mattar says she and Marek plan to marry after they both divorce. She says she will convert to Judaism. 'I can't go back to live among the Arabs,' she said. But she is worried that Marek's return to Israel may change him. He has been heavily criticised in the Hebrew press.

Marek now faces a military tribunal to explain the liaison. His defence is that he was only fraternising with Mattar in a patriotic endeavour to recruit her as a spy. At the moment observers are not betting on a happy ending to the tale.

Desperately seeking answers in the Arafat slipstream: Yasser Arafat

5 June 1990

The Times

When people know you have spent a year making a film about Yasser Arafat, the question they ask most often is 'Were you ever afraid?' At times I felt frustrated, angry, despairing and very tired, but not afraid. In his manner, Arafat is one of the less threatening people you are likely to meet.

Making a documentary of him takes endurance, not courage. We had flown into Tunis for a scheduled interview to begin our filming. But Arafat was in Baghdad. The film opens with a Tunis to Baghdad telephone call. It is 2am and Arafat seems to think the only way we can get a connection in Baghdad in time to meet him is to find a boat to Paris. We agree instead to fly separately to China where he is due for a state visit, then fly back together in his borrowed Iraqi jet.

This scene must cause great pain to BBC accountants. But at the time it seemed the ideal trip. We would film behind the scenes in an exotic location while the terrorist-turned-statesman wheeled and dealed, then have him as a captive interviewee for the hours it took to fly back to the Middle East. The latter was the most alluring. Arafat grows bored in interviews and will often stand up, unclip his microphone and thank you as he walks out.

But the Chinese Foreign Ministry called Arafat while we were somewhere over Pakistan and said: 'We cannot receive you, the students are causing trouble.' We headed back to Tunis, arriving in

Marie with Yasser Arafat, *c.*1994.

time to board his borrowed Iraqi jet and set off to the summit in Casablanca. But the China trip did pay off. Arafat takes everything personally. Had we decided not to go it would have signalled a lack of commitment, however well-founded our misgivings.

When we finally caught up with him, he owed us one. We were instantly famous in PLO ranks as the crew that had gone to Peking to see the 'Old Man' and been stood up. Everyone had a similar tale; this time it was not Arafat's fault, but it usually is. People around him, a travelling entourage that is both family and staff, began helping with tips on the etiquette of living alongside him. One of my journal entries notes a word of advice from a senior aide: 'When I break your foot, you have gone wrong.'

Arafat's schedule is exhausting and it wears down everyone around him. Half the hotels in Tunis seem to be filled with people waiting to see Arafat. Fighters with blood rivalries meet in the lobby of the Hilton and turn their backs. Arafat maintains his own rigid personal organisation within the chaos around him. Days are for seeing to problems such as parents seeking university tuition for their children. Serious business takes place at night, dating from the time the PLO was an underground organisation. Meetings begin about 9pm and rarely end before 3am. Everyone is expected to be at Arafat's call.

He never tells anyone, even close aides, his schedule in advance for security reasons. When you fly with him you do not know your destination until you take off. Asking a simple question at breakfast such as 'What are you doing today?' brings startled stares from aides and silence from Arafat.

The PLO is Arafat's life and he expects the same commitment from everyone around him. He accepts planes and villas from Arab leaders, but remains a nomad and just out of their control. All his villas look the same – sterile, furnished with a print or two of Jerusalem, a television, some nondescript sofas and a desk. The head of the Palestinian government travels in four suitcases: one for his uniforms, one for his fax machine, one for 'in' and 'out' faxes and one for a blanket to curl up in for cat naps.

His obsessive precision can be maddening. He arranges his keffiyeh headdress meticulously every day in the same way. It must hang down his shoulder in the shape of the map of Palestine. He empties his machinegun pistol precisely as his jet takes off, carefully lining up the bullets on his tray. He marks every single fax sent to the PLO with a felt-tip red pen. But doubts begin to set in when one spends a lot of time around him. Does Arafat really have to read every single fax? Does he have to control every disbursement of funds, the purchase of an office desk in Singapore? It is Jimmy Carter as PLO leader.

Arafat is up on every detail of running the organisation, but never takes time to review policy, listen to advice or plan ahead. The PLO is run from moment to moment from Arafat's head. The main criticism one hears in the ranks of the PLO is of this autocratic style. Arafat brooks no criticism and, as a result, many educated and independent Palestinians have opted out.

Now, when he desperately needs good advice on the workings of the western world as he tries to convince it that he is sincere in his current drive for a peaceful settlement with Israel, few around him know its ways. He himself is unsophisticated about the West, not surprisingly, as he spent most of his youth organising a resistance movement and has been banned from most of it for his adult life.

So why do Palestinians follow this unlikely leader? In person, Arafat is warm and inspires devotion. Palestinians who disagree with his views respect his devotion to the cause. He has always managed to compromise and lead by finding the highest common denominator within the fractious Palestinian movement. Arafat has no political ideology. He wants one thing: to liberate the homeland of his people. He has become more than a leader. For most Palestinians he is a symbol of their aspirations.

Arafat today is a desperate man. He is 60, has no heirs, and wants to achieve something tangible before he dies. In renouncing terrorism and recognising Israel in 1988, he played his best card and cannot understand why he has not received more support from the United States in convincing Israel to make a similar concession.

Arafat is now flying around even more obsessively than when we were filming, trying to stave off attacks from radicals within his own organisation and from Arab states who say he has given everything in return for nothing. Arafat is hoping to convince enough people to stay with him, hoping to keep the organisation together long enough, hoping to stay alive long enough, so that he can one day land his own plane in Palestine.

Home alone in Palestine: Suha Arafat

19 September 1993

When Yasser Arafat went to Washington, his wife stayed in Tunis. But she wasn't hiding away. Marie Colvin profiles the determined Mrs Arafat.

Suha was never going to have it easy. She faced an entrenched PLO bureaucracy where proximity to Arafat meant power. But there was little they could do: by all accounts it was a love match. For the historic peace deal last week, Yasser Arafat wore a uniform, a keffiyeh that caught the slight breeze like a jib sail, and the designer stubble it might be said he pioneered. His wife Suha wore red. But while he was standing on the White House's South Lawn, the PLO leader's 29-year-old, French-educated wife was sitting at home in the couple's whitewashed villa in Tunis, while the wives of Bill Clinton and Yitzhak Rabin were escorted to their seats on the South Lawn.

Arafat would no doubt have liked her to attend, but his advisers counselled him that bringing along his chic young wife would set Palestinian conservatives and radicals alike clucking away that he was treating the signing of the Palestinian–Israeli peace accord as a social event. They shuddered at the imagined sniping: Palestinians are dying in Gaza and she is parading herself in the White House.

So the Arafats were foiled. Well, not quite. She snapped on her gold earrings, donned her favourite Paris couture suit, a tasteful scarlet number decorated with jewelled buttons, and invited the CNN correspondent Richard Blystone to come and watch the ceremony *chez elle*. Blystone brought along a satellite dish and broadcast Suha's thoughts and plans live to the television audience of several million watching the historic ceremony.

Standing on the mosaic portico of the marital home, she told Blystone how she was happy 'to stay with my people in Tunis to share with them this great historical moment'.

She spoke of her future role as the first lady of Palestine in echoes of Hillary Clinton. 'I think I have to assume great responsibilities. I must concentrate on health care for the casualties of the intifada and for all the Palestinians all over the world, to compensate for their long years of suffering.'

The public relations coup epitomised her deft manoeuvring since Arafat, a confirmed bachelor who for years had vowed he was 'married to Palestine', shocked the Palestinian community in July 1991 by wedding a pretty blonde less than half his age.

She recalls first hearing of her future husband when she was four years old and 'hiding in fear' in her family's basement in Nablus as Israeli soldiers searched the West Bank city for a resistance leader named Arafat. In 1988, because of her fluent French and the long association of her mother Raymonda with the PLO (she founded the first Palestinian news agency in the occupied territories), Suha was asked to help out during an Arafat visit to Paris where she was living after finishing her education at the Sorbonne.

Within weeks Arafat asked her to come to Tunis as his personal assistant. Soon she was flying around the world with him and had supplanted his long-time secretary, Um Nasr. When he married Suha, there was a hair-pulling cat-fight between the two women at Arafat's office. Um Nasr, a forty-something woman who had dedicated her life to the revolution, felt that she would make a much better wife.

Much of the resentment of Suha seems inspired not by anything she has done but rather by what she is. She is neither a traditional Arab wife in a culture that is still very conservative, nor is she the politicised revolutionary that many assumed Arafat would choose were he ever to wed. She likes French fashion and perfumes and visits Paris to stock up. Her upper-class trappings rankle among Palestinians more than the difference in age or religion (she is a Greek Orthodox Christian, he a Sunni Muslim).

For years Arafat's nomadic existence and paucity of possessions had been a symbol of his refugee people; now Palestinians had a first lady who said: 'It's so difficult to take all of the luggage and go all over.'

But Suha is no bimbo. She comes from a prominent Palestinian family; her father is a wealthy banker and likes to talk of how her ancestors lived in a crusader castle. She is trying to carve out a middle role, somewhere between being a traditional wife and a public figure in her own right.

She recently took along a film crew with her to visit a Palestinian orphanage in Tunis to publicise their plight. Arafat has symbolically adopted all the children, most of whose parents are considered martyrs of the Palestinian cause. And she has founded a society to care for Palestinian children.

But unlike Hillary Clinton, who seems to tolerate Bill's presence only because it gives her the power to implement her own programmes, Suha genuinely seems to adore Arafat. She pours him tea in the morning and nags him to rest. His schedule is less erratic these days, although he still maintains his nocturnal habits, often meeting with other PLO officials until three or four in the morning.

'She is suffering with me,' Arafat said last week during his Washington visit. 'I am working 18-hour days.'

But she has given the PLO leader the chance to think of a home as well as a homeland.

Arafat thrives amid cut and thrust of peace

MIDDLE EAST

9 January 1994

For a man who was supposed to be going mad under the gruelling pressure of negotiations with Israel, Yasser Arafat, the Palestine Liberation Organisation leader, was in an extraordinarily good mood last week.

He opened a meeting of Palestinian engineers in Tunis, joking that if his political career did not work out he could always join their ranks and resume his former profession. He met for three days with a delegation of disgruntled Palestinians from the occupied territories.

He dispatched Farouq Qadoomi, the PLO foreign minister, to try to patch things up with King Hussein of Jordan. He met an all-party group of British MPs and a Gaza businessman with plans to build a floating port.

He also delivered a New Year's Day address from his Tunis headquarters to a carphone in Yarmouk Square in Gaza; and he persuaded the executive committee, his cabinet, to stand firm in the latest contretemps with Israel over talks on the implementation of their peace accord. All the while, faxes and telephone calls flew back and forth between Arafat, his representative in Cairo, and Israel to resolve the deadlock in negotiations.

It was all in a week's work. Arafat has changed very little in his last three decades as a Palestinian leader, much less in the three months since the peace agreement was signed in Washington. But at 64, he has been rejuvenated by Israel's recognition of the PLO, working more hours than ever before, impatient with constraints. On New Year's Eve he paused only for a piece of celebratory cake before signing his first working paper of the year at five minutes past midnight.

Arafat wants the peace accord to go ahead and he is twisting arms, using financial pressure, threatening those who do not agree with him and playing off internal rivalries for all that he is worth. He even bangs the table in meetings of the executive committee, and, heaven forbid, has been known to shout.

He is acting like a leader; yet this behaviour has led to charges that his style of governing is undermining the peace process and even to absurd reports that he is mentally unstable.

Perhaps this is because he has actually done something he has been criticised for not doing during his entire leadership of the Palestinian movement. It has long been the conventional wisdom that Arafat is incapable of taking the bold steps required of a leader, insisting instead on securing the consensus of even the most radical PLO faction.

When he signed the peace accord with Israel last September, Arafat took a bold and dangerous step for the first time, leaving behind anyone whom he could not convince to join him. He felt Yitzhak Rabin, the Israeli prime minister, was offering the best deal possible and that if he waited to bring along every fractious member of the PLO, that handshake on the White House lawn would still be merely a dream. In his view, those who are now accusing him of being autocratic are the same people who previously lambasted him for failing to take the initiative.

The second criticism that has lately been floated is that Arafat's style of leadership has opened serious divisions in the PLO and that this threatens the peace process. Israel has tried to play on these divisions, making it clear for example that it would prefer to deal with Abu Mazen, the senior PLO official who signed the peace accord in Washington.

This is a serious misinterpretation of what is going on inside the PLO. In its decades of scrutiny of its enemy, Israel may have missed the forest for the trees. Although the Israeli intelligence services can identify which individual Palestinian mounted such-and-such an operation, they do not appear able to explain to their government how the PLO works.

In fact, titles mean little. Power is based on shifting internal alliances, party membership, past history, and money. Arafat is the unquestioned leader because he works the system best and because he rises above all of them as the lasting symbol of Palestinian nationalism.

Even Arafat's most vocal opponents have not called for his replacement; they know there is nobody else who can keep the organisation united behind this peace accord. There is criticism in the PLO ranks, but this reflects the changes in Palestinian politics rather than any change in Arafat.

For years, there have been divisions along ideological lines, from the Marxist left to the Islamicists on the right. That is all irrelevant today. The divisions are now social and economic, and Arafat is having to juggle them, conducting the peace talks while he tries to put together a reliable and competent team for his new government.

He has to balance the demands of returning guerrillas and wealthy Palestinian businessmen who have made their money in the diaspora and who now want to run the economy of the new Palestinian entity; between Palestinian technicians who have worked in the West and loyal political appointees who are afraid there will be no place for them; between Palestinians inside the occupied territories, who feel they have borne the brunt of the occupation, and those returning, who feel they have sacrificed normal lives for the revolution.

The entire situation is in flux; nobody knows what his future will be, so everyone has a word for or against any move Arafat makes. But it is self-defeating for Israel to search for chinks at the top of the PLO.

There is a danger of misinterpreting events. Last week a delegation, headed by Haidar Abdel-Shafi, a soft-spoken Gaza doctor who led the PLO negotiating team in Washington, came to Tunis with a petition signed by 118 Palestinians. The visit was seen outside the PLO as an attack that could break Arafat; in fact, he had invited the delegation to discuss criticism of the way he has been proceeding with the implemention of the accord.

They talked for three days. They did not get all they wanted but Arafat agreed that Abdel-Shafi should head a 'national debate' on the future of the Palestinian entity. As he left, Abdel-Shafi said: 'Arafat is monopolising power but we cannot blame Abu Ammar [Arafat] when no members of the executive committee stand up to insist on sharing this power.'

Arafat talks openly about criticism: 'We are now facing a new era, and in this new era no doubt we can expect hesitation, criticism, worries, misunderstandings. I am not leading a herd of sheep.'

Rabin complains that dealing with Arafat is like dealing in a 'Middle East bazaar'. Why is he surprised? Arafat is trying through any means to get the best he can out of what Palestinians see as a pretty bad deal. Arafat faced severe criticism for making too many compromises when he signed the peace agreement. Now that he has refused to compromise further, his support is growing daily.

The PLO leader is difficult to deal with. That is why he has survived. He has managed to slip through the grasp of every Arab state trying to control him – Jordan, Syria, Egypt, to name just a few. He survived in 1970 when the Jordanian king turned his army against the Palestinian guerrillas in Black September, and in 1982 when Israel turned its might against him in Lebanon.

Rabin, when he shook Arafat's hand in Washington, seemed to be acknowledging that no matter how much he despised Arafat, the PLO leader was the only possible partner for peace. Since then, the Israeli prime minister has conducted peace negotiations not as if he was dealing with a partner but with an enemy that must be controlled and contained to the most minute detail. The last Israeli negotiating document stipulated that there should be opaque glass between the partitions at crossing points.

In making such details the focus of negotiations, and in seeking to divide and conquer, Israel has lost sight of what it agreed to do in Washington – make peace with the PLO, led by Arafat, for better or for worse. Rabin should begin dealing again with Arafat as a partner in peace. And the judgement of Arafat should be left to when it really matters, when he enters his homeland and heads the government.

Rabin last week told his cabinet: 'We will let them sweat.' Who? The PLO?

'Look at me,' said Arafat on Friday night. 'I'm not sweating.'

Libya

Frightened Libyans await the next blow: sanctions

TRIPOLI

19 April 1992

The omens had been bad all week. Colonel Muammar Gadaffi lay tucked up in bed with tonsillitis, UN sanctions had closed off the country and Russian military advisers haggled for suitcases in the souk before making a break for the border. When the chill Hamsin wind blew in off the desert it seemed that even the weather was conspiring against the Libyan leader.

Out on the streets, Libyans felt anxious, vulnerable and isolated. While the sanctions imposed last week caused inconvenience not hardship, they were a severe psychological blow. Once again the Libyan people felt trapped in confrontation with the West. They are dreading the next turn of the screw. Oil sanctions? Another air strike?

The disgruntled middle-class expresses resentment only in private. At a dinner party in Tripoli last week guests lamented how Libya's wealth had been frittered away, siphoned off to military and revolutionary movements all over the world.

'We are only 4m Libyans and we export 1m barrels of oil a day,' a businessman said. 'We could be like Saudi Arabia. Instead look at us.'

His expansive wave of disgust took in the shabby clothes of his countrymen, the dirty hospitals where patients often sleep two to a bed and the vast, grimy supermarkets like the Souk al Jumaa that stand empty or display rows of plastic candelabra from Romania.

Such anger is, of course, impotent because Gadaffi brooks no opposition. After rumblings of discontent, he has reinstated his 'revolutionary committees', the young shock troops that were stood down three years ago after an outcry over their 'excesses'.

The escalating tension evoked memories of the weeks leading up to the American bombing of Tripoli and Benghazi in 1986, during which at least 70 civilians, including Gadaffi's adopted daughter, were killed. On television, announcers condemn George Bush as 'unjust' and read telegrams of support. 'The crusaders think they can humiliate these people, the Libyan people, but they are mistaken,' raged one Muslim preacher in a televised sermon. 'We will bend our heads only to Allah.'

The appeals may be the same but there is a key difference. Gone is the fury of the organised daily demonstrations; one protest in Tripoli's Green Square drew only about 50 young men who danced to Algerian rai music before drifting away in good humour.

Gadaffi was chastened by the bombing and has so far forsworn the revolutionary rhetoric of 1986. As he lay on his sickbed, he was no doubt pondering the dilemma of whether to surrender the two Libyan intelligence agents accused of planting the bomb that exploded aboard a Pan Am jet over Lockerbie three years ago, killing 270 people.

Although his old friend Yasser Arafat, the PLO leader, returned to Tripoli saying 'I must stand by Libya and my brother Gadaffi', solidarity is in short supply. The Soviet Union, Gadaffi's long-time backer, is no more and Arab leaders refused landing permission to the planes he sent out in defiance of the UN sanctions.

It is no easy choice. Should Gadaffi surrender the accused men unconditionally, they may implicate more senior Libyan officials and prompt further demands. 'If you hand them over, you are lost,' one Arab envoy advised him last week. 'The Americans will come back with a list of 100 names, then the name of Abdelsalam Jalloud [Gadaffi's second-in-command], then your name.'

Jalloud, a rough-spoken major and Gadaffi's close comrade since they seized power with a gang of young officers in 1969, is said to be arguing fiercely against surrendering the two suspects, both members of his tribe.

For many Libyans, fed up with 22 years of revolution and crisis, the new openness of Gadaffi's own brand of perestroika now appears under threat. Should Gadaffi play a wrong move in his poker game his people are unlikely to forgive him, even though few think the West's demands are just.

His low-key response suggests that he has been seeking a compromise behind the scenes to have sanctions against air travel, diplomats and arms lifted. He does not wish to repeat the mistake of Saddam Hussein, and knows that taking foreign workers as a 'human shield' would only unleash a violent reaction.

But Libyans are disillusioned. Today only the revolutionary committee apparatchiks believe the new sign on the road to the airport: 'We are all Muammar Gadaffis.'

Adie's minder cracks up: Saleh

TRIPOLI

26 April 1992

Saleh is a broken man, his health uncertain, his job insecure. But his plight has little to do with the political pressures on the beleaguered Libyan regime that employs him. Recovering from a nervous breakdown, Saleh sums up his woes in two words: Kate Adie.

Assigned as a government 'minder' to the roving doyenne of the BBC, Saleh looks back on it all from his sickbed with the horror of a man plucked from the deck of a sinking ship in shark-infested waters. 'Oh dear,' he moaned. 'Kate Adie has been very bad for my health. I have very tender nerves.'

Adie, a veteran of Tiananmen Square, Tripoli and the Gulf, succeeded where sanctions had failed: she had brought the government to its knees.

The extent of the Libyan anguish emerged last week in an extraordinary telex to the BBC, in which Tripoli bemoaned the pugnacious temperament of Adie and pleaded for her to be withdrawn.

'All our attempts to obtain a common and satisfactory solution were gone with the wind,' lamented the telex. 'We are demanding never ever send Kate Adie to Libya whatever the reasons are.'

By that stage, Saleh was at his wits end. Wandering into the lobby of the Bab al-Bahar hotel, he fainted. Coming round, he muttered, 'If you ask me to choose Kate Adie or prison I would not hesitate to choose the prison.'

Grimacing as he relived their last encounter, in a crowded hotel lobby, Saleh said: 'She said she should be filming demonstrations. I told her there were no demonstrations or clashes. But she insisted we find some.'

Deploying ruthless hyperbole, Adie said Libya was treating the foreign press 'in a manner that had gone out of fashion with Stalin'.

Saleh respectfully suggested Adie should leave. But that was like waving a red flag at a bull. 'If you are throwing me out it will be very bad for your country,' she stormed.

Saleh went on: 'I felt shy, so small, like an ant. I am from a good family but she was treating me as if I was a slave or an illegal boy [bastard]. But because of her age I am not allowed to shout or attack her. I must treat her like a mother or a grandmother.'

His next step was to assign an underling to Adie. The colleague was soon on the phone. 'He was calling me all the time and begging me to release him. He said, "Saleh what have you done to me?"'

The ministry adopted new tactics. The BBC was banned from filming, as were other television crews. But Adie soon found her way round that. 'Kate Adie said I had to choose between going to the souk [market] with her or have her shout at me. I took her to the souk,' recalls Omar, the replacement minder.

As a last resort, the information ministry hosted 'a farewell dinner' in which, it was hoped, Adie would get the message. The next day, to their horror, officials received intelligence that she had embarked upon another embroidery square, her favourite method of whiling away time.

In the end, she left on Thursday. 'We have sanctions,' said one official, 'but even worse is Kate Adie.'

Lockerbie drama turns to farce

3 October 1993

Although Muammar Gadaffi, the Libyan leader, is on the brink at last of surrendering the two men suspected of the Lockerbie bombing, justice is far from being done.

After one of the biggest international investigations ever mounted, the expenditure of more than £12 million of British taxpayers' money, and interviews with 16,000 witnesses in 53 countries, most of the evidence indicates that those who made the decision to bomb Pan Am flight 103 will be nowhere near the court.

Libyan sources said yesterday that, under threat of increased United Nations sanctions, Gadaffi had decided to hand over the suspects for trial in Scotland.

Few who have investigated the case think these men, Abdel Baset al-Megrahi and Al Amin Khalifa Fhimah, initiated or planned the operation.* They are low-level intelligence operatives. One is obviously slow-witted. They are accused of smuggling a suitcase bomb aboard a plane from Malta to Frankfurt, where it was loaded aboard the Pan Am flight that exploded over Lockerbie, killing 270 people, at Christmas 1988.

Critics say the American and British governments have ignored evidence that the attack was ordered and paid for by Iran, in retaliation for America shooting down an Iranian jet, and that Iran contracted out the bombing to Ahmed Jibril's PFLP-GC, a radical Palestinian faction based in Damascus, with Syrian connivance.

According to a well-documented line of investigation, Jibril only turned to Libya for help in completing the operation after his own men were arrested by German police. Neither Washington nor London wanted to alienate the Syrian and Iranian leaderships at the time of the investigation, which coincided with the Gulf War.

Relatives of the victims are enraged. 'It's like trying the hit man and ignoring the person who paid him to pull the trigger,' said Susan Cohen, whose daughter, 20, was killed. 'Nobody thinks that these two guys sat in a café and decided to bomb an aeroplane.'

Even the conviction of the Libyans is by no means certain. Prosecutors fear they may have insufficient evidence. No witness,

---

* Al Amin Khalifa Fhimah was found not guilty and acquitted of 270 counts of murder, conspiracy to murder and a breach of the Aviation Security Act 1982 by a panel of three Scottish judges sitting in a special court at Camp Zeist, Netherlands.

fingerprint or any other forensic evidence links either of them directly to the explosion.

None the less, all the might of the British and American governments has been brought to bear on Gadaffi through the UN to surrender the men, and Libyan sources said yesterday that he had finally been convinced that neither country would accept any compromise.

Travel and diplomatic sanctions were imposed last year, and on Friday the UN security council tabled a draft resolution imposing further sanctions if Gadaffi does not surrender. Apparently at the request of Boutros Boutros-Ghali, the UN secretary-general, the vote has been delayed to give Gadaffi time to declare his intentions. The denouement could come this week.

Gadaffi has been assured that the pair will get a fair trial in Scotland, where the stringency of evidence laws would give them the best chance of acquittal. He has also been promised that they would not be interrogated by MI6 or any other security agency. Security sources see this as an important concession because the men cannot be forced to reveal any Libyan secrets.

The British have even told the Libyans that Scottish cells are 'very comfortable' and that the men will be taught English – a puzzler for Libyan negotiators, who thought the Scots spoke Scottish. The farce continues.

Gulf War

Under fire

27 January 1991

Hussein stood alone in the carpet souk on the eastern bank of the Tigris, fingering his ivory worry-beads and gazing at the huge sun setting behind the Ottoman tenements on the far side of the river. The dying sunlight washed his dishdasha robe a wintry red.

The market square of the souk usually bustled at this time of the early evening as people stopped to gossip or do last-minute shopping on the way home from work. But it was 15 January, the United Nations' deadline for Iraq's withdrawal from Kuwait. Baghdad was silent and edgy. The souk was deserted.

Hussein greeted me with far more warmth than our acquaintance merited. I had visited him on and off in his shop over the past five months, using the excuse of fingering a Kurdish bangle, or looking at a carpet, to pick up the rumours and rhythms of daily life in Baghdad. For him, it had been an excuse for a rare talk with a foreigner, something that for an Iraqi is akin to a visit to the confessional.

Now, in this chance encounter, we seemed the only people left in the capital. We walked to his shop under the vaulted roof of the souk. Inside, there was none of the usual salesmanship or the ritual cup of sugared tea. 'Would you like a whisky?' he asked, and picked up a half-full bottle of Whyte & Mackay. He poured us two tea glasses full.

Amid the clutter of piled up carpets, silver necklaces, antique frames, heavy Kurdish belts and, beside the ubiquitous picture of Saddam Hussein, a likeness of President John F Kennedy beaten into a copper plate we discussed whether he should stay in Baghdad or take his family to a place safe from American bombs, as other merchants had.

Tareq, who owned the House of Antiquities across the street, had taken his wife and sons to Kurdistan in northern Iraq. 'The Americans like the Kurds, they won't bomb them,' he had said.

Hussein agonised. Baghdad was home; perhaps thieves would come to the empty souk and steal his carpets; but there was no business anyway because everybody was hoarding their money.

We drank another tea glass of whisky, standing up, too edgy to sit down. His wife, five children aged two to 12, younger brother and mother were at home waiting. His children had their school exams on the 20th; if they missed them, it would mean losing a year of school. 'But perhaps it is better that they lose a year than that they lose their lives,' he said.

Darkness was falling and we walked out of the shop. He said: 'If you have any problems you can come to my house. Really.' For an Iraqi, it was an enormous act of faith. A visit by a foreigner in this tightly controlled society meant a follow-up visit by the security police. But these were extraordinary times. It was a way of saying we were not enemies. I drove back to the Rashid hotel through dark and deserted streets.

Baghdad is normally a bustling city. Although its glorious antiquity was long ago buried under drab concrete, its spirit was irrepressible, even at the height of the first war in the Gulf, when taxis returning from the front with coffins on their roofs raced among the fierce traffic on its highways. To see the city now was chilling.

Many middle-class families had closed their homes and left to stay with relatives in the country after the failure of the talks in Geneva between Tariq Aziz, the foreign minister, and James Baker, the American secretary of state. Others held out, fiddling for good news between the BBC, Voice of America and the pan-Arab station, Monte Carlo.

They had heard the ominous tone in Saddam's speech on Friday to an Islamic conference in Baghdad. They had heard Joe Wilson, the American chargé d'affaires, dramatically announce as he left on Saturday: 'This is the last flight out.' They knew most western diplomats had left with him.

But even illiterate taxi drivers held an irrational faith that Javier Perez de Cuellar, the United Nations secretary-general, might be able to avert war when he arrived to see Saddam at the weekend. 'Maybe Saddam will leave Kuwait,' the taxi driver said as he drove me to Perez de Cuellar's news conference at the airport. When the secretary-general said 'only God knows' if there would be a war, it was the last straw. Iraqis knew Saddam was ready to take on the world.

Everybody was jumpy. We lost our way leaving the airport and when we drove up to a checkpoint to ask a soldier for directions, there was an audible click as he flipped the safety catch off his AK-47 and walked up to the car with the barrel pointed through the window.

There were many poignant moments in those days overshadowed by the deadline. The most striking thing perhaps, to somebody who had been visiting Iraq on and off since the crisis began, was the sudden openness of the usually careful and closed Iraqis.

This is a society that usually keeps its head down and offers no political opinions. Most dissidents are dead or in exile. The tiny middle class would, in general, be glad to see Saddam's regime fall; but the merchants did well out of the war against Iran and reached an accommodation with those in power. The urban poor, who have enjoyed cheap, and even free, housing and subsidised food under Saddam, are compliant to his will. The long war against Iran united society and now I found that his stand against the world was filling many Iraqis with pride as well as fear.

After seeing Hussein in the souk hours before the deadline expired, I went into the Al-wiyah club with Falah, an Iraqi businessman. It is a former British club now frequented by Iraq's elite, a place of contrasts. A huge Saddam portrait greets arrivals in the club car park, but members still leave their own private bottles of whisky behind the bar, their names printed on them, in the old British club tradition. We were the only customers, but there was still food, some salads and chicken.

Falah spoke over dinner about statistics, trying to put on a brave face that Iraq would somehow continue. He had been helping as a consultant to the government in what he called 'food security' since the crisis began. He had managed to cut sugar consumption by 60% by closing down ice-cream and confectionery shops; Iraq was now making its own liquid sugar from dates. Farmers had had to kill most of Iraq's chickens because of the shortage of grain, but cows had been switched to grass and still gave milk. Wheat was a problem; Iraq produced 4 million tons annually and consumed 6.5 million but increased subsidies for farmers would make up much of the shortage. Meanwhile, rationing filled the gap: his office had made charts of human consumption, added 20% and produced rationing amounts and distributed coupons.

Such statistics are usually impossible to come by; but I had barely the energy to commit them to memory (you don't take notes in public in Iraq). Falah relaxed, dropped his beloved subject and lapsed into tales of his childhood.

The club was significant to him and to the current situation. He had come here first as a young and proud university student, the first Arab of his generation to visit it, brought by a British professor as a reward for being number one in his class. 'You realise for us this is much more than a war between Iraq and America. For us, even for the Arabs who are not with Saddam, it is a struggle for our dignity. The West has humiliated us and we see Saddam as a leader who has finally stood up to the West and said we want our dignity.'

On the way home, I went by the French embassy where André Jenier, the last western diplomat in Baghdad, was preparing to leave in proper French style. He had laid out the embassy's last French cheeses, pâtés and salamis and served champagne until midnight, when he and his few remaining staff clambered into their cars and drove through the night to the Jordanian border.

At the Hotel Palestine, previously the Meridian but now run-down and shabby after a change from French to Iraqi ownership at the start of the economic embargo five months ago, I stopped at a 'challenge the deadline' celebration, an Iraqi version of an end-of-the-world party.

Kadum Al-Sahir, a popular singer, was on the floor amid a group of men who danced and waved Iraqi flags. But most of the rest of the hall was filled with sombre beer drinkers, sitting at their tables without much enthusiasm. Most were government recruits; the only guests who seemed to have paid the 20 dinar ($35) entry price were 10 Palestinians who had come in a delegation from Jordan to show solidarity with Iraq. A wedding party had been recruited to build up the numbers.

I went to bed in my room at the Rashid hotel and waited for the worst.

The Americans had announced that the deadline would fall at midnight New York time, 8am local time next day, Wednesday the 16th. When I woke, a heavy fog had settled across the flat city. For a moment, looking out of the hotel window, unable to see anything but white mist obscuring the skyline, I thought perhaps the attack had come and I had slept through it.

Downstairs, among the government 'minders' who watched the comings and goings of the few of the 40 or so journalists left at the Rashid hotel, there was premature euphoria. 'You see, I told you there would not be war,' said Karim, one of the men from the information ministry.

Baghdad thought otherwise. Driving around town, I saw only a few knots of men in quiet discussions. Rashid Street, the main thoroughfare, lined with colonnaded mock-Ottoman buildings from the 1930s, was usually packed with cars. Instead, it was a wide deserted avenue at 9am.

Windows were taped over against bombs for the first time. The Mandarin restaurant on Karada Street, once Baghdad's busiest fast-food joint but closed for months because of a ban on serving meals, had its wide windows taped in large Xs. At the Shorjah souk, Baghdad's most popular market because of its cheap clothing, household items and canned goods, only four of the 200 stores had opened. One man, hanging up flannel robes from the ceiling of his shop, said: 'We will open for an hour. If it stays like this, we will close.' Schools had opened, but with few teachers and fewer students they quickly closed for the day.

There was no sign of backing off by Saddam. The headline of the government newspaper, *Al-Jumhuriya*, said: 'We shall never compromise on Iraqi and Arab rights.' Midday television news showed perhaps the unluckiest people in the world that day: 177 former prisoners of war descending from an Iraqi Airways flight to Baghdad after years of captivity in Iran.

Sources were fast disappearing. I telephoned the foreign ministry to try to see Nizar Hamdoun, the under-secretary. But the ministry's number had changed and its officials had moved to a new location. The last time I had seen Hamdoun, he was sitting in his office, morosely watching CNN television. 'I feel like I'm watching a bad fiction movie,' he had said.

During his tenure as Iraqi ambassador to Washington, Hamdoun had been the architect of the Iraqi–American rapprochement of the 1980s. He still felt Iraq could be America's best ally in the Middle East. It was the only local power able to enforce stability in the region under Bush's new world order; it had oil America needed; it was a potentially wealthy market; and it would guarantee American interests. But by 16 January 1991, policy was long out of the hands of thoughtful diplomats such as Hamdoun.

At the ministry of information that evening, the receptionist at the office of Naji Hadithi, the director-general, was watching cartoons. Inside, Hadithi and I watched a film showing Saddam visiting troops in Kuwait. The president looked confident as he had in every appearance that week, although rather awkward as he sat wrapped in a huge greatcoat with troops who looked terrified by his presence. He asked them oddly personal questions. 'Have you had your dinner?' he said to one. A long pause … 'Is this place warm?' he said to another.

Hadithi switched to CNN and we watched a demonstration of allied fire control in Dhahran, where Saudi, American and British forces are based. A lieutenant-commander was interviewed, saying his men were prepared. Hadithi commented: 'The only thing missing from this is reality.'

He meant on the allied side. It was a cherished belief of many Iraqis I spoke to, even those who were desperate to avoid war, that if it came to a battle, Iraqi soldiers, hardened in the war against Iran, would defeat their better armed but inexperienced enemy.

As Wednesday evening drew on, Marlin Fitzwater, Bush's spokesman, caused the first real worry among the foreign press corps. He said any journalists in Baghdad were in danger and should leave immediately. All American print reporters had left on the 14th, but the American television networks remained. Now they started getting prearranged signals from Pentagon sources that an attack was imminent.

Larry Doyle of CBS received the message: 'Your family is fine but your children have colds.' Doyle, a veteran journalist who reported on the Vietnam war, put down the phone and said simply: 'Shit.'

A delegation of journalists hurried to Hadithi's office. Some wanted to move out of the Rashid hotel, located in central Baghdad near most of the ministries and the presidential palace, all obvious targets for attack. But Hadithi said: 'We are still here. Our ministry is a dangerous place and yet we did not evacuate.'

John Simpson of BBC Television said in his understated manner: 'The Americans have 2,000lb bombs which could make things extremely unpleasant.'

Latis Jassim, the information minister, arrived and reassured us. 'You are safe. This is a commitment on our part. We are willing and eager to offer you the necessary services so that you can report the facts as you see them. But at no time will communications fail completely.'

It was midnight. We went back to the hotel. The attack could come at any moment. Nobody knew how bad it might be. We waited.

I took a small bag down to the bomb shelter below the hotel, just in case. Already women and children were huddled along the walls wrapped in blankets. Somehow the warning had swept through the hotel.

The lights in the shelter flickered. I had to see what was happening. I turned and started up the steps but was met by a flood of panicked people coming down the stairs, women with crying children, Sudanese waiters still in uniform, an Iranian delegation staying at the hotel.

At entrance-hall level, I could hear booms from outside. Upstairs, from the fifth-floor BBC office, we saw out of the window a spectacular display of tracer fire shooting across the sky. Tracers spewed up as if from a Roman candle. Others shot across the sky as if following an unseen and unheard enemy. White flashes illuminated the tops of buildings on which, during the last five months, we had watched the crews of anti-aircraft guns shelter first from the August sun and lately from January's rain and cold.

Strange video game noises filled the air. The staccato thud-thud-thud of heavy artillery sounded. Bob Simpson of BBC Radio had a microphone out of the open window and leaned on his elbows on the windowsill as he calmly described the spectacular display. Down the hall, a CBS cameraman knelt on the floor, his camera out of the window, and filmed through a down-tilted eye scope.

Huge yellow flashes appeared on the horizon. Something to the right thudded and the impact threw me back across the room. Smoke rose from the building. There could no longer be any suspicion that it was a false alarm or jittery anti-aircraft gunners. It was 2.35am Iraqi time and Baghdad was under attack.

Doyle, spotting the flashes on the horizon, narrated for those of us less knowledgeable about armaments. 'Those are the big boys, the cute 2,000lb bombs,' he said. 'Unfortunately I've been through this before. They are just pounding the hell out of that place.'

The bombing appeared to be about 20 miles off, probably at the Rashid military complex. The attack slackened off, then started again at 3.35am. The city, which had remained lit up, went completely black. The anti-aircraft fire stopped and started again in almost 15-minute intervals, sometimes directed above our hotel, filling the skies but seeming to have little effect.

About 4.25am, hotel security guards came into the room and tried to drag us downstairs to the shelter. They settled for taping over the emergency light that had gone on when the hotel lights failed. From below, during a lull, an earnest ABC reporter yelled up: 'What are your departure plans?' Somebody yelled down: 'Up in the air at the moment.'

I wandered back to my room at 6am as dawn broke and the attack appeared to have stopped. A man I had never seen before was asleep in my bed still wearing large boots. I went down the hall and took a nap on the floor of the BBC office.

Morning came cold and misty again when I woke at 7.30am. After the drama of the night, it was strange to see the city skyline unchanged. Smoke from a fire behind the hotel drifted through the hallways. But little damage was visible from the hotel room. We clustered around to hear Baghdad radio for the first communiqué of the war. 'This is communiqué number one. The mother of battles has begun. President Bush will regret this attack. Victory is near.' The voice announced the immediate call-up of reserve soldiers born in 1954, 1955 and 1956. The radio returned to martial music.

My driver had disappeared. He was born in 1955 and had been worrying about the call-up for the last month. 'War is very bad,' he had said to me. 'I fought eight years in the war with Iran. No wife, no children. Now maybe I have to go to Kuwait.' His fears had been realised.

I grabbed a taxi on the street and drove around the city. The first evidence of attack was at the international post and telecommunications building. It had been hit by at least four missiles that had left gaping holes and dangling wires. Chunks of building and glass littered the streets, but no surrounding buildings suffered damage more than broken windows.

A bit further on, the Ba'ath party headquarters had taken a direct hit in the roof. Again, no surrounding buildings were touched. On Abunawas Street, across the river from the presidential palace, a car tilted crazily into a 30-foot crater already filled with water. But, other than that, there seemed to be almost no damage to civilian targets.

Anti-aircraft guns sounded again at 9am and 10am. Soldiers in uniform lined the roads at bus stations trying to flag down cabs or cars to head south to register with their units. The few families that had left it too late to leave stood, suitcases and children in hand, trying to do the same.

At 10.30am I was standing in front of the ministry of information, now deserted despite the minister's brave words just hours earlier, as a thud sounded and a mushroom of smoke went up from the defence ministry about half a mile away. Two more thuds shook the building. Neither a plane had been visible nor an engine heard. Anti-aircraft fire went up but it was too late.

Driving by the ministry – an old Ottoman building still marked the Abbassid Palace on tourist maps and so secret that a government official once told me it was a museum – I could see flames in the central section. A wing had been flattened as if by a giant fist.

The reaction from soldiers in the barracks across the street from the defence ministry was as surprising as the suddenness of the attack. They stood standing and watching the fire as if it was a show unconnected to them. Nobody seemed to be in much of a hurry to put it out. Like the foreign ministry, the defence department must have transferred its operations elsewhere in the days before the deadline.

As I drove around town, the calm and lack of panic were impressive. Orderly lines formed for bread and cars queued for petrol. It was a far cry from the day after the bombing of the Libyan city of Tripoli, when Libyans crashed their cars into each other trying to flee, the government disappeared and rumours that Colonel Gadaffi had been overthrown filled the capital.

Baghdad's militiamen had appeared overnight to keep order. In the Amriyah area, a civilian neighbourhood, six teenagers dressed in jeans and jackets walked along the streets with Kalashnikov assault rifles casually slung over their shoulders. A man in a cheap suit and a keffiyeh Arab headdress manned an anti-aircraft gun placed in the bed of a Nissan pick-up truck at a crossroads. But there were no new checkpoints, nor was there hostility towards foreigners.

Saddam came on Baghdad radio at 12.40 in the afternoon, speaking in calm and confident tone: 'At 2.30am the great duel started. The valiant sons of Iraq, your brothers, sons and fathers, confronted the invaders. Damn King Fahd, the traitor of Mecca, damn the invaders, damn these criminals. We shall win. The dawn will break and they will be damned.'

My taxi driver, taking me back to the hotel, said he was not at the front because he had a piece of shrapnel still in his head from the Iran war. It hurt when the weather got cold. Like most Iraqis that day, he appeared worried but unfazed. 'I did not think we should have taken Kuwait,' he said. 'I don't agree with this. But the Americans should not come to Iraq. Iraqi soldiers will fight for Iraq and for Saddam. We have fought for eight years against Iran and they cannot frighten us.'

This was the mood of Baghdad under fire. An Iraqi businessman explained to me why people were so calm. Listening for weeks to the propaganda from Washington, they had expected Armageddon. Now that the bombing had come at last and they had survived, he said, their attitude was: 'Well, if that's it, we can take it.'

People had even begun to listen for the first time to Iraqi radio, and to believe its propaganda, because they felt that the BBC and Voice of America had lied about allied successes against the air force and missile sites in the first attack.

In addition, the government maintained at least a semblance of control. The city was without water or electricity, and the streets began to smell of sewage and cordite. But soldiers directed traffic in place of traffic lights, papers continued to publish daily, and the television news appeared every night at the same time, with its usual announcer, and on the same television studio set.

Only a few shops opened; and prices were astonishing: I saw a bottle of whisky, a packet of cigarettes and three Mars bars bought for 147 dinars, the equivalent of $441 at the official rate and equal to three-quarters of the monthly salary of a middle-ranking government official.

But in the poor neighbourhoods such as Saddam City, where more people had remained because they had no way of escape, and which the regime regards as its centres of support, government lorries distributed bread under normal ration regulations.

Anti-aircraft fire erupted sporadically during the day. Tracer fire, the thud of guns and falling bombs filled the night, but there were few civilian casualties.

There were makeshift shelters to be found almost anywhere in the city. Driving back to the hotel, I ducked into Baghdad Hotel when anti-aircraft guns went off at the nearby presidential palace. The discotheque had been turned into a bomb shelter and guests were handed candles at the door. People were worried but there was still an air of unreality. 'Palestine seems closer than it has for 40 years,' said a Palestinian businessman also sheltering inside.

Baghdad's survival and the news that Saddam had launched Scud rockets at Israel had many Palestinians and their Iraqi supporters still believing that he would achieve his goal of some-how freeing Palestinian land from Israel.

As the sun set on Friday, I watched two orbs of light streak low across the city skyline, just missing the rooftops, and smash into the Dora oil refinery. A huge ball of fire erupted and smoke drifted back over Baghdad.

Bombing continued sporadically that night and at dawn the refinery had only three instead of four chimneys. The 20-storey communications tower which had lost its top three storeys to an unseen missile on Friday, as if to an invisible hand, had completely disappeared from the skyline by Saturday morning.

On Saturday afternoon, I was gazing idly from a fifth-floor window across the Zawra zoo park opposite the hotel when I suddenly realised that a cruise missile was heading above the trees straight for us. It seemed to be white. I could see its little fins. There was no smoke trail coming from it.

I thought it was going to hit the hotel, and I yelled out. But it turned right and skirted the building, as if following a street map, and hit the old parliament building about half a mile away, sending up a white pall of smoke.

Another cruise landed even closer, disappearing with a deafen-ing crash into breeze-block staff quarters next to the hotel. The huts burst into flames and shrapnel showered the lawn and swim-ming pool. Glass from broken windows littered the hotel lobby as hotel workers dragged an electronic circuit board into the air-raid shelter, dancing around it, ululating and shouting that they had downed an American plane.

It was a relentless afternoon attack. At least two more missiles hit the Dora refinery again, sparking a fire that lit Baghdad with a beautiful rose glow late into the night.

Conditions at the Rashid hotel were becoming primitive. Electricity remained off and journalists worked at night by candlelight. Sanitation had broken down, toilets could not flush, and we had been washing in the swimming pool.

The officials minding us had had enough. They had stayed in the shelter for days and had not seen their families nor been able to contact them by telephone. They were worried about our safety and about the detail of what we were reporting. We were ordered to leave.

On Saturday night, as I packed and sat up late with other journalists discussing our departure, a Palestinian friend stopped by to say farewell. An articulate, educated man, he was trying to explain why so much of the Arab world had come out in support of Saddam despite his invasion of Kuwait and oppressive policies at home.

'You must understand that if Saddam goes, no Westerner will be safe walking down an Arab street. I will pick up a machinegun and fight the Americans. A year ago I would have told you I hated Saddam and his regime. But he has become a symbol for us. Saddam is the result of the humiliation of the war of 1967 and of all the humiliations we have suffered from the West. If we let you destroy Saddam now, you will destroy all of us Arabs again.' He added: 'It is a question of dignity. Saddam came along with his rockets and stood up to you and we said, "Why not?"'

I rose at 5am to the incongruous sounds of a cock crowing and another barrage of anti-aircraft fire, this time a light and sparkling scattering of shots of tracer into the air. The government newspaper headline read: 'Hussein rockets answer the call of Palestine. The road to Jerusalem is open.' Uniting under attack behind Saddam, people might even believe this hyperbole.

Downstairs the taxi drivers demanded the exorbitant sum of $3,000 a car to the Jordanian border, because a convoy of cars that had left on Saturday had been bombed near the town of Rutba in the western desert.

We drove out of Baghdad on the deserted highway, past military camps on the city's perimeter that appeared surprisingly intact, with anti-aircraft guns still manned on mounds along their boundaries. Government army lorries trundled south towing anti-aircraft guns, but there was little other traffic. The journey through flat, unbroken rocky desert was uneventful. Iraqi guards stamped exit visas into our passports at the desolate border station of Trebeil. Among the shabby breeze-block buildings we left behind the stacks of abandoned cheap luggage from earlier refugees and drove across the no man's land into Jordan.

Ghosts of war stalk Basra's empty streets

SOUTHERN IRAQ

23 August 1992

The fat singer in the smoky gloom of the Eastern Nights Club in Basra was just getting into her stride when the lights went up. The laughter at a table of rich merchants died instantly.

An unsmiling officer in khaki swept through the beads hanging across the door followed by eight soldiers, who fanned out between tables draped in red velvet and dotted with bottles of Scotch. The customers froze. They knew that last month Saddam Hussein executed 42 merchants for profiteering.

The officer scanned the room, but he had no interest in the traders or the soldier sitting with a buxom prostitute. His eyes fell on a table of eight young men.

Two soldiers moved forward, ordering the men to their feet with the flick of a Kalashnikov. The officer pulled out battered papers.

The first passed and was motioned to sit; the second was led away.

'Oh, he didn't even have time to change his clothes,' lamented Ishar, a young prostitute. A second glance told the story: the arrested man still wore his olive army trousers under a white shirt and maroon jacket. He was a deserter. Four more of his companions were led away.

As the soldiers left, there was a moment of silence. Then the manager strode to the dance floor and, with a grandiose flourish, restarted the band and the singer. The lights dimmed and laughter flooded the room again – the forced laughter of relief.

Basra, capital of the south and home to Iraq's Shi'ite majority, is a city under siege. Whereas Baghdad has been largely rebuilt since the Gulf War, Basra still bears the scars of allied bombing and the rebellion that saw officials of the ruling Ba'ath party slaughtered in the streets and government buildings and hospitals looted and torched.

Today, fear of Iranian infiltrators, army deserters and fugitive rebels empties the city's streets after 9pm. Food is scarce and expensive. The factories, port and oil plants are closed; its hospitals desperately short of medicine and filled with malnourished babies.

Fifty life-sized statues of dead heroes of the Iran–Iraq war line the corniche on the Shatt al-Arab, their arms pointing across the water towards the old Iranian foe. Locals, fearful of the enemy within, joke that they should point in every direction.

The man charged with keeping order in Basra is Brigadier General Latif Omoud, a governor who sits behind a desk with 10 telephones. It is impressive, but unconvincing.

The city's telecommunications have not been restored since the end of the Gulf War 18 months ago, and a line has to be installed to each number he wants to call. 'The pink telephone is for my girlfriend,' he joked.

Dressed in a neatly pressed uniform and with his hands manicured, Omoud appears unbowed by the calamitous state of the city he took over after Iraqi forces crushed the Shi'ite rebellion in March last year.

He has not been amused, however, by the news that Britain, France and the United States were preparing to enforce an air exclusion zone south of the 32nd parallel to protect the Shi'ites in the southern marshlands from destruction by Saddam.

Any Iraqi plane or helicopter that flies will risk being shot down. Since Basra is 100 miles south of the 32nd parallel, Omoud was angry and perplexed. The general, who sees himself on the front line with Iran, claims to have quelled the 'security problem' in Basra.

But the road south from al-Amarah to Basra remains a no-go zone at night; checkpoints are attacked, soldiers killed and civilians robbed. It will get much worse, said Omoud, if the allied plan is enforced.

'We have arrested many infiltrators in Basra,' he said. 'They come from Iran to commit acts of sabotage. We should be allowed to fly our planes and helicopters to counter the Iranian menace.'

He made no apology for the attacks on the marshes, insisting they were a haven for rebels and Iranian agents. The West, Omoud said, was short-sighted: 'The Iranians are still interested in exporting their revolution.'

Then the governor was off, speeding away in his armoured white Mercedes followed by a jeep with a mounted machinegun and two cars full of soldiers. Behind him, sweltering in the 53°C heat, bricklayers continued rebuilding his governor's garrison, which had been gutted during the rebellion.

The real picture in the south is difficult to piece together in a tightly controlled nation of nervous people. But it is clear that the government has won the upper hand in the war with the 30,000 rebels in the Hawaiza marshes, a 6,000-square-mile swampland of waterways and reed banks.

The attacks against insurgents in the marshes, according to diplomats in Baghdad and interviews in Basra and al-Amarah, began around 21 July. There is little doubt they were brutal. Diplomats believe that Iraq used helicopter gunships and artillery against the marsh Arabs but has not sent in ground troops because of the treacherous terrain.

The rebels had little chance. Besieged, they were killed or forced to flee or surrender. Many civilian marsh dwellers also died. The season favoured the army; in July and August the marshes dry up, making operations easier. One source said 9,000 rebels had surrendered or been captured.

The few townspeople in al-Amarah willing to talk say the roads are too dangerous to travel at night. At the Saddam Hussein general hospital, Dr Ayad Abdul Aziz said there had been constant attacks on civilians and soldiers in the area near the marshes.

But operations by the Iraqi army seem to have ended. The military appears to be in defensive positions. Nightly on Iraqi national television, captured rebels make their confessions.

One Iraqi, a PoW from the Iraq–Iran war, claimed he had been forced to fight for Iran: 'It was decided to start a sabotage campaign. I received verbal instructions to go on a fact-finding mission in Iraq. We needed information on the security status. I carried false identification, money and a pistol.'

He said he met rebels who had plentiful supplies of explosives and weapons, and sent back information to Iran. The interviewees show extraordinary calm while making their confessions; it is widely assumed they are executed afterwards.

'Of course they are calm,' said one Iraqi viewer last week. 'They know it is the end of their lives.'

Critics are silenced as Saddam rebuilds Iraq

BAGHDAD

4 October 1992

Arc lights on the roof of the National Conference Palace shone through the night and into the pink dawn last week as construction workers hammered and welded round the clock to repair the bombed building. It might have been an unremarkable scene in a city recovering from 43 consecutive days of air attack, except for one thing: it was the last important building to be restored.

Little more than 18 months after the Gulf War ceasefire, you have to scour the back streets of Baghdad for any sign of the heavy bombing it underwent. Iraqi engineers have repaired all but one of the bridges destroyed during the hostilities and rebuilt the 14-storey central telephone exchange on the bank of the Tigris, bombed so often that by the end of the conflict it was just a concrete shell with steel and wires curling from the windows. Gutted ministries have been reconstructed, rubble removed.

The main power plant, which was lit almost nightly by flashes from explosions, is working at 90% of its pre-war capacity. Soon after the bombing ended, an engineer at the plant said it would take at least two years to get it working again; but there was not one blackout during the blazing hot summer, when Baghdadis ran their air-conditioning at full blast.

The list of achievements goes on. Oil production is back to about 800,000 barrels a day, although United Nations sanctions prohibit Iraq from selling its petroleum abroad. Restored refineries supply more than enough petrol and heating oil for Iraq's domestic needs and exports to Jordan. Iraqi experts say they could now pump 2 million barrels a day.

The six-lane highway from Baghdad to the Jordanian border, littered with craters from nightly raids, is now a smoothly surfaced superhighway. Three weeks ago the evening news showed Saddam Hussein congratulating workers for finishing repairs on the presidential palace.

In fact, much of the current construction in Baghdad is of new buildings. Enormous villas are sprouting in the wealthy Mansour district, financed by war profits. Newspapers report the progress of the Third River project, the construction of a 350-mile canal that will drain the rising water in the Tigris-Euphrates basin to reclaim land.

Yesterday, Saddam announced that construction would resume, using Iraqi designs and expertise, of an enormous petrochemical complex which the war forced foreign companies to abandon. When finished, it will be the largest in the Middle East.

What happened? Just 18 months ago, Saddam sat in a windowless bunker, wrapped in a heavy woollen greatcoat because there was no heat and in dim light because even the president had to rely on a diesel-fuelled generator for electricity. Outside, his country lay in ruins. The electricity grid was destroyed. Sewerage and water systems, telephones, even traffic lights did not work. His oil refineries were reduced to tangled machinery and holed tanks. He had just been kicked out of Kuwait, his army was in disarray, a rebellion raged in 14 of his 18 provinces, and much of his air force was parked on the territory of his enemy, Iran.

Since then, Iraq has been rebuilt without money from oil exports, without the teams of foreign experts that once staffed the military and civilian industries, without the $4 billion of assets frozen in overseas banks, and under strict sanctions that ban the import of spare parts or construction materials.

The key to the revival is Saddam. According to those around him, he did not even falter in the face of devastation so massive that allied leaders believed his downfall to be inevitable. Saddam never, ever, gives up, they say. This mentality was a liability during the Gulf crisis, when he refused to leave Kuwait, but it was crucial to the rebuilding of Iraq. He went from the Mother of all Battles to the Mother of all Reconstructions without missing a beat.

Saddam emerged unrepentant from his bunker and ready to rebuild. The 53-year-old president knows his people well. He needed to remove the daily reminders of the war, and his responsibility for it. 'I don't want to see any war damage in the capital,' an Iraqi official quoted him as saying. In a dictatorship as absolute as Iraq, such an order concentrates the mind. Construction crews began working 24 hours a day, even on Saturday, the Muslim Sabbath.

Saddam was fortunate in the resources he commanded. When UN sanctions were imposed in August 1990, Iraq had two years' supply of spare parts in storage. There were millions of dollars in overseas slush funds, which his brother, Barzan al-Tikriti, Iraqi representative to the UN in Geneva, used to buy spare parts that were smuggled in through Jordan. Perhaps most important, Iraq is home to the best educated and disciplined people in the Arab world. He had no need for foreign technical expertise.

Saddam identified himself with the reconstruction effort. News programmes regularly broadcast East-European-style footage of him inspecting repaired factories.

A special Order of the President was created to reward those who excelled in the rebuilding effort, and the annual conference of the ruling Ba'ath party was named the Jihad (Holy War) of Reconstruction Congress.

Nothing proved too insignificant for Saddam's attention. During a nationally televised meeting, he advised education officials to 'give special attention to sanitary facilities for students. The student who cannot go to the bathroom all day because it is dirty cannot concentrate.'

There has been no let-up in the momentum. Saddam warned his ministers last month: 'From now on, those government officials who fail in their responsibilities will be considered as being involved in economic sabotage. Stringent measures will be taken against them, similar to the strict measures taken against the traitors who were involved in profiteering and monopoly.' It was an undisguised reference to the 42 merchants executed in July for profiteering.

The success of the reconstruction has won Saddam the admiration of his greatest critics. Ordinary Iraqis, who love their bridges and modern buildings the way Europeans love their nation's art treasures or scenic vistas, are proud that Iraq has rebuilt its infrastructure quickly, and without outside help.

The country still has serious problems, though. Inflation has wrecked the economy, with prices spiralling higher almost daily – last week rice sold for 8½ dinars ($25) a kilo, a spare tyre for 2,000 dinars. The country's future wealth is mortgaged to old debts and war reparation. On Friday, the UN security council voted to seize $1 billion of Iraq's frozen assets to pay for UN operations.

But the dissatisfaction of Iraqis with their financial lot is irrelevant. Along with his bridges, Saddam has reconstructed his formidable security apparatus. The army has been restored to 40% of its pre-war capacity, with about 400,000 troops under arms; the ubiquitous Mukhabarat security men are back on the streets. The south is under undeclared martial law; generals have replaced civilians as governors in every southern province.

Saddam's success has also undermined Washington's attempts to persuade Iraqis to oppose the regime. I heard again and again in Baghdad, albeit in hushed tones, that Saddam and Bush had a secret deal: why else would the allied forces have stood by as the Republican Guard crushed the rebels?

In case anyone in Baghdad needed a reminder that Saddam's rule has been restored as surely as his capital, they need only look to the shore of the Tigris in the exclusive Adamiya district of Baghdad. An enormous building, designed on the lines of a Sumerian palace, has begun to emerge from its scaffolding. It is a new presidential palace.

Shadow of evil

IRAQ

22 January 1995

Latif Yahia spat in the mirror when he saw himself for the first time after being forced to undergo plastic surgery. But it was too late. He now looked exactly like Uday Hussein, the eldest son of the Iraqi president.

He spent the next four years as Uday's double, a time he now refers to as 'years of blood'. He was trapped at the heart of one of the most secretive, paranoid and brutal regimes on earth, learning its secrets while treading a tightrope between the pampered privileges of the inner circle and the terror of knowing that he could be shot at any moment.

Yahia has now spoken for the first time about how he was tortured into taking on the role, how he was turned physically and mentally into a terrible imitation of Saddam's murderous and licentious son, how he eventually escaped, and how he is now trying to exorcise the evil persona that entered him.

He has also revealed that Saddam, like Stalin and Churchill, has his own series of doubles, who are forced to undertake potentially dangerous public appearances. The present 'Saddam' replaced one who was assassinated in an attempt on the dictator's life.

Yahia attended public parties and football matches in his assumed role and posed with soldiers at the Kuwaiti front so that Uday would face no danger but the Iraqi people would believe Saddam had sent his son to serve in the Mother of all Battles. Yahia survived nine assassination attempts.

Only once did he give thanks for his hated new identity. When Yahia finally fled Iraq, soldiers manning checkpoints leaped out of the way and saluted as he sped north in his Oldsmobile, also a double for one of Uday's cars.

He came to think of himself as a monster. The man he had to impersonate is feared as much as his father in Iraq. He is a spoilt, brutal playboy who flies into uncontrollable rages when crossed and whose violent excesses are covered up by the security forces.

Uday even fell out with his father when he beat to death Saddam's favourite retainer in a drunken rage in 1988 and was briefly exiled to Geneva. Father and son now appear to be reconciled; last year, Iraqi exiles reported that Saddam had executed three senior military officers after they suggested Uday was not up to the job of defence minister that his father wanted to give him.

Since the Gulf War, Uday has tried to make his image more serious by founding *Babil* newspaper and a radio and television station that broadcasts popular western entertainment. But Yahia witnessed the sinister private activities of Saddam's son, which he said included earning millions of pounds from black-market deals in whisky, cigarettes and food while normal Iraqis suffered under international sanctions, and entertaining friends with torture videos shot in his father's prisons.

Yahia's story is fascinating, not just as the tale of a man pushed to unbelievable psychological limits, but also because it gives a remarkable insight into the most secretive of worlds, the life of Saddam Hussein and his family.

Now in Vienna as a political exile, the 30-year-old refugee is trying to recover his lost identity. It is disconcerting to meet him. He still looks exactly like Uday, still dresses in the same sharp European suits the dictator's son favours, sports the same heavy gold jewellery and black Ray-Ban sunglasses. He smokes a Cuban cigar with the same motions and has the same beard that distinguishes Uday from other Iraqis, who have only moustaches.

He is soft-spoken and polite, but old habits die hard. Taking out a cigar, he holds it until somebody lights it, even though the retainers that swarmed around him in his old role as Uday are long gone. He has, however, stopped beating his wife: the violent streak he picked up from his double now sickens him.

Yahia wants to destroy Uday, but he has not changed his appearance because he has no other identity, a dilemma that would have fascinated Sigmund Freud, who lived in the same Vienna street where Yahia's hideout is.

Yahia's case is like none Freud ever came across. He grew up in Baghdad, the son of a wealthy Kurdish merchant, and attended the exclusive Baghdad High School for Boys. Uday was in the same class and the two boys resembled each other. 'But I did not welcome looking similar,' he said. 'Uday had very bad manners with people even then.'

After graduating from Baghdad University in 1986 with a law degree, he went off to fight in the Iran–Iraq war, like most young Iraqi males. He was a first lieutenant serving in a forward reconnaissance unit in September 1987 when he received a presidential order to report to Baghdad.

Uday welcomed him in an ornate salon in the presidential palace. There was chit-chat about their schooldays and polite questions about his family before Uday came to the point. 'Do you want to be a son of Saddam?' he asked. Wary, Yahia answered: 'We are all sons of Saddam.'

'Well, I would like you to be a real son of Saddam, working with me. I don't want you as protection but as my double.'

Yahia recalled: 'I was afraid. I knew this was a government of criminals. So I asked him what would happen if I agreed, and what would happen if I refused. Uday told me that if I agreed, "all that you dream will happen". He said I would have money, servants, houses, women. If I refused, he said, "We will remain friends".'

Uday left him alone, desperately trying to think up an excuse. When he returned, Yahia had formulated what he thought was a diplomatic way out. 'All Iraqis want to serve the president,' he said. 'I am serving my president as a soldier and I would not like to be more than that.'

Uday's eyes reddened in rage; he tore the military epaulettes from Yahia's shoulders and called in security officers. Yahia was blindfolded, driven for an hour in a car (later he would realise he had only been driven around the presidential grounds), and imprisoned in a tiny cell that was painted entirely blood-red.

'I suffered every kind of torture,' Yahia recalled. He said he was beaten with a cable, hanged from the ceiling by his hands, fed only bread or rice and water at different times of day so that he would become disorientated. He was told that if he continued to refuse, he would spend the rest of his life in the cell. After a week, he cracked.

Four days later he signed papers promising he would act as Uday's double and reveal nothing about his activities. The contract ended with a warning: any violation and the penalty was death by hanging. Two weeks later, surgery began at the Ibn Sina hospital in the palace complex. Dentists removed his front teeth and replaced them with teeth like Uday's; doctors cut a cleft into his chin.

'I hated myself,' he said. 'All my family and friends hated Saddam; so looking like his son, I was disgusted with myself.'

He began his 'special education': 16 hours a day watching videos of Uday walk, dance, drive, talk, get in and out of cars, light cigars, drink Scotch. A trainer would then take him through each movement over and over 20, 30, 40 times, day after day until he got it right.

'I never drank before, or smoked, or danced. I was very correct with people,' Yahia said. 'I had to learn to drink Dimple (Uday's brand of whisky), smoke cigars and talk differently. And I had to learn to be rude with people, like him.' He also learned intelligence and sabotage techniques, and was taught to check under cars before getting into them.

After six months of intensive training, Yahia made his first public appearance as his double at a football match at the People's Stadium, where he was surrounded by people who knew the president's son. With a trainer by his elbow every moment, even driving the black Mercedes 500SL that was Uday's favourite car, Yahia passed muster. He remembers thinking when he arrived back at the sumptuous villa Uday had given him: 'Latif Yahia doesn't exist any more.'

Four lost years followed. Yahia appeared as Uday and travelled with him to London, Geneva and Paris. Whenever Uday wanted a suit – he preferred Christian Dior and Yves St Laurent – he bought two: one for himself, one for Yahia. Uday owned more than 100 luxury cars, and selected them daily to match the colour of his suit.

Outside Baghdad, Yahia would travel in a security convoy as Uday, sometimes with as many as 72 bodyguards. By the time of the Gulf War, Saddam had so much confidence in Yahia that he used him in a cruel confidence trick against his own people. Every Iraqi remembers the visit by Uday to troops on the Kuwaiti front; in fact it was Yahia, sent there with a television crew to counteract truthful reports that Saddam's family had fled to safety outside Iraq.

During the years of their 'partnership', Uday gave him only one rule: 'Don't touch my girls.' At one point, Uday sent him to prison for 21 days because a girlfriend of Uday's became angry with Yahia, and told the president's son that he had tried to seduce her. When he was released, his double gave him a Mercedes by way of apology.

Uday often beat his guards, so in public Yahia would have to do the same. He had to learn to curse people; now, in an embarrassed voice, he repeats Uday's favourites. 'I would have to say "Your mother is a whore" and things like that,' Yahia said.

Gradually his public life merged with his private; he is ashamed to admit that he began to beat his wife, Bushra. 'I would kill Uday if I saw him again,' Yahia said. 'I would cut his body into small pieces and feed it to dogs. He made out of me a criminal like himself.'

Yahia was at a party on the river Tigris given for Suzanne Mubarak, the wife of the Egyptian president, when Uday committed one of his worst outrages. Uday hated Kamel Hanna, his father's favourite retainer, for serving as the go-between for Saddam's mistress, Samira Shahbandar, wife of the president of Iraq Airways. When Hanna failed to invite Uday to the Mubarak reception, he threw a party nearby out of spite; hearing shots at midnight, he crashed drunkenly into Hanna's celebration.

Uday saw Hanna firing into the air, Yahia recalled, and ordered him to stop shooting. 'I only take orders from the president,' Hanna replied. The night degenerated into violent chaos. Uday cut Hanna's neck and beat him, then downed pills at the thought of his father's anger. Both were taken to hospital, where Uday met Saddam waiting for word of his aide.

'Saddam grabbed Uday by the shirt and said: "If Kamel dies, you die",' Yahia said. Hanna died that night, but Uday's mother intervened to save her son. Yahia worried that he would be executed instead of Uday, but there had been too many witnesses.

Life was not all misery. Yahia had three villas, six luxury cars, all the money he wanted, beautiful women in droves. 'But I was always afraid,' he said. 'I was afraid Uday would kill me. I was afraid of being killed instead of Uday. Nine times I suffered assassination attempts.'

The attempts to kill him were sometimes by family members outraged that Uday had dishonoured their women, sometimes by political opponents. Once, he recalled, an outraged man burst into Uday's office at the Special Olympic Committee, which he headed, claiming he had raped his young daughter. The father said he had killed his daughter because of the dishonour and wanted satisfaction from Uday.

'Uday pulled out his pistol and shot him on the spot,' Yahia recalled. 'I sat in his office, six metres away. I was not shocked. I had seen it before. I knew I could do nothing.'

Yahia described a permanent atmosphere of fear in the presidential palace. Even those closest to Saddam refrained from speaking openly; everyone was afraid that they would be reported as disloyal, and the penalty was death.

He said Qusay, Saddam's younger son, who now heads the presidential intelligence agency, was the Iraqi president's favourite and heir apparent. 'Uday never called his father "dad",' Yahia said. 'Even in private he addressed him as "your excellency".'

One of the few people with whom Yahia could relax was Saddam's double, Fawaz al-Emari. He was the second man trained to impersonate the Iraqi president; his predecessor was killed posing as Saddam in 1984.

Emari had undergone far more extensive surgery than Yahia. His face had been entirely remodelled in Yugoslavia, and Russian doctors in Baghdad had operated on his vocal cords so he would speak exactly like Saddam. 'Sometimes when I met him, for a moment I would be afraid, thinking he was Saddam. And we were good friends,' said Yahia.

He and Emari would practise target-shooting together in the palace grounds, which included a swimming pool, cinema, theatre, hospital and sports centre. 'We spoke about general matters, but never about what we really felt or our activities. We were both too afraid one would betray the other,' he said.

Both doubles had to undergo weekly medical examinations. Doctors at the presidential palace would check that they were still the same weight as their masters, that their health was good, and that their surgery work remained sufficient for impersonation.

Saddam's double remains in the palace to this day, a virtual prisoner of his identity. 'Fawaz had a much more difficult life than me,' Yahia said. 'At least Uday went out all the time to restaurants, parties and discos, so I could. Saddam never did these things so Fawaz never could. He could not even go outside and walk on a street looking like Saddam; he would have been killed. He was banned from ever leaving the palace except when he was working.'

Work meant big formal occasions, including a hugely publicised swim by 'Saddam' in the Tigris on 26 July 1992. The swim was staged to prove that the president was alive and in good spirits despite the devastation of the Gulf War. In fact, he was afraid to appear in public and exposed his double to danger instead.

Yahia made the decision to flee almost a year after the allies liberated Kuwait in February 1991. His relationship with Uday had become increasingly tense.

'We were at a party at the Rasheed hotel,' Yahia recalled. 'Uday was invited by the president to receive four medals for his role in the Mother of all Battles. I joked, "You are not worth receiving these: I was in Kuwait instead of you." Uday said there was no difference, but he was not happy with me.'

The danger sign came the next night at another party, when Uday's 'love-broker', who procured girls for the president's son, upbraided Yahia for refusing to sell him a car. Then Uday also turned on Yahia.

The master apparently sensed that his double was going to make a break for freedom and decided to stop him. As Yahia stepped from a lift into the lobby of the Babylon hotel in Baghdad the next morning, Uday suddenly appeared and shot him. The bullet hit him high in the chest, missing vital organs.

Bleeding heavily, he says, he managed to get to his car and drive north towards the UN-protected safe haven in Kurdistan. To his surprise, Iraqi guards had not been alerted. 'At every checkpoint, nobody stopped me, they just waved me through. I would see them saluting in my (rear-view) mirror.'

Yahia has the scars to support his story: a round wound in the top of his right chest, an exit hole out the back. As he approached Kurdistan, he needed urgent medical treatment and feared the reception he would get from the Kurds. 'I could not go directly to Kurdistan. If the Kurds saw me, they would think I was Uday and kill me. So I abandoned my car in the woods, and went to a friend's house. I am from a Kurdish family, so they helped me.'

Through the Kurdish underground, he reached the American operations headquarters in the Kurdish town of Zakho. The Americans, wary at first, flew in four intelligence officers to debrief him. His wife, who had gone into hiding, was helped out by the same Kurdish underground, and their baby daughter was smuggled to Jordan by friends.

With the help of the Americans, he was granted political asylum in Vienna where many Iraqis live. But an import-export company he set up has failed to prosper and, because of Vienna's close connections with Baghdad, the city has a high number of Iraqi government representatives. Any one of them, he fears, might be a potential assassin.

His anxiety heightened last September when he received a letter from the Iraqi embassy saying he had been granted an amnesty and should return to Baghdad. The message came on his personal fax machine, even though he is living in hiding and gives the number only to close personal friends.

Yahia is afraid to send his daughter, Tamara, now five, to school in case his whereabouts can be traced through her. He keeps his wife, daughter and Omar, their 18-month son, with him even at the office.

Most of all, he finds it difficult to recover any sense of himself. 'Uday stole my life, my future, my identity,' he said. His wife agrees. Watching videos of Yahia posing as Uday in Baghdad, she shivered when she saw the man on the screen roughly grab a tissue proffered by an aide.

'He changed so much in his manners,' she said. 'Before, he was a normal person, but after he was tough and violent. He would hit me or kick me, and many times I thought of getting divorced. But I know now he is trying very hard to recover himself.'

Blood feud at the heart of darkness

8 September 1996

Terrible deaths in the family of Saddam Hussein illlustrate the brutality of a tyrant still powerful enough to shake the world. Marie Colvin reports from Oman.

In the glistening marble and gilt palace of Hashemiya, high on a hilltop overlooking the Jordanian capital, Ali Kamel, nine, spent many hours of his exile drawing brightly coloured pictures for his grandfather. Ali never learnt why he was living in this strange place. He was too young to be told his family had fled there in terror of the grandfather he loved: Saddam Hussein.

Hussein Kamel, Ali's father, had been the Iraqi tyrant's closest adviser. He had risen from lowly bodyguard to head of military procurement, and had been put in charge of rebuilding his country after the Gulf War. Kamel even married Saddam's favourite daughter, Ragda. But he fell out with the dictator's son, Uday, a thug who had repeatedly killed on impulse.

In August last year, Kamel was in such fear of his life that he took Ragda, Ali and his two daughters across the barren Iraqi desert to seek safety in Jordan. Other members of the family accompanied him in a fleet of black Mercedes.

There was a brother, Saddam Kamel, who had been responsible for the dictator's personal security. His wife Rana, Saddam's second daughter, came too, clutching their three children. A second brother followed, with a sister, her husband and their five children.

The family's terrible fate, details of which are disclosed here for the first time, gives a chilling insight into the methods used by Saddam to retain power despite isolation from the world and hatred at home.

The defection of so many family members was a devastating blow to the tyrant. In the days that followed he retaliated: scores of Kamel's relatives and followers disappeared. For months afterwards Saddam plotted his revenge with the cunning and lethal aggression that was so much in evidence again last week in his latest challenge to the international order.

Kamel's family settled comfortably at first into the luxury of the palace provided for them by King Hussein of Jordan. Stuffed with Persian carpets and other finery, it provided them with a secure home behind the shelter of tall, white stone walls.

Ali took lessons from a private tutor. Although the boy did not excel in his academic work, it did not take him long to work out that all was not well with his parents. Kamel had expected to be seen by the world as the potential successor to Saddam. But he had too much blood on his own hands. The Americans came only to pump him for information about the Iraqi military establishment. Even the Iraqi opposition shunned him.

Early in February, Ali often saw his father walking in the palace garden despite the cold and rain, speaking on his cellular telephone. Hussein Kamel had become so disillusioned with exile that he had begun discreet negotiations to return to Baghdad.

It was part of Saddam's game plan that he responded by making strenuous demands. Not only would Kamel be obliged to return millions of dollars he had hidden in a German bank; he would also have to provide a detailed written account of everything he had told his western interrogators, a lengthy process for a man who was barely literate.

His departure was precipitated by the growing impatience of his hosts with public statements in which he criticised the king. On the first day of the Muslim feast of Eid, he was visited by Prince Talal of Jordan, who told him he was 'free to go', the unspoken message being that he had outstayed his welcome.

Kamel strapped a pistol to his hip, drove to the home of the Iraqi ambassador and sat in animated discussion with him in the reception hall. Then they went to the embassy and telephoned Baghdad.

Once he was sure that Kamel had fulfilled the conditions set for his return, Saddam sent a video of himself, in which he promised he had forgiven his son-in-law. 'Come during the feast,' he said. 'The family will be together.' He implored him to bring all his relatives back with him. A written amnesty followed from the Iraqi leadership council.

Kamel made his decision abruptly. 'We are going home,' he announced to a family gathering. Ragda and Rana, suddenly frightened, began crying. At the last moment, Ragda telephoned her mother, seeking reassurance. But the phone was answered by Uday, who, in his latest outrage, had shot an uncle in the leg in an argument over an Italian car that he wanted to add to his collection of classics.

Ragda begged her brother to tell her the truth: would they be safe if they came home? '*Habibti* [Arabic for my love], I give you my word,' he said.

Hours before he left, Kamel telephoned one of his few friends to say goodbye. The man, a fellow Iraqi, was appalled. 'You know you are going to your death,' he said. Kamel bragged that he had obtained personal assurances from Saddam. 'To this day, I don't know why he trusted Saddam,' the friend said last week. 'He was one of them. He should have known.'

Arriving at the border, the returning defectors were greeted by a smiling Uday in sunglasses and suit. The men were separated from their wives and children. Kamel would never see Ragda and Ali again.

With his brothers, he was taken to one of Saddam's presidential palaces, where they were rigorously questioned about their experiences in Jordan and their contacts with western representatives and opponents of the Iraqi regime. After three days, they were released and went to the home of Taher Abdel Kadr, a cousin. Here, they were joined by two sisters and the women's children. But their relief and jubilation were short-lived. Within 48 hours, they learnt from a statement broadcast on television that their wives had denounced them as traitors and had been granted divorces.

As dawn filtered through the windows of their villa on 20 February, a cousin who still worked at the presidential palace woke them with the news that they had been betrayed. He brought weapons. Grimly, the Kamels prepared for their assassins as the children slept on.

Their killing was a family affair. While army vehicles and police cars blocked off the neighbourhood, an armed gang led by Uday and Qusay Hussein, Saddam's second son, surrounded the house. Uday and Qusay were accompanied inside by the former husband of one of Kamel's sisters. He showed his loyalty to Saddam by opening the firing on his family's house.

The attack, carried out with assault weapons, was ferocious. Although Kamel's men fired back, they were swiftly overwhelmed.

Some of the family were killed in the initial onslaught; others when the armed men entered the house. They included Kamel's elderly father, all the women and at least five young children, gunned down in their nightclothes.

Outside in a parked Mercedes sat Ali Hassan Al-Majeed, a cousin of Saddam's who had earned the nickname 'The Hammer of the Kurds' after gassing villages in northern Iraq with chemical weapons in 1989. Al-Majeed was on a mobile phone, describing each step of the assault to Saddam as it happened.

'We have 17 bodies,' he said. The only member of the family who was missing was Kamel himself. Saddam barked: 'I want his body.'

As bulldozers were brought in to destroy the house, Kamel, naked to the waist, wounded and bleeding, burst from a hiding place inside and appeared at a door brandishing his personal pistol and a machinegun.

He had barely fired a shot before he was riddled with bullets. When the gunfire ceased, Al-Majeed walked up to the body and emptied his pistol into it. He dragged Kamel by one foot through the sand, yelling to his men and to neighbours cowering behind closed doors: 'Come and see the fate of a traitor.' The bulldozers moved in and the house was razed.

The massacre was a vivid reminder to the people of the ruthlessness of the regime under which they live. If Saddam was willing to eliminate close and even innocent members of his own family in such a fashion, there was no limit to what he could do to them.

During the summer, however, came two further reminders of the apparent futility of resistance. In June a member of the presidential bodyguard fired shots at Saddam and was executed. Less than a month later, according to western diplomats and Iraqi exiles, a rebel group of Iraqi officers planned to kill Saddam by bombing a presidential palace from a plane that was to have taken off from Rasheed airport in Baghdad.

The conspiracy was discovered and hundreds of members of Saddam's armed forces were arrested. Between 1 and 3 August, 120 of the officers were executed.

Iraqis have grown used to atrocities since Saddam came to prominence. His first known political act was an attempt in 1959 to gun down Abdel-Karim Qassem, then the Iraqi leader. When he became president 20 years later, he began by accusing 21 senior members of the leadership of treason. He formed a firing squad with his remaining colleagues, and together they shot all the condemned men.

In the years that followed, his people learned to voice their opposition only to close friends and family. Criticism of Saddam is punishable by death, and the security services are ubiquitous. Iraqi couples do not even speak in front of their own children for fear they might innocently repeat something and bring down the wrath of the regime.

The long series of confrontations into which Saddam has led Iraq has made life immensely difficult in a country whose citizens should be as pampered as those of Saudi Arabia. Iraq, unlike most Arab states, has both oil and water. Two huge rivers, the Tigris and Euphrates, nourish the land, and before the imposition of United Nations sanctions following the invasion of Kuwait in August 1990, Iraq earned $10 billion a year by lifting 3m barrels of oil a day.

Much of the money was spent on creating not comfort, but the largest army in the Middle East. Within a year of taking power, Saddam ordered the invasion of Iran, starting a bitter war that lasted for eight years and left 1 million people dead.

The attack on Kuwait was another miscalculation. The 43 days of allied bombing, supported by Arab countries afraid of his might, destroyed not only military sites but roads, bridges, oil refineries, communications, sewage facilities and the rest of an extensive infrastructure built by oil revenues.

Last week's conflict, in which Iraqi support for one group of Kurds against another provoked two waves of bombardment with American cruise missiles, was by no means the first test of the allies' resolve since the Gulf War. But after previous confrontations, Saddam has simply waited out his enemies. Those close to him say he is proud to have outlasted in office both George Bush and Margaret Thatcher, who led the coalition against him in 1990.

The few who have risen in revolt have been crushed, but his inner circle has tightened around him and now consists almost solely of relatives from Tikrit, his home town.

According to Arab dignitaries who have visited Saddam, he has become so paranoid about his security since the Gulf War that he maintains 250 safe homes. The staff in each house prepares dinner every night as if he is to arrive; nobody knows where he will sleep until he shows up at the door.

The Kamel clan was not the first to betray him. Last June he was shaken by a coup attempt led by the powerful Dulaimi clan from his Sunni heartland that had been a pillar of his armed forces. Provoked by the torture and death of a clan member accused of involvement in a previous coup attempt, General Turki al-Dulaimi led his troops in a bold but suicidal march on Baghdad. The rebels were defeated in a day.

It has not escaped the attention of most Iraqis that while the latest confrontation has occurred less than six years after the Gulf War, the reaction around the world this time has been quite different. America's use of missiles was backed wholeheartedly only by Britain, Canada and Germany. Although he lost a few isolated radar and anti-aircraft batteries, Saddam succeeded in dividing the coalition that had been ranged against him.

The main reason for the change was the nature of Saddam's offensive. He did not roll his army across an international border and occupy another country, but sent a limited force of tanks and infantry into Arbil, a Kurdish city 12 miles inside the Kurdish 'safe haven' patrolled by allied jets.

He was also invited in by the Kurdish faction that represents the majority of Kurds, the Kurdish Democratic party (KDP). Other Middle Eastern countries saw the American intervention as a blatantly inconsistent piece of interference in an internal problem. The United States had not objected when Turkey sent 35,000 troops into northern Iraq last year to attack bases of rebellious

Kurds; nor when Iran sent 3,000 troops across the border into northern Iraq last month.

Turkey and Saudi Arabia, among the countries that are the closest allies in the Middle East, refused Washington permission to launch strikes from their soil. The Arab League, for once in agreement, denounced the attacks on Iraq.

Just as striking, the first criticism of the American bombing came from a Gulf newspaper, condemning the action and saying that all Arabs should oppose it 'as a matter of honour'. It was the first time since the Gulf War that any paper in the region used the word 'brothers' to refer to Iraqis.

France was critical and Britain was unable to get a resolution denouncing the Iraqi incursion through the UN security council following strong opposition from Russia. By the end of the week, Saddam's tanks were still dug in in northern Iraq and the allied coalition was in tatters.

For now, Saddam may have little choice but to accept the establishment of a security zone inside its territory by Turkey, which says this is needed to fight Kurds battling for independence from Ankara. He should not be expected to be quiescent forever, however. He has every prospect of increasing his power and has a lot of grudges to settle. Those who know Saddam say the one certainty is that he never forgets and never forgives.

For the ordinary Iraqi, life seems likely to get harder. While the so-called 'war rich' who have profited from the black market in Baghdad continue to work on new palaces, most people are worried about food prices driven to new peaks by the crisis.

Privations, large and small, continued last week. People had to shower at 4am because electricity cuts meant there was no water during daytime. In a hospital in Baghdad, surgeons who no longer had paediatric surgical equipment operated on children with adult-sized instruments. 'It is butchery,' one doctor agonised.

Saddam's offensive put into limbo a UN-negotiated deal that would have enabled him to sell oil for food. There now seems little hope of relief in the near future.

Life is more comfortable but barely less bleak for Saddam's two daughters and their six young children. They were not in the villa where Kamel and his other relatives were killed, but face a dark future.

The two young widows were forced to move into the house of their mother's sister, where they are virtual prisoners. They cannot go out. Their children were taken away and they have been told they may never see them again. Sources in Baghdad said Rana, who was close to her husband Saddam Kamel, tried to kill herself and had to be hospitalised.

Ali, his sisters and cousins are living a sequestered life in Tikrit, Saddam Hussein's birthplace. Ali may still be drawing pictures for his grandfather in vain. He and the other children are being raised to know that their parents were traitors.

Middle East

The Hawk who downed a dove: assassination of Yitzhak Rabin

12 November 1995

Marie Colvin and Jon Swain

Her name was Nava, and she was everything that Yigal Amir, a rather serious student at the religious university of Bar Ilan, wanted. Amir, his friends say, was an arrogant man, lonely and aloof, who had never had a girlfriend before because no girl had been good enough.

He began pursuing her as soon as they met in the spring of 1994. 'She was rich, pretty, clever, pure and religious. She had it all,' said a fellow student. They dated for five months. 'They never broke the limits of what is permissible between a religious pair, but there was a huge commitment.' So intense was the relationship, they planned to marry.

Then, in January this year, she abruptly left him for his best friend, Shmuel Rosenblum. Amir was stunned. 'The talk on campus was that her parents had disapproved of her marrying him because he was poor and of Yemeni extraction,' the friend said. A month later Nava married her new boyfriend.

Amir changed. He had always been fiercely nationalist, with a deep religious belief that God's holy land had to be zealously guarded by the Jews. He was utterly opposed to Yitzhak Rabin, the prime minister, and his policy of trading land for peace with the Palestinians.

Now he became outrageous, outspoken and dangerous. The extremist, angered and rejected, had tipped over into a potential assassin. 'I think that not only political views caused the murder, but also his feeling of disappointment in his personal life,' the friend said. 'Suddenly we heard him talking about the duty to kill Rabin.'

A fellow student, Shmulik, recalled: 'His arguments were always based on the Torah [the body of Jewish sacred writings and traditions].' Amir would tell his friends that, since Rabin had given up parts of the land of Israel, it was a mitzvah (positive obligation) to kill him.

Eight days ago, on a Saturday night in Tel Aviv, he walked up to Rabin, pumped two exploding bullets into him, and discharged that obligation.

In the weeks before, Amir was on such a public rampage that it now seems astonishing that he was able to get near the prime minister with a gun in his hand and a clear line of fire. All last week, stunned Israelis asked why nobody had been watching him.

Amir had made no secret of his deadly intentions. He was a member of an extremist Jewish group that denounced Rabin for treason; he was dragged away by security guards for heckling Rabin at meetings; before he succeeded last Saturday, he had already made two unsuccessful assassination runs. Weren't the groups of fundamentalist Jews who vowed to stop the peace process at all costs under any kind of surveillance?

The murder raised other, more profound questions. Nobody had believed a Jew would ever kill a Jew; despite the venomous rhetoric that had followed Rabin's peace treaty with Yasser Arafat, the Palestinian leader, nobody believed that taboo would be broken. So what was this nation of Jews if the land had become more important than an individual's life?

The shock and incomprehension deepened as Israelis learned more details about the killer in their midst. Amir grew up in the heart of Israel, the Tel Aviv suburbs, and served in an elite brigade of the army. His background might have given him something of a chip on his shoulder; he was a Sephardi, an Israeli descended from Jews who came from Arab lands, rather than an Ashkenazi, the elite of Israel who came from Europe and founded the state. But he had done well.

Born in 1970, the second of eight children, he was raised in a two-room house by his father, Shlomo, a scribe who supplemented his income with the ritual slaughter of chickens, and his mother, Geula, a large, warm woman who supported the family with a creche in the back garden. They had come to Israel in the 1950s from the Yemen.

Religion played a strong role in Amir's life from the beginning, first at Wolfson, a school run by the ultra-orthodox Aguda movement and dominated by Ashkenazis. He was out of place as a dark-skinned Sephardi, but he surpassed everyone in his work.

When most of his fellow religious students opted out of armed service, allowed for those pursuing religious studies, he joined the elite Golani brigade while continuing to study the Torah at the fiercely nationalist Yeshiva Kerem De'Yavne institute.

In October 1993, a month after Rabin signed the agreement with Arafat in Washington to hand over land occupied by Israel in the 1967 war in return for peace, Amir entered Bar Ilan University. There, too, he was unable to forget his Sephardic background.

Although he was a top student in the most difficult of Israeli studies – a triple course of law, computer and Torah studies – he always
felt a misfit. When Nava left him, he felt it even more keenly: she
was Ashkenazi.

As his politics became more virulent, he spent most of his time
in the Institute of Advanced Torah Studies and in fierce religious
and political debates. He began organising student demonstrations, obtained a gun licence and bought a short-barrelled Beretta
9mm, the gun he shot Rabin with. He wore it ostentatiously, tucked
in his left trouser hip pocket, the handle protruding over his belt.

Somehow, though, he escaped the attention of Shin Bet, the
Israeli version of MI5, even when he joined Eyal, a violently anti-
Arab group operating in the West Bank and a venomous agitator
against the Rabin government. He became a friend of its founder,
Avishai Raviv, who was under surveillance and had been arrested.
Still Amir went unnoticed.

In the final weeks he was a publicly angry young man who was
hiding nothing. The incidents mounted. On 30 September, he went
with other Bar Ilan students to Hebron, where about 20 Jewish
families live at the heart of a city of 100,000 Arabs. There they went
on a tour with a settler, Maisha Meishcan, a man who defiantly
walks the streets with a cowboy hat on his head and an Uzi on his
shoulder, and visited the site of a 1929 pogrom against Jews.

There, Meishcan revealed last week, Amir 'beat up' two Christian
women pacifists, dragging them 20 yards, before police arrived.
Two of the group were arrested but Amir slipped away.

A week later he was stopped and his identity details taken by
police at a demonstration outside the home of a right-wing Israeli
minister who had revealed his support for Rabin over the second
phase of the peace agreement. There were other demonstrations.
He was twice arrested and released.

On 23 October, Bar Ilan reopened. The last time fellow students
remember seeing him was on 2 November, the Thursday before the
assassination, at a computer class. He arranged with a friend for a
lift to the university that Sunday. He never went.

On the evening of 4 November, at 5:45, Amir locked himself in his family's garden shed and loaded his Beretta. This time his plan would work.

He had made his first attempt to murder the prime minister months earlier, in June, but at the last minute Rabin had failed to show up at a ceremony at Yad Vashem, the holocaust memorial in Jerusalem. Thwarted, he tried again in early September, when Rabin was opening a new road in Herzliya, near Amir's home. He joined right-wing demonstrators against the premier, gun in pocket, and got close before security 'closed like a clam' around the prime minister.

Now Amir loaded his gun with special hollow-point bullets prepared by his brother, Haggai, 27. In the previous weeks, while Amir was demonstrating, Haggai had painstakingly drilled holes in the heads of about 20 bullets, filling the tiny space with mercury. Ordinary bullets pass cleanly through a target, but hollow-points flatten like a mushroom on impact, bounding around in the body and ripping apart flesh and bone. Amir was now ready.

He walked out of the shed, past the family car and took a bus to the Kings of Israel Square in Tel Aviv, where more than 100,000 Israelis had gathered for a demonstration in support of the peace process. It was the largest rally in Israel since 1982, when Israelis protested against their country's invasion of Lebanon. Rabin was on stage and in a more ebullient mood than anyone could remember.

Out of the public eye, the security operation was under way to protect the prime minister. Its code name: Operation Sunrise. The special techniques for protecting VIPs in Israel are so straightforward that they can be written on one side of a sheet of paper.

But on the night of Rabin's murder, the much-vaunted organisation was preoccupied. Evidence is emerging of recent infighting that may have weakened Shin Bet's morale, upset its discipline and damaged its capabilities in the crucial weeks leading up to the assassination.

The trouble began six months ago when a new head of Shin Bet was appointed amid vociferous praise in the Israeli intelligence community. The fact that this man, who cannot be identified under Israeli censorship laws, spoke only broken Arabic was considered of minor importance; he had other vital qualifications, principally his expert knowledge of Jewish extremist organisations.

While at university in the 1970s he had written a thesis on Jewish fringe groups and how to deal with them from a legal point of view. Here was the man to carry Shin Bet into the new era of the peace process between Israel and the Palestinians.

But when Yaakov Perry, the outgoing head of Shin Bet, who was a close friend of Rabin's, chose him as his heir, the result was devastating. Six section heads resigned when they realised their way to the top was blocked by the appointment, creating a serious vacuum within the organisation.

Even during Perry's last years as director-general, signs of unease within Shin Bet had become discernible. Part of these were about Perry himself, who was nicknamed the 'trumpeter' for his taste for boisterous parties and wild music. There were two commissions of inquiry into Shin Bet's activities during Perry's tenure. But Rabin, in keeping with his customary loyalty to his friends, overlooked the reports against him.

In the words of a leading Israeli security specialist, Shin Bet had grown 'complacent, sloppy and corrupt'. In common with many other bodies in Israel, a malaise had set in, derived from the deep divisions in Israeli society, the lack of a common goal and the pursuit of peace amid continuing terror.

None the less, it knew that an assassination was in the wind. Three weeks earlier, the heads of Shin Bet summoned leaders of the Jewish settler movement to meetings in Tel Aviv where they were urged to help build a profile of a potential assassin. They refused, saying that as leaders of their communities their involvement with the security services was inappropriate.

They assured Shin Bet that it was highly unlikely that a settler would assassinate a Jewish leader anyway. It would be better, they warned, for the security service to concentrate its energies on the Israeli heartland – the suburbs of Tel Aviv, for example.

They were right, and the view is that the new head of Shin Bet, as an expert on Jewish extremists, should have evaluated their advice better, and followed it. Like Britain's naval guns guarding the fortress of Singapore in 1941, Shin Bet was pointing the wrong way last Saturday night.

The plain fact is that everyone knew the prime minister was in danger that night. In the days leading up to the peace demonstration, the intelligence services had publicised their fears of an attack, perhaps by sniper fire or a car bomb. The assumption was that it would come from Palestinian extremists.

There was extra surveillance around the square, with more than 1,000 policemen on duty, snipers crouched on rooftops and checks on hundreds of apartments.

Even so, Rabin failed to take the most elementary precaution of wearing a bullet-proof vest. One Israeli security expert last week laid some of the blame for this on the chummy relationship between the prime minister and the man in charge of VIP security, Colonel Benny Lahav (since resigned) of Shin Bet. It meant that Lahav could not exercise his authority. 'Had I been in charge,' the expert said, 'I would have told the prime minister that either he wore a bullet-proof vest or I would, that I could not protect him without it. Such a firm stand would have got through to Rabin.'

Error was compounded by error. Shin Bet's rules require the prime minister to be in a 'sterile zone' at all times, surrounded by a minimum of three Shin Bet bodyguards, preferably six. Last Saturday there were only two near him as he took his place on the stage with Shimon Peres.

By that time a vital breach in security had already taken place. The original plan had been for Rabin to arrive at a nearby municipal building and go to the rally via a basement door through a secure area not open to the public.

Instead, the premier's car was parked next to the stage and he climbed to it up an open flight of stairs. 'I don't know why the change was made, but it cost Rabin his life. Under the original plan, he would not have been exposed to the public at all,' said a security official.

Just after 8pm, Rabin took the microphone to address the cheering crowd. 'Allow me to say that I am excited. I was a military man for 27 years. I fought as long as there was no chance for peace. I believe there is now a chance for peace that must be taken.'

Surprisingly, since he was awkward in public and usually fled after speaking, he stayed with Peres and other Israeli personalities to sing the Song of Peace, an anthem that was banned in Israel when it was released in 1969. Nobody had ever seen Rabin sing in public. It was a sign of his joy that after all the criticism of his policies he felt that the unprecedented numbers at the rally validated his decisions.

Then, 15 minutes before Rabin took his fatal walk down the stairs from the podium, two more security lapses gave Amir his chance. Shin Bet should have been guarding the car parking area beneath the stage. They were not. When an officer noticed that this area had not been secured, he ordered police to do so. By then, Amir was already inside, explaining to the police that he was a VIP driver called up for extra duties. Nobody challenged his story. As he waited behind a barrier for the right moment to strike, the Beretta lay hidden in his clothes.

By now, the Shin Bet officer in charge had reason to be distracted. Over his radio he received a tip-off that a shooting was imminent. 'The tension was immense, and he wanted to get Rabin off the stage as fast as possible. But he was convinced that the main threat was from Palestinians,' said a security official.

At the end of the demonstration, Rabin came down the stairs to his car, failing to make sure the bodyguards were around him. Another blunder. The police unit in the parking area had not received a message that Rabin was arriving, so no safe channel was formed. 'We let down our guard,' said the security official. 'We felt that the rally had passed peaceably and that we had done our job.'

At 9.44, as Rabin was getting into his armoured Cadillac, Amir stepped forward. From 5 feet away he drew his pistol and fired.

Ingeniously, he shouted to the police that it was 'only an exercise' and he was firing blanks. They believed him.

Rabin's bodyguard, hit in the shoulder, knew otherwise. He bundled the prime minister, a bullet in his stomach, another in his back, into the car and they sped off. At the hospital, there was the final blunder: nobody was ready to receive them. In the confusion nobody had radioed ahead. The chief surgeon, summoned to an emergency on a badly wounded man, found he was treating the dying prime minister.

One top Jewish counter-terrorist expert said of the colossal foul-up: 'It is beyond negligence of the most simple basic procedures. Rabin was abandoned.'

Amir told security officials who surrounded him immediately after the killing, the gun still in his hand: 'God told me to do it. I have no regrets.' The fact that he believed he had a religious mandate shocked Israelis.

So did the crass statements by supporters. One student at Bar Ilan sent a message on the Internet: 'Happy holiday everyone. The witch is dead; the wicked witch is dead.' The West Bank settlement of Maale Amos hung out a sign: 'We are all Yigal Amir.'

'I am very happy that the dictator Rabin is dead,' said Aryeh Bar Yosef, a resident of Kiryat Arba, a radical settlement outside Hebron, which has made a shrine of the grave of Baruch Goldstein, who gunned down 29 Palestinians at the Hebron mosque last year.

'I hope that the Nazi Arafat and his friend Peres will die like Rabin. Rabin, the head of the traitors, got what he deserved. Praise be to God. Yigal Amir redeemed us from the terrible situation we were in.'

Such statements have forced Israelis to face the dark netherworld of Jewish extremist groups. Eyal follows the teachings of Meir Kahane, a Brooklyn-based rabbi who moved to Israel and founded the extremist Kach movement.

Kahane was assassinated five years ago – eerily, on exactly the same day as Rabin – while making a speech in New York and his movement was outlawed last year by the Israeli government after

Goldstein's massacre. With Kach banned, groups such as Eyal, with the same ideology and many of the same members, have become increasingly active.

Even more disturbing for Israelis is the realisation that these groups flourish among young people from comfortable, ordinary homes. When police searched the Amir family house and the kindergarten run by his mother they found a cache of ammunition and explosives. Car tyres that were used as swings for children were packed with explosives. One of those arrested as part of the alleged conspiracy to kill Rabin, Ohad Skornik, is the son of Yehuda Skornik, an eminent surgeon at Ichilov hospital, where Rabin died. It has made parents all over Israel wonder what their children are up to.

Last week, the issue confronting Israel was the allegation of a conspiracy to kill Rabin. There is no doubt Amir was a member of an extreme right-wing group that considered Rabin a traitor.

Eyal, founded in 1991 by Raviv, good-looking, arrogant and, like Amir, a student at Bar Ilan, is fanatical, albeit in an immature way. Members are given a Hebrew code word, and go through a dramatic swearing-in ceremony at the graveside of Avraham Stern, the leader of the Stern Gang terror group that fought the British mandate.

It is believed to take orders from Baruch Marzel, a Boston-born settler based in Hebron who is a former member of Kach but resigned when it became illegal. Last week, he would not support the killing, but blamed Rabin for his own death. 'When you force people underground, when you shut their mouths, their hands work and you have violence. There will be more, I am sure. Israel is heading to civil war.'

Before last Saturday, though, Eyal was 'known for words rather than actions', said one security official. That is indeed what Raviv said when he denied all knowledge of Amir's plans to kill Rabin. 'Yes, he was very close to us, but we knew nothing of his intentions,' Raviv said after his arrest. 'I am in complete shock. The guy ruined his life. We knew he said that Rabin must be killed but he didn't speak more than anyone else here. We all shouted all kinds of things at demonstrations.'

In fact, Raviv was shouting those very things the night of Rabin's assassination, with a few dozen right-wingers who staged a counter-demonstration in a side street at the peace rally in Kings of Israel Square. Amir was seen to join them briefly, then leave after talking to Raviv.

Was there a conspiracy? A total of six people are now in police custody, charged with complicity in the killing. All are religious men in their twenties.

Along with Amir, his brother Haggai, Skornik and Raviv, police also have in custody two other students, Dror Hadani and Michael Epstein. All deny any connection.*

The signs are that Amir acted alone on the day. He took a bus to the rally and later told investigators: 'I never believed it would be so easy.' Investigators believe Amir would have aborted his plan had the opportunity not been there. 'He didn't know he was going to do it until he pulled the trigger,' said one.

But while he may have acted alone on that night, police believe the others helped him procure weapons, and did not report the possibility of his plans to police. 'We think there was a connection between a group of persons ... who established a form of organisation to assassinate the prime minister and other political persons based on their ideology to try to prevent the peace process,' Moshe Shahal, the police minister, said.

All week, mourners visited Rabin's grave side at Mount Herzl cemetery and his widow's home, leaving flowers, candles in makeshift cans or just a handwritten note. Tonight, at the end of seven days of mourning, hundreds of thousands, the largest crowd ever seen in Israel, are expected to gather at the Kings of Israel Square in Tel Aviv for a ceremony renaming the plaza where Rabin died in his honour.

---

* Haggai Amir and Dror Hadani were convicted of conspiring to assassinate Rabin, conspiring to carry out attacks against Arabs, illegal weapon production and illegal weapon possession. Michael Epstein and Ohad Skornik were not prosecuted. Avishai Raviv was acquitted of charges that he failed to prevent the assassination of Rabin.

Peres, the acting prime minister, will try to move on. He plans to push forward the peace process, which he helped broker and which cost Rabin his life. It will be a difficult task. Rabin, a gruff old soldier, was trusted by Israelis to look out for their security. Peres's language is visionary, but he lacks his predecessor's credibility.

The process is too far advanced, however, to be easily derailed. Arafat has ruled Gaza for more than a year and, starting this week with the Israeli withdrawal from the West Bank town of Jenin, will take over the West Bank in a phased process that will culminate in elections in January. The hard decisions have been pushed through. Rabin's death may help move along the peace process that he came to reluctantly but once converted pursued like one of his military campaigns. A poll released on Friday showed the proportion of Israelis supporting the peace process had risen by 31%.

And the outrage Israelis feel at the assassination of Rabin by a Jewish fundamentalist may win Peres support from those who now see the right as tainted because it provided fertile soil for such an extremist as Amir. With the death of Yitzhak Rabin, Israelis may no longer see a peacemaker as a defeatist, but as a hero.

Israel's peace hopes wither: Netanyahu victory gives voice to the hardliners

2 June 1996

Marie Colvin, Gaza; Andy Goldberg, Tel Aviv

It was a mournful gathering. Meeting for lunch in Gaza yesterday, Palestinian politicians mulled over the results of Israel's election with an air of grieving relatives at a wake. The surprise election of Binyamin Netanyahu as prime minister, they grimly concurred, could prove a mortal blow to peace. Even the menu seemed to symbolise their worst fears. They were eating roast dove.

The Likud leader, they recalled, had vowed his first act would be to close Orient House, the Palestinians' diplomatic outpost in Jerusalem.

What is more, he plans to ignore Shimon Peres's promise to withdraw Israeli troops from the West Bank city of Hebron, which was to be the next step on the road to a permanent peace. 'We feel the Israelis have voted against peace,' sighed Um Jihad, a Palestinian minister. 'There are difficult days for us ahead.'

The shock at the rise of Netanyahu was not limited to the Palestinian camp. President Bill Clinton congratulated him, as did Peres, his defeated rival and Labour leader. Yet they were stunned. Clinton had urged Israelis to vote for peace, in a thinly disguised endorsement of Peres.

Another worried man was Yasser Arafat, the Palestinian leader. He had stayed awake until 7am on Thursday after the previous day's voting. He watched the returns on television in anxious disbelief. Netanyahu won the vote by just one percentage point. Yesterday an adviser said the Palestinian leader was 'in a state of shock'. Israel's political status quo had been turned on its head.

The man responsible relaxed yesterday with his wife and children at their home in Jerusalem. Within hours of his victory he had begun to look as if he had been a prime minister all his life. He waved regally to a crowd before stepping into a chauffeur-driven Cadillac for a trip to the Wailing Wall, where he slipped a thank you note to God into a crack. To the delight of cameramen, he ruffled the blond locks of his two young sons as they arrived home.

He has never even held a cabinet post and at 46 is a beginner by contrast with Peres, who had counted on five decades of experience and a Nobel prize for peace to secure him victory. Yet Netanyahu espouses an old idea: Israel's paramount need, he believes, is for strong government that can provide security for Jews. He has consequently ruled out an Israeli withdrawal from the Golan Heights, effectively scuttling any chance of a peace deal with Syria. He has promised to resume Jewish settlement in the West Bank and said he would send the army and Shin Bet, the Israeli intelligence service, back into what is now autonomous territory patrolled by Palestinian soldiers.

By contrast, Peres seems to have believed he was leading a nation converted to peace, satisfied with a booming industry and improved economy. It was a fatal miscalculation. A wave of suicide bombings by Hamas extremists in which dozens of people were killed left the country feeling pessimistic about Peres's vision of a new and peaceful Middle East.

Supporters of Peres made pilgrimages to the grave of Yitzhak Rabin, the prime minister who was assassinated in November by Yigal Amir, a right-wing student. One left a note saying 'Sorry, friend', a melancholy echo of Clinton's 'Goodbye, friend' uttered at Rabin's funeral.

Netanyahu had been unrelenting in his opposition to Rabin, who led his country into the historic peace agreement with the Palestinians in 1993. Netanyahu would stand among the corpses left by an Islamic fundamentalist attack aimed at stopping the peace process, blame the government for the deaths and call for the revocation of the Oslo accord. He turned a blind eye to posters at Likud rallies depicting Rabin in Nazi uniform. Rabin's widow, Leah, refused to shake Netanyahu's hand at his funeral and was said to be in despair at Likud's victory.

Rabin's death had left Peres with a seemingly unassailable 26-point lead. But ironically, it was Peres's attempt to 'get tough' that led to his downfall. With his approval, Israel's security services used a booby-trapped mobile phone to assassinate Yehia Ayyash, a Hamas bomber revered by the Islamic fundamentalist group. Israel hailed the death as a glorious blow against terrorism: but then Hamas struck, killing 63 people in revenge suicide bombings. Peres's lead was wiped out overnight.

Sensing the newly subdued mood in Israel, Netanyahu restrained his accusations and let the bloody scenes on television do the talking. He moved to capture the political centre, refining his position on the Oslo accord from outright rejection to acceptance of the agreement as a fait accompli that needed revision.

And, in what would be the deciding factor in the campaign, the worldly Netanyahu wooed the ultra-orthodox vote, 10% of the electorate. Netanyahu took to wearing a skullcap and adopted the phrase 'with God's help'. He persuaded the rabbis that Likud's belief in Eretz Israel or the greater Israel that includes the biblical land of the Jews was preferable to Labour's commitment to territorial compromise.

One of the most dramatic moments of Netanyahu's campaign came with his endorsement by Rabbi Yitzhak Kadurie, a 106-year-old mystic, 36 hours before polling. Every Israeli newspaper and television station showed pictures of the frail rabbi, his hands resting on the head of a reverential Netanyahu, saying: 'Bibi, Bibi, Bibi, may God grant that next week you will be premier.' More than 90% of the ultra-orthodox community voted for Netanyahu. This tipped the election.

Netanyahu was also helped by the disastrous Labour campaign. While Likud was stealing Labour's message of peace, Labour tried to dress up as Likud. Peres bombed southern Lebanon to hit Hezbollah, the Islamic fundamentalist group, but everyone saw it as an election ploy. The operation backfired when Israeli artillery fire killed 100 Lebanese civilians in a United Nations camp at Qana, losing Peres some of the Israeli Arab support.

In a final blow, Likud mounted a scare campaign that touched on racist themes. Posters proclaimed 'Netanyahu is good for the Jews' and warned them that Peres was the candidate of the Arabs.

But Netanyahu still might not have won had Peres not practically given the election away. While a brash and confident Netanyahu pressed ahead, Peres was advised to ignore him and act like a statesman. It is a role that has never worked for him. He has lost every election campaign he has waged, including two earlier runs for prime minister. He could not shake off his image of a loser. The contrast between the two could not have been more noticeable when the results were announced on Friday night. A jubilant Netanyahu greeted crowds as he entered his home in what was an old Arab neighbourhood before 1967, shouting they should welcome 'a new Israel of peace and security'.

Peres spent the day in seclusion in his 12th-floor apartment in a luxurious suburb of Tel Aviv. He emerged briefly, looking exhausted and speaking in a flat voice. 'This was not a choice between two parties,' he told waiting reporters. 'It was a choice between two different ways. We shall remain loyal to our way.' But at 72, he can do little to implement his vision. There will be no more elections.

This week will see the first steps towards Netanyahu's 'new Israel'. The West and Israel's Arab neighbours are hoping Netanyahu will be more pragmatic than his campaign rhetoric suggested.

But there are few early signs of moderation. He owes enormous debts to right-wing nationalist and ultra-orthodox religious parties, which themselves won unprecedented numbers of seats in the Knesset. To put together a governing coalition Netanyahu will have to give the right-wing and religious parties ministries and a say in policy.

The lineup for his cabinet includes retired generals Ariel Sharon, the former defence minister who launched the 1982 Lebanon war, tipped for the finance portfolio, and Rafael Eitan, candidate for the Ministry of Domestic Security (police), who as Sharon's chief of staff enforcing the siege of Beirut announced the Arabs were 'trapped like drugged bugs in a bottle'. Netanyahu's new Israel is likely to bear little resemblance to the vision many have had in their sights in the past three years.

Israeli bulldozers rev up for showdown in Jerusalem

JERUSALEM

16 March 1997

Sasson Shem-Tov drives a black Jaguar and wears sunglasses whatever the weather. He does not usually take much interest in politics. But this week he finds himself in the middle of a dispute between Israel and the Arabs that risks bathing his country in blood.

Shem-Tov is about to order his bulldozers into Arab east Jerusalem to help build a Jewish settlement that the Palestinians have vowed to stop by any means. Even America, which is usually supportive of Israel, has denounced its plan to build 6,500 homes for Jews on a hill within sight of the church spires of Bethlehem. On Thursday the United Nations general assembly called for construction to stop.

Yasser Arafat was so angry that he twice refused to take calls from Binyamin Netanyahu, the Israeli prime minister. It is not only the settlement plans that have provoked Arab ire: Netanyahu recently announced that the first step of a three-phase withdrawal from rural areas of the West Bank, mandated under the Oslo accords, would include only a fraction of the territory Palestinians expected. The prime minister then ordered the closure of four Palestinian offices in Jerusalem, a move whose legality is being debated.

King Hussein of Jordan sent a bitter letter charging that the Israeli prime minister was 'dragging the peace process to the edge of the abyss'. When a Jordanian gunman opened fire on Israeli schoolgirls on Thursday, killing seven of them, commentators in both countries suggested he had been angered by Netanyahu's intransigence and insinuations.

Shem-Tov, a wealthy Israeli construction magnate, is unperturbed. 'We are going in next week,' he said over his car telephone. His yellow bulldozers were already in place near Har Homa, the pine-covered hill Israel seized from Jordan in the 1967 war, which he has been contracted to clear for the new homes. To him, it is just business. But for the right-wing Israeli government, the settlement means much more.

If built, Har Homa will close the last gap in a half-moon of Jewish settlements constructed on hilltops around the outer edges of Arab east Jerusalem. By encircling the Arab area with these self-contained Jewish townships, right-wing Israelis want to create 'facts on the ground' to ensure they will never have to cede an inch of Jerusalem to the Palestinians, who claim east Jerusalem as their capital.

Under the Oslo accord, the final status of Jerusalem is supposed to be decided in talks scheduled to conclude in 1999, but Palestinians argue that there will not be much to talk about if Israel keeps building. Netanyahu showed no sign of backing down. 'I am building Har Homa this week and nothing is going to stop me,' he said in an interview. The Israeli cabinet on Friday reaffirmed his decision, and government sources said the bulldozers are likely to move in tomorrow.

The army will no doubt be called in to keep back protesters, who have vowed to lie down in front of Shem-Tov's machines. Palestinian leaders have pledged that the demonstrations will be peaceful, but emotions are running so high among Palestinians that they are widely expected to explode into violence. 'The minute the bulldozers go in I think only God knows the consequences of what will happen,' said Saeb Erekat, a Palestinian minister involved in the Israeli–Palestinian negotiations.

Yesterday Arafat made a last-ditch effort to thwart Netanyahu diplomatically. Amid Israeli condemnations, he gathered American, European and Arab sponsors of the peace process to an emergency conference at his seaside headquarters in Gaza to seek their help in stopping the Har Homa settlement and putting the peace process back on track.

Although the Americans used their veto in the United Nations vote, they showed their opposition to the settlement plans by sending Edward Abington, the American consul in Jerusalem, to the talks, despite a direct Israeli request that Washington should boycott the meeting. The Palestinian president is making no secret of his anger. 'The situation is really serious,' Arafat told envoys to yesterday's meeting. 'We are facing a plan to destroy the peace process.'

The conference in Gaza is not expected to make any difference on the ground. Arafat called the meeting to send a signal to Netanyahu that he is not alone; the governments who sent envoys wanted to reassure Arafat of support, which they hoped would head off an explosion of Palestinian violence.

The threat of bloodshed is no secret. Under the codename Thornbush, Israeli army units with tanks have been practising manoeuvres to re-enter cities on the West Bank controlled by Arafat's Palestinian authority, in case Palestinians fight to stop the building at Har Homa. Israeli intelligence sources said yesterday that the army wanted to be better prepared than it was in September, when 60 Palestinians and 15 Israeli soldiers were killed in clashes after Netanyahu's decision to open a tunnel in Jerusalem.

Given the reluctance on both sides to fight, there is still a good chance violence can be avoided. Crises have come and gone since Netanyahu's government took over from Labour in May, and generally he has compromised.

Nor is Arafat in a strong position. His army is no match for the Israeli forces. If he had to fight, the peace process that would finally win a homeland for Palestinians would be shown up as a failure. He would then be vulnerable to Islamic extremists.

Netanyahu needs the support of the ultra-right-wing parties in his coalition government. But he may well have miscalculated the strength of anger his moves have inspired among Palestinians. The test of that will come when the bulldozers close in on Har Homa.

Arafat encircled in battle for Jerusalem

6 April 1997

In his first interview with a foreign journalist since the latest Middle East crisis erupted, the Palestinian leader tells Marie Colvin in Gaza why the new Israeli township must be stopped.

It was an odd spectacle: Yasser Arafat marched briskly around his modest office, arms swinging, eyes fixed on the carpet. He might have been deep in thought. But the diminutive Palestinian leader calls his compulsive pacing 'speed walking', a form of daily exercise that seems a perfect metaphor for his political predicament: he has little room for manoeuvre.

Sweating in the heavy military jacket he wears in all seasons, he marched round and round on Friday, skirting the conference table and ignoring the breathtaking view from his windows of the sparkling Mediterranean sea. After half an hour's wear of the dull, grey carpet, he sat down, mopped his forehead with a yellow Kleenex and turned his attention to a visiting reporter.

On his desk were reports of yet another day of violent Palestinian protests in the West Bank against the decision by Binyamin Netanyahu, the Israeli prime minister, to build a new Jewish settlement in Arab east Jerusalem.

'I am asking Netanyahu to understand exactly the sensitivity of the question of Jerusalem,' Arafat said, swivelling his chair to face the sea, then turning it abruptly back again. 'I am astonished at how he does not understand it. Or perhaps he understands it but insists on challenging the Palestinians, Arabs, Christians and Muslims.'

On the eve of Netanyahu's summit with President Bill Clinton tomorrow, Arafat knows he has no alternative but to continue the Israeli–Palestinian peace process. Yet if he accepts the new Jewish township he will lose any credibility among his own people.

From the Israeli side, Arafat is faced with overwhelming force and an intransigent prime minister. The Americans, meanwhile, are pressuring him to halt street protests. They also want him to arrest extremists who have dispatched three suicide bombers to attack Israel since the bulldozers began clearing the way for homes to be built for 30,000 Jews on a pine-covered hill known as Har Homa to the Israelis and Jebel Abu Ghneim to the Palestinians.

An Arab League decision last week to sever Arab ties with Israel gave Arafat some support for what he calls 'the battle for Jerusalem'. But the backing of other Arab countries has been largely rhetorical. Thus Arafat feels very much alone as he marches in his headquarters by the sea.

For his part Netanyahu, say those who know him, believes that if he can force Arafat to accept the new settlement, the Palestinians will 'lower their expectations' in future peace talks. Yet Arafat, already under attack for conceding too much to the Israelis in the Oslo agreements, cannot give up any more if he is to survive as leader.

'Netanyahu must stop this settlement on Jebel Abu Ghneim,' he insisted, adding that this was a condition for Palestinians returning to the peace talks. 'Netanyahu must return to the honest and accurate implementation of the peace process. Nothing less.'

Arafat says he has 'no contact' with Netanyahu these days. He has ordered his security chiefs to stop sharing intelligence information with their Israeli counterparts. Netanyahu's generals have warned that this is dangerous. Since Arafat took over Gaza and the West Bank cities, shared information from Palestinian security forces has prevented several planned attacks against Israeli targets.

But the Palestinian leader has lost faith in any idea that Netanyahu can be a partner in the peace process. Instead, he sees him as dangerously dependent for his political survival on the support of religious and ultra-right-wing parties who believe in Eretz Israel, or greater Israel.

'I am sorry to say Netanyahu is following the ideology of the (Jewish) fanatic groups,' said Arafat. 'He must remember he is committed to Oslo, which was signed by the previous Israeli governments, or we will be at a real impasse.'

For a few moments, Arafat stared through his heavy black-framed glasses into the middle distance, as if trying to see the way ahead. There was none. 'We are at a real impasse now,' he sighed.

One possible hope is American mediation. 'The peace process now needs the attention of the American administration – especially President Clinton,' the Palestinian leader said. 'The agreement was signed under his supervision. This is not a bilateral agreement. It is an international agreement.'

Arafat has not yet received an invitation from Washington to take part in a meeting with the Israelis. But some analysts believe the Americans are trying to work out a deal. Sources in Washington say the Clinton administration is trying to piece together a compromise that would include delaying the settlement, rather than definitively stopping it, while simultaneously speeding up the schedule for final negotiations.

At the moment, however, the Americans, who have generally supported Netanyahu's position that the Palestinians must stop their protests before peace talks can resume, seem intent on winning concessions from Arafat.

Last week Madeleine Albright, the secretary of state, telephoned Arafat twice to seek his approval for three-way talks. She urged him to try to calm the violence in the West Bank, arrest Islamic extremists and resume security co-operation with the Israelis.

In one lengthy telephone call, Arafat explained that as Netanyahu had ignited the crisis with his 'violent' action of sending in bulldozers, she should be asking the Israelis, not him, for concessions. He could not return to security co-operation before the political negotiations resumed.

'Let's not get into a discussion of which came first, the chicken or the egg,' Albright responded. To which Arafat replied, cryptically: 'But we have to remember that in the end there is the hen and there is the egg.' The response of the new secretary of state is not recorded.

Kosovo

The centuries of conflict
over a sacred heartland

8 March 1998

Like earlier Balkan wars, the battle in Kosovo, the impoverished southern province of former Yugoslavia, has its roots in history. For the Serbs
the region is the sacred heartland of their long-lost medieval state. For
the ethnic Albanians who make up 90% of its population, it has been
home for centuries.

The rise of virulent Serbian nationalism was the trigger for the
current conflict. In the Yugoslavia of Josip Broz Tito, the former
communist leader, Kosovo, although extremely poor, enjoyed a
degree of formal autonomy within Serbia.

Under Slobodan Milosevic, the bullet-headed Serbian nationalist, everything changed. In 1989, two years after he came to power
as Serbian Communist party leader, he visited Kosovo and
proclaimed himself the protector of local Serbs claiming to be the
victims of discrimination. He rescinded Kosovo's autonomous
status later that year.

The province is seen as the spiritual home of the Serbian
nation: in 1389, at Kosovo Polje, the Serbs lost a battle with
Turkish troops that consigned them to 500 years of rule by the
Ottoman empire.

Milosevic's initiative to reclaim Kosovo prompted riots in 1989
and 1990. He sent tanks against the protesters and their leaders fled
or were killed.

The ethnic Albanians have never given up their demand for
independence. They have ignored the state network, setting up a

'parallel society' of schools and hospitals. The driving force behind
the policy of passive resistance has been Ibrahim Rugova, known
as the 'Gandhi of the Balkans' – a quiet intellectual who is president of the self-styled republic of Kosovo.

The present violence appears to have been provoked by younger,
more militant Kosovans who feel frustrated at Rugova's failure to
win concessions for them. The Kosovo Liberation Army, an armed
guerrilla group, emerged 18 months ago, claiming responsibility
for the killings of Serbian policemen and informers. It appears to
be funded by Kosovan emigrés in Germany and Switzerland.

By last month the attacks had grown so lethal that the Serbian
police withdrew from much of the Drenica region, a stronghold of
separatists northwest of Pristina, the capital. Milosevic responded
last week by ordering troops to raze villages there.

The fear now is that fighting in Kosovo, which was largely unaf-
fected by the conflicts that engulfed Croatia and Bosnia in the early
1990s, may lead to a wider Balkan war. This could drag in Albania
and Macedonia, which has its own ethnic Albanian population.
Turkey is sympathetic to fellow Muslims in Kosovo, while Greece
could be drawn in on the side of the Orthodox Serbs.

Kosovo's silent houses of the dead

PREKAZ

15 March 1998

All 11-year-old Basorta Jashari knew was that the artillery shells had
stopped crashing into her house. For hours, the noise had been
unbearable.

As she hugged herself tightly beneath the table her mother used to prepare bread, the ceiling had collapsed and the walls had appeared to explode. Now it was the silence that was terrifying. Choking on smoke and dust, she screamed for her mother.

Weeping as she crawled through the rubble, she found her sisters, Lirie, 10, Fatima, 8, and seven-year-old Blerina. She tried to shake them awake and was covered in blood by the time she realised they were dead.

Then Basorta saw her brothers: Selvete, 20, Afeti, 17, Besim, 14, and Blerin, 12. They had always seemed so strong. Now, all were dead.

Finally, there was her mother, Ferida, whose dark shiny hair and beautiful voice Basorta had cherished, lying with her limbs protruding at impossible angles. She would never again respond to her daughter's cry of 'nene' (mummy).

Basorta climbed through a hole in the wall and ran round the house, shouting: 'Anybody ... is anybody still alive?' When nobody answered, she crawled back under the table.

The pause in the shelling was all too brief. Basorta would spend the night and the next day alone, with her family dead all around her, as the Serbs' rockets came again and again, smashing into the whitewashed house with red-tiled roof that had once been home.

A bright, happy pupil at school, Basorta was the sole survivor of an attack that can now be revealed as nothing less than a calculated, cold-blooded massacre.

The house in Prekaz, a village in a pastoral landscape of neatly tilled fields and rolling hills, had sheltered 22 members of the families of two brothers, Hamza Jashari, Basorta's father, and Adem Jashari, her uncle – ethnic Albanians in Kosovo, the southernmost province of what remains of Serb-ruled Yugoslavia.

Their deaths were no accident of war. I pieced together the horror last week from the account Basorta – now in hiding in the nearby town of Srbica – gave to relatives who managed to escape from other homes in Prekaz. I saw the gaping holes in the roofs and walls of the three Jashari homes in the compound – one for

Basorta's grandparents and one each for Hamza and Adem – and the brown pockmarks left by close-range machinegun fire on the walls.

In the muddy farmyard lay strewn the detritus of domestic life: a little boy's shredded sports bag, postcards from relatives in Germany and a satellite dish dented by bullets. The nose cones and tailfins of two rockets were scattered amid the debris.

Yesterday all that moved in the compound that once teemed with children were two black and white cows and a flock of chickens pecking at the rubble. On the other side of the dirt road that runs in front of the compound were 51 fresh graves with mounds of dark earth and wooden crosses.

These were the final resting places of the Jasharis who died in the house, four relatives who were killed nearby and neighbours who got in the way of the Serbian forces.

There is little doubt that the Jashari brothers were connected to the Kosovo Liberation Army (KLA), a militant force that emerged last November dedicated to fighting for the interests of the ethnic Albanians who make up 90% of Kosovo's population.

They had grown impatient with the policies of the mainstream Kosovo Democratic League. The league advocates passive resistance to the strong-arm tactics of Slobodan Milosevic, the nationalist Serbian president of Yugoslavia, who revoked the province's autonomous status 10 years ago.

However, this was not the killing of suspected terrorists in a firefight, nor the ambush of dangerous outlaws. It was a military assault on three family homes without warning: on men, women and children asleep in their beds.

The Serbian offensive in the Drenica valley, a region of farming villages that is the stronghold of Albanian resistance, began on 28 February, the day after four Serbian policemen were killed in an ambush as they chased KLA guerrillas. The Serbs moved first against the village of Llaushe, killing 24 Albanians. Then they prepared to attack Prekaz, where the Jasharis were the principal family.

Jetish Durmishi, a bus driver, was alerted to danger when a friend telephoned from his home near the local police station in Mitrovica with the warning that a convoy of buses full of Serbian police was moving towards Prekaz.

Durmishi escaped to the woods, leaving his family behind; in the past the Serbs had targeted only men. He saw what happened from the woods above the Jashari compound.

'Within minutes it seemed, the police came and the village was surrounded by a cordon of Serbs,' Durmishi said. 'They were standing about half a yard apart all along the road and up across the hills.'

The artillery fire came at 6am from a Serbian base above Prekaz. There was no warning. The first to die were the Agas, members of a gypsy family who panicked and tried to flee their house.

The mother, a small boy and a girl were gunned down in their garden. The next victim was Nazmi Jashari, who ran a kiosk in Prekaz selling cigarettes and sundries and lived opposite the main family compound.

He tried to carry his elderly mother, Naile, out of the back door, and was shot in front of her. The signal was clear. Anyone seen leaving their home would be a target for Serbian snipers.

The extended Jashari family gathered in what they thought would be the safest room, which had a new brick wall. But they were trapped: they faced gunfire if they came out or bombing if they remained inside. Soon, the shells were coming through the roof, then the walls. Basorta's last memory of her family is that her uncle, Adem, was singing Albanian folk songs above the noise to keep up their spirits. She remembers the moment he stopped singing. Then, for 36 hours, there was only the sound of the bombs.

When they thought everybody inside was dead, the police entered the house, throwing grenades into several rooms ahead of them. One officer stood guard while another sprayed the bodies with bullets.

Perhaps they had had their fill of killing when they found Basorta cowering. Perhaps they thought she was too young to accuse them. Or perhaps they could not look a terrified schoolgirl in the eye and shoot her. But she is the reason the truth can be told.

'I tried to pretend I was dead,' she said to her uncle Hilmi. 'But one of the soldiers put his hand on my chest and he felt I was alive.'

Still dressed in her red shirt and black trousers, by now covered with blood, she had to step over the bodies of her family to leave the room, surrounded by Serbs. She was taken to the military base nearby and interrogated for three hours.

Basorta believed her only chance was to lie. She denied that she was a Jashari, claiming her father was abroad and she was merely a guest in the compound. 'They asked about my father and about Uncle Adem,' she said. 'I told them nothing, nothing.'

The Serbs dumped her on a road in Srbica and she ran to the home of a school friend. Yesterday, shocked and finding it increasingly difficult to speak, she was being moved from house to house for protection.

Unbeknown to Basorta, the bodies of her father, mother, uncle, aunt and all her cousins were lined up by the police at a bus depot in Mitrovica last week.

When nobody from the family turned up to identify them and friends tried to insist on post-mortem examinations, the Serbs dumped them in the graveyard they had dug opposite the remains of their house, leaving the coffins poking through the earth. The surviving villagers came back in the night to finish the job with respect.

All that was left of Basorta's family was a pile of numbered black bin bags at the bus station, each filled with the bloody clothing they had been wearing when they died.

Kosovo guerrillas fight Serb shells with bullets

25 April 1999

Marie Colvin, the first reporter to enter Kosovo from Albania, is with a KLA unit fighting to open supply lines. She braved sniper fire and shelling to send this report.

At night, the foothills of Kosovo are silent except for the sporadic sound of gunfire. The silence makes them even more terrifying to walk through. Serbian snipers are in the woods but we do not know where they are. The anticipation of a shot at any moment is unnerving. Nobody speaks.

There are no civilians left in these woods or villages. It is dark and cold and when the shooting starts the crossfire can be petrifying. Bullets slam into trees.

I walked in single file on Friday night with a KLA special forces unit advancing towards the distant lights of the city of Djakovica. The Serbs were 500 metres away.

We walked through a village of six houses. All the red roofs had been holed by shells and half of one house was a pile of rubble. First the Serbs had driven out the ethnic Albanian farmers, then the KLA had driven out the Serbs. There is little for the families to return to.

Our goal was a gully in the forest overlooking Serbian positions in the village of Batusa. It was cold and wet and I slipped off a log when I was trying to cross a stream. A soldier held me up with the butt of his Kalashnikov.

Camp for the night was in camouflaged tarpaulins strung over branches. A pile of sleeping bags stashed earlier was sodden with the cold rain that had fallen all day and into the night. It is difficult to sleep in a flak jacket on a slope; it is like being an upended turtle with a detached shell. I keep slipping down the slope.

A patrol set out into the darkness and the night was broken intermittently by gunfire: single shots, automatic weapons fire and the crack of snipers' rifles resounding off the hills. At 1am there was a long exchange of fire. Shells boomed intermittently though none landed close. One man in a returning patrol said he had killed a Serb, but nothing is sure here.

The watch came in for breakfast and a soldier passed round packets of cigarettes, bread and tins of sardines. This unit travels light. We overheard the Serbs on the radio asking to go back to their bunkers.

Every night has been like this for the past two months for this unit on the front line of the KLA offensive. The last weeks have been the worst. The Serbs have not attacked on foot; they have just shelled. Their tanks and artillery are beyond the hills. Two shells landed during breakfast.

It is heartbreaking for these men to hear Nato planes fly overhead on their way to Belgrade and Novi Sad. Everyone asks me when Nato will start bombing Serbian tanks and artillery and when the Apache helicopters will arrive.

The men in this special forces unit are different from the raw recruits one sees in most of the KLA camps. They have been fighting together for a year and seem like the units seen in old war movies.

There is 'Doc', who looks after communications as well as the wounded and to whom most of the men turn in time of crisis. Their commander was killed by a sniper 10 days ago. Another soldier, Morina, remembers his village and how the old men wept when he left. Another refuses to get out of bed, saying he cares more about the cold than the Serbs.

Few have heard from their families for months. They accept that there will be no news until the Serbs leave.

The KLA holds a small but strategic foothold in Kosovo at this point. The group I am with has so far penetrated about 8 kilometres from Kosare, a Serbian border post captured by the KLA just over two weeks ago.

Kosare is in a small cleft between the mountains and the KLA holds the mountains, including a towering, snow-bound peak where KLA soldiers sleep in 3 foot of snow. They will dominate the valley as soon as they take Batusa, the next target.

The KLA is trying to meet up with other units inside Kosovo who have been besieged and are running low on food and ammunition. They can hear that the Serbs are low on food and ammunition and constantly requesting to go back to their bunkers. The spirits among the units are rising.

There is still a big question of whether any of these units will be able to join up with the inside forces because of the superior armaments of the Serbs. They have tanks and artillery and the KLA is fighting with Kalashnikovs and a few modern Nato-issue guns; but their spirit and courage are extraordinary.

On the first day when the KLA fought its way into Kosare, the Serbs replied with a welter of shells; now shells fall three or four times a day. Shards of broken flowerpots cover two unexploded shells in a concrete courtyard outside the former Yugoslav barracks – now KLA headquarters in Kosovo – and there are six shellholes in its red-brick facade.

When the sun came out for a moment on Friday, I took a bowl of bread and soup outside for my lunch. Within minutes there was a whistle of a shell, which burst 100 metres away. As I moved inside, another whistled down.

In between shells, the men waited to go on their 24-hour shifts at the front, smoking, sleeping, talking about home. The uniforms are from Switzerland, Germany and America – all bought by the KLA recruits on their way to war. One man wears a black jacket that says 'Let's go!' on the sleeve. Most have good boots but some set off to battle in black rubber wellingtons.

Those returning from patrol collapse onto iron bunk beds still in their clothes. The beds are warm from those who have left to replace them.

It is a barracks with no comfort. The windows have been blown out by shellfire. Off-duty soldiers cook on wood-burning stoves, heating up big pots of stew from tins left behind by the Serbs. There is no electricity. There is a generator but the base commander thinks it makes too much noise so it goes unused. At night those who cannot sleep stand in the halls lit by a fire and talk of home – never of war.

Coffee, cigarettes and sometimes bread arrive by donkey from Albania. Soldiers cluster around to greet them. Days are spent cleaning out the barracks. A sodden pile of detritus from Serbs is in the courtyard – fatigues, sweaters, playing cards, empty soft-drinks bottles and letters. Soldiers amuse themselves by looking through photographs of Serbs in uniforms with their girlfriends.

Last week they passed around one letter that horrified even these people who are used to news of Serbian attrocities. It was written by a Serbian doctor, Bojan Mihailovic, to his son at the front. It closed by saying: 'When you come back home, can you bring me the body of one dead Albanian so that I can cut its neck.' The letter went on to say love from 'Jasna, mother Anka and grandmother Milica'.

From the front line overlooking Batusa yesterday, a landscape that would under normal circumstances be a lovely valley of red roofs, farmhouses and green fields instead looked empty and dangerous. We could see through binoculars that Djakovica, in the distance, had been burnt and shelled. Only Serbs were left.

All the ethnic Albanians fled or were bused out. All the villages I have walked through are empty. Many of the men with me know these villages. There is almost nothing left behind in them. Whatever was not stolen has been smashed or broken.

On two days last week the Serbs fired shells that emitted white smoke. It seemed to be some kind of chemical. Those who breathed it suffer red eyes, an inability to breathe, small pupils and disorientation. Doctors do not know what it is. A few gas masks have now arrived.

The spirit of the men here is extraordinary. Many are young and have no experience. Most have families in Kosovo and are constantly worried about mothers, fathers, children, sisters and brothers.

There is Burim, 19, an architectural student, who after being expelled from Kosovo by the Serbs joined the KLA as soon as he crossed the border.

Angel left his restaurant in Sweden and told his mother he was going to find a wife in Albania. 'I am not a soldier and I have no experience, but I have come to Kosovo with all my heart,' he said.

Pren left his friends and family in Zurich without a word because he feared they would try to stop him.

All are very young. It is somehow more heartbreaking that some of these men will die with the end of Serbian occupation in sight.

Massacre in a spring meadow: war in Europe

2 May 1999

In a war of numerous atrocities Marie Colvin talks to over 100 witnesses of the most horrifying slaughter Kosovo has endured.

Seven-year-old Egzon Zyberi interrupted adult conversations late last week with a childish monotone. 'Long live Milosevic!' he chanted. 'Kosovo is Serbian!'

The little boy in orange trousers seemed to want an explanation, his brown eyes darting about for a reaction.

They were strange words to hear from a young Kosovan refugee but everyone around him knew what had happened.

They were what Serbs in uniforms and black masks had made Egzon, his brothers and cousins shout as the children watched their fathers and grandfather being dragged away to a killing field at the village of Meja in southwestern Kosovo on Tuesday morning.

'I didn't feel well to say this,' Egzon muttered to a translator, when asked what had happened at Meja.

Egzon's 40-year-old father, Dani, his 30-year-old uncle, Skandar, and his 65-year-old grandfather, Burim, were all pulled out of a refugee convoy by the Serbs. Arbur Hajosaj, a 16-year-old boy they had picked up on the road with his grandmother, was also taken.

They appear to have been some of the many victims of what is emerging as the worst Serbian atrocity of the war in Kosovo.

The women and children last saw them being escorted into a field in the centre of Meja where lines of men already sat in the open under the barrels of what they described as hundreds of Serbian gunmen. Then the Serbian forces on a narrow road shouted at the family to move, move, move. There was no chance to say goodbye.

None of the women knew how to drive a tractor so a 12-year-old neighbour jumped into the seat. 'He kept bumping into the other tractors,' said Egzon, perking up at something he could talk about. 'He didn't even know how to drive.'

Egzon and what remains of the Zyberi family now live in a tent in a muddy field outside the city of Kukes in northern Albania. Snow-capped peaks tower over them. Their tent shelters Egzon's mother, grandmother and two aunts, his three small brothers and his two little cousins, one only two months old.

In a corner, weeping silently, is Fawze Hajosaj, the elderly woman who lost her grandson to the Serbs. The Zyberi family does not know her; but she has nobody else so they have taken her in.

The Zyberis are far from alone in their affliction. They are in a camp, run by Médecins sans Frontières which shelters most of the families who arrived last week from the latest wave of Serbian ethnic cleansing around the city of Djakovica.

Women wash clothes in brightly coloured plastic basins, children play in the dirt, a few old men gather in little clusters. But in row after row of dark green tents there are no fathers. Family after family tells the same story and it always ends with Meja.

Yesterday the Zyberi women were still hoping their men had somehow escaped the Serbs. They had not been told that other families who passed through Meja after them had seen a pile of bodies in the field in the centre of the village. 'There has certainly been a mass killing,' confirmed the United Nations High Commissioner for Refugees (UNHCR).

Estimates of the total dead ranged yesterday from 200 to more than 1,000. Whichever proves correct, the Serbian forces are now killing on a scale that matches their bloodlust in the Bosnian and Croatian wars. In Bosnia, they reached a peak of savagery shortly before their strategic position began to deteriorate.

The trigger that turned Meja into a killing field may have been the assassination there of a senior Serbian officer and several of his bodyguards by the Kosovo Liberation Army (KLA) about 10 days ago. Shortly afterwards, a renewed wave of ethnic cleansing began in the area.

The Zyberi family had already been 'cleansed' once from its farmland around a remote village called Molic.

A month ago, under pressure from the Serbs, Nushe Zyberi, the grandmother and matriarch of the family, took her husband, her two sons and their families to live with her sister's family in the village of Dobros. They hoped to sit out the Serbian offensive there and return to their farm instead of ending up homeless in Albania or Macedonia.

There was no work and little food. The only shops open in nearby Djakovica were Serbian and the owners had started refusing to sell food – even bread and milk – to ethnic Albanians.

Last Monday night, the adults and children went to sleep as usual crowded together in blankets on the floor. Tuesday morning dawned cold and rainy. While the children slept, the adults rose early. The women started a wood fire and began baking bread.

At 6am gunfire sounded throughout the village. The children awoke, crying and frightened. Dobros had been surrounded by what seemed to the Zyberis like hundreds of Serbs with tanks.

Soldiers were firing into the air. Others were shouting at the villagers to leave their homes: 'Go to Nato if you like them so much. Go to Albania, this is not your home, this is Serbia.'

The time had arrived at last to submit to Serbia's systematic programme to 'cleanse' Kosovo of its 1.2 million ethnic Albanians. The men moved quickly. Dani and Skandar hitched their two tractors to metal carts and the families piled in. Their wives, young children, mother and father went into one cart, driven by Skandar; their mother's sister and her family were in the second, with Dani at the wheel.

There was no time to take clothes or supplies. They grabbed some blankets to wrap the frightened children in and tacked a plastic sheet over the carts to protect them from the rain, before heading for Albania. They had only been on the road for a few minutes when the farmhouse burst into flames behind them, torched by the Serbs who were rampaging through the village.

Similar scenes were taking place in other villages around Djakovica, once a lovely city of white stone houses but now an armed Serbian encampment, and the road towards the border was becoming clogged with tractors, trailers and their human cargo. Serbian soldiers and police with tanks and armoured personnel carriers lined the route.

At Meja, a hitherto insignificant village on the route, Serbian soldiers and paramilitaries began stopping the convoy. The Zyberi family reached Meja at about 8am. They saw Serbian soldiers walking down the convoy, pulling men from tractors and beating and kicking some of them by the roadside. There was nowhere to turn off and escape.

Skandar Zyberi twice ignored Serbian demands to get off his tractor; then they hauled him off by his sleeve. Describing the scene later, his wife Sheribone, 28, wept and cuddled their two-month-old daughter, Ezuntina.

Skandar's brother and father were ordered out of the cart at gunpoint by Serbs wearing black masks. 'The children started crying and yelling "daddy, daddy" but the Serbs laughed,' said

Nushe, who watched in horror as her husband and two grown-up sons were led away.

'Then they made the children say the Serbian things, terrible things. The children were so frightened.'

The last the family saw of the three men was their backs as they walked at gunpoint into the field where several hundred men were sitting surrounded by armed Serbs. With his hands clasped on his lap, Egzon apes the way they sat.

Another member of the family, Aphrodite Zyberi, 19, said the Serbs had shouted: 'You killed seven of us; we will kill 700 of you.' In Yugoslavia during the Second World War, the Nazis killed 100 people in retribution for every German slain by partisans.

Family after family reaching the refugee camp outside Kukes last week was interviewed separately yet described the same scene at the same place. Males aged from 16 to 60-plus had been forced from their families into the meadow at Meja. Serbs had shouted and beaten anyone who did not move quickly enough.

Xhamal Rama, a 58-year-old farmer, a neighbour of the Zyberis in Dubros, had held out for as long as he could at home; but at 9am he had also piled his wife and 10 children into a cart and had driven off on his tractor. His brother and family followed. 'The Serbs were firing their guns and setting fire to the houses,' he said. 'They had masks and some had red handkerchiefs. They ordered us to leave and we could do nothing.'

Reaching Meja after the Zyberis, he found the Serbs behaving like 'beasts'. Three of his nephews were hauled off his brother's tractor and taken to the field, where about 250 men were being made to show the Serbian three-finger sign and shout, 'Long live Serbia.'

Zek, 55, another farmer, who would not give his full name, had bruises on his arm and said he had been beaten by the Serbs for shouting, 'Leave him alone', when they took his 16-year-old nephew. Zek looked far older than his years, which may have saved his own life.

A slight, frail woman called Birami described how Serbs had arrived early on Tuesday at her village, Dalasaj, shooting and shouting that they would kill anyone who did not leave in five minutes.

Her husband, Alban, had piled their four children and their parents into his tractor-drawn cart and departed. As houses went up in flames behind them, Alban balanced Blerim, his blonde, five-year-old son, on his knee.

On reaching Meja, said Birami, they were confronted by masked Serbian paramilitaries or soldiers; she was not sure which.

Ordered off his tractor, Alban handed her Blerim and walked away into the meadow to join the other men. She could not drive and a neighbour had to take the wheel.

Another of the families caught in this terrible exodus had already been in a fleeing convoy a little more than two weeks ago but had been attacked from the sky.

'A tractor in front of us burst into flames,' recalled Fana, the mother of the family, who had seen too much to reveal her full name. People had been burnt in front of her eyes. Other people had jumped from their tractors off a bridge and drowned.

Nato later admitted it had mistakenly bombed the convoy but – like all the refugees – Fana and her family would not say a word against Nato. They insisted the plane must have been Serbian.

After that incident, they had camped in a ruined house in a village called Dalas. At 7am on Tuesday, they said, Dalas was surrounded by Serbs, some wearing black balaclavas, shooting in the air. The family took to the tractor again – and, again, the houses went up in flames behind them.

'Serbs with guns and tanks stopped us at the village of Meja,' Fana said. 'They took my nephews and my son, he was only 16. We began to cry and scream but we could do nothing because they had guns. They were pushed to the ground and then made to walk into the field where other men were sitting.'

Her youngest son, 12-year-old Vilsan, began driving the tractor. 'I couldn't see for my tears,' Vilsan said quietly as the family replayed the scene at the refugee camp.

'They knocked my father down on the ground and beat him with their guns. But we had to drive because the Serbian soldiers said move immediately. I was afraid to look back.'

Vilsan is now the oldest male in the family. Two young women, the wives of Fana's nephews, sat crying near him surrounded by young children. They had only the clothes they were wearing.

Several miles after Meja, the family had been stopped by other Serbian soldiers and robbed of all their money, DM700. Another family, the Salihus, had travelled from the village of Ramizi on foot after Serbs forced them to leave at 5am. They reached Meja at dusk on Tuesday.

'We were so afraid,' said Rucka Salihu, 23. 'I saw dead bodies in a field in the middle of Meja. I was too frightened to look for long. I could only see that they were lying across each other on their stomachs, in this pasture near some bushes. Hundreds of them. Maybe 200.'

She crossed her hands, one over the other, to show how she saw the bodies lying. She said other men were sitting in the meadow, still alive and under Serbian guard.

Serbian soldiers pulled her uncle, Niman Salihu, 50, and a neighbour off the road into the meadow. Two soldiers then spotted Rucka's brother, Kiytim, 18, who is small and dark and looks young for his age. 'Two Serbian soldiers shouted to me to put down my bag and stop,' said Kiytim. 'The bag was full of bread. Then my sisters began weeping and surrounded me and I was so afraid I was sick.

'One of the Serbian soldiers, the older one, shouted at me again but the other one said, "Oh, let him go, he's too young", and we kept walking and I was surrounded by my family and they just let me go. My sisters' tears saved me.'

He cannot forget the sight of the meadow in Meja. 'There were bodies in the field. A pile of bodies. I was too scared to make any accurate count. I tried not to look for long because the Serbs would notice me.'

After five minutes of walking, the Salihu family heard a burst of gunfire that went on for about 10 minutes.

The first news of the massacre at Meja came in the hours after the refugees started crossing into Albania at the Morina border post under a full moon late on Tuesday night.

Nobody expected them, as the Serbs had closed the border days earlier. The only aid agency to meet them was Action Hunger whose workers began dispensing hot tea in the chilly air. UNHCR officials raced to the border.

In all, 47 tractors hauling carts full of women and children and a few elderly men reached Albania that night. The first arrivals looked merely anxious.

By the time the last tractor rolled across the border, the road down to the refugee camp at Kukes was a trail of misery. Their faces etched with horror, the last to arrive could barely speak.

More refugees from Djakovica poured across the border all week, with 10,000 arriving on Friday alone.

Madeleine Albright, the American secretary of state, has announced that the events at Meja will be investigated as a possible war crime. But no international outrage comforts the families who had to leave their men in Meja. 'I feel like I want to die,' said Safeta Zyberi, Egzon's mother.

THE MACEDONIAN BUSINESSMAN

Petrovski Gupco runs an import/export company in Skopje.

'I can no longer see a future in Macedonia for me or my children. We were lucky to avoid the war, but it will go on around us for many more years. You cannot look for serious investment. When you have poor neighbours, you cannot expect your economy to grow. Albania is the poorest country in Europe. The Serbian economy is destroyed.

'I am seriously considering leaving, to live in a normal country, maybe to Singapore. If these refugees stay in Macedonia, no one will be happy. They cost money. The UN and Nato help out, but it also costs our government. We have 200,000 unemployed and now we have the same number of refugees. We have excellent relations with the Albanians who have lived in Macedonia for generations.

'I have visited the refugee camps. The conditions are very poor. I feel sorry for them. But there is a background to this. This century, when Serbs began to rule Macedonia, they started to kill Albanians. When Bulgarians took Macedonia in World War Two, they killed Albanians. After the war, Albanians killed the Macedonians. But I do not approve of Milosevic. Only a madman would.'

THE TEENAGER

Arta Abizi, 15, a refugee with a family in Kumanovo, Macedonia.

'When we were forced to leave our home in Pristina by the Serbs, I just cried. Not only because we were frightened, but for the things I had to leave behind. I left my photographs that told my whole life's story from when I was three. I left my rings, my earrings, my nice socks. Emin, my brother, who is nearly 12, had to leave his parrot.

'We tried to go to the border but we were turned back to Presovo, a Serbian town near the Kosovan border. The soldiers made us walk back in a line along the tracks. We had to sleep in the open but we could not light a fire because they told us Nato would shoot us. The nights were so cold. When we finally got to the border, we spent six nights in no-man's land. I did not sleep one night. I was frozen and it was so very dirty that I was afraid to sleep.

'Since I came here I have started going to school in Kumanovo. People from the school invited me to come to class, because I was a refugee. I hate being a refugee; you have nothing and everything is so uncertain. I don't want to stay here. Every day, all day, all I think is what am I doing here?'

Letter from ... Kosare

4 June 1999

The Times Literary Supplement

The Kosare Barracks of the Kosovo Liberation Army was never much to look at. The fight to capture it from the Serbs had been fierce. Six shell-holes pierced one red-brick wall and there was a hole in the roof. When the wind blew at night, glass fell from the shattered windows. It looked lonely. To get there, you had to walk down a narrow path from Albania, across a barbed wire fence that used to be the international border, past a deserted farmhouse now half tumbled into stones and the corpses of four horses in a grassy field pitted with craters of black soil. Everyone said the border minefield had been cleared, but everyone stayed on the narrow winding path which bore the comforting footprints of those who had walked that way before.

The barracks stood alone in a narrow valley between mountains covered with scrub oak. No one ever sat outside in the spring sun; the Serbs might see you and fire off a shell. There was no electricity. The Serbs were on the next hill and the commander thought the noise of the generator might attract their attention, although since they had lived there first and clearly knew where it was, that really didn't make too much sense. But there were always bean stews cooking in cauldrons over wood-fired stoves, and there was always someone to talk to at night when you couldn't sleep.

When I heard Nato had bombed the KLA barracks at Kosare, it was those late-night conversations I thought of. They never started out as war conversations. Someone would come out of the sleeping rooms that were crowded with bunk-beds and Kalashnikovs hanging over the metal bedsteads and pour some oil in a tin pot or whatever he could find, dip in a rag until it was soaked, light the cloth and then a cigarette. It would draw the other non-sleepers and we would stand around, offering each other cigarettes, smoking. There was always the boom of artillery in the background, but no one talked about it – it wasn't close enough to worry about – and we had learned you only really had to worry when you heard a whistle that meant an incoming shell was close, and then there was not much you could do except dive for the ground. It was from Kosare Barracks that KLA units walked out at night, in single file, up into the mountains to fight the Serbs, to push them back. The gains and losses were unspectacular but dependable: a mile a week, a comrade killed when he was shot trying to lob a grenade into a Serb bunker. Kosare Barracks, for all its discomforts, was somewhere safe before you had to walk out and try again.

The talk would always start with families, now lost in Kosovo. We were in Kosovo, of course, the young men talking at night were proud that they had fought and captured this small piece of their homeland, but the Serb army was between us and where their families lived. The only villages we saw were those we walked through late at night, remaining silent in honour and in awe of the bombed and destroyed homes and the absence of people.

Perhaps in all barracks in a war there is a camaraderie that – intensified by the ever-present possibility of sudden death – thrives on deep and immediate intimacy, that removes the need for formalities, and that, once established, is only broken by death. One night in the hole lit by the flicker of an oil fire, Xhavit said it was his son's sixth birthday, and showed us pictures of his boy and two older daughters. He was a big beefy man and had been working in Switzerland, sending home money when the war started. He hadn't seen his family for four months and now he didn't know if his son had turned six or was dead. He was a sniper. He didn't even need to say why he was there; everyone in the barracks had reached a point where years of Serb oppression meant they were ready when the time came to pick up a gun. Burim, who had left his restaurant and his girlfriend in Spain, where he had lived for fourteen years, would tell us again about how he found his sister in the mountains. He had not seen her in all that time, but had found her lying exhausted on the ground with her three children, the nephews and nieces he had never met. He had taken his sister and her children to a refugee camp in Kukes in Northern Albania and returned to join his fellow KLA guerrillas. He told us this story every night in the barracks, as if by telling it he would somehow understand how that miracle could happen.

Standing in the oil-lit hallway, everyone knew when the next patrol was due to return, but never talked about it. When the returning KLA soldiers walked in, tired and wet after three days in the mountains, the group around the fire would line up and solemnly, ceremoniously, embrace the arriving men and, anxiously but without saying it, never asking, look to see if anyone who had walked out of Kosare three nights ago had not come back.

Eventually, the talk would always turn to Nato. The KLA soldiers, young men who had grown up quickly or at least tried to seem as if they had, were proud that they were now allied with Nato; when they said it, it was as if they stood a bit straighter, looked a bit taller. They were fighting for their country and it had to turn out okay because Nato, the West, the Americans and the British, those countries where people had unimaginable choices, unimaginable freedoms, were on their side. They would always talk about Nato with awe in their voices. They liked to joke that Nato was the KLA air force. And yes, they would always ask when the Apaches were coming.

The Apaches, of course, are helicopters. That was important because the KLA are fighting with light weapons. Some had bought themselves expensive kit in Europe, but mostly they all carried battered Chinese copies of Russian Kalashnikovs or even just single-round hunting rifles. They were trying to fight their way across Serb lines, but they faced three emplacements of artillery and tanks – at Batusha, Mount Plahnik and Morine. Against all odds, they had captured not just Kosare Barracks, but fought their way ten kilometres into Serb-held Kosovo, and taken the mountains for another ten kilometres horizontally along the front (Kosare Barracks is at the centre), carving out a foothold of almost

100 square kilometres. Testimony to the continued fighting came
to Kosare every day when KLA soldiers carried back injured
comrades, and put them on donkeys for the journey up the narrow
path to Albania, where they would be put on carts pulled by tractors and, it was hoped, arrive at a hospital two hours away.

Nato could break this stalemate, could destroy those tanks and
artillery in hours. If the KLA rushed those positions head on,
however, with no weapons other than Kalashnikovs, they would
lose hundreds of men. Nato did not strike. There was news of
bridges bombed, oil refineries hit, electricity grids destroyed, but
never those artillery guns or tanks. The positions of the Serb heavy
weapons were no secret. KLA commanders would call Astrit
Huskaj, the KLA–American liaison officer in Kukes, give him the
co-ordinates of the Serb positions and the KLA positions so that
there could be no mistakes. Everyone at Kosare Barracks believed
that one day, soon, Nato would take out those Serb tanks and guns
blocking their offensive. They all heard the BBC reporting on the
reluctance of Nato to send ground troops, but for these KLA men
that made no sense. Tell them, they would say to me, an American
working for a British newspaper ('so you must know them'), tell
them just arm us and we will go in. We need weapons against
tanks, not much more. Our families are there. Our homes are
there. We can fight, we have to.

That was before Nato bombed the Kosare Barracks and killed
seven of these young men, men I knew, although no one has bothered to list the names of the dead. It was a small place. There is no
doubt it was a mistake. The KLA has been anxious to say they
understand mistakes can happen and Nato must continue bombing, because it is the only way to end the reign of their enemy,
Slobodan Milosevic. Since returning from Kosovo, I have heard all
the reservations about arming the KLA, but none has really made
sense when I thought of the young men I met and with whom I
travelled into the mountains. There was Ramis, very proud that a
British journalist was with his unit, a village boy whose family was
only about ten miles away in the village of Ratkovac, if they were

still alive. We could see the lights of Djakovica, the nearest city, at night, and the fires of the houses the Serbs were burning. He would point to where his village was and tell me it was dark because people slept early, but neither of us believed that. He told me about how the old men in the village had cried when he left and how he told them not to worry: his generation would free Kosovo. There was Ghani, a young philosophy student who would never talk seriously but made a bet with everyone else in the unit that he could eat eight hamburgers and drink two pints of beer when they arrived in Pristina, Kosovo's capital. Doc, laconic, bespectacled, who held the unit together after their commander was shot in the head and killed by a Serb sniper. Doc never talked about bravery; no one did. He had had to travel outside Kosovo for education because Albanians cannot become doctors under the Serbs.

'You don't understand freedom,' he said one day, during a lull in fighting, sitting in a freezing mountain bivouac: 'you can't. You grow up with freedom, you've never thought about it. I picked up a gun because there is no way we can live under the Serbs any more. This will be over soon. The West understands that.'

I'm not sure how any of these young men feel now that the planes we saw flying overhead every day and that were supposed to destroy the artillery and tanks between them and their villages and families have instead bombed their barracks. I'm not sure whether they are still alive. I do think anyone who met them would also feel it is hypocritical for a Nato spokesman to get up on television every day and talk about the success of hundreds of warplane sorties, and for diplomats to brief journalists that Nato is doing all it can to defeat Milosevic, and not to help the only people who are fighting his troops and paramilitaries every day and are willing to die doing it. There was no talk in the Kosare Barracks about zero tolerance for returning body bags. They saw too many.

The neighbour who burned with hate

DJAKOVICA

20 June 1999

Bozhidar Dogancic was a loser who for the duration of the war had the power to decide whether his neighbours lived or died at the hands of the Serb paramilitaries, reports Marie Colvin in Djakovica.

In Djakovica, a quaint, cobbled town that used to be home to many of Kosovo's leading writers, artists and intellectuals, Bozhidar Dogancic was a nobody.

He lived near the bus station in a concrete, single-storey house with peeling paint and dirty curtains. His front windows looked out on to a dank garden of earth and weeds, darkened by unkempt trees that hid the property from passers-by.

Dogancic, known in his neighbourhood as Bozho, liked to sit on his porch and drink slivovitz from half-gallon bottles, shouting, singing and talking with friends. What he enjoyed talking about most of all was how much he hated Albanians.

The day before Nato troops entered Kosovo last weekend, Dogancic dumped all the food from his refrigerator into a rotting heap on his living room floor. He could not take it with him and he did not want to leave it for his neighbours. They were Albanians and Dogancic was a Serb.

Dogancic, 65, left Kosovo, knowing he could never return. There was too much blood on his hands.

In almost any other country, he would have remained nothing more than a resentful loser. Neighbours regarded him as something of a bully and avoided him. He rarely troubled them except when his noisy drinking sessions kept them awake at night.

But this was Kosovo and for 10 years, since Slobodan Milosevic rose to high office with passionate promises to protect the Serbs of Kosovo, Dogancic had also exercised power.

Milosevic rode a wave of Serbian nationalism that led to a decade of war in the Balkans. Dogancic did the same thing, on a smaller scale, in his little district of Djakovica. His power over Albanians enabled him to exact intoxicating revenge for slights, imagined and real.

The son of a saddler, Dogancic grew up in Djakovica's tiny minority community of Serbs and worked for local government. His job was to patrol the forests to stop people felling trees illegally. He was a handsome youth and married a pretty local girl, Radmilla. They had four children.

Albanians, who made up 90% of Kosovo's population, dominated senior positions in the government at that time and ran most of the businesses. Many had big houses and sent their sons abroad for education and work. Dogancic lived in squalor with little money and few prospects. Everything changed when Milosevic rescinded Kosovo's autonomy in 1990 and Albanians were kicked out of their jobs. Dogancic had what were considered the right opinions. He told anyone who would listen that Albanians should be deported from Kosovo. After all, he would say, they had Albania, didn't they?

His mentors were two pairs of brothers from similarly inauspicious backgrounds. Momcilo and Sava Stanovic, and their first cousins, Milan and Jokica Stanovic, are infamous among ethnic Albanians in Djakovica.

There was little education among them; Milan was a sheep farmer, Momcilo a building inspector's clerk. Under Milosevic's regime, however, they were able to establish a semi-autonomous dictatorship. Jokica Stanovic, who had friends in Milosevic's circle, was appointed mayor by Belgrade in 1991. He made Milan his police chief.

Momcilo, his cousin, became a local minister in charge of government property, including state factories. He gave Dogancic, the lowly forest patrol man, the job of director in a brick and tile plant.

In 1996 Momcilo took over as mayor when Jokica became a deputy in the Yugoslav senate. He built several Serbian Orthodox churches and soon became a priest. But his religious beliefs did not stop him from intensifying repression of Djakovica's ethnic Albanians.

He built up a private police force and was under investigation by the Organisation for Security and Co-operation in Europe for suspected war crimes when it became obvious that Nato was about to launch its airstrikes and the OSCE pulled out.

While Milan arranged for the deportation of countless local Albanians from Djakovica, Momcilo directed squads of special police and paramilitaries into the town. The separatist Kosovo Liberation Army had waged guerrilla warfare against these forces in the surrounding area since early this year. The hatred between them was fierce.

Djakovica, with its thuggish Serbian leadership, ruthless para-militaries and poorly defended Albanian community, was about to became a microcosm of Kosovo as it was torn apart. Dogancic would exercise the power he held in his community to devastat-ingly lethal effect.

The local Albanians had been growing increasingly fearful of Dogancic for years. He walked around with a pistol in his belt. Serbian police and members of the security forces in civilian clothes came in and out of his house. Whenever he had an argu-ment in his part of town, the neighbour concerned would be taken into the local police station and beaten.

The danger in the rise of such a man is evident now in the devastation that surrounds his house. The homes of all his Albanian neighbours – mechanics, shopkeepers, barbers – are blackened ruins with overgrown gardens. No more than a cher-ished rose bush still blooms here and there.

Dogancic has gone, but there is no jubilation at his departure. His neighbours paid too high a price for living next door. Last week, as the first of them returned to begin clearing out their homes, they spat his name with fury and contempt.

The Serbs started burning Djakovica on 24 March, the night Nato began bombing. About 100 high street shops were looted and then torched. The homes of professional men and anyone who had had contact with international organisations were set alight.

For the first few days, people were killed one at a time. Izat Hima, Djakovica's most prominent ethnic Albanian doctor, was shot dead on his doorstep. Paramilitaries cut the throat of Kujtim Dula, a lawyer who had defended political prisoners, in front of his wife.

But as the bombing went on, the Serbs launched a systematic campaign to murder the Albanians who remained in the town and to empty the surrounding villages.

Dogancic would walk through the streets pointing out houses to long-haired men in dark camouflage uniforms with black cowboy hats characteristic of the so-called Frenki's Boys, a para-military group that reports to Frenki Simatovic, Milosevic's state security chief.

'The paramilitaries didn't know the neighbourhood,' said Xhavet Beqa, a heavily built man who got his wife and four chil-dren out to Albania but stayed in Djakovica, slipping back to his district through Serbian patrols. 'They needed Bozho to tell them where to go. He told them who was in hiding.'

Beqa said Dogancic, his wife Radmilla and their eldest son, Nebojsha, a 26-year-old policeman, had stood in the middle of his street, arms folded, as they watched Beqa's three houses burn. The paramilitaries surrounded Dogancic, he said, joking and congratu-lating themselves on a job well done. Radmilla also had a pistol.

After choosing which houses should be the first to burn, Dogancic asserted his authority over the fate of people. He meted out virtual death sentences, simply by identifying places of concealment.

Beqa led me through the overgrown back garden of the building opposite his home to a cellar where Dogancic had pointed out the hiding place of the Vesja family. They were poor and frightened and did not want to risk fleeing to Albania. Twenty-four people were hiding in the basement when Dogancic and the paramilitaries arrived.

Five men ran; they had been taken in by the Vesjas and had no relatives to worry about. Lurzim Vesja, a shopkeeper, stayed with his family.

Scorched bed springs and a child's partly burnt boot are all that is left to testify to their presence in the shelter. Nineteen men, women and children, including Lurzim, were led to a row of garages behind the house. The paramilitaries shot them in one of the garages and set fire to the row. Nobody escaped. They were people Dogancic would have seen every day.

Few traces of the massacre remain. There are bullet holes in the scorched grey walls and shells on the overgrown garden in front. The bodies lay untouched for two days. Beqa and other men from the neighbourhood who were too afraid to give their names – 'I know we are free now, but you can't know how deep the fear is in us' – saw them that night, a charred huddle.

Finally, gypsies pulled up with a tractor and cart and hauled the bodies away for burial in the Djakovica cemetery under wooden markers with numbers and a date. 'I saw them put the bodies in the cart,' Beqa said. 'I couldn't believe how small they were.'

If you have ever seen a charred body, you know he was telling the truth. The human body, when burnt, is reduced to an almost childlike size. It is a horrible piece of knowledge that comes with reporting from Kosovo. In house after house, village after village, I have seen those bodies, so small that it seems they must be those of children, yet they are not.

Dogancic's reign of terror did not end with the Vesja family. Around the corner, amid the burnt-out skeletons of other houses, is the home of the family of Skandar Dylatahus, a barber. In front of the walled garden is a jar of pickles and a silver-plated tray. This family also tried to hide rather than risk their men on the road to Albania.

Dogancic knew they had stayed. Nobody in the neighbourhood understands how, because they had laid in supplies and never gone out. But paramilitaries directed by Dogancic found 17 people in the basement of the two-storey home.

This time they were more merciful. They told 10 women and children to leave, saying: 'Go to Albania, that is your home.' They lined seven men up in the garden and shot them, then put their bodies back in the basement and torched the house. Dogancic stood in the road, again staring into the flames.

Today Djakovica looks like Dresden at the end of the Second World War. Beautiful old buildings in the centre and big mansions in the suburbs have been reduced to blackened shells. On the main street, every shop is without its roof. In the old bazaar, where traders sold cloth, books, bric-a-brac and tiny cups of coffee, there are only charred walls.

The cemetery contains 238 new graves, each marked with a flat wooden stake. A name, or sometimes just a date and number, is written in marker or pencil. Semi-literate gypsies did the burying, so most of the names are misspelt. Next to the graves are two large areas of disturbed earth, each covering about 20 yards by 50. About 1,500 men are missing in Djakovica – the highest number of any town in Kosovo – and many are no doubt dead.

In the countryside within a few miles' radius, the atrocities committed by Frenki's Boys and other paramilitary groups with the aid of local agents such as Dogancic are no less in evidence.

In the village of Celin, to the west, Serbian forces from Djakovica set up on three hills on 25 March, the first day after the Nato bombing began, and started firing artillery at 8am. Several thousand villagers hoping to escape to Albania made for another hill less than two miles away. There, they were surrounded by 'Frenkis' who demanded jewellery and cash.

The first to die was Agim Ramadani, 23, a student who was accused of being in the KLA, told to run for his life and shot in front of his mother when he did so.

The villagers were goaded for most of the day. A Serb named Banzic Novica from nearby Opterusa recognised Hait Bytyqi, 35; they had worked together in a factory. 'Hait, come here,' Novica yelled. 'I'm going to show you I'm your God. Give me 1,000 deutschmarks [£330].' Bytyqi's father collected the money from people standing around in terror, but Novica shot the top of his head off anyway. Bytyqi was the father of a young son and daughter.

Finally the men were separated from the women. Some lived; some died. Twenty-one are buried at one spot, eight lie in a shallow grave covered with daisies and thistles at another. Altogether there are 86 graves.

In Meja to the south, where more than 100 people are thought to have been shot in a single incident, I followed a smell to the bodies of three men, dressed in the rough suits of peasants, lying under the bushes. Many others are said to have been removed from a mass grave.

Momcilo Stanovic, the mayor of Djakovica, fled from his flat on the day of Nato's arrival. He was in a small police car with no escort.

Stanovic left behind rooms full of dark wooden furniture, oriental carpets and marble. Every cabinet is filled with foreign liquors. At the door is a bucket of empty beer bottles. From the two terraces where he drank, Stanovic would have seen Djakovica burning.

The flat is now inhabited by Skandar Dubruna, 62, a bearded, bespectacled intellectual whose family was active in the party of Ibrahim Rugova, the moderate ethnic Albanian leader. Dubruna and his wife Shyretta have painted their Albanian name on the door so that nobody attacks them by mistake.

'He burnt down our house,' Dubruna said. 'So I came and took his house.'

It will probably matter little to Stanovic. He moved his family to the palatial villa he had built in Montenegro a month before the bombing campaign, and will no doubt join them there.

As for Dogancic, he and his family escaped with their belongings piled high on their Yugo car. They are unlikely to taste power again. But the enduring horror of Djakovica is that Dogancic was not alone. There were many like him: little men whose brief rise to unrestrained authority led to the destruction of a town and a society.

British detectives on trail of men behind massacres

27 June 1999

Marie Colvin in Bela Crkva reveals how Serbs mowed down fleeing families.

A pile of clothes on the bank of the River Belaja tells you who died here. There is a child's pair of black rubber boots, size 28; another little pair of bright red rubber boots, size 35; tiny blue-and-green pyjama bottoms, with a bullet hole in the left leg; a baby's bottle, half-filled with what looks like apple juice; and a hand-knitted, sage green woman's vest, unravelling around two bullet holes.

Five yards from the pile of clothes is a mound of dark earth that covers 14 bodies. British war crimes investigators are due to arrive at this scene, near the village of Bela Crkva, today. They will dig up the bodies, bag the clothes and sift the earth for the copper-coloured 7.62-calibre bullets – Kalashnikov issue.

They will also walk upstream to the graves of 65 men who were shot in cold blood after being forced to strip to their underclothes: husbands, fathers, neighbours of the women and children in the riverside grave. The evidence will go to the international criminal tribunal for the former Yugoslavia at the Hague.

The deaths are listed in the tribunal's indictment of Slobodan Milosevic, the Yugoslav president and commander-in-chief responsible for those who killed 79 men, women and children of Bela Crkva on the night of 25 March.

The language of the indictment is matter-of-fact. The dead women in that riverside grave are listed as 'Spahiu, FNU (first name unknown), wife of Xhemal' and 'Zhuniqi, FNU, wife of Clirim'. There are four listings of 'Spahiu, FNU, daughter of Xhemal'. But the villagers who survived knew these people, and guarded their graves last week, waiting for the British team.

'Zhuniqi, FNU, wife of Clirim' was Lumniya Zhuniqi, 35, who fled into the cold night with her husband, 40, and their five children, desperate to hide them from the Serbian forces that had surrounded the village at 4am and from the tank shells that had begun crashing into its terracotta tile roofs at 5.30am.

Sabri Popaj, a neighbour, found the Zhuniqis trying to cross the river to what they thought would be safety. Popaj was hiding from the Serbs but he heard children crying. 'I carried one of Lumniya's babies across, a little boy, maybe two years old, and she and Clirim helped the others. I handed the boy up to her where she stood on the bank.'

Also with Lumniya was her grandfather, Qamil Spahiu, 77, his daughter-in-law and her five children. Popaj left them hiding under the lip of the bank and fled across a field. 'We thought they would kill the men, but not women and children,' he said. He heard machinegun fire soon afterwards. About 20 Serbs dressed in camouflage uniforms with white bandannas around their arms stood on the bank and fired down at the cowering families. Popaj crawled back half an hour later.

'Lumniya was spread out over her children. She was trying to hide them from the bullets. Heads were burst open. I walked a few metres and sat down and smoked a cigarette. I couldn't think anything.'

He did not know it, but the two-year-old boy had survived under Lumniya's body. Another villager found the child, and hid him in blankets. A woman from the village took him with her own children to Albania.

The Spahiu and Zhuniqi families were killed at 6.30am. The 20 Serbian soldiers – probably paramilitaries – continued walking upriver. About half a mile away, they found several hundred villagers hiding near a narrow railway bridge.

The Serbs stood on the bridge and fired into the air, shouting for the villagers to move into a field. Men, women and children emerged. It was 9am, cold and foggy.

Isuf Zhuniqi, a small, wiry man with the weathered skin of a farmer and now a bullet scar in his shoulder, is another survivor. With the other men of the village, he was separated from his family: his wife Nuriya, 37, and his four children. His four-year-old son Adnan ran after him, screaming in terror, and Serbian soldiers took the boy and bashed his head against the track.

While Popaj was hiding near the bodies of the slain families, his wife Fedayia, 35, and two sons, Shendet, 17, and Agon, 14, his only children, were forced into the field; Agon was torn from his mother's arms. She screamed that he was just a child, but he was big for his age: he liked boxing and worked on his physique.

The women and children were kept in a field on one side of the river; about 50 or 60 men were forced to cross to the other. 'The river was so cold. We were all frozen,' Zhuniqi said.

'The Serbs pointed their guns at us and said, "Take off your clothes." They went through our pockets and took any money. Then they told us to put our clothes back on.'

The Serbs told Sabri Popaj's son Shendet to lie down with his hands behind his head. Nobody knows why he was singled out. Nesim Popaj, 43, Sabri's brother and the local doctor, tried to talk to the commander, saying: 'This is not right, what you are doing.' The commander ordered him out of the group, shouted: 'F*** your mother,' and shot him.

He turned and shot Shendet in the head. Then the Serbs opened fire on the group with Kalashnikovs. Men fell wounded and dead on the field as they fled towards the river.

'I was in the water. The shooting was everywhere. Dead bodies fell on me,' Isuf Zhuniqi recalled. 'The Serbs came down the riverbank and shot anyone who was moving with automatic pistols. I thought I was dead.'

After 20 minutes in the freezing water, he heard the Serbs leave. Around him were bodies without arms, heads split open, blood in the water. He knew all the men. Somehow he made his way to the nearby village of Zrze, where the women had taken refuge. 'Everyone is dead,' he told his wife. 'Everyone.'

Sabri Popaj returned to the river that night with his wife. He found Shendet on the riverbank. The body of his younger boy, Agon, was in the water.

The couple buried their sons and Popaj's two brothers on the bank, with their names on a slip of paper in a soft drink bottle to mark the spot. Thirty other men are buried next to the four Popajs, all with soft drink bottles and their names. The rest lie further along in the fields beside the river.

This weekend, Popaj is alone in his burnt-out house. A wooden cradle painted in blue with white flowers stands on the porch. He carries photographs of his sons in a small bag, and a handwritten list with the names of the bodies in the graves in his pocket.

As we left the place where he had buried his boys, he found a hypodermic needle the Serbs had left behind and placed it carefully in a shoe lost by one of the slain men.

He was waiting for the international war crimes investigators and justice.

Milosevic and four of his inner circle have been indicted on three counts of crimes against humanity and one of 'violation of the laws or customs of war'.

The indictment lists seven 'incidents of mass killings' – the murders of several hundred Kosovars at Bela Crvka, four other villages and the town of Djakovica, in southern Kosovo. Too many crimes were committed, too many thousands killed, to list them all.

British and American investigators have begun compiling evidence to help prosecutors prove the charges in court. The British team started work in a house in Velika Krusa, where 40 men had been herded together on 25 March, then shot, covered with straw and burnt.

Clive Donner, a big, beefy detective with 27 years' experience in Scotland Yard, is not easily shocked, but he was appalled by what he saw. The bodies had decomposed into each other because the men had tried to flee the gunfire and died in a heap. Scavenging dogs had dragged off limbs. 'I'm from the anti-terrorist squad, and I've never seen anything as bad as this,' Donner said.

The team's report to the Hague will explain what happened in Velika Krusa. 'There is "stratification" at the site,' said Dave Halliday, the team's fire expert. 'That tells you something. The first layer is bodies. On top of the bodies is broken glass, then the bullets, then straw. Roof tiles are the final layer. That tells you that the men were there first, the killers broke the windows, fired the bullets through the windows, and laid the straw on top after the men were shot.'

Their colleagues from the FBI are up the road in Djakovica. They have roped off a single-storey white house, scorched by flames. Xhamal Caka, 68, slumps nearby with a school photograph of granddaughters whose bones lie among the broken roof tiles.

Dalina, 13, sits in the front row, a tall brunette wearing a yellow T-shirt; Delvina, 8, a little blonde stands in the second row in her red-and-white striped top, her chin tilted upwards a little as if she is trying to look taller. Diona was two on 2 April, the day Serbs in uniform shot her and her sisters.

Caka is filled with regret. Valbona Caka, his daughter-in-law, the girls and his 10-year-old grandson Dren spent 2 April in his house. They went next door to hide in a basement when the Serbs began shooting.

'I keep seeing them and wishing I had stopped them. But we didn't think the Serbs would kill women and children.'

His son Ali, the children's father, thought the same. He was hiding elsewhere when his family was killed. Shortly after 1am, he heard Dren shouting in terror. Dren was on the other side of a garden wall and could not climb over. He had been shot in the arm.

The boy had seen what no 10-year-old should see after Serbian police had fired through the windows of his hiding place. 'Dren remembered who was shot first and he remembered exactly one by one who was shot after that,' Caka recalled. 'He escaped when the Serbs started a fire.'

Twenty people died in that house on Milos Gilic Street, 19 of them women and children. Their names are listed in the Hague indictment.

Apart from Milosevic, the war crimes tribunal has indicted Colonel-General Drogoljub Ojdanic, the chief of staff of the Yugoslav army; Vlajko Stojiljkovic, the Serbian minister of internal affairs, whose police went into the villages with paramilitaries to deport and kill; Milan Milutinovic, the president of Serbia;* and Nikola Sainovic, Milosevic's deputy prime minister responsible for Kosovo. A second indictment is expected, of men in lower ranks.

Investigators are documenting not only the work of the killers but their chain of command. Major-General Vladmir Lazarevic is one of those likely to feature in further indictments; he commanded the Third Army, known as the Pristina Corps, which deployed in Kosovo.

It would have been his men who surrounded the village of Bela Crkva, shelled the red-roofed houses and gave protection to the interior ministry police or paramilitaries who went in and did the killing. Most of the men who pulled the triggers and killed Shendet and Agon Popaj, and Dalina, Delvina and Diona Caka, will probably go unpunished. There are too many of them.

But Sabri Popaj will greet the British investigators today with his piece of paper listing those killed in Bela Crkva and where they are buried.

Popaj's grieving wife left for Canada last month, and his mission is the only thing he cares about now. 'I think justice may help,' he said as he stood on the riverbank where he had hidden his dead son's jacket in the weeds to give to the investigators. 'I don't have the words for anything else.'

---

* Milan Milutinovic was acquitted on charges of war crimes.

The enemy within

15 August 1999

With Serbs now the target of revenge ethnic cleansing and British troops caught in the crossfire, Kosovo has all the ingredients to become a Balkan Northern Ireland, writes Marie Colvin in Pristina.

Godsa Draza was the darling of the Royal Hussars. When all the other Serbs of the village of Donje Ljupce fled, including her two sons, the 78-year-old grandmother decided to hold her ground. She remained in her cottage, as she had throughout the Nato bombings, tending her two pigs and a scattering of chickens and weeding her vegetable garden.

The Hussars, based in nearby Podujevo, visited her once or twice a day, never at the same time, to show her Albanian neighbours that she had protection. She would brew cups of thick, sweet Turkish coffee. The soldiers laughingly called their visits the 'granny beat', but they admired her courage.

When the Royal Hussars arrived last Wednesday, there was no answer to their knock. They went around the back.

Her two withered feet were sticking up out of a pile of hay that had been dumped on the rubbish tip at the bottom of her garden. Some time on Tuesday night, Draza had been shot in her bed, shot again at the back door of her house, dragged down the garden and hidden. None of her neighbours admitted hearing or seeing anything unusual.

'The boys were pretty cut up. They had become very attached to her,' said Captain Tom Mallinson of the Royal Hussars. 'She meant no harm to anyone.'

It was not a good week to be a lonely old Serbian woman in Kosovo, one of the diehard matriarchs who have stayed behind to tend the animals, hoping that their families will some day come back.

On Thursday, Mica Stolic stood in her garden in the village of Gornje Brnjka, weeping and wringing her hands as military investigators sifted through the smashed furniture and appliances inside her farmhouse.

Stolic was lucky. At 5.30am, Irish Guards patrolling the village in a Warrior had heard shooting. They arrived at the scene in minutes and chased two Volkswagen Golfs along the winding dirt road at high speed. When a man in the back seat started firing at them, the commander remained cool. Rather than responding with his cannon or machinegun, which would have obliterated the car, he fired back with a rifle.

Four ethnic Albanian men, two of them wounded, were captured when the cars slewed to a halt; a fifth man was arrested later that day when he sought treatment for a wound at Pristina hospital.

The cycle of ethnic hatred has turned in Kosovo. About 100 houses along the dirt road through the village of Zhiti, 25 miles south of Pristina, have the Serbian symbol painted in white on their courtyard gates – a cross with four backward Cs into the four right angles.

During the Nato bombing, the sign protected the Serbian farmers from marauding Serbian paramilitaries who drove out their Kosovar neighbours. They survived the war unscathed, but last week the Serbian families of Zhiti had had enough. Four of their men had been shot dead in the eight weeks since the war's end.

The Zhiti Serbs were escorted to the border by their supposed protectors, the 82nd Airborne, American troops serving with Kfor [Kosovo Force]. Their homes were looted and burnt in their wake, the crosses that once ensured survival now inviting destruction. All that remained of Zhiti's Serbian community were burnt and roofless homes, their courtyards littered with cooking pots, charred window boxes and blackened geraniums.

An Albanian farmer prised a charred window frame from a house as a dozen Albanian youths with bicycles and a football occupied the street. 'We are very happy the Serbs have left. Very happy. But of course it was not us who burnt their homes,' said one.

During the war, the Serbian army and paramilitary forces drove into exile three-quarters of the ethnic Albanian population of Kosovo – 800,000 men, women and children – and laid waste their homes. Almost every surviving Kosovar has lost a father, brother, child or cousin; almost every village has a mass grave; 1,500 men are still missing.

Even the most moderate Kosovar shrugs off the thought that not all Serbs are guilty, insisting: 'We were targeted because we were Albanians.' The Balkan creed is familiar and unforgiving: an eye for an eye, a tooth for a tooth.

In this cauldron, two parallel forces are trying to shore up the idealistic policy that Kosovo must remain a mixed Albanian-Serbian entity. Kfor, the international army, is charged with enforcing law and order, which has in recent weeks come down to protecting the 50,000 Serbs who remain. Unmik, the United Nations Mission in Kosovo, led by Bernard Kouchner, the flamboyant former French health minister, is responsible for civil administration, which is almost non-existent. Kouchner is on his summer holiday.

The violence last week seemed to indicate that the euphoric welcome given to Nato troops had worn out and Kosovo was spiralling out of control. Given the increased number of attacks on Kfor troops and nightly incidents of intimidation against the dwindling Serbian community, can the peace be kept in such a scarred and divided population? Is this another Northern Ireland in the making, another example of a community turning on its liberators?

Major-General Andrew Ridgeway, chief of staff to General Sir Mike Jackson, the head of Kfor, and his replacement while Jackson is in Britain for a working holiday, says Kfor cannot protect every Serb. But he insists that his troops have a hold on the situation.

'Multi-ethnicity is not a concept on everyone's lips in the Balkans,' Ridgeway said over dinner in a tent at Kfor headquarters.

He is an informal sort of general: dinner was chicken pie and vegetables, and staff officers pitched up on the benches around the picnic table at will. The red wine was the only touch that distinguished his table from others, as he joked with noisy soldiers holding a going-away party nearby. But he is very serious and well-experienced from a term in Bosnia, where he believes serious mistakes were made.

'We're just looking for tolerance, for Serbs and Albanians to live together in some areas without killing each other,' Ridgeway said. 'But, of course, forcing people into that creates tensions.'

Despite the murder of Draza and the daily scuffles with French Kfor forces in the divided city of Mitrovica, statistics support Ridgeway's words. On Friday night the only incident reported in Pristina was a brick thrown through the window of a Serbian home. 'Must mean the buggers have run out of grenades,' joked the British soldier first on the scene.

The number of murders in Kosovo has steadily fallen, from 33 in week one after Kfor's arrival to 18 in week eight. Given that almost 600,000 Albanians have returned in the interval, the figures are even more striking. Arson, almost non-existent in week one, jumped to 187 incidents in mid-July, when Kosovar Albanians returned to their destroyed villages and avenged themselves on Serbian property, but fell again to 75 in week eight.

Who is attacking the Serbs? It is not as simple as it seems. The Kosovo Liberation Army (KLA) is most often blamed because it is the most obvious opposition force. Yet every authority in Kosovo – from Ridgeway to Bishop Artemije, the spiritual leader of the Serbs – rejects the theory that the KLA leadership is ordering the attacks.

'The chaps behind these attacks have nothing to do with the KLA,' Ridgeway said. 'The leadership does not condone them. Most of it seems to be organised crime. That is not to say that there are not some KLA radicals who are as keen to drive out the Serbs as we are to keep them. There are certainly some who believe they are the victors and to the victors belong the spoils.'

In the British sector, the men of 'Britfor' say they have been increasingly successful. 'We're beginning to get good intelligence and arrest a lot of these people,' Ridgeway said.

In a 24-hour period last week, 11 of 15 ethnic Albanians arrested in Pristina carried KLA cards. None, however, was on the official list of the KLA that Kfor has put together.

The problem is that the KLA is a mixed bag. During the war regulars were joined by overseas recruits, villagers, students. Now, everyone in Kosovo claims to have fought.

Kfor and UN investigations have shown that while crimes in the villages are almost certainly revenge attacks, most of the crimes against Serbs in the cities are committed by criminals using a 'political' cover.

'If a gang knows Serbs are living in an apartment, they go and intimidate them. They know they sound even more frightening if they say they are KLA,' said Bill Okula, a former American police officer now serving with the UN police, who are due to take over eventually from Kfor.

'They either chase them out or buy a DM100,000 flat for DM1,000. It's straightforward crime for gain. No politics there.'

Much of the anti-Serbian violence is committed by a group called the BIA. Since the return of Nato troops, BIA has been scrawled on city walls alongside KLA graffiti. Kosovan sources say the BIA comprises young former fighters. The initials stand for Bahria, Ilyir and Agron, three Albanian youths from Pristina who joined the KLA and were killed.

'Ilyir and Agron were killed before the war, and Bahria died fighting with the KLA during the war,' one Kosovan source said. 'They are revered by the boys of Pristina because most of the fighting was done by the people from the villages and these were city boys. They are famous here.'

Although the BIA no longer has connections with the KLA, the sources doubt that members are unknown to the leadership; but stopping their activities is another matter.

According to an undertaking signed with Jackson by Hashem Thaci, the prime minister of the self-styled KLA-led 'transitional government', the KLA must disband as a military group by 19 September. Thaci is in negotiations with Kfor over the KLA's continued existence. Getting into a war with young radicals is not something he needs at a time when he must convince his followers to lay down their arms and take up politics.

The belief in Pristina is that if the transitional date of 19 September is met, the tensions will lessen. Kfor proposes that Thaci and his leadership should become a political party, while their fighters could become an unarmed 'Rescue and Protection Corps'. That would allow them to remain militarised but not as an army.

As the bargaining continues, the remnants of the Serbian community are terrified. Artemije, holed up in the Serbian Orthodox monastery of Gracanica near Pristina, says that unless anti-Serbian violence is stopped, the community will disappear.

'I try to persuade people to stay in their homes. I tell them that as long as we are here Kosovo will be ours. It can never be only Serbian, but at least it will not be only Albanian,' said the bishop, a small rotund figure with a wispy grey beard, dressed in a black robe and turban.

His cloistered receiving room is a dissonant mix of ancient and modern: faded icons adorn the walls and priests who enter kiss his hand, while in the background two black-robed priests tap away at computers. British soldiers guard the gate of the monastery.

He is desperate. 'I have only words,' Artemije said. 'Every grenade is saying something else. The international community cannot sit by while they [the Albanians] finish the ethnic cleansing of Serbs.'

Chechnya

Wrath of Moscow leaves no place for Chechens to hide

19 December 1999

Pinned down by fire, Marie Colvin shares the anguish of the Chechen rebels.

Everyone in Chechnya travels at night. In mud-smeared 4x4 vehicles on dirt roads pitted with pot holes and bomb craters, the Chechen rebels head to the front to fight, or back to the mountains to rest.

Convoys of refugees, many in Ladas, drift by carrying families too scared to leave on roads that are bombed all day and often at night. They are even more scared to stay.

Fires started by the bombs burn on mountain ridges. The planes are bombing villages and roads indiscriminately and most of the victims are civilians, judging by those being treated in the few hospitals still functioning. There is no way of predicting when the planes will come.

I spent 12 hours yesterday pinned down in a field by a road south of Grozny. The planes, evil machines with the sun glinting off their sleek silver bodies, circled again and again. They trailed thunder, dropping bombs that whined as loudly as high-speed trains as they fell.

The car I was travelling in was blasted by shrapnel, its windows blown out. The quiet field where I took refuge, with only bracken and beech trees denuded by the winter for cover, felt like a death trap.

It takes no imagination to understand the fear of civilians who have to endure this day after day and who must decide whether to flee and face a day's drive on the open road, or take their chances in a basement.

Alkayez and his wife, Taus, have tried three times to escape along the supposed 'safe corridor' established by the Russians to Ingushetia. They are now living in a cave with four young children, not far from the ruins of their home in Vashenkali.

Outside is their car which has been hit by a missile. A woman and a man were killed in the explosion and were buried beside the road, but nobody knows their names.

The cave measures about 10 yards by 20 yards. One bed, where the whole family sleeps, lies on the rocky dirt floor and there is a crudely built brick wood stove. A bag of potatoes, a sack of onions and some flour they took from home are piled by the walls.

Family life is lit by two oil lamps that burn all day. Taus, 41, says they have no desire to leave the cave; they panic even to hear the engine of a passing car.

Three-year-old Kazishet, with blonde curls to her shoulders, sits in her mother's lap, chewing on a dummy. Eight bombs were counted on Thursday during my visit. 'The children are facing death with all the bombing,' their mother said. 'They bomb the village day and night.'

The few hospitals offer only primitive care to those injured on the roads. In Shattoi, a town of single-storey houses that has been bombed so often that it looks like a miniature Dresden, the hospital has somehow survived intact. But there are no windows and it has no electricity. Inside it is so cold that you can see your breath.

Two rooms are filled with the injured. There is one doctor and, according to one of the patients, 'he is only good for changing bandages'.

On one bed, lying on his back, is a frail, middle-aged man with a bloody towel wrapped around his head. Each breath is loud and laboured. His name is Khoja Khamoratov; he was on his way to his cousin's funeral in Tetoy when his car was bombed near Dai village by a Russian plane.

His brother, the driver, was killed instantly. The top of Khoja's skull was blown off and there is no treatment for him here. His face is still streaked with dried blood. 'We don't know what to do with him,' said the doctor.

In the other room is 15-year-old Timur Patirov, who has his arm in a sling. He was travelling in a Lada near Gote with his brother and cousin, trying to escape Ingushetia, when Russian tanks opened fire on them.

Heider Kaurnukoy, his sister, is holding the hand of her unconscious brother, Arby, 44. Half his foot has been amputated after their house in Khalkiloy was struck by a 1,000-pound bomb.

'How could we have believed they would hit our house?' she said. 'When I came to my senses my brother was lying in a pool of blood. He loves children. I want the world to feel ashamed of what has happened. The world is doing nothing while we are being slaughtered.'

The view from the mountain looking over the plains stretching from the village of Komsomolskaya to Grozny in the distance makes one wonder how a pilot can bomb in the way the Russian pilots have.

From the mountains, Komsomolskaya looks as it must from the cockpit of a plane – a place of white roofs, dirt streets and barn yards of cows and chickens. Smoke rises from the few chimneys, yet pilots dive on this village day and night. All last week Russian artillery crashed into homes.

The inhabitants of the village are no different from villagers anywhere. It is no military base. The victims are the old, the poor and women and children. Any sons who may be fighting with the rebels are not here.

The worst hit so far have been the Zakriyev family. They are too poor to have a basement. Dakov, the 51-year-old father, works as a labourer on building sites and their house is made of mud and straw bricks.

Last week the family was asleep on the floor of the front room when a missile crashed into the house and exploded. Adem, Dakov's 18-year-old son, died instantly.

'I was knocked out,' said Virlant, 39, his mother. 'The crying of the children woke me.' The youngest of her four surviving children, two-year-old Medina, is now a very quiet child who clings constantly to her.

The family buried Adem just before dawn because, they say, the Russians have been bombing funerals. Komsomolskaya is a village in shock.

In Grozny itself, it is difficult to see how the Chechen fighters can hold out indefinitely. They are faced with overwhelming numbers of Russian troops and the constant threat of helicopters and artillery.

However, for all the Russian superiority in numbers and weaponry, there could yet be a repeat of 1996 when the Russians last captured Grozny, only to lose it soon afterwards.

This is fighting country, with mountains that are almost impenetrable and studded with rebel strongholds. I stayed at one such base last week – a camp in which fighters recuperate after time at the front. The mountains were bombed daily but nothing changed in the rebels' grim, craggy faces.

General Hussein Isabayev is the base commander. There is a concern for individual fighters in the Chechen army that is rarely seen elsewhere. Each commander is required to build a resting post, just as he builds bomb shelters on the front lines. 'We don't have many people, so each one is precious to us,' said Isabayev.

Like most of his peers he pays for his unit's expenses – food, guns and ammunition – and most of the men are related to him or come from his clan.

Conditions are primitive: the house he occupies is built from flat stones hewn from the mountains and there is one long bed on a raised platform where at any time between five and 20 fighters are sleeping or resting and watching television.

Sometimes there is the odd sight of some young rebels watching a Russian pop video while more devout fighters kneel on the bed in prayer, leaning towards Mecca.

The atmosphere is sometimes excessively relaxed: when I curled up to sleep one night I pulled out from under me some annoyingly lumpy objects, only to find they were two hand grenades.

Isabayev's wife is known as the 'deputy commander'. She constantly brews up tea and cooks meals from big chunks of slaughtered wild goat that hang from the rafters outside.

A poster of Dzhokar Dudayev, the Chechen president killed in 1996, hangs on the wall next to a collection of weapons, including Kalashnikovs, a 1920s hunting rifle and a shoulder grenade launcher. Ammunition is stashed under the bed.

The soldiers have no doubt about their cause. Turpal Ali, 35 and a nephew of Dudayev, is in a special regiment known as Duki. He has not worked since the 1994–96 war, when a piece of shrapnel pierced his neck and cut a nerve, disabling his left hand. Before that he was a director of a trading company.

He has a bearded, thin face and speaks with a soft voice. 'I wouldn't be able to look into my friends' eyes if I didn't stand in a line of fighters,' he said, explaining his return to uniform.

Isabayev is a father figure to the young men here and has a tendency to philosophise. 'The trouble with the Russians is that they did not understand the psychology of the Chechens,' he said.

'They thought that by bombing and striking, they could divide our nation. These strikes will not do anything. They imagine that these people in occupied villages are theirs. That is not true. The villages are on our land. Every bit of this land is ours, every piece of soil. In every bush lurks an enemy to Russia.'

The final assault on Grozny began on Wednesday evening, when a column of Russian armoured tanks and transports drove in from the Khankala area to the east. Brigadier General Aslandek, leading the defence of the city, claimed that his troops were holding their positions.

Aslandek, 36, another veteran of the 1994–96 war, is seen by Chechens as a master strategist. Reached by radio yesterday, he sounded calm but said the fighting had been 'terrible'.

The Russians had attacked from Khankala every day, co-ordinating simultaneous advances from the north and the northwest.

The events of Wednesday night had raised Chechen morale, however. The first Russian column to penetrate the city centre had been destroyed, an armoured car had been captured and many Russians had been killed with rocket-propelled grenades and machineguns.

'We did not stop to calculate how many corpses were lying on the ground,' Aslandek said.

Escape from Chechnya to a trial by ice

2 January 2000

As Russian paratroopers cut off her last line of retreat, Marie Colvin was forced to flee with Chechen help by the only route left open: a range of 12,000-foot mountains.

The two moonlit gravestones were the only signs of humanity in the mountain range that stretched far around us. Magomet Amin Katayev, our guide, sat in their shadows and seemed to find comfort from them.

A small wiry Chechen who has spent his life on these slopes, Magomet had agreed to lead me and Dmitry Beliakov, a Russian photographer working for *The Sunday Times*, across these mountains from Chechnya to safety in Georgia. We had jackets and boots but little else for a trek across the 12,600-foot peaks.

The journey began four days before Christmas. It continued for eight increasingly desperate days, ending in rescue by helicopter last week from a snow-bound field in Georgia.

It was a trip that was not supposed to be necessary. I had been smuggled into the country from Georgia on 10 December in a four-wheel-drive vehicle to report first-hand from the towns and

Marie reporting from Chechnya, 1999.
Photograph by Dmitry Beliakov.

villages under bombardment. I had planned to leave by road. But then Russian paratroopers seized Melkhist, an ancient centre known as the Dead City, taking control of the only road to Georgia. They shot at any vehicles that tried to pass. I was trapped.

If we travelled a day north, we would reach the so-called safe corridor into Ingushetia set up by the Russians. But I knew that road and was not going back to it. On the way in, Russian fighter planes had attacked and destroyed the vehicle I was travelling in and had returned again and again, firing missiles into the field where I had taken refuge under a stunted beech tree. The pilots tried to scare us into making a run for it so that we would be easy targets. It was torture to listen to the babble of a stream in the silence after each attack, only to hear the returning roar of the jets.

I had also met refugees who had reached the 'safe corridor' only to be attacked from the sky. They had taken refuge with their injured in caves, or in the dark, unheated ruins that passed for hospitals, where the few doctors left could only stop the bleeding.

The alternative route, east over the border to Dagestan, was blocked by fighting. Sitting in a mountain hideout, we agreed that a trek over the peaks was preferable to being hunted from the skies.

For hours on the day we hoped to set out, Tuesday 21 December, planes attacked the slopes nearby with rockets that set brush and trees on fire in great arcs of flame. We left our hideout just after sunset. As we reached the gravestones, where Magomet said a friend would meet us, the dark ridge above us began glowing orange. One of the fires was burning our way. 'It will take 15 minutes to cross this field,' Magomet said. I asked why we were sitting there. 'We are waiting for my friend.' There did not seem much point in arguing.

Valed, Magomet's friend, showed up before the fire reached us. Unlike our laconic guide – who was dressed in a sheepskin coat, jeans and lightweight climbing boots – Valed was in full combat camouflage gear with a Kalashnikov over his shoulder. He told us about his ambition to join the Foreign Legion.

Valed said he would escort us until there was no more danger from kidnappers and smugglers. That was the first we had heard of them, but to Valed the perils seemed as commonplace as a weather report. He kept up a stream of patter, walking ramrod straight and talking about how he needed training missions like this. Dmitry and I struggled behind the silent Magomet.

Within an hour we were zigzagging up a mountain on a 6-inch-wide path covered in snow and ice. I was carrying a pack with a satellite telephone and a computer, and wearing a flak jacket. I felt every ounce.

I tried to time my breath to my strides, but it was impossible. I struggled to breathe and the air kept getting thinner. Magomet paced silently in front. I looked down to the spectacular depths below us and the snow-covered slopes across the gorge, then thought better of this and kept my eyes on the path. I regretted every cigarette I had ever smoked – and I had smoked a lot in the past few days: cheap Russian tobacco that gave some respite from the bombs and the decisions. Without a word, Magomet took Dmitry's camera bag and Valed shouldered my rucksack.

We stopped at a spring where, like all those we would come across, a tin cup had been left on a stone. Valed took off his shoes and socks and washed his feet in the freezing water, then knelt to pray while I collapsed and tried to breathe.

'Normal?' asked Magomet.

'Normal,' seemed the only response. I would find out during the next days that 'normal' was Magomet's way of indicating anything from 'okay' to 'will you survive?' – and that 'normal' to a Chechen and to me were two different things.

The path was ghostly grey in the moonlight and seemed deserted. But it was alive. Three human shapes appeared along it and Magomet and Valed stiffened. The meeting was like one between suspicious dogs. Both parties circled each other, speaking quietly, until some obscure test was passed and grins broke out and all five embraced.

Some agreement to travel together had been reached. The newcomers – Leche, Mussa and Omar – took our baggage and one of them put on my flak jacket. I was sure we would be bombed as soon as I relinquished it, but I was beyond caring about anything except the relief from the weight on my back. I was thirstier than I can ever remember being and scooped up handfuls of snow to suck. I thought of the Chechen refugees who had fled along this route.

About midnight, after almost six hours of walking, we reached the top of a peak, where a roofless stone hut provided shelter from the wind. Magomet lit a fire and said we would eat. I lay on a bed of woven saplings covered with damp sheepskins and fell asleep. When I awoke, the Chechens were breaking out bread and opening tins of salty Russian stewed beef. I drank a cup of hot water but could not eat anything.

Magomet insisted we get going. The path took us towards another mountain that looked so close in the moonlight that it seemed hyper-real, a dark shape lined with white veins of snow. It was a moment of pure beauty, but when we reached the bottom of the slope it turned out that one of the white veins was the path we would have to climb up.

Dmitry sat down and said he could not continue. 'Leave me here. Someone will find my body.' I sympathised but we had to get over the mountain before dawn or the Russian planes would find us. Magomet sat down beside Dmitry and quietly talked him out of suicide.

We walked up the slope, looking down thousands of feet into a gorge that one slip would take us into. Magomet hauled me by the hand to the last summit. I slept for an hour sitting against a stone in the snow until Magomet woke us at dawn with a warning that we were still in Chechnya and would have to move.

We slid and walked down the mountainside, but the way forward over a mountain river was blocked. The river had frozen into a stream of silver ice, 30 feet across. This was pure ice with no footholds and a drop of about 1,000 feet. We detoured back up the slope, then down across fields towards another river and another path. Suddenly, two Russian fighter planes flew overhead. We froze.

It was a discouraging day. Travelling up the next river, I stepped in the wrong spot and plunged through the ice up to the hip into the raging torrent below. Our three fellow travellers went ahead but returned to say they had reached the head of this half-frozen river and could not find a pass over the mountain. They declared that they were going back because 'we cannot see any chance for success in this mission'.

We had now been walking for 24 hours. As night fell, Magomet lit a fire on the ice of the frozen river and then set off on his own. He returned at about 10pm and told us he had found the pass. He said the departure of Leche, Mussa and Omar should not concern us. They were young town boys, wannabe weapon smugglers out to make some fast money, and had decided that this route was too difficult.

I remembered Leche hauling me up 200 yards of an almost vertical slope and reflected on the Chechen meaning of 'town boys'.

Without my noticing, Valed had also gone – replaced by another Chechen, Murad, who was walking to Tblisi, the Georgian capital, to buy a weapon.

The next 12 hours were passed in a daze, one foot in front of the other, up and over another mountain. The air was so thin that I could not fill my lungs, and the wind was so strong that several times I was almost blown off the mountainside. Just before dawn we reached a snow-covered field amid the peaks. It looked like the top of the world. Dmitry could not walk, so Magomet placed him on a small tree and hauled him across.

There was a pile of stones ahead – the Georgian border. Two shots rang out. We dived into the snow and another two shots sounded. It seemed unfair that here, yards from the border, we would die. Magomet began shouting in Chechen and the shots stopped. We crossed the border. But we had not yet reached safety. We could not find Giveri, the Georgian village that was our goal.

I had been dreaming of coffee and a bed. Magomet said Giveri would have been deserted anyway as it was winter. Despair, for the first time, set in. I fell asleep on an exposed bluff, impervious to the wind and cold. When I awoke, Magomet had found an abandoned shepherd's hut.

It was Christmas. The symbolism of spending it in a shepherd's hut seemed a better omen than the graves at the start of our trek. I got a call out over the satellite phone to *The Sunday Times* foreign desk to say that we had crossed the border, and I also managed to reach Georgian contacts in Tblisi who had promised to pick us up by helicopter. There were no roads here and it was the only way out. The helicopter was promised for 11am the next day.

We foraged through the hut and found some flour, which we boiled up with melted snow into a gluey porridge. We took it in turns to stoke the fire, working in four-hour shifts.

Christmas turned out to be a time of disappointments and broken promises, however. Timor, one of the Georgians who was supposed to be organising the helicopter, kept promising and not appearing. The battery on my satellite phone was running out. We were marooned.

For the next two days we lived in the shepherd's hut on flour and water. I supplemented the porridge once with wild onions. They tasted horrible but they would give us some vitamins. Magomet gave me a pistol loaded with nine bullets – telling me not to shoot a wild animal until it was 10 metres away but to shoot a man the moment one appeared – and set off to find a way forward.

After his return, we walked down a river valley into Georgia. Magomet said that in the Caucasus, people built their villages along the rivers and we might find some inhabitants. He was right: we found Giveri, a collection of dark stone houses. All were open and unlocked but had been abandoned for the winter. We found a house with beds, a stove, some more flour and a can of peas.

Using the last power in the satellite phone battery, I made my final, brief call to Sean Ryan, foreign editor of *The Sunday Times*. Could he take over and try to get a helicopter here?

In fact, Ryan was already in touch with Georgy Gvasaliya, a Georgian general who was helping to provide the helicopter. The general had painted him a false rosy picture: Dmitry and I were being cared for in a village with traditional Caucasian hospitality, downing great stews and sleeping in warm sheepskins, he said.

On 28 December, a storm set in and we were down to the last of our flour. We decided to try to walk out. According to the map, about 30 kilometres down the river was a town and a road. I fried up the last of the flour into five flatbreads and we set out along the valley. After walking for five hours, we found another shepherd's hut and spent the night in the cold, eating half our bread.

The dawn was clear and cold. The storm had passed but left about 1ft of snow. In a village along the river we heard a dog barking and found an elderly couple, Bartanz and Elizabetha Kacunkubev, too poor to leave for the winter.

They took us into their tiny stone house, where a portrait of Stalin looked down from the wall, and gave us fried potatoes, preserved cabbage and a shot of vodka each. Bartanz then drew a map, showing us how to get to another village, Omala, which he said had a radio and was only 5 kilometres away.

Setting out for it, we walked until an hour before dark, when we heard a helicopter. We waved madly. The helicopter ducked its nose and landed below us in a field. The Georgian general had let us down but *The Sunday Times* had sent my colleague Jon Swain to Tblisi. He had gone to the American embassy and told them a US citizen was missing in the mountains on the frontier. I was never happier to have an American passport.

I walked down the slope to be greeted by an Ernest Hemingway figure with a white beard and blue snow jacket, who said: 'Jack Hariman, American embassy. Are we glad to find you ...'

He told us Omala was much further away than the old couple had said. We would have spent another cold night on a mountain-side with no shelter. Instead, the helicopter lifted off, whirling over the frozen landscape of snow and dark fir trees towards Tblisi.

East Timor

Trapped by the terror squads in city of death

DILI

12 September 1999

Marie Colvin is one of three foreign journalists who stayed behind in Dili after hundreds of colleagues withdrew in response to warnings that their lives were at risk. Her broadcasts on the BBC, CNN and Sky enabled a worldwide audience to follow events in the United Nations compound where 80 staff and 1,000 refugees sheltered from militia attacks. Colvin, 43, an American citizen, has been a *Sunday Times* foreign correspondent since 1986 when she witnessed the American bombing of Tripoli. She has covered several Middle East conflicts and remained in Baghdad throughout the bombing of Iraq during the Gulf War in 1991. Earlier this year, braving snipers and shelling, she became the first journalist to enter Kosovo from Albania with KLA guerrillas after the airstrikes had begun. Yesterday she said she was astonished that all her male colleagues had left the compound as the danger intensified, commenting drily: 'They don't make men like they used to.'

The first sound of trouble was the screams of two little old ladies who slashed themselves on the razor coils topping the walls of the United Nations compound, desperate to enter.

Militiamen were in the UN car park next door to the compound, firing in the air, terrifying the refugees in an overflow camp outside and the 1,000 slightly luckier ones who were inside the walls.

The militia had just seen most of the UN staff being evacuated, leaving behind a small and vulnerable group of UN officials, a host of refugees, and three foreign journalists – myself among them.

The swaggering militiamen wanted a UN car and they walked up to the blue iron bars of the compound and demanded one. They carried a grenade. Indonesian soldiers on the perimeter were supposed to provide security, but they stood back as more militia poured in.

General Razaz, the dashing Bangladeshi commander of the UN's unarmed military mission, arrived with his bamboo walking stick. The militia fired off more rounds.

The commander of the Indonesian guards said he was under orders not to shoot at them. 'Give them a vehicle and we can solve this. What's the problem?' he asked. To emphasise the point, the militia began smashing windscreens and looting UN vehicles. Two Indonesian soldiers helped them.

It was proof, if needed, of what everyone has known all along: 'The military and militia are two sides of the same face,' as a

UN liaison officer said. For all the denials of the military, UN analysts believed that many of the militia are moonlighting soldiers.

Surrounded by 'defenders' who are in league with their besiegers, the remaining occupants of the UN compound were still holding out yesterday after a week of terror. UN officials insisted they would not leave the refugees to die. They pointed out that the Timorese had voted for independence in a UN-sponsored election and the UN had promised to stay and protect them through to the transition. Yet Dili was in ruins. There were now 200,000 displaced people in the country.

The UN was helpless. The least its officials could do was to save the comparatively few refugees who had reached the sanctuary of their compound.

The siege of the UN compound began last Monday, a day when Dili was a city in hiding. No cars moved on the streets except military vehicles and the motorbikes and vans of the militia. Buildings had begun burning overnight and the militia had rampaged through the residential neighbourhoods, shooting wildly, threatening death to anyone they met.

Foreigners were fleeing. Several cars of election observers, driving to the airport with their local staff, were pursued by two militiamen on a motorcycle. The pillion passenger started firing and one driver managed to force the motorcycle off the road. When the convoy fled to a nearby police station, the militiamen walked in the door.

Gillian Flies, of the East Timor Observer Mission, said the police forced the delegation to sign a statement admitting dangerous driving and speeding, to say they had not been fired at and to pay the militiamen for damage to the motorbike.

Monday was also the day when the East Timorese found there was no limit to what their Indonesian enemies would do. About 1,000 refugees woke at dawn in the International Red Cross compound. Sleepy children played amid the piles of bedding, suitcases and plastic carry-alls that held the few possessions their parents had been able to carry to what they had thought would be a safe refuge in the walled rear courtyard.

These refugees had come to the Red Cross because they believed it offered international protection, like an embassy. But they were wrong. At 11.30am soldiers in camouflage uniforms and wild-eyed militia dressed in T-shirts, the black shirts of the Aitarek (Thorn) militia and bandannas poured into the compound. They fired into the air, shouting curses and commands.

I was in the Turismo hotel next door. A cacophony of screams and shouts sounded from the Red Cross compound. Dodging patrols of soldiers running through the hotel with guns pointed forward, I reached a balcony and looked down on a terrifying scene. Women rolled on the ground of the compound in terror, clutching children. A soldier stood in the centre, pointing his assault rifle at a woman and shouting and gesturing at her as she held her hands over her head. Other women scrambled for their children and were kicked or hit with rifle butts. Militiamen roamed around the courtyard, shouting and firing in the air.

It was all over in about half an hour. Women, children and men were marched at gunpoint into the street, while international Red Cross staff were driven away to the airport to be evacuated to Darwin.

The deserted courtyard was strewn with food, blankets and overturned cooking pots. The silence was broken only by the crowing of a rooster. While police stood around the walls, a militiaman smashed open suitcases and searched piles of refugee possessions. He paused to look for identification when he found an East Timorese independence banner, and took the banner and a wallet with him. In another suitcase he found a woman's beaded purse and pawed through the jewellery inside, pocketing a string of pearls. His search completed, he walked out to where the refugees were being held at gunpoint.

About 200 people, mostly men, were separated from the 1,000 who had been in the compound and were marched east down the beach, in the direction of the huge statue of Christ on the cliffs overlooking the city. There has been no news of these men since. Their families were allowed back into the compound to collect their belongings. Weeping women bundled cooking pots and clothes into blankets and fled.

Down the corniche from the Red Cross, a simultaneous attack had taken place on the refugees in the seafront compound of Bishop Ximenes Belo – a co-ordination which gives the lie to Jakarta's attempt to blame the violence on militias who had run amok. At the Turismo hotel, soldiers tried to find the journalists who had witnessed the brutality. They banged on doors but nobody opened them.

John McCarthy, the Australian ambassador to Jakarta, came to the rescue, arriving with consulate cars and his defence attaché. On the way, his clearly marked diplomatic vehicle had come under fire and he was angry. We were not allowed to collect our bags. 'What do you want, your life or your clothes?' the ambassador shouted at one journalist before we were driven to the walled UN compound in a former teacher-training college in the Matadoro neighbourhood.

The situation was hardly better there. Militiamen invaded the refugee encampment outside, shooting automatic fire almost at the refugees' heels as they fled. Men and women threw themselves over the walls into the compound, slashing themselves badly on the coils of razor wire that had protected the UN personnel. Children were caught in the wire. The UN clinic treated 50 people for cuts.

Refugees streamed in steadily on Tuesday with tales of terror. Sister Esmeralda, an elfin nun in a grey habit and gold spectacles, led 800 people to safety from her convent. The nun, just 4ft tall, held a Bible in her tiny hands as she softly described how a commander of the Aitarek militia jumped over the wall, yelling: 'Out, out, out. You are going to Polda [the police compound].'

'He was like in a horror movie. The people were crying: "They will kill us, madre." I say to the people: "Calm. Stop crying. We will go to the United Nations." They looked at me: "Who is she? She is so small."

'I organised the people and said: "We will not go running." I lined them up and told the people: "Silence." We came out like you see in television and we walked toward the Aitarek and Brimop [army unit] in front of the convent and I led the people through them and they parted for me. I led the way to the United Nations.'

One of the luckiest to make it there was Aida Ramos Horta de Assis, the sister of Jose Ramos Horta, co-winner of the Nobel peace prize with Belo and a hate figure for the forces roaming the streets. This tiny woman in shorts and flip-flops knew she was a target and had fled to a relative's home with her five children before the announcement of the referendum result.

On Monday night the military had surrounded the house, yelling and banging, but a neighbour said nobody was home. Aida said she heard them talking about killing and needed to hear no more. She fled at dawn but had to leave her husband behind. 'He said to me, "Don't wait for me, save the children".'

By late Tuesday the compound was filling up. The dwindling number of UN staff occupied two-storey houses with tin roofs. Refugees slept on concrete pathways and patches of ground if they could not find a space in the open-air conference hall.

In the morning the tiled floor of the conference hall was cleared and scrubbed down by its temporary occupants. Women washed their children's little frilly dresses and baby clothes and hung them on the barbed wire.

Columns of smoke rose from the city, just below the compound. Night-time brought a spectacular view of fires leaping hundreds of feet into the air. The UN transport compound had been torched and the militia were driving the streets in UN vans.

We heard that there were 200,000 refugees and that many were being forced to Indonesian-controlled West Timor, by boat or overland. More than 10,000 people were being held at the Dili police compound and refugees with missing relatives were terrified of what would happen to them. Rumours of mass executions circulated.

Word came that the Aitarek had ordered: 'No white faces will be seen on the streets.' Journalists were executed here in 1975, so it was a warning to be taken seriously. McCarthy advised all the journalists to evacuate and many took him up on the offer. They were driven out with some UN staff, lying in the backs of open lorries, surrounded by Indonesian soldiers.

An American officer briefed a convoy setting out to the airport to rescue a group of terrified UN staff workers, all local Timorese, who had arrived from a UN outpost in Bacao. The convoy was in danger, as the militias and army were targeting UN workers. Ten had been reported killed already. 'Pack them in,' said the officer as the rescue column headed out. 'The good news is they're all small.'

The convoy returned with a weeping group who said militiamen had overrun their Bacao outpost that morning, the first attack on a UN compound. There was shooting all around the compound, breaking windows and doors.

They had fled to a church next to the UN post, but many were left behind when a UN convoy headed for the local airport. Those that made it were promised they would be flown to Darwin, but at the airport the Indonesians allowed only international staff to continue.

Manuel, 40, who did not want to give his full name, last saw his wife, Maria, 42, a UN interpreter, hiding in the St Anthony church in Bacao. His seven children, aged from one year old to 20, are missing in Dili, where they were staying with his sister while he and Maria worked for the UN during the election campaign.

Numbers still grew in the UN compound. Food stocks dwindled and fuel for the pump that drew water from the well was running low. UN security men were more confident by Wednesday morning, despite the continued gunfire. They had been told that the local Indonesian troops guarding the UN compound had been replaced by Kostrad, an elite force with no connections to the local militia. 'I looked into their eyes and I saw commitment,' said Alan Mills, the Australian commander of the UN civilian police.

The confidence proved ill-founded. Guarded by two trucks of the new soldiers, a convoy set out for the UN warehouse near the port to pick up supplies. They were ambushed by 50 militiamen while the guards stood and watched.

'As soon as we opened the warehouse door and started loading boxes of water, the militia opened fire,' said Ronnie Wahl, a Norwegian driver in the convoy. 'They tried to smash the windshields with machetes, clubs and sticks.'

The convoy drove off, leaving the doors of the warehouse open for potential looters.

This disaster left things desperate in the compound which was by then a sanctuary for about 2,000 refugees, plus the 208 international staff and 63 local staff, many with their families. There were only 400 ready-to-eat meals and enough rice for one more day. The Australians, who had decided to evacuate, offered a bottle of whisky, packets of biscuits and six bright yellow tennis balls.

That night, the mood in the compound darkened. The gunfire was relentless and for the first time a bullet was fired into the compound. It swished through a tree and hit a UN car about 10 feet from where I was talking to Brian Kelly, a lanky UN information officer from Ireland. 'Heavy leaves here,' Kelly said, rolling his eyes.

The security men examined the car and went quickly to the office of Ian Martin, the UN mission head. Children walked around holding hands, oblivious to the crisis atmosphere that was developing.

'You look around at these kids and it's hard not to get emotionally involved,' said Michael Holworth, a police officer with the UN who comes from Sussex. 'Luckily I'm used to it from police work – but not on this scale, of course.'

There was a nervous twitter in the camp as I walked through, giving out the Australians' yellow tennis balls. Everyone knew that the UN was preparing to evacuate.

Was the UN really going to leave all these people behind? Privately, Kelly confirmed that it was, but we were not to report this. Clearly deeply upset, Kelly kept a calm exterior and said local UN staff would be evacuated with their families.

Refugees began asking what was happening. 'Just tell me the truth and I will tell the people calmly. We cannot have panic,' said Dr Nilton Tilman, a softly spoken Timorese doctor who had emerged as a leader in the camp. 'They know they will die if the UN leaves, but I will try to calm them. Just tell me the truth.'

People were already panicking. Babies squalled. An exhausted and tearful local UN worker stayed awake all night for fear that the UN would sneak out while she was sleeping. Another, Angelita Buak, who worked for the UN for five days during the election as a voter identification officer, was not on the list to be saved. She was threatened by the militia and had to move house during the election to stay safe, but only full-time staff were being evacuated. Tiny, scared and clutching a Bible with a coloured picture of Jesus on its cover, she begged to use my satellite phone and called her sister in Australia.

'Sister, sister, save me,' she howled into the phone in Tetum, the Timor language. 'Sister, they will kill us. We are going to die. You must do something tonight, now.'

Her howls drew everyone and spread terror. People started trying to leave the compound through the back, climbing under a coil of barbed wire and up a stone culvert. The escape route then passed through large boulders and up a steep hillside. Everybody was silent, even the smallest child. A little boy fell between two boulders and his mouth opened in a silent scream.

Firing broke out as soldiers camped outside noticed what was happening. The refugees were forced to stop. Teresa DeGama, 19, was halfway up the hill with her family when the shooting started. Terrified, she left them and ran back down again. Now she stood alone, staring blankly at the wire, holding the sack of rice that was to have been her family's only food for the coming weeks in the hills.

At midnight, Sister Esmeralda asked if she could use the satellite telephone to call her mother superior in Rome, surrounded by seven other nuns in dove grey robes and head-dresses, all with tissues to their eyes. Over the phone, she said in Latin, 'We are ready to die but what about the people we brought to this place? There are many women and children.'

She listened to the answer, hung up and embraced me. Her head came to my waist. She wept, but then she straightened and said, 'God is strong.' She and her seven sisters marched out into the night.

There were other forces at work. UN staff started signing a petition saying they did not want to leave and would remain whatever the security situation. 'The refugees – we can't leave them,' said a jolly, middle-aged American woman who ran the now non-existent supply operation. 'My government tried to order me home but I told them I work for the United Nations. Stuff 'em.'

At 1.15am, Kelly arrived with another statement. The evacuation would be postponed for 24 hours. Local staff and families would be evacuated as well. And a solution would be found for the refugees.

On Thursday morning I slipped out of the compound. The Aitarek militia ruled the roads, driving by on motorcycles or in vans with assault weapons pointing out of the windows. One Aitarek with a machete told me not to continue, it was dangerous. He pulled his finger across his throat to illustrate what he meant.

Two soldiers pulled up in their truck and invited me to meet their commander, a lieutenant, who turned out to be articulate and professional. 'We came here for a civic action,' he said. 'We have failed. We have failed to win the hearts and minds of the Timorese people.'

I told him I was trying to get to my hotel, where I had had to leave all my baggage. 'I know you are a reporter,' he said. 'No matter. Have some breakfast and I will drive you. My orders are to protect foreigners.'

Over noodles and an omelette, my first hot meal in days, we talked about his ambition to go to West Point, the American military academy. His orders not to fire on the militia clearly grated.

We drove through a devastated city in his pickup truck with four soldiers in the back for protection.

It was an apocalyptic vision. Hundreds of militia roamed the streets, some walking, some riding three to a motorcycle with one carrying looted goods, the second an assault rifle, the third driving. It was a frenzy of looting. The post office was still burning, but most of the other buildings were burnt-out skeletons. Gunfire sounded nearby.

The lieutenant drove grimly. There were no civilians or cars on the streets. It was as if the barbarians had taken over. One motorcycle passed us, the militiaman on the back waving his pistol at us and smiling maniacally, showing no fear of the army vehicle or its occupants.

The police compound was the centre of their activity; militia families waited under trees, loot piled high next to them in boxes and bags, while militia drove in and out depositing their latest gains. The Turismo, my hotel, had been looted but not burnt. Oddly, the militia had taken all my underwear but left behind my flak jacket.

Early the next morning the evacuation of most UN staff from their compound began at last. Many had debated all night whether to get on the plane.

At 5am, 120 UN staff, 160 local staff and their families and 23 journalists got on the trucks heading to the airport, sitting in the back surrounded by Indonesian soldiers. Those staying behind watched sombrely.

'Goddamn way to run an international mission – going out on my belly like a dog,' complained one Australian policeman who had wanted to stay behind.

Courage knows no gender

10 October 1999

Award-winning war reporter Marie Colvin, who has roughed it in Kosovo and East Timor, argues that women don't have to use feminine wiles to win the battle for stories.

Do women report wars differently from men? The question used to make me bristle. It irritated me to think that I would be judged as a woman war correspondent rather than as a writer, taking the same risks and covering the same story as my male colleagues.

My feelings were hardly new. 'Feminists nark me,' wrote Martha Gellhorn, one of the great war correspondents of the century. 'I think they've done a terrible disservice to women, branding us as "women's writers". Nobody says men writers; before, we were all simply writers.'

I have been covering wars for 13 years now, ever since the Americans bombed Libya in 1986. In those days war reporting was very much a man's world. It seemed important to blend in and the only way to do that was to be 'one of the boys'. Now, roughly a quarter of the correspondents covering any conflict will be female.

The image of the glamorous female correspondent, weighed down by mascara, fluttering her eyelashes and showing a bit of leg, is as dated as a 1950s *Life* magazine spread, if it ever was true. Yet Ann Leslie, foreign correspondent of the *Daily Mail*, has just revived the myth in a book, *Secrets of the Press*. Acting the 'harmless bird brain', 'chirruping' about cooking and 'twittering' about babies, helps to land the scoops, she argues.

I have only to think of myself in Kosovo and East Timor to laugh.

In March I walked over the Albanian mountains into Kosovo with a unit of the Kosovo Liberation Army. The war was being reported second-hand from videos and briefings in Nato headquarters and from tales told by fleeing refugees. I wanted to see what was happening at first hand. That doesn't seem to me a very male or female notion, just a commitment to what all journalists should be doing – trying to find out the truth for ourselves.

The idea that I was glamorous would have seemed pretty comical to the guerrillas who took me in. I walked and slept in the same clothes for days. I had to carry my own gear and, as far as I was concerned, a satellite phone was heavy enough. A change of clothes just wasn't a priority. I was quickly covered with mud up to my knees. On the one day that the sun came out, I took off my flak jacket. I was so smelly, I quickly put it back on. Even I couldn't stand the odour. And when you are huddled in a cold gully under shellfire with 12 men, fear is as great an equaliser as dirt.

My decision to stay in the United Nations compound in East Timor incited a lot of comment, because the three journalists who refused to leave were women (the other two were Dutch reporters). Again, there was little glamour involved. I was sleeping rough, mostly on the ground, and was once again short of clothes. I had been forced to leave my hotel when it was overrun by angry Indonesian soldiers and militiamen and, in my haste, I escaped with only a computer and satellite phone.

It underestimates men to say they are suckers for women who behave like sex kittens on the battle front. There are very few soldiers on a front line who wouldn't take up the offer of a drink or a flirt with a woman correspondent – not least because there is not a great deal of female companionship around. But that doesn't mean the femme fatale will land the story – she may get a drink at the price of enduring a really boring hour or two. Most likely, she will then be considered a lightweight and the object of her wiles, if he has a big story, will give it to somebody he considers a serious journalist. Men aren't fools all of the time.

That said, there are differences. I don't have to dab Chanel under my ears or play dumb for it to be easier for me to get through a checkpoint manned by surly militiamen with automatic weapons. They do react differently to me simply because of my sex. They feel less threatened by a woman, and however crazed they are, some vestigial feeling of protectiveness towards the 'weaker sex' means they are more likely to help, or at least less likely to hurt.

This happened in East Timor, when I was trying to walk into the centre of Dili and was accosted by a militiaman with a machete, who drew his hand across his neck as a warning of what would happen to me if I continued on my way. An Indonesian officer rescued me, and drove me around the burning city.

I also think that gender can work in men's favour. Male reporters can play on the boys' club mentality, swapping dirty jokes with soldiers, or discussing the merits of different weapons. I've never been interested in types of guns, just what the people firing them mean to do.

There are other differences which are more difficult to pinpoint. Women, I think, tend to try harder to understand what is really happening to people on the ground. They are less inclined to settle for writing an analysis of a situation and leaving it at that. I think of Maggie O'Kane of the *Guardian*, who covered Bosnia and most recently the East Timor conflict with fearlessness; her war reporting is marked by vivid observation and tireless interviewing. This is a huge generalisation, and by no means always true, but writing about the 'big picture' seems to carry a certain prestige that, to me, often misses the point of journalism.

I remember talking to a male colleague after writing a story about a man whose wife and five young children had been executed by the Serbs. It didn't seem enough for me to simply report on his loss. I sat for hours with him, by their grave on a river bank, staring at a bloody and bullet-ridden romper suit, listening to his memories and his guilt.

My colleague mused that he simply would not have stopped. 'There would have been other things to do that day, a briefing, whatever, more important or not. I would have written down his details and moved on.'

Why? That's hard to work out. From experience I know men think differently from women, but since I've never been able to figure out their behaviour in other walks of life, I find it just as impossible to explain why they think differently in wars. Again, Gellhorn said it best describing her 40 years of reporting wars. 'Beware of the Big Picture,' she wrote. 'The Big Picture always exists. And I seem to have spent my life observing how desperately the Big Picture affects the "little people" who did not devise it and have no control over it.'

There is probably a darker side to all this. Fewer women than men become foreign correspondents, and even fewer cover wars. Those of us who do are probably more driven than most, simply because it is harder to succeed. Maybe we feel the need to test ourselves more, to see how much we can take and survive. Bravery is personal.

But it is wrong to say that women are inevitably more sensitive. Since my return from East Timor, people have said to me that I must have stayed in the UN compound after my male colleagues had left because I felt more strongly about the women and children who would have been slaughtered had the UN evacuated it.

I felt proud that my reporting contributed to the reversal of the UN's decision to pull out. I embarrassed the decision-makers and that felt good because it saved lives. It is rare to see such a direct result in journalism. I was moved by the children, who greeted me with 'Hello, Mister' as I walked through the compound. But for me, it was a moral decision, made passionately but not out of sentimentality. I simply felt it would have been wrong for the UN to have promised these people protection and then to have abandoned them to certain death. It would have been a betrayal. I can't believe that is a judgment that has a gender.

PART TWO

Marie at the entrance to a smuggler's tunnel in Gaza, 2005.
Photograph by Seamus Murphy.

Ethiopia

Horror of Ethiopia's living dead

9 April 2000

Five months ago, Miyir Mohammed thought he was a well-off little boy. His father had 40 cattle and 50 sheep and goats, and was middle-class by the standards of southern Ethiopia. Miyir helped to herd the smaller animals.

I never got to meet him. Miyir, 4, died of hunger on Friday morning as I drove into his camp. Hours later, his father was still waving flies away from his tiny body, which was wrapped in his mother's headscarf. It looked far too festive for such a tragic thing as the death of a child.

There was little joy in Miyir's last days. His family's livestock began dying as the drought in Ethiopia moved into its third year. For months Miyir's parents, Hassan and Safia, and their five children drove their herd for hundreds of kilometres, criss-crossing the Nogup region in search of pasture, hoping that somewhere it would rain. It never did.

Sometimes the boys would haul up a sheep or a goat and help it to walk, but the animals always died anyway. There was simply nothing for them to eat.

Two months ago Hassan and Safia gave up their nomadic life when the last animal died. The herd had been their life: it provided milk and meat, which they sold when they needed anything from town.

The family walked to Danan, a village where they had heard there was some food. They walked for four days, resting at midday when the temperature passed 40°C.

A donkey carrying their belongings died and they had to leave behind everything except plastic water containers. The parents could carry only the younger children. 'We came here with nothing, nothing,' said Safia as she gazed down at her son's body.

In Danan, Hassan and Safia had no money and no way to earn it. They built a small dome shelter on the edge of the village, piling straw mats and grass on top of a structure made from branches. By last week, 6,300 nomads were living in a makeshift refugee camp, all of them in similar straits.

The Mohammed family lived for a while on one meal a day: porridge made from wheat distributed by the government. Then the children began to die.

Fadoma, 12, their eldest girl, died two months ago. Two weeks ago it was one-year-old Mohammed. Finally the couple lost Miyir. He had slipped in and out of consciousness for two weeks, able to eat only water and sugar.

There is a doctor at the local clinic – which is two rooms in a building erected as a school – but they had no money to pay for the oral rehydration salts and intravenous dextrose that might have saved Miyir.

In death, his face is peaceful but painful to look at: chocolate-coloured skin is pulled tight over sharp cheekbones. His neck is so thin that his hairless head looks far too big for his body. His tiny shoulder blades almost cut the skin of his back. His eyes are half-open. It is the face of famine.

Safia is so stricken that she cannot cry. She tells her story in the monotone of shock. Her six-year-old daughter, Amran, is ill; only her son Noor, 9, is still healthy, although he is very thin. The children cannot live on the food that the government distributes, Safia says. It is only wheat, which they have never eaten before.

'Miyir could not digest this wheat,' she said. 'We were used to eating meat and milk, and sorghum that we bought from selling our animals.'

In the afternoon, Safia washed Miyir's body in the red dust outside their hut and wrapped him in a white shroud. Hassan and some male relatives built a wooden stretcher to carry him 2 kilometres to a cemetery that is expanding on the outskirts of Danan.

They buried him in a double grave with a four-year-old boy he had never met – Abdi Baalul, who also died from hunger on Friday. The two families dragged the leafless branches of an acacia bush over the grave.

New arrivals who pass this place need no signpost to know they have reached Danan. Before the first hut comes into view, rows of desiccated carcasses appear along either side of the dirt road – big packages of hide-covered bones for cows, small ones for sheep and goats.

The population of Danan, the epicentre of Ethiopia's famine, has swollen to 10,000 with the coming of starving nomads. Their stories are heartbreaking.

A year ago Fadoma Sultan had four children and a husband, 30 cattle and 200 sheep and goats. A year ago her husband died; six months ago she lost the last of her livestock. She was destitute.

Fadoma, a tiny woman with fine features, hardly seems strong enough for the trials she has endured, but she decided to walk to Danan where she had heard there was food. The family walked for five days.

Fadoma carried her youngest child, Trishi, an 18-month-old girl, and some water. Her eldest child, Mohammed, who would be six now, died on the road and she had to bury him in the dirt with nothing to mark his grave.

There was food in Danan but that was no guarantee of survival. In their six months at the camp, Fadoma and her remaining three children ate one porridge meal a day. Last Wednesday Trishi died, too.

'She could not swallow,' Fadoma said. 'She had diarrhoea and stomach problems for a long time, but I could not find her soft food or milk. She could not digest this wheat.'

Her two remaining children cling to her blue and yellow robe. Oba is five and Derq is four, but they are so thin that it is almost impossible to tell which is a boy and which a girl. 'They are not healthy, but they are living,' Fadoma said.

There is death in the camp every day, but the most terrible sight is of those who are clearly about to die. They can be saved with so little – the right food, the right drugs – but there are not enough of either and so they will die.

They seem resigned to it. Their eyes are blank and there is no expression in their faces. They no longer wave away the flies on their faces. They wave away food, weakly. The families of those who are dying have seen the look before. Osman Hashi Ahmed is one of the desperate ones. He insists that I come to his hut to see his daughter and leads me at marching pace, the tail of his white turban waving behind him.

Four-year-old Nasteho is lying on the dirt floor fanned by Fatimo, her mother. She tries to pour water into Nasteho's mouth but the little girl lets it run down her cheek.

Nasteho is skeletally thin. She has a big head, tiny neck and arms and her legs are so narrow that they are just little sticks. Ahmed carried her to the clinic on Thursday but the doctors had nothing to treat her with. He thinks Nasteho is going to die and he can tell by my silence that I also think so.

Ahmed is one of those who knows the face of death. Five days ago he washed the body of his two-year-old daughter, Shukri, in front of this same hut. Shukri joined her sisters, Fordoza, 5, and Nasri, 6, in Danan's cemetery.

This is a proud man who, with his 60 cows, 100 sheep and goats, was wealthy. He now has to watch his family die one by one in the camp where he brought them for refuge.

I cannot help his daughter but he has two more children and a plea. 'We have prayed for Allah's help, but we need assistance. Tell the other nations they must send us food and medicine or we will all die.'

Danan provides a glimpse into the depth of the horror of a famine that could grip much of Ethiopia. This is not like the 1984–85 famine when 1 million people died in a disaster that Band Aid drew to everyone's attention. So far, enough food relief has dribbled in to keep the strong alive. But the situation is more desperate by the day.

Wheat was delivered to Danan in March, enough for 4.5 kilos per person. The April delivery is said to be 'in the pipeline', but it is late and there is no sign of it.

Much more desperately needed are supplementary rations: a high-energy mix of cereal, skimmed milk and vitamins which is needed by the young and elderly alike.

At first glance there appear to be a lot of people in Danan who are skinny but look healthy enough. Then you realise that there are no old people and few toddlers.

American aid has pledged 480,000 tons, but the next delivery is of only 85,000 tons and not until 15 April. According to Oxfam, the European Union has provided little more than half the food it promised last year. It has pledged only 50,000 tons and says this could take up to nine months to deliver. The distances are vast and the roads are poor. A huge airlift is urgently needed. But some donors are wary of sending food to a country whose government is spending millions fighting a border war with Eritrea.

Britain has halved its aid to Ethiopia from £39.3 million to £19 million because of fears that renewal of war with Eritrea would stop the money reaching projects designed to tackle poverty.

Some 230 trucks that were previously used for relief have now been sent to the front line.

Still, there is a chance in the first year of the new century to stop a disaster before it happens. The politics of aid distribution mean little to children such as Miyir. But food means everything.

Zimbabwe

Rape is new weapon of Mugabe's terror

MUREWA

28 May 2000

The manicured lawns and bright red poinsettia shrubs of St Paul's Catholic mission school in Murewa, 50 miles northeast of Harare, made it seem a safe haven in the eyes of Tabitha, a 16-year-old cook. That was before she became the victim of a campaign of systematic rape and violence by the thugs terrorising Zimbabwe's countryside on behalf of President Robert Mugabe's Zanu-PF party.

A tiny, delicate teenager, too young to vote in next month's elections, Tabitha has no understanding of the brutal politics behind the attack on her as she walked to nearby shops with her friend Florence. She simply sits on a couch, wraps a white woollen shawl tightly around her body and talks in a quiet monotone about the day that ended her hitherto happy life.

'I have lost my virginity and I want only death,' she said.

St Paul's mission became a target for Zanu-PF activists after they entered the school and found T-shirts signifying support for the opposition Movement for Democratic Change (MDC). They beat up two teachers and accused the school of disseminating MDC propaganda. The teachers were stooges, they said, for white imperialists who would destroy Zimbabwe.

Until their arrival, Tabitha had loved her job at the mission. She earned money for her family of subsistence farmers, and could sit and gossip with other young girls between preparing meals.

One afternoon earlier this month she finished cooking lunch, put on her new blue dress and strolled out of the compound with Florence, also 16. The two girls chatted as they walked down the dirt road that leads from St Paul's to the nearby Musami shoping centre to buy meat for the following day's meal.

Tabitha was proud to be trusted with the mission's money. It was like play-acting for the role of wife and mother she dreamt of for her future. She had no fears: Murewa is a village of traditional round brick houses with thatched roofs, where people instinctively look out for each other.

The girls might have felt differently had they paid more attention to national politics. The ruling Zanu-PF is facing its first real challenge since independence 20 years ago. Its reaction to the emergency of the MDC has been to bus young supporters and war veterans into villages across the country.

They have been unleashed in an attempt to cow communities into voting for Zanu-PF. In Murewa, the party enforcers had taken over the local Shavanhwoye nightclub, just a grassy slope away from the shopping centre.

It was dusk when two men wearing Elections 2000 Zanu-PF T-shirts approached Tabitha and Florence, and prevented them from passing. The men carried newly cut switches. The girls turned and ran.

They did not get far. More Zanu-PF men came running out of the fields and chased the girls down 'like animals', Tabitha said. 'They tore off my dress and I had only my panties left. I was screaming, "Mother, mother, save me," but nobody came.'

Two men dragged Tabitha behind the nightclub, threw her to the ground and covered her face with a Forward with the Land Zanu-PF banner. One held her arms while the other raped her, then they switched positions.

'I felt a huge pain between my legs,' she said. 'I thought I was looking at my death.'

Covered in blood, Tabitha was left to crawl away. Her screams finally brought a local shopkeeper. He took her to a hospital in the

St Paul's compound, where she stayed for three days. Florence was found by the side of the road, badly beaten about the head, back and arms.

Physical and psychological pain are not the only traumas faced by rape victims such as Tabitha, who is now stricken with nightmares. One in four Zimbabweans is HIV-positive, so there is a chance that she may have been infected with the Aids virus.

Two white women who were raped by war veterans on a farm near Harare last month flew abroad for treatment with a cocktail of drugs to stave off potential infection. Tabitha is a poor black girl and does not even have the money for a blood test.

'They told me at the hospital that, if I start feeling ill in some months, I should come back,' she said.

Cruel though it was, Tabitha's ordeal is virtually routine today in the rural areas of Zimbabwe. Few such incidents are reported: the police are either allied with the perpetrators or seem powerless to stop them.

The deaths of four farmers focused international attention on the plight of whites in the build-up to voting on 24–25 June, but most of those falling prey to Zanu-PF's campaign of terror are black. The violence is about politics, not race or even land.

'There is what I would call a low-intensity war going on in the rural areas,' said Tony Reeler, of the Zimbabwe Human Rights Organisation. He estimates that 6,000 men, women and children have fled the rural violence for refuge in the capital.

Tabitha is one of at least eight women to have been raped in her small village alone. All the victims say their attackers came from the Zanu-PF encampment.

Fideline, 33, a tall, handsome mother of two, with high cheekbones and almond-shaped brown eyes, said she felt luckier than some. Now hiding with relatives in Harare, she showed three knife slashes the war veterans had left on her skull and a horrific 6in wound on her breast where she was beaten with barbed wire.

She was left unconscious on the side of the road after she and her friend Gladys, 33, were attacked by a group of about 30

Zanu-PF men as they walked home from Good Friday services at St Paul's church. Gladys suffered most. She was dragged into a field and raped by four men. She still cannot walk, Fideline says.

'The shopkeeper who found me thought I was dead,' she said last week. 'I remember as they beat me, I thought, "Now I am going to die."'

The reign of terror shows no sign of abating. Many parents in Murewa have sent their children to the city for safety. Those left behind have no protection from the Zanu-PF raiding parties.

The one home where they found an MDC T-shirt was burnt to the ground. The party enforcers go from door to door, accusing people of being MDC supporters, seemingly at random.

Eveline, 16, and her 18-year-old sister Susan were forced from their home by intruders who found her washing the breakfast dishes before going to school. The girls were marched through the village as the Zanu-PF men forced more and more young women onto the street. 'They told us if we ran away, they would catch us and we would not go home any more,' Eveline said.

The raiding party eventually gathered a group of about 30 girls and marched them to the village of Ngomamowa, where they arrived in the late afternoon.

Eveline, a pretty, chubby teenager, can barely utter the words to explain what happened. She speaks almost in a whisper, picking at her hands as she talks.

She and Susan were forced to cook sadza, a maize porridge, and elephant meat for their captors. Then they sang party songs and danced for hours.

During the night, the so-called war veterans took some of the girls into a local grain mill and raped them on the concrete floor. 'I don't know how many were raped. Many,' Eveline said.

She and Susan were released in the morning. Others were held for days.

There appears to be no stopping the excesses of what Zanu-PF calls its election campaign. Anyone who believes Mugabe's promise of free and fair elections should spend a day in Murewa.

Hunzvi's surgery is turned into a torture centre: Africa in crisis

14 May 2000

It is an evil inversion of the oath sworn by every doctor. In Harare, men can walk when they pass through the door of the surgery of Dr Chenjerai 'Hitler' Hunzvi, the physician who has led the war veterans occupying farms throughout Zimbabwe. But they leave so bruised and battered that they can barely move.

Hunzvi's surgery in the Budiriro neighbourhood of the capital looks innocent enough at first glance. It is a single-storey concrete building with a tin roof, painted a pale blue and emblazoned with 'Dr C Hunzvi, Surgery' in block capitals across the front.

But merely stopping in the road outside draws an angry swarm of menacing men through the front gate, who try to prevent the car from leaving when they see a white face. This former place of healing has become a torture centre.

A week and a half ago, about 50 men calling themselves war veterans moved into Hunzvi's surgery compound and began sending out gangs to kidnap local residents they suspected of supporting the opposition.

Once through the doctor's gates, their victims were subjected to hours of beatings and sadistic abuse. Their move into Harare was evidence that the violent campaign to intimidate people into voting for President Robert Mugabe's Zanu-PF party had widened from the farms to the cities, the stronghold of the Movement for Democratic Change (MDC), the main opposition party.

A man who can be identified only as Emanuel was forced into the centre on Thursday. When I met him in the casualty ward of Harare hospital, he wore a detached blue hood to try to hide his injuries. His left cheekbone was swollen and his left eye blood-red.

He could barely hear because the 'war veterans' had boxed his ears so ferociously. His back was a mass of bruises and welts that went all the way down his thighs. The welts on his buttocks were bleeding.

He wouldn't show me the worst of his injuries and I didn't want to look. His captors had tied a rubber strip tight around the tip of his penis and kept it bound for the 13 hours that they held him in the surgery, preventing him from urinating.

Emanuel's sin was to buy a membership card for the MDC, the party that hopes to challenge Zanu-PF in elections due by August. 'About 12 of them picked me up near my friend's shop at about noon,' Emanuel, 28, said. 'I had no chance. They said you are MDC and drove me to Hunzvi's surgery.'

Two other men were already on the floor, naked and bruised. His ordeal began at once.

'They beat me with electric cables and wooden poles like table legs,' he said. 'They kept shouting, tell us the names of your MDC members. I kept telling them I am just a simple man, I am not participating in the party, but they didn't care.'

The Zanu-PF thugs based in Hunzvi's surgery are terrorising the neighbourhood. Residents call the surgery 'the concentration camp'. They named three other men who had been abducted, taken to the surgery and beaten, and said many more had suffered the same fate.

Hunzvi toured the country last week in a government helicopter with a delegation of white farmers, claiming to be seeking an end to the occupation of farms that has provoked weeks of violence.

On Friday, just hours after Emanuel was released from Hunzvi's surgery, the physician turned politician sat to Mugabe's left at a negotiating session with white farmers to resolve Zimbabwe's crisis. Three white farmers have been killed by his followers.

Mugabe, say those who have met him in recent weeks, turned on the farmers not so much because he wanted their land but because he was furious that they were helping finance the MDC, led by Morgan Tsvangirai, the trade union leader.

Sierra Leone

Drug-crazed warriors
of the jungle

FREETOWN

3 September 2000

It is hard to talk to Junior Savage. He has sewn the front half of a rat's pelt to the baseball cap that is pulled down low over his forehead, so the beady eyes of the dead rodent stare at you as a human voice talks from somewhere below. The tail and another bit of the pelt hang off the back of the cap – every once in a while he turns it around and then you look into the dead, flat eyes of a young West Side Boy.

The young men who captured 11 British soldiers are members of Junior's gang. Embittered by years in the bush and lack of recognition, they are maddened by constant drink and drug use – and by the knowledge that they are not going anywhere.

It is that volatile state of mind that is most dangerous to the British major and five non-commissioned officers from the Royal Irish Regiment still being held by the West Side Boys in their jungle base last night. The servicemen were seized just over a week ago, together with five other soldiers, when they apparently took a wrong turning in the jungle.

In another time and place, Junior might not have turned out to be a bad guy. He speaks softly, his chin almost on his chest, the rat eyes staring out from above the peak of his baseball cap.

His tone does not change when he talks about the drug he was given before military operations. It is called brown-brown and is probably a cocaine derivative.

'They put this white powder in a big bowl and they squeezed lime juice over it to make it liquid. Then they injected us.' Asked who 'they' are, he says: 'My colleagues.'

Did he ever have any doubts about taking the drug? 'No one among us can say no. And when you get the injections, you are feeling good. Death is in front of you and you don't feel her. If anyone gives you any order, you do it.'

Junior has just come out of the Occra hills, where about 500 of his fellow West Side Boys live in tin-roofed shacks in the jungle about 50 miles east of the Freetown peninsula.

The story he has brought with him does not bode well for the Britons still being held – much less for this beautiful and war-ravaged country.

Most Sierra Leoneans view the soldiers – part of a contingent of 220 sent to train government troops – as their saviours. They are appalled that troops they believed to be invincible could be seized by a gang of young bandits like Junior.

Ironically, the West Side Boys actually fought under the direction of British soldiers in May in the battle against the Revolutionary United Front rebels. The British, who they respected, gave them rifles and ammunition during the fight to protect Freetown. But several months ago, the West Side Boys reverted to banditry. The soldiers they have taken hostage have become merely a means of getting what they want.

The West Side Boys evolved out of the Armed Forces Revolutionary Council (AFRC), a group that overthrew what was seen as the country's then corrupt government and took power in 1997. Nigerian-led Ecomog troops forced the AFRC out of power in 1998. Then, with the return to power of President Kabbah, AFRC members such as Junior, together with thousands of other rebels, fled into the bush.

'Sometimes we were sitting there and crying, asking "Why are we here?"' he recalls. The long march was made through the jungle with no food and no medicines against malaria and other diseases.

The rebels came under the leadership of a man Junior knows as Commander Bomblast, born as Papeh Kamara in Freetown.

The self-styled Commander Bomblast was the disillusioned son of a Sierra Leonean sergeant who, after 40 years' service, was kicked out of the army and as a thank-you was given only a bundle of corrugated iron, used here for roofing.

Bomblast, of whom there is no known photograph, has long been a hero of the rebels here. He has only come to world attention because he is now in Pademba Road central prison and his release is the key demand of the West Side Boys, who are holding the British hostages.

He earned his name from his fighting stance. 'When we would fight, Bomblast would hold two RPGs [rocket-propelled grenades], one on either hip, and fire both at the same time,' Junior said. 'Any other man would have been blown backwards from the recoil.'

There is little likelihood of an early release for Bomblast, who is held with Foday Sankoh, the rebel leader, awaiting an international tribunal under United Nations auspices.

Human Rights Watch, the international organisation, has catalogued a file of offences committed by men under Bomblast's command that would constitute war crimes. These include rape, destruction of property and summary executions, and most date back to the January 1999 attack on Freetown by the West Side Boys.

Bomblast was actually put in prison because of a gun battle with a rival commander over a four-wheel-drive vehicle in May, coincidentally on the day when Robin Cook, the foreign secretary, arrived to review British troops. Security was high and both men and their supporters were carted off to jail.

British military sources here are still unable to explain how an experienced Royal Irish Regiment unit could have fallen into the hands of drunken, drugged and demoralised young men like Junior.

The unit of 11 British soldiers – accompanied by a Sierra Leonean officer – had travelled to Masiaka, about 40 miles east of

Freetown, on 25 August. They lunched with a Jordanian UN unit and were travelling back to the capital when they turned off on a side road heading to Foradugo – a known base of the West Side Boys.

Kai Kai, the president's spokesman, said he did not know why they were on that road but believed the British soldiers had been surrounded by armed children, as young as 11 and 12, and decided to surrender without a fight rather than hurt the youngsters.

'My information is that they were surrounded by the child soldiers, 11- and 12-year-olds who have been abducted and made soldiers of the West Side Boys,' he said.

'How would it have looked if you saw on your television screens the bodies of these little tiny children and were told that they had been killed by British soldiers who were defending themselves?

'I think the British had no choice when they were faced with these children.'

British military sources in Sierra Leone agree with the government that Bomblast should not be released in exchange for the six remaining hostages. The danger now is that the West Side Boys' demands have escalated.

Last week, speaking on a British military satellite phone that was traded for the release of the five junior soldiers, the rebels increased their demands to say that they wanted Bomblast's release but also required the dissolution of the government of President Kabbah and the formation of a power-sharing administration that would include leaders of the West Side Boys.

Tony Camp, a British military spokesman here, said he had spoken on the phone to a British captive on Friday but there was no contact yesterday.

Negotiations, meanwhile, have been continuing in a roundabout way. The British high commission representative has been meeting relatives of the West Side Boys in an attempt to convey messages to secure the soldiers' release.

This volatile group seems daily to change its demands. The crisis may ultimately be resolved more easily, though, than the escalating demands would indicate. When I left Junior, he asked me for money to pay for a pair of shoes to replace his plastic flip-flops. In return, he agreed that he would attend church today.

How the hi-tech army fell back on law of the jungle and won

17 September 2000

Marie Colvin, James Clark and Peter Conradi

The first Chinook C-47 flew low over the jungle as the African sun started to rise. There was just enough light for the pilot to see where he was going – but not enough for his helicopter to be seen – as he swooped towards Rokel Creek in the heavily wooded Occra Hills of Sierra Leone.

His target was a camp sprawling over both banks of the muddy creek, where six British soldiers had been held in sweltering heat for more than two weeks by heavily armed members of the rebel militia that called itself the West Side Boys.

On board the Chinook and four other helicopters that followed were more than 120 paratroopers and members of the Special Air Service (SAS) trained in hostage rescue. Their mission: to recover the six members of the 1st Battalion, Royal Irish Regiment and, if possible, to capture Foday Kallay, the rebels' 24-year-old leader.

Operation Barras, co-ordinated from Permanent Joint Headquarters, the army's nerve centre almost 2,700 miles away in Northwood, northwest London, had received the green light from Tony Blair four days earlier. Within 20 minutes of the first landing last Sunday, the British hostages were being flown to safety, their 16-day ordeal over. Within hours, at least 25 of the West Side Boys had been killed and Kallay was on his way to jail.

For the military planners it was a textbook operation, worthy of study for years to come and marred only by the death of Brad

Tinnion, a 26-year-old member of the SAS snatch squad, who was shot as he jumped from his helicopter.

'You cannot resolve a situation like this with a laser-guided bomb from 30,000 feet,' said Brigadier Andrew Stewart, who monitored the operation from Northwood. 'As a purely military operation, it knocks the lifting of the Iranian embassy siege into a cocked hat.'

Few of the hostages would have dared envisage such an outcome during the dark days after they fell into the West Side Boys' hands on 25 August. At one point, they were subjected to a mock execution at a place known as the dead zone, because so many of the West Side Boys' enemies had been shot there.

Eleven members of the Royal Irish – five of whom were subsequently released – had been returning to their Benguema base after visiting a Jordanian peacekeeping battalion in Masiaka, east of Freetown, when Major Alan Marshall, their commander, turned sharp right off the main road, down a narrow red dirt road that led for seven miles to the West Side Boys' camp at Magbeni.

Marshall thought there were only a few rebels there. He was wrong. His men were overwhelmed, he was beaten and all were taken across the creek in dugouts with outboard motors to Gberi Bana, Kallay's headquarters on the north bank.

There they were stripped of their uniforms and searched. Kallay personally stuffed possessions ranging from watches to spare clothes into a bag, putting their rings on his fingers and admiring the glitter of the gold. He later put on a spare British uniform as he swaggered around the camp, and used one of the three British Land Rovers to check on his followers.

Kallay visited his captives every day, repeatedly demanding to know why they had driven to his camp. 'Explain your mission or I will shoot you,' he would say.

Several days after their capture, Kallay hyped himself up with cocaine and decided he had had enough. The six soldiers were taken to the dead zone and placed in front of wooden poles that had been hammered into the ground about a yard apart.

Their hands were secured behind the poles with cuffs twisted out of twine. The bodyguards lined up, stony-faced, pointing their weapons at the captives, awaiting the order to shoot.

As the rest of the Britons fell silent, Marshall tried to reason with the rebel leader, who, maddened by cocaine, was shouting: 'I will kill you! I will kill you!'

'Even when he was tied to the stake, the major continued to speak to Kallay,' said the rebel leader's chief bodyguard, who styled himself Corporal Blood. 'He was very cool. He told Kallay, "We just came to see you, to tell you to forget fighting. We did not come with any bad intentions. If you kill us, it will not be for any reason."'

Then, after half an hour of threats, Kallay relented and ordered the men to be returned to their hut in the main camp. He gave no reason.

Unbeknown to the rebels or their captives, Kallay's increasingly erratic behaviour was being monitored by a handful of SAS men who spent a week in the jungle before the rescue.

While the British Army continued to negotiate with Kallay in the hope of a peaceful resolution, the SAS's task was to supply intelligence that would facilitate any eventual rescue mission.

Working in pairs, they lay in shallow trenches, just below eye-line, dressed in 'ghillie suits' – a type of overall to which they attach twigs, leaves and branches picked up from local vegetation as camouflage. Eating carefully packed rations, and urinating into bottles, they used night-vision, thermal and infrared scopes to provide commanders in Northwood with information so detailed that a replica of the West Side Boys' camp was built for training purposes.

The mango swamps along the creek in which they were hidden are heavily wooded. Anyone concealed there would have faced water snakes in the river and the danger of being given away by curious monkeys.

On 6 September, 'H hour' was set for 6.16am local time on Sunday – 7.16am in London. Three of the giant Chinook C-47s and two smaller Lynx craft took part in a two-pronged assault. One group of Paras was assigned to destroy the positions held by the rebels at Magbeni, on the south bank of the creek. This was intended to give the helicopter heading for Gberi Bana camp, on the north bank, the chance to land without taking fire from two sides.

Captain Danny Matthews, aide-de-camp to the commander, Major Matthew Lowe, was apprehensive as his Chinook came in to land. At 22, Matthews had already had one tour of duty in Sierra Leone and been a platoon commander in Kosovo. This time, the risks were far greater.

'We knew the West Side Boys had lots of equipment, mortars, rifles, machineguns and heavy machineguns,' he said. 'There is obviously no set format and obviously that plays on your mind – not being able to predict your enemy's intentions or reactions.'

The West Side Boys had little more than a minute from the moment they heard the clatter of the helicopters to prepare to defend themselves.

From their camouflaged positions, as close as 180 feet from the camp, the SAS men could see the rebels take up their firing positions. They sent a snap radio message back to Northwood warning that the landing would be made under fire. The first target was the hut in which the hostages were being held. As the Chinook touched down in the centre of the village, it came under fire from West Side Boys shooting from a captured Land Rover.

The helicopter responded with machinegun fire. The SAS men in the jungle opened up, causing panic among the rebels by firing from behind positions they had thought were safe.

The West Side Boys retaliated with British-made general purpose machineguns and Kalashnikov AK-47 assault rifles. Heavy fire also came from Magbeni, where the rebels had heavy-calibre machineguns and a double-barrelled anti-aircraft gun. But they were no match for the British.

'We never experienced anything like this,' said Blood. 'We saw the soldiers coming down to the ground. I fired my RPG [rocket-propelled grenade] two times, but both times the helicopter balanced [swerved] and I missed.'

As the battle raged, SAS men came sprinting towards the hut where their colleagues had reported the hostages to be, firing bursts from their 5.56mm Canadian assault rifles and hurling grenades. 'It was all about speed,' said one British-based special forces officer. 'They had to be in and out very quickly.'

The assault was brutal: the government claimed last week that 25 of the West Side Boys were killed. One source close to the operation said the death toll would prove higher. 'If you followed every blood trail into the jungle you might well be able to quadruple that figure.'

Inside the hut, the SAS found Marshall, his men and a Sierra Leonean liaison officer who had been captured with them.

On the south bank, meanwhile, a Chinook loaded with Paras had landed in front of a swamp, leaving Matthews and his fellow soldiers to wade up to their midriffs for at least 10 minutes, each man weighed down by as much as 60 pounds of kit. They then had to hack their way through 150ft of jungle.

The platoon successfully took its first objective – a crumbling one storey-building – but came under heavy fire as it approached a second. A mortar bomb exploded in front of the men, injuring seven, who might have been killed had it not sunk so deep into soft ground. The wounded included Lowe, who went down with shrapnel wounds to his legs. 'The OC [Lowe] called me up and told me I was to take over command of the company,' Matthews said.

As another Chinook braved enemy fire to pick up the wounded, Matthews sent his three platoons in different directions to secure the area and retrieve the British vehicles. A Lynx helicopter touched down at speed to the north to collect the hostages.

It was an audacious piece of flying, but Tinnion, a new recruit to the SAS, was shot from behind shortly after getting out of the helicopter.

The bullet passed through his body and out through his shoulder. Under heavy fire, his colleagues treated him as well as they could. He died shortly after reaching medics aboard Royal Fleet Auxiliary Ship *Sir Percivale*, off the coast near Freetown.

The mood in headquarters in Northwood changed dramatically: 'Within 20 minutes of the go, we knew all the hostages were safe and away from the scene, but within a minute of that we knew Tinnion had been hit and looked unlikely to survive,' said Stewart.

The carnage the SAS left behind them was considerable. 'There were many corpses and wounded people lying on the ground moaning,' said Unisa Sesay, 16, one of the West Side Boys' child soldiers, who reached the base just after the British had left.

'One commander was standing and his friend was trying to remove a fragment from his shoulder. The rest of the people were on the ground.'

Another soldier, who gave his name as Cyrus and his age as 17, said they had been told the wounded would be shot and thrown into the river because there were no medical supplies. Both boys said they saw too many corpses, and were too shocked, to count. The dead included a 14-year-old boy soldier and one Sierra Leonean hostage who panicked and ran into the firefight.

General Sir Charles Guthrie, the chief of the defence staff, had been booked three months earlier to be interviewed that morning on BBC1's *Breakfast with Frost*. At about 9.20am, Major Tom Thornycroft whispered to Guthrie in the wings of the studio confirmation that all the hostages were safe. Guthrie then broke the first news to the nation that an operation was under way in West Africa.

The prime minister, who had spent the weekend at Chequers approving the last details of the plan, had already received a call from Guthrie informing him of the success. Blair returned to London and made a statement to television cameras in Downing Street.

Kallay, meanwhile, had been captured at his hut and flown by British helicopter to JordBat2 [second Jordanian Battalion] on the Freetown–Masiaka highway. He was hustled into the base, his hands secured behind his back with white plastic cuffs, his oversized Calvin Klein T-shirt flapping almost down to his knees.

He was stripped naked and searched. Then British soldiers threw him to the ground and exploded in anger. A large black boot was placed on his back and another on his legs, pinning Kallay to the ground, face down. He peered around, not responding to shouts from soldiers who had spotted the rings Kallay stole from the British hostages.

One soldier with a heavy Irish accent shouted, 'You f****** f***, stealing f****** soldiers' rings' as his colleague, one by one, twisted and pulled until all the rings were back in British hands. Kallay grimaced in pain, but did not let out a single cry.

The operation terrified the West Side Boys. More than 50 have surrendered since the raid. But defectors revealed that a hard core had regrouped at a base inland from Gberi Bani.

In London, jubilation was tinged with sorrow at the death of Tinnion, who had served with distinction in 29 Commando Royal Artillery. The army believes he was almost certainly killed by a round, believed to be of 7.62mm calibre, from a self-loading rifle (SLR) of the type provided by Britain to pro-government forces in Sierra Leone. The West Side Boys' militia supported the Freetown government until a few months ago.

On Friday, as Marshall faced the prospect of disciplinary action after taking the blame for his men's capture, Tinnion's parents and girlfriend were at his graveside after he was buried with full military honours at his regiment's base in Hereford.

Anna Homsi, his girlfriend, who is seven months pregnant, described him as 'the man of my dreams'. She added: 'We are obviously deeply shocked and devastated by Brad's death, but enormously proud he died doing the job he loved.'

Under army rules, neither Homsi nor the unborn child would be eligible for Tinnion's pension or other money. However, the Ministry of Defence is preparing to make an exception. One SAS officer said: 'Because of the level of danger the lads face, the wives need to know somehow that there is security for the family there if it all goes wrong. It's in the regiment's interests as well as the blokes' and their families.'

Sri Lanka

Fighting Tigers talk of peace deal

15 April 2001

Marie Colvin, the first foreign journalist to visit Tamil-held Sri Lanka since 1995, reports from Mallawi.

Conciliatory words do not come easy to Thamilthevlan, the second-in-command of the Tamil Tigers. His walking stick is a legacy of the three times he was shot in battle since joining the founding ranks of one of the most ruthless guerrilla movements in the world.

For the first time in 18 years of armed struggle that has cost 60,000 lives, however, he claims the group is now ready to settle for an autonomous homeland rather than continue fighting for an independent state in northern Sri Lanka.

His message, direct from Velupillai Prabhakaran, the reclusive Tamil leader, is far removed from the uncompromising rhetoric long the signature tune of the Liberation Tigers of Tamil Eelam (LTTE).

'There must be a political solution,' Thamilthevlan told *The Sunday Times* last week. 'The name is immaterial. Federation, confederation, northeast council, autonomous region, we can accept any of these solutions as long as we are guaranteed our equal rights, our dignity and justice. We don't want a lifestyle decided by Buddhist monks in Colombo.'

The decision does not appear to spring from military weakness. Last April the Tamil Tigers overran a huge Sri Lankan military complex to capture Elephant Pass, the neck of land that controls access to the Jaffna peninsula, their heartland. They swept the army out of Vanni, the four northern Tamil provinces on the mainland,

and today control more than 50% of the ancestral land they claim as their own.

Rather, the LTTE decision to enter the diplomatic water appears to come from a realisation that even while they cannot be defeated militarily, neither can they win on the battlefield. They are increasingly isolated and not just politically: the Vanni region is ringed by the army and navy and under an economic siege. Journalists are banned by the Sri Lankan government from entering.

Travelling to Tamil Tiger headquarters in Mallawi was an education in the LTTE networks. I left Vavuniya, the northernmost town controlled by the government, in a car with civilian LTTE sympathisers who held army passes and told me to say that I was going to 'Kanthaudaiyarpuvarsankulam' at checkpoints. Fortunately, nobody asked.

Fed by a family of farmers, I slept on the floor of a school near Mannar on the west coast, sitting up late into the night with the principal, hearing how government oppression of the Tamils had turned him from a moderate to a militant. 'I don't want this war,' he said. 'But I can't see any other way to win our rights.'

At dawn, 10 Tamil Tiger fighters arrived dressed in bits of camouflage and flip-flops. All were armed with automatic weapons and grenades. Nobody seemed concerned that we were in government territory.

We rode by tractor through a ruined cashew plantation, until the dirt road became too narrow and the jungle too dense.

The thick foliage overhead turned into a green tunnel; the air was so thick with humidity that my arm felt as if it was furred when I swung it.

Scouts ranged ahead across open fields, checked for Sri Lankan army soldiers, then motioned us in single file across at 10-yard intervals – if one of us were unfortunate enough to step on a mine, at least nobody else would be hurt by the blast.

By sunset another obstacle lay across our path: a river. Following the lead of my Tiger guides, I waded tentatively through the water as the level swiftly rose to my chest.

By 9pm we crossed the main road between army territory and the Tamil Tiger area, and on to the group's headquarters in Mallawi. The sense of relief was overwhelming.

En route the guerrillas had told me their stories. Most of those in the patrol were village boys and all were from families living as refugees. They are fanatically loyal to Prabhakaran, who they speak of reverentially as 'national leader'. He sounds a strict master. Tamil Tigers cannot smoke or drink alcohol and must remain celibate until they are allowed to marry; women at 24, men at 28. They receive no wages.

All Tigers, even those in the political wing, wear cyanide capsules around their necks – they know they will be tortured if captured and are ready to die rather than reveal information. This is not paranoia. The American State Department reported last year that 'torture continues with relative impunity'.

Until the 1970s the Tamil protest movement eschewed violence. The LTTE emerged in 1983, when Sinhalese mobs turned on the Tamils, slaughtering hundreds with machetes and burning tyre necklaces and sending thousands fleeing north.

The youth turned to Prabhakaran's advocacy of armed resistance and secession. The LTTE's ruthless reputation comes from the Black Tigers, an elite suicide unit. They have bombed government buildings, assassinated a president and killed Rajiv Gandhi, the Indian leader who sent a taskforce to Sri Lanka in 1987.

Although the government claims the Tamil Tigers intimidate civilians, there is evidence of extensive popular support in the areas they control. 'The Tamils would be all dead, shot up, without these Tigers,' said Father Xavier, a parish priest. 'My parishioners want an end to war, but they say to me, "We have lost our lives, our properties, our land, we need a settlement that guarantees us our rights so that we don't have to go through all this again".'

The government has alienated Tamil hearts and minds. Ministers in Colombo deny that there is an economic embargo on the Vanni, the Tamil area on the mainland, while checkpoints on the internal border enforce a ban on items ranging from fuel, cement, and plastic sheeting to instant noodles and vegetable oil. Even sanitary towels are not allowed; they can presumably be used to dress wounds.

The Vanni region, which covers 2,000 square miles, has no mains electricity or telephone service; its roads have deteriorated to potholed dirt tracks. Most people travel by bicycle because of the fuel shortage.

The embargo has created a huge but unreported humanitarian disaster for the 500,000 civilians who live here, more than half of them internal refugees. The majority live below the national poverty line of about £12 a month.

Colombo prohibits international aid agencies distributing food. International aid agencies estimate that 40% of the children in the Vanni are undernourished or malnourished.

Pushiparani, a teacher, 52, has been displaced seven times after she fled Jaffna with her six children when the army captured the city five years ago. This is fertile recruiting ground for the Tamil Tigers. One of her sons died in battle and a daughter now serves as a Sea Tiger.

In Killinochchi town, a thriving commercial centre of 300,000 until it was bombarded by the Sri Lankan army in 1996, classes are held in the bombed-out shells of school buildings; hospitals are chronically short of surgical supplies.

'Last week one of my cardiac patients walked into the jungle leaving behind a note that said: "I have suffered enough. Suicide",' one doctor said. 'I had no medicine to give him. I feel helpless.'

A unilateral ceasefire declared by the Tamil Tigers on Christmas Eve, and renewed every month, is due to expire on 24 April. The group said this weekend that the ceasefire would be renewed to give Norwegian mediators more time.

After two weeks in the Tamil-held area, I set out southwards late in the evening. Government lines lay a 24-hour walk away; my Tiger guides promised to lead me back across them under cover of darkness. The river lay beyond.

'The shot hit me. Blood poured from my eye – I felt a profound sadness that I was going to die'

22 April 2001

Last Monday, award-winning reporter Marie Colvin was attacked as she returned from a rare interview with Tamil Tiger leaders in Sri Lanka. From her hospital bed in New York she writes about her escape.

It was the most difficult decision of my life. I was lying in an open field with a clump of tall weeds on a slight rise for cover. The moon had not yet risen and the night was pitch black. Every five minutes or so a flare, fired from the nearby Sri Lankan army base, seemed to expose every blade of grass. Advancing soldiers intermittently raked the field with automatic weapons fire. They had to be as scared as I was.

I just wanted to lie still and wait for it all to go away. I thought I would not mind lying here for hours. I noticed little things. One of my trouser legs had come up to my knee and that meant my white calf might draw attention in the dark.

There were three options. I could crawl away. But if one soldier had night-vision goggles – didn't even the poorest armies these days? I would be the only moving object on the field and would be shot.

If I was not spotted, I would still be alone in the jungle with no shoes. If I lay here until the soldiers stumbled on me, they would shoot first. If I shouted and identified myself as a journalist they might shoot anyway. There was no fourth option.

It was 10pm, on the forward defence line of the Sri Lankan army at Parayanlankulam, about 3½ miles from the Madhu road junction. I thought of how I came to be here. There didn't seem to be any one moment when it all went wrong.

A week earlier I had secretly entered the Vanni, a 2,000-mile area of northern Sri Lanka that has been the refuge of the rebel Tamil

Tigers since the government captured the Jaffna peninsula in 1995. The Sri Lankan government bans journalists from travelling there.

The ban meant journalists could not talk to the leadership of the Liberation Tigers for Tamil Eelam (LTTE), even though the government was involved in negotiations with them through a Norwegian envoy to begin peace talks. The only news of the problems with those negotiations came from the government.

More important, the ban prevented any reporting on the plight of the 500,000 Tamil civilians, 340,000 of them refugees, bottled up in the Vanni suffering under an economic embargo that the government denied existed.

I had travelled through villages in the Vanni and found an unreported humanitarian crisis – people starving, international aid agencies banned from distributing food, no mains electricity, no telephone service, few medicines, no fuel for cars, water pumps or lighting.

I had filed the story and had been trying to leave the Vanni to return to the government-controlled south for three days. This involved walking 30 miles a night through jungle and the knee-deep water and mud of marsh and rice paddies – only to end up sleeping on the same straw mat, on the same dirt floor, in the same mud hut. Even the bugs were starting to look familiar.

Each night I tried to leave, guided by local Tamils. But each time they decided it would be too risky to cross army lines. On Sunday night we came within 50 yards of the border between the two sides. The leader studied the army post we were supposed to slip past. Suddenly, he made a somersaulting motion with his hands and started walking back.

There was no argument; we used hand signals and observed silence until several miles from the army line.

'My mistake,' he said. 'Military alert. Too dangerous.' I watched my guides' tireless brown feet, clad only in black rubber flip-flops, pad unceasingly ahead of me until we reached the base house near the Catholic church at Madhu, home to 10,000 refugees living in tents and huts. At dawn I collapsed into sleep.

Monday night was meant to be third time lucky. As the sun slipped below the horizon, I sat with my guides under a banyan tree, looking out over a silvery lake, waiting for dark in a rare moment of peace and beauty.

We were a motley group. The civilians with me were dressed in a collection of shorts and sarongs. An emaciated old man carried a string shopping bag with two bottles of Pepsi, our only drink. A teenager kept trying the little English that he had learnt in St Patrick's college in Jaffna before the army overran the town and killed his father.

'Tonight, you will be in my father's house sipping milky tea,' the leader of the group said. He was the only one who was armed; he carried an old rifle to protect us from wild boar or elephants. 'We are going a way that is safe and secure.'

The plan was to reach his family's house in the government-controlled area that night. The Tamils would return before dawn and I would get the morning bus to Vavuniya. I had a last cigarette as the sun went down; there would be no smoking, talking or even coughing as we walked the next seven miles to sanctuary.

We trekked single file along narrow jungle trails, sometimes pushing our way through thickets of thorn trees; we waded waist-deep round the edges of a lake, eyeing the lights of an army base on its far edge. They are dotted along the Mannar–Vavuniya road that marks the border we would have to cross. At about 8pm, we crept through dark scrub about half a mile from the road, then waited crouching in a marsh – letting the mosquitoes bite because slapping could alert a soldier – while the group's leader scouted ahead.

I took off my shoes to walk more quietly. At a signal from the leader we followed him to the road. Half-crouched, we negotiated our way through barbed wire on both sides of the road and seemed safely across.

We were running through the last dark field for the line of jungle ahead when the silence was broken by the thunder of automatic weapons fire about 100 yards to the right.

I dived down and began crawling, belly on the ground, for some cover. For a few minutes, someone was crawling on top of me – protection or panic, I don't know. Then I was alone, behind weeds.

A tree was 10 yards away, but it seemed too far. The shooting went on and on. Flashes and light came from an army post nobody had seen.

The shooting stopped and dark and quiet descended. There had not been a sound from my side. I could not tell where anyone was. The only sound was the occasional bellow of a cow which had been hit.

I had a few mad moments of thinking it was over, I had survived. But I knew this was not true. We had been spotted. The army would think this was a Tamil Tiger patrol and would come after us. They would be scared and trigger-happy.

The reputation of the two forces is that the army has superior manpower and weapons, the rebels superior manoeuvrability and commitment. The advantage was to the army this night. I was lying in a field with a decision to make: run for it, lie still or shout.

I lay there for half an hour under the penetrating glare of the flares. I turned my face to the earth when one came drifting down directly above me, worried that my white skin would reveal my hiding place.

Bursts of gunfire began across the road about half a mile away. The search and destroy patrols had come out. I heard soldiers on the road, talking and laughing. One fired a burst from an automatic weapon that scythed down the weeds in front of me and left me covered in green shoots.

If I didn't yell now, they would stumble on me and shoot. I began to shout.

'Journalist! Journalist! American! USA!'

A soldier sighted on the sound and fired. This army was not taking prisoners.

The shot hit me with an impact that stunned me with pain, noise and a sense of defeat. I thought I had been shot in the eye.

Blood was pouring from my eye and mouth onto the dirt. I felt a profound sadness that I was going to die.

Then I thought it was taking an awful long time to die if I was really shot in the head (it was actually shrapnel), so I started yelling again. 'English! Anyone speak English?'

There were more shots, but they seemed half-hearted, and lots of hysterical shouting from the soldiers. This was bad. They were as scared as I was. I did not really care because it seemed that I would die anyway, so I just kept shouting.

Searching for a word that non-English speakers might recognise, I fixed on doctor and shouted over and over that I needed one. Finally a voice screamed in English: 'Stand up, stand up.' He fired a few more shots for emphasis.

I stood up slowly, hands in the air, saying, 'Don't shoot, American,' and whatever else I could think of just so that they would keep hearing a foreign voice.

'Take off your jacket,' came the voice. I dropped my blue jacket and stood straight up, hands in the air. Blood poured down my face so I could not see much. Someone yelled, 'Walk to the road.' I stumbled forward.

Every time I fell, feeling faint, they would shout hysterically, afraid that I was pulling some trick, and I would struggle up again. I made it up the incline to the road and was shoved to the ground, flat on my back and kicked by shouting soldiers. A bright light shone in my face. I could not see any of my captors.

I am not sure how long I lay there on my back. I was searched for weapons, then told to walk at gunpoint, prodded by the weapons. The soldiers live in fear of women suicide bombers carrying explosives underneath their clothing.

The LTTE has a ruthless reputation as a result of the activities of the Black Tigers, an elite unit for suicide missions, who have bombed government buildings, assassinated a president and killed Rajiv Gandhi, the Indian leader.

I thought the soldiers were taking me somewhere to shoot me. I remember thinking that they were all scared and that I should act scared and vulnerable. I reached the limit. I could not walk any more and fell, telling them to get a doctor. They relented and put my arms round the shoulders of two men. But they pummelled me again when my hand fell and a soldier shouted that I was going for his grenade.

The nightmare seemed endless. We reached some lighted space outdoors and I was thrown on the ground on my back. A bright light again was in my face and questions shouted in Sinhalese and broken English. Someone ripped open my shirt and pulled it off. They shouted for my weapons. I kept saying, 'Journalist, I need a doctor.'

An officer, or someone in authority, came on the scene and the questions changed into an interrogation: 'Where did you get your training? How many people were with you? Where is your vehicle? Ah, you say you are American but you have no vehicle?'

Things were calming down and my sense of the ridiculous returned. If I had a vehicle, why would I be lying in a field on a dark night?

'Admit that you came to kill us,' he said. 'At least admit that your side fired grenades first. This is true, is it not?'

I said, 'No sir, there was no fire until your soldiers shot at us.'

Then began an endless series of journeys. I was put in the back of a truck and driven, bouncing over potholes, hyperventilating because I could not seem to breathe. I thought it was shock; later, I found that my lungs had been bruised by the shock of the grenade and were filling with fluid.

Someone kind was in the truck. He kept telling me in English: 'We are taking you for medical treatment, you are going to be okay.' I fixed on his voice, and he held my head up so that I could breathe.

At the first hospital I was taken to, the military hospital in Vavuniya, shrapnel was taken out of my head, shoulders and chest. I realised I could not see out of my left eye and I think the doctors panicked the soldiers into some sanity.

I was put in the back of another truck and driven for an hour to Army Victory hospital in Anuradhapura, where an x-ray revealed shrapnel in my eye. A truck took me to a third hospital, the Anuradhapura general hospital. I was never out of army custody.

The doctors seemed scared for me and I asked one to call the American embassy. But an army surgeon kept insisting that they should operate immediately.

'You are going to lose your eye anyway. I can operate now,' he said. I fended him off, but he would appear again, sharpening his imaginary knives, asking to operate.

Telephone calls were being made. It seemed that my request to be taken to Colombo was going to more senior people. At one point I heard a conversation in English. A soldier was saying, 'No, she cannot come to the phone. What is your message?'

I heard him trying to pronounce the name of Steve Holgate, the personable public affairs officer of the American embassy. I shouted: 'Give me the phone.' I had a huge sense of relief that someone knew where I was.

At dawn, someone in the Sri Lankan army hierarchy relented. I was put aboard a military helicopter and flown to Colombo. At the eye hospital, I was shoved on a stretcher against a wall in the crowded emergency room surrounded by hostile soldiers.

Miraculously, Holgate showed up moments later, clipboard in hand, and simply told the soldiers he was taking me into the custody of the American embassy. It was like the moment in a classic Wild West movie when the quiet guy faces down the armed and dangerous gang. I was safe.

Why do I cover wars? I have been asked this often in the past week. It is a difficult question to answer. I did not set out to be a war correspondent. It has always seemed to me that what I write about is humanity in extremis, pushed to the unendurable, and that it is important to tell people what really happens in wars – declared and undeclared.

War has changed remarkably little over the centuries. Do not believe the nice clean videos where Gameboy jets hit Nintendo tanks framed in a satisfying and sanitary 'X'. War is not clean. War is about those who are killed, limbs severed, dirt and rock and flesh torn alike by hot metal. It is terror. It is mothers, fathers, sons and daughters bereft and inconsolable. It is about traumatised children.

My job is to bear witness. I have never been interested in knowing what make of plane had just bombed a village or whether the artillery that fired at it was 120mm or 155mm.

War is also about propaganda. Both sides try to obscure the truth. Foreign journalists arriving in Sri Lanka are told in a government handout that parents in the rebel area keep their children home from school because the Tamil Tigers are recruiting them for service. But the parents told me they keep their children at home because they are hungry and faint in the classroom and do not have money for school supplies.

The Sri Lankan government reacted with anger to my presence in the Tamil-held area of the Vanni. It made no apologies for what had happened to me. I had no permission to go there, the government said, therefore I must have had a 'secret agenda'.

I had no secret agenda. I had a journalist's agenda. I went to the rebel-held areas because talking to the Tamil Tigers and writing about a previously unreported humanitarian crisis are important issues.

I am not going to hang up my flak jacket as a result of this incident. I have been flown to New York, where doctors are going to operate on my injured eye in about a week's time. They have told me it is unlikely I will regain much use of it as a piece of shrapnel went straight through the middle. All I can hope for is a bit of peripheral vision.

Friends have been telephoning to point out how many famous people are blind in one eye. They seem to do fine with only one eye, so I'm not worried. But what I want most, as soon as I get out of hospital, is a vodka martini and a cigarette.

GRATITUDE FROM TAMILS WORLDWIDE

Sri Lanka, April 2001

Colvin was the first foreign reporter in six years to enter Sri Lanka's dangerous northern Vanni region where the Tamil Tigers are waging a civil war against government forces. She went to interview the leaders and was ambushed while trying to walk out of the area last Monday. After reports of Colvin's ordeal last week *The Sunday Times* received many letters from Tamils all over the world offering their support.

This one was typical:

'We Tamils are so proud about your brave foreign correspondent Marie Colvin …We [are] all aware of the risk she undertook and we appreciate her visit to [the] Vanni area of north Sri Lanka for bringing the news to the outside world. We are deeply concerned about her health and wish her to get well soon. Thank you.'

Signed Elan Ramalingham, Carleton University, Ottawa, Canada.

Fighting back

15 July 2001

Marie Colvin, who was blinded in one eye three months ago while reporting the Sri Lanka conflict, reveals the lingering physical and psychological scars of the ordeal – and describes her new life as 'the lady with the pirate patch'.

Lying on the operating table in New York, sleepy but still awake and very nervous, I could hear the two surgeons chatting as they began cutting into my left eye.

'That lens has to go,' said one.

A tiny pulling feeling. The 'buckle' they were sewing into my eye seemed to be causing problems. More tiny pulling sensations. I started feeling claustrophobic under the green mask that covered my good eye but left the injured one exposed to their blades.

I knew what was going on because I had opted to go under the knife with a local anaesthetic. I'd been warned the operation was likely to take so long that recovery from a general anaesthetic would be uncomfortable.

The surgeons weren't sure what they would find when they went in. A 6mm piece of shrapnel had blasted through my eye, entering the front right side and tearing out through the retina that lines the eye, detaching it completely. The tiny missile had taken some of my iris with it and lodged against my optic nerve. I had been warned the prognosis was not good.

'How are you doing in there?' asked Dr Stanley Chang, the eye surgeon who had invented some of the microsurgery equipment he was using to operate on me.

'Stop the whale music,' I managed to croak. Whale music was playing in the operating room, and I suppose it was meant to calm me down in a new age sort of way, but I've always found it incredibly irritating. Something Brazilian came on. They got on with cutting.

From their conversation, I could tell that blood was the main problem. The shrapnel had caused extensive haemorrhaging in the eye and blood had pooled behind the retina. To reattach the retina and save the eye, the blood needed to be scraped out, bit by microscopic bit, so as not to damage the retina further.

Scrape, scrape, scrape; I was now about four hours into the operation.

The days before the surgery had been full of dread.

I had been exhausted but hopeful the night I arrived in New York by air medivac from Sri Lanka. It was late on 19 April, three days after soldiers fired the grenade that injured me. My mother and my sister Cat were waiting for me at Columbia Presbyterian hospital. So was Chang.

He examined my eye and then sat with me in his darkened office to give me a verdict I had not expected. He said he would try to save the eye, but didn't think the chances were good with such a traumatic injury.

I appreciated his honesty – he is a quiet-spoken man whose manner inspires unquestioning confidence – but it hadn't occurred to me my injured eye might have to come out. I went to sleep in tears, the first time I had cried since being shot. I think it was because it only hit me then that my life would never be the same.

In the next few days, I wrote myself questions to ask the doctor in a pre-op examination. Rereading them last week, I relived my fears.

'Are you saying that I may wake up from the operation with only one eye?' I wrote. It was a new and very strange world. 'You were talking about shrinkage of the eye. How does that happen?' Although I knew I had probably lost my sight, the idea of my eye being removed was unbearable.

The worst part of the operation came towards the end. Chang tried again and again to reattach the retina, but couldn't do it. I remember at one point hearing him saying with grim determination: 'We are going to attach this retina,' in a voice that made it clear he was not going to give up.

Five hours into the operation, the pulling in my eye became unbearable and I asked for more anaesthetic. Finally, Chang succeeded and silicone oil was placed into my eye to keep the retina in place. The operation had taken five and a half hours.

Claustrophobia overwhelmed me and I tried to pull the head covering off. A nurse calmed me, took it off and wheeled me into recovery.

The ordeal had just begun, however. Nurses were under orders to lay me on my stomach to keep the retina and oil in place in the eye. Waves of nausea and pain engulfed me. Every bump of the bed knifed into me as I was wheeled to my room. It was a reaction to the anaesthetic.

I lost any sense of politeness, yelling at the nurses to please give me something to stop the pain. It's an impossible position, having to lie on your stomach and keep your head down, when all you want to do is vomit and have the pain go away.

The next three days passed in a haze. I remember thinking I want this eye out, regretting ever agreeing to surgery to save it, just wanting the pain to go away.

Chang was unexpectedly poetic when I saw him to hear his verdict on my operation. 'Your retina was like a morning glory folded in on itself,' he said, making a slow, clenching motion with his hand to illustrate the floral image. 'A morning glory full of blood.'

The good news was that I would keep my eye. I had lost the perception of light and dark; that was depressing. But I would keep the eye, blind as it now was.

The other good news was that there was no evidence yet of 'sympathetic ophthalmia', a condition which can blind the second eye once one is injured.

On the fourth day, I went to a rented service flat in New York City to recuperate. My eye was covered in a bulky white bandage. I presented a bizarre spectacle to the curious, because I had to walk looking at the ground to keep the retina and oil in place.

I was still under doctor's orders to lie on my stomach for a week. This seemed torture just to think of. But there was one thing I had to do before getting into bed.

I smoked a couple of cigarettes and went into the bathroom. I took off the bandage and looked up into the mirror for the first time.

No flower comparisons came to mind. The pain made my eye feel like the enemy. The eye itself looked even worse.

It was swollen to the size of a peach, bright red, with a thin line – like that little indentation that peaches have across their middles – the only evidence that the two lids had ever opened or would ever open again.

I went and lay on my stomach, my head off the foot of the bed, looking face down through a weird contraption that seemed like an inverted and padded toilet seat. With one eye, I examined the carpet.

Recuperation is not always restful. Friends sent books and flowers, and one provided the most thoughtful, if daunting, of gifts, a box of 84 tapes entitled *Great Minds of the Western Intellectual Tradition*. I thought I might make up for all those university lectures I skipped.

My former husband, Patrick Bishop, with whom I'd been reunited about a year ago, flew from London and turned out to be a pretty good nurse, squeezing into my swollen eye endless drops of steroid and antibiotic drugs.

My mother sent home-cooked comfort food. The most successful was meatloaf, which Patrick, being British, had only seen on *The Simpsons* cartoon show.

With nothing to distract it, my mind began playing endless reruns of what had happened to me. I didn't feel the need to consult Freud; my subconscious was clearly seeking an outcome it liked better. The pain of being shot was not the focus of my nightmares, but that didn't make them much more bearable.

I had been wounded trying to leave the northern, Tamil area of Sri Lanka and re-enter the government-controlled south at the end of an assignment to visit the Tamil Tigers, the LTTE.

Leaving LTTE territory was not a simple matter of hitching a ride. For the past six years, the government in Colombo has banned journalists from the area, hoping to hide the catastrophic humanitarian crisis engulfing 500,000 Tamil civilians bottled up behind a siege line of army bases. I had to cross this line clandestinely.

For three nights my guides led me from a hut at Madhu, a shrine to the Virgin Mary and home to 10,000 refugees in tents and wood shelters, to the army lines. We padded along jungle paths, sloshed through abandoned rice paddies and waded waist-deep through lakes surrounded by banyan trees.

As I lay face-down in the New York apartment, I remembered cascades of white butterflies in shafts of sunlight that penetrated the emerald foliage. The air had been filled with the cries of peacocks, which sounded more like deranged cats, and we came across the spoor of elephant.

For two nights the guides decided it was too dangerous to cross. The third night, 16 April, after we had squatted for hours in a rice paddy, bitten by mosquitoes I couldn't swat for fear the noise would be heard, the lead guide waved us quietly forwards.

Ahead lay ditches, a road and a deep expanse of open ground. In the distance was the jungle. I took my shoes off; one of the things I had learnt was how difficult it is to walk in water wearing shoes. A young man grabbed my hand to haul me more quickly between the two barbed wire fences that lined the road, whispering 'bang, bang' to himself. I wasn't the only one who was frightened.

As we ran, stooped low, towards the safety of the jungle, a rolling flash erupted from the right. Sri Lankan soldiers in a forward listening post had opened fire. I crawled on my belly as long as the gunfire lasted, frantically, as if I could somehow escape. Flares went up, arcing high into the sky and falling slowly, turning night to day. I was trapped in a field, behind a clump of weeds, alone. And that's where the nightmares always begin.

My mind has recorded in exact detail what happened next, except that the tape is slowed down and spools endlessly. Soldiers are coming for me in the night, and I have to make a decision. They come forward inexorably, endlessly.

In reality, I think I only lay in the field for about half an hour. Finally, aware that if they stumbled on me they would shoot me, I shouted 'journalist'. They fired a grenade at the sound of my voice. Shrapnel hit me with a shocking impact of pain and noise.

Usually that wakes me up, but sometimes the dream continues and I am walking forward – as I did that night when I figured out I wasn't going to die, and I kept yelling, and someone speaking English told me to stand up, and I went on walking and falling down at times from weakness and shock and loss of blood. Only, in the dream, I am being shot at each time I fall, and I can feel what it is like to be shot across the chest.

The dream now has flashes of the horrific injuries I have seen in other wars – an old man lying in a basement in Chechnya, the back of his head blown off by a rocket fired from a Russian plane, somehow still rasping out breath until he died. A body I found under a bush in Kosovo, his chest riven by bullets, still wearing the worn wool suit of a peasant who has dressed up for the day. The knowledge of the fragility of the human body never leaves you once you have seen how easily flesh can be rent by hot flying bits of metal. What shocked me after the operation was my sheer exhaustion. I asked Chang what was wrong. 'Let's recap,' he said. 'You've been hit by a grenade in Sri Lanka. You've travelled halfway across the world, not to mention the trauma. You have just undergone a 5½-hour operation, and we're not even taking into account what is going on in that stubborn head of yours. And you ask me why you're tired?'

The first time I went out alone on the street with my new pirate-patch look, I couldn't cope. I had left my bag of clothes – along with my computer and satellite phone – behind at the scene in Sri Lanka, and I thought it would be a simple matter to buy some more.

I like shopping, but I had got only two steps into Barney's department store before I just had to get out again. People were coming at me. I couldn't trust the steps.

People on the street glanced at my eye patch and looked away, but the doorman at my apartment block asked: 'What the heck happened to you?' American friends said they loved the patch but wanted to see what was behind it.

On a week's recuperative holiday on the Ligurian coast, I was told by Italian men that the patch was very sexy. Back in London, I find that friends are surprised I don't appear worse. People in the street still glance away, but children ask me why I am dressed as a pirate, which is delightful.

Everyone professes to like the patch. A designer friend offered to make me a party patch with rhinestones for evening wear; and even the Prince of Wales pronounced it 'very fetching' when I was introduced to him at a reception.

I have become very fond of my patch. At home I usually take it off; but when I see myself in the mirror without it – rarely, as I am not a great looker in mirrors – I am taken aback. What I see doesn't look like me. So I put the patch back on as it makes it clear to my mind what has happened to me.

In some ways it is harder to cope with the frustrating tiredness. I used to be so energetic. Now I have to have a nap after lunch like a little child. I also can't drive, which is fine as I have always hated driving in London. But the Underground is also out, as I don't trust myself on the escalators. I now know what 'blind-sided' means.

Ridiculously, I can't even light a cigarette – I'm always lighting them in the middle or waving the flame two inches from the end – and I'm learning again to pour a glass of wine without missing.

At the back of my mind all the time is the fear for my good eye and the phenomenon of sympathetic ophthalmia. As I understand it, the auto-immune system can react to the injury and operation in one eye by attacking the other. At Moorfields hospital two weeks ago, I was assured there was no sign of this. But I discovered that the retina in the injured eye had become detached again. This isn't unusual, but it was depressing.

Next month, I'll go to New York to consult Chang about another operation. It's a toss-up, of course, as further surgery could increase the danger to the good eye.

I have been asked if my trip to Sri Lanka was worth it. One blunt BBC reporter last week argued in an interview, not unkindly: 'Some people would say it was stupid, Marie.' Was it? That's a hard question to answer.

Certainly, Sri Lanka is a forgotten conflict. Some 60,000 people have died since the country exploded in civil war in 1983, a loss barely noticed except by their families. The public message for the Sri Lankan government that I was given by the Tamil Tiger leadership was barely noticed, either. They said they were willing to negotiate for autonomy rather than the independence they had sought for 18 years. After I left, they ended a four-month unilateral ceasefire, saying the government had refused to reciprocate. Fighting has resumed. On a smaller scale, however, the trip did seem to me worthwhile. I may be exhausted and haunted, but not all the images that flash back to me evoke dread. I remember a government agent in a town in the Vanni – the region controlled by the LTTE – who put his neck on the line just to give me information. He received me late at night in his office, very formal but resolute. He put a suit on and asked me not to reveal his name for fear of retaliation from the very government that paid his salary.

He had facts and figures of the type that make on-the-ground reporting worthwhile. I wanted to resolve two contradictory stories: the government in Colombo claimed to be distributing food to Tamil civilians on the same monthly basis as the rest of the country, yet in village after village people told me they received little. Many were painfully thin.

This government agent explained. He said he notified Colombo monthly that 36,400 families in his district (about 140,000 people) qualified for food aid. They sent him food for 8,900 families (about 35,000 people), claiming he had inflated his figures.

'So I hold the first shipment, and divide up what I have to distribute every two months,' he said. 'There is no basis for this misery.'

Not everyone was as easily persuaded that I was worth talking to. Father Xavier, the Roman Catholic priest of Mallawi, was garrulous, opinionated and angry. He told me he had given up on the West: nobody cared about the plight of the Tamils, why should he waste his time talking to me. So what if I was the first journalist to come to the Vanni in six years? Western television cameras went to famines in Africa every year. They sent back pictures from Kosovo of Serbian killings. What about here?

When he calmed down, he served me sweet tea and we talked about his parishioners. He said people were tired of the war, mostly, but that it had its own dynamic.

'People tell me they feel they have suffered so much, it is not worth ending the war to return to the same situation,' he said. 'They have lost their homes, their land, their sons and daughters. The only way to end the war is for the Tamils to have their self-determination.' The government siege had turned people to the Tamil Tigers. 'I know you in the West say they are terrorists,' he said. 'Here, they are the only people that have protected us Tamils from being chopped up.'

Weeks after my operation, a letter arrived wrapped in brown paper. It had been smuggled out somehow by Father Xavier – no doubt at great risk, there being in the Vanni no electricity, few cars, much less any postal service.

'I was sorry to hear of your injuries,' he wrote. 'You are remembered here as a brave and honest person.' It meant a lot to me.

A surprising amount of mail arrived from Sri Lanka during my weeks of recuperation. Messages from Tamils were mostly sympathetic. None was under the impression that I supported their cause, but they sent heart-rending appreciations for providing the first report on their homeland in years.

The Sinhalese majority was divided. A man wrote from Colombo: 'I am not a Tamil, but if there were more journalists reporting the truth as you did, this war would be over in 24 hours.'

Others were less kind. One of the more printable Sinhalese critics – a woman claiming to be a doctor – wrote: 'If you sleep with dogs, you wake up with bugs.'

So, was I stupid? Stupid I would feel writing a column about the dinner party I went to last night. Equally, I'd rather be in that middle ground between a desk job and getting shot, no offence to desk jobs.

You can only describe what I do as 'stupid' if you agree wars shouldn't be covered by journalists, or think they should be reported by way of government press conferences. If journalists are to report on what really happens in war, on the atrocities and pain and death, they are going to face risks.

For my part, the next war I cover, I'll be more awed than ever by the quiet bravery of civilians who endure far more than I ever will. They must stay where they are; I can come home to London.

Bravery is not being afraid to be afraid

21 October 2001

Marie Colvin, Woman of the Year, defined in her acceptance speech the complex nature of courage.

Receiving the Woman of the Year award is a great honour – not least because I got to meet Ellen MacArthur, who's done the only thing I ever really wanted to do – sail round the world. And also Pam Warren, whose experience embodies the concept of the award: bravery.

This is a tough time to be a war correspondent (let alone a grounded one, as I am, for medical reasons). The need for front-line, objective reporting has never been clearer. We are engaged in a war that will affect us all, yet know almost nothing about events on one side.

Marie reporting from the mountains of Chechnya, 1999.
Photograph by Dmitry Beliakov.

There are no western journalists in Taliban-held Afghanistan.

Equally, the risks of going and getting that information has been made clear by the experience of Yvonne Ridley, who could have paid with her life. What level of risk should we take? What is bravery, and what is bravado?

I, too, almost didn't make it. In April I was hit by shrapnel from a grenade fired by the Sri Lankan army. I had gone to the northern Tamil area to report on the plight of 500,000 people under government siege. There was no medicine, little food, an unreported war that had left 340,000 of them refugees. The government had not allowed journalists into the area for six years. I entered illegally, and lost the sight of my eye. Worth the risk? Brutal question – one I've thought about a lot. I did think so at the time, and have to say I do now.

Simply: there's no way to cover war properly without risk. Covering a war means going into places torn by chaos, destruction, death and pain, and trying to bear witness to that. Not so much as to what kind of toys are being used – I've never been able to figure out if that is a MiG or a Tornado shooting at me, or 105mm or 155mm artillery. I care about the experience of those most directly affected by war, those asked to fight and those who are just trying to survive.

Despite all the videos you see on television from Pentagon or Nato briefings, what's on the ground has remained remarkably the same for the past 100 years. Craters. Burnt houses. Women weeping for sons and daughters. Suffering. In my profession, there is no chance of unemployment.

There is no easy way to cover a war. In Chechnya, the war could not be reported from the Russian side, so I travelled into Chechnya from Georgia to report on the indiscriminate bombing of civilians. I stayed with Muslim fighters in the mountains: as I walked in to their base, little more than a one-room hut with a 20-foot bed for everyone, the commander put his devout Muslim fighters at ease by saying: 'There is no woman here, only a journalist.'

I went from village to village. I remember an old man, lying in a basement, his skull cracked and brains leaking out and somehow he was still breathing. His wife sat next to him holding his hand. She knew he would die: there were no doctors, no medicine, the Russian planes would come again soon, but she wanted to be there to his last breath. That's bravery.

One of the rules I have in covering war is: don't be afraid to be afraid – perhaps more important for a woman because you are often with men trying to prove they're macho and watching you for signs of cowardice. In Chechnya, I was pinned down in a snowy field as Russian planes came back, over and over, bombing the field. After hours of this, a Chechen fighter lit a fire, saying with great bravado that impressed his fellow rebels: 'It is better to die warm than to live cold.' I said: 'Put the fire out, you idiot.' They all thought me a coward. I thought I'd rather survive.

My strongest memory of East Timor is walking through the besieged United Nations compound and being stared at, with fear, by all the women and children who were camping on the ground under palm trees. They knew that, if I stayed, they had a chance to live. If I left, they would die. I was a kind of human shield.

The compound was besieged by militiamen wielding machetes and guns, and likely to be overrun at any moment. The UN decided to evacuate, leaving 1,500 women and children behind. Except for two Dutchwomen, my journalist colleagues made the decision to get out on the last flight. I decided to stay – and had the most irritating conversation with my foreign editor. 'What do you mean everyone's left and you're staying?' he asked.

'Don't know. I'm staying.'

'Well, why have all the men left?'

In exasperation, I said: 'I guess they don't make men like they used to.' To his great credit, and my embarrassment, he printed that comment in the paper. It's been tough getting dates ever since.

I stayed, and reported to anyone I could over my satellite phone – CNN, BBC, Australian television – that the UN evacuation was a death sentence for these women and children. Women barred from entering the compound threw their babies over the walls, into barbed wire, to save them from the militia. Three days later, the UN reversed its decision and evacuated all 1,500 women and children. That risk was certainly worth it.

The war in Afghanistan worries me. Let me make clear, I am not from the 'yes, but' brigade. I despise what Osama Bin Laden stands for. I despise the ways of the Taliban. But this war is being fought in our names, and it is our business. Explaining something, trying to help people to understand it, does not mean support. I wish there was reporting from both sides – at the least, it keeps governments and generals honest. In the words of Martha Gellhorn, one of the bravest war correspondents of her generation: 'Never believe governments, not any of them, not a word they say; keep an untrusting eye on all they do.'

I worry when I hear phrases from the Pentagon that American missiles destroyed the 'command and control centre' at Kandahar airport. I was there – there's a mud building and a guy with a phone that can take only incoming calls.

Going to these places, finding out what is happening, is the only way to get at the truth. It is not perfect, it is a rough draft of history. But historians can come later. You see such huge injustices happening and, as a reporter, you have the chance to tell people about that.

To me, bravery is not something gigantic and definitive. I don't go into a war thinking I have to prove myself brave: that would be about me and that would be bravado. Bravery is secondary. When you are covering a war, you have to be 'brave' over and over again because it means going to places where you could be killed, and where people are being killed, and putting one foot in front of the other – however afraid you are.

The point is to try to report as truthfully as you know how, about what you see and make that part of the record. You can't get that information in a war without going to a place where people are being shot and they are shooting at you. The real difficulty is having enough faith in humanity to believe that someone will care.

Middle East

A bitter taste for vengeance

RAMALLAH

7 April 2002

Marie Colvin, Uzi Mahnaimi, Tel Aviv; Tony Allen-Mills, Washington;
Peter Conradi and Tom Walker, London

Behind its campaign to crush militant Palestinian factions, Israel has embarked upon a brutal conflict that has escalated into all-out war. As the death toll mounts, Marie Colvin reports from Ramallah on the human impact of the political posturing.

Soraida Abu Gharbieh probably died because she believed that Israeli soldiers would not shoot civilians. She was born in America and had idealistic views. But as her husband drove her around the corner to her father's house, she was shot in the head and killed. When he pried their 10-month-old son from her arms, the baby was chuckling. He thought it was a game.

Last week Soraida was buried in a mass grave in the car park of Ramallah hospital. The city was under curfew, her family could not retrieve her body and the mortuary was overflowing with the dead. Soraida's husband remembers the last word that she spoke – his name, Murad – as she keeled forward, her body around the chubby boy in her lap.

The family's crime was to be frightened. When Israeli tanks began shelling buildings on the first night of the incursion nine days ago, Soraida thought they should go to her father's house because it was larger and lower down the hill.

'We were sleeping when we heard the explosions,' Murad said. 'The drive to my father-in-law's is only 200 metres. The soldiers began shooting at the car and I stopped. They were five metres away. Then came a rain of bullets.'

Murad was hit in the shoulder and neck; he remembers the soldiers walked up to the car, looked in and laughed.

He struggled out, carrying tiny Muhsin, then fell and began screaming for help. Neighbours who tried to reach him were raked with gunfire. Farhan Saleh, his father-in-law, finally dragged him into the house. They found Soraida the next day, slumped in the front seat.

The silver Renault Clio is still there, its windows shattered by bullets, dried blood staining the steering wheel and her seat. 'She was the smartest of my children,' said Saleh, who brought his family back to Ramallah after 24 years in America because he was afraid of the crime and drugs in Washington DC. 'And she thought her baby was the smartest, best baby in the whole world.'

The Abu Gharbieh family was not alone in mourning last week. By Friday night 27 people had been killed in the city. Buried in the car park next to Soraida was Wadeed Safran, a grandmother in her fifties.

She had been shot dead by an Israeli sniper as she walked from Ramallah hospital on her cane. She had broken the curfew because the cast on her leg had become too painful to bear. 'She was nothing, nothing, no danger to the Israelis,' said Dr Ahmed Haleem.

Across the West Bank there were similar stories of heartbreak and despair as Israeli forces rolled into all the cities they had withdrawn from in the mid 1990s – Ramallah, Qalqilya, Jenin, Bethlehem, Nablus and finally Hebron.

In Bethlehem, the siege of the Church of the Nativity entered its fifth day yesterday as an estimated 200 Palestinian fighters continued to seek refuge in the ancient building. The stand-off began on Tuesday as Israeli soldiers chased local militiamen into Manger Square. By Tuesday afternoon, panicked and exhausted, the Palestinians shot the lock off a door of the church and in so doing dragged the Arab–Israeli fighting into one of the most sacred shrines of Christianity, the birthplace of Christ.

The cloister was quickly surrounded by Israeli tanks and snipers, ensnaring not only the resistance fighters but also the monks and nuns of the three religious orders who live and work inside the compound.

The religious community suffered its first victim at dawn on Thursday when Samir Salman, a Palestinian Christian, walked into the open from his nearby house to ring the church bells, as he had done for 30 years. He was shot dead and his body was left where he fell, in the middle of Manger Square.

More violence followed when the Israeli artillery reportedly struck a metal gate to the rear of the basilica. Convinced that an Israeli offensive was imminent, a few Palestinian militiamen tried to break out of the basilica but a heavy gun battle ensued, sending a clear message to those remaining inside that there would be no escape, only surrender.

The Pope sent a fax appealing for those trapped inside to trust in prayer. Israel pledged not to storm the church, but those inside were still not safe. Yesterday morning Father Ibrahim Faltas, the church's Franciscan superior, was shot at as he tried to open a window. Food ran low. 'We haven't got much left,' said Sister Lisetta Vingi, 69, a Roman Catholic nun. 'We try to give a piece of bread to everyone. But we won't be able to hold out much longer.'

Elsewhere across the region the casualties mounted as Israel continued its occupation of every West Bank city except Jericho. In Jenin, tanks and armoured personnel carriers tried to enter the narrow alleys of the refugee camp on Friday night, protected by Apache helicopters. A local journalist filming the incursion was shot dead; residents said ambulances were prevented from entering the area so nobody knew how many were killed or wounded. Other reports said that the town's Al-Razi hospital was hit by gunfire and vital supplies of water and oxygen had been damaged.

If the Israeli offensive was designed to wear down the will and capability of local fighters, then it has had little success so far. In the face of mounting opposition, Palestinians have learnt new tactics of resistance. When Israeli soldiers tried to enter the house of a wanted man in Jenin, Islamic militants lying in wait exploded a bomb in the house. Wounded Israeli soldiers were ferried out by helicopter. Residents of the nearby refugee camps are also said to have been equipped with explosive belts and hand grenades, with one Palestinian woman blowing herself up yesterday when Israeli troops approached her door.

In Nablus, an Israeli tank appeared to have been targeted by a home-made bomb, while fierce street fighting led to the death of at least a dozen militants as support for the fighters mounted.

In the words of one resident: 'I am 32, but I'm more radical than Arafat. My nephew is 15 and more radical than me. We are all with the resistance now. What choice do we have?'

Another Palestinian fighter said that many had been inspired by Arafat's telephone interviews from his besieged compound in Ramallah. 'We have seen that Abu Amar [the familiar name that Palestinians use for Arafat] is standing steadfast. We are standing steadfast for this reason. We don't need orders.'

He added that the divided militia factions had now combined – gunmen from Fatah, Hamas and Islamic Jihad (see below) were fighting side by side.

Whether he intended it or not, the military operation launched by Ariel Sharon, the Israeli prime minister, has progressed from an incursion into all-out war.

Demonstrators poured into the streets of Arab capitals. Thousands protested in Jordan and Egypt, the two countries that have ties with Israel.

'Sharon's actions are threatening the whole region,' said Marwan Muasher, the Jordanian foreign minister, who headed for Washington with a letter of appeal for President George W Bush from King Abdullah. Even Israelis, largely supportive of Sharon's operation, began to wonder if he had an exit strategy.

By Thursday the Americans had begun to rethink their hands-off approach. A week after the tanks had rolled into Ramallah,

Bush announced that he was sending Colin Powell, his secretary of state, to the Middle East.

Bush criticised Arafat, saying the desperate situation that the Palestinian leader found himself in 'was of his own creation', but for the first time he demanded that the Israelis make political concessions, anathema to Sharon, who has insisted that there must be a ceasefire before any peace negotiations can resume.

The Israeli leader has refused to listen to western diplomats, who believe no ceasefire can be brokered unless Arafat can offer his people political gains.

Arafat, despite the criticism, was heartened by the Bush speech. 'He told me that he understood Bush is under heavy pressure,' said a senior adviser trapped in the compound. 'Contrary to news reports, Arafat thought the Bush speech was very positive.'

He said Arafat had focused on the concrete issues in the speech: Bush's request for the Israelis to withdraw from the West Bank cities, stop the expansion of Jewish settlements in the occupied Palestinian territories and seek a solution that would see the creation of a Palestinian state alongside Israel.

Bush repeated his demands yesterday, calling on Israel to 'withdraw without delay' from Palestinian territory. Sharon responded by saying Israel was aware of the Americans' wish for a quick end to the military offensive. In a statement, his office said: 'Israel will make every effort to accelerate Operation Defensive Wall.'

Israel has shown little inclination to bow to American pressure. On Friday Israeli soldiers fired on journalists who were trying to report on the arrival of General Anthony Zinni, the American envoy, in Ramallah. Sharon also refused to allow Zinni to meet a delegation of senior Palestinians, appointed to follow up his meeting with Arafat. Palestinians feared that Powell's predicted arrival towards the end of this week would be too late, with the Israelis stepping up their action before the diplomatic mission arrives. A repeated call by Powell yesterday that Israel should begin an immediate withdrawal appeared to have fallen on deaf ears.

'The partial pullback will not take place this week,' said one Israeli military source. 'We are not driving a speedboat that can be easily diverted. We are like a big ship which takes some time to turn around.'

Others suspect more sinister motives. Along with destroying the 'infrastructure of terror', Sharon's army has been busy systematically dismantling the Palestinian Authority civilian infrastructure built up since the mid-1990s. Such a wholesale operation will take time. Shaul Mofaz, the Israeli chief of staff, said last week that his army needed 'four full weeks to complete the operation, and four more weeks to establish security'.

Late on Tuesday, tanks and helicopters began shelling the headquarters of the Preventive Security Force, the Palestinian MI5, on the edge of the industrial zone. If the aim of the Israelis was to catch terrorists, it was a bizarre choice of targets. The PSF, armed and trained by the US Central Intelligence Agency, was the only force carrying out the Israeli demands and arresting known militants, often to the anger of the local population.

Other Israeli attacks in Ramallah struck directly at government buildings. During a brief curfew on Friday, Naim Abu Hummus, the Palestinian education minister, visited the shattered remains of his former headquarters.

Israeli soldiers had gone from room to room destroying as they went. 'At each room, they threw me in first,' said the caretaker. 'I was their human shield, even though I told them there is nobody here.'

Smashed computers and ceiling tiles littered the floors alongside trampled pages of high school results. The ministry safe hung open, scorched by blast marks. The ministry accountant said 40,000 shekels (£5,800) was missing.

'I am sick,' Abu Hummus said. 'Our education ministry is sacred to us. If they want to search, I understand. But this is not the way to search. What can I tell our future generation about peace when they see this?'

Across a square, the building of the Palestinian Legislative Council was a similar scene of destruction. Both departments had been set up with millions of dollars from Europe, Japan and the World Bank. By the time the troops withdraw there may well be no government left to run the West Bank.

Sharon's plan may be to weaken or remove Arafat and return to the situation a decade ago when an Israeli military administration ran the occupied territories. No Palestinian, however critical of Arafat, thought this could succeed, but now many are wondering whether Sharon may have gone too far down the line to stop.

Even as the heavy fighting subsided, Palestinian families were struggling to come to terms with what had befallen them.

Near the Greek Orthodox church in central Ramallah, the Ziadi family was yesterday still holding a vigil for Majd, their 19-year-old son, taken by Israeli soldiers on Tuesday night with his father and the other men of the building, rounded up as house-to-house searches continued.

'The soldiers came and started shouting, "You are Hamas, you are Hamas",' recalled a neighbour. 'We told them, "No, we are Christian", but they would not listen.'

Mohamed Ziadi, Majd's father, was also taken but later released. Forty-eight years old and bespectacled, he was still in shock yesterday. The Israelis forced everyone from their building, then separated the men from the women and children. All the men were made to walk to the Israeli headquarters, their hands on their heads, in front of a tank that herded them through the streets.

When they were blindfolded and taken by bus to a nearby settlement for questioning, the soldiers' behaviour turned sadistic. 'One soldier called a friend in Tel Aviv on his mobile phone and said: "Listen to this."

'He held out the phone and began to beat one of us. The man screamed in pain. Then the soldier came back to his mobile phone and asked his friend, "Did you hear that?" He was laughing.'

Ziadi was kicked in the stomach and beaten. After questioning, he was released and walked three miles back to his house in the rain. Majd is still missing.

The family insists he is no militant; his room, now littered with the clothes and debris of smashed wardrobes from the Israeli search, seems to bear this out. There are no pictures of the martyrs that normally adorn the walls of militants.

As Powell prepares for his tour of surrounding Arab countries, rallying support to drive a peace plan forward, such tales of Israeli brutality will do little to aid America's cause. Well-meaning missions and verbal posturing do not count for much in a region where the common language is violence.

As one normally moderate Israeli put it last week: 'We gave these guys all the chances in the world to live in peace with us. They rejected every possible proposal, one after another, and started a war against us. They asked for a war and they got a war, so they should not complain now.' It is one of the many tragedies of the past fortnight that such views are no longer the exception.

THE PALESTINIAN MILITANTS

HAMAS

Founded in 1987 during the early days of the first Palestinian uprising, this Islamic resistance movement was centred on the mosques of Gaza, where funding from Saudi Arabia enabled it to provide welfare services for the local population. It later gave rise to a more militant faction whose long-term goal is the destruction of Israel and the creation of an Islamic state. It was a Hamas attack on a hotel in Netanya two weeks ago that prompted the recent incursions, but the group now enjoys even greater popularity among the Palestinian population than Arafat's own party.

PALESTINIAN ISLAMIC JIHAD

Although sharing much of the ideology of Hamas, Islamic Jihad is even more militant in its aims, pressing for the immediate over-throw of Israel. Following the assassination of the group's former leader, Dr Fathi Shikaki, by Mossad agents in 1995, it experienced a brief decline but the second intifada has given it fresh impetus and attacks have been stepped up with funding from Iran. Although its hardline approach is only supported by a minority of Palestinians centred on Gaza, its small size and independence make it a difficult group for Arafat to control.

HEZBOLLAH

A fundamentalist Shi'ite organisation that was established in 1982 in response to the Israeli invasion of Lebanon. Although primarily concentrating on military targets across the Israeli border, it carried out the bombing of the Israeli embassy in Buenos Aires in 1992, causing hundreds of casualties and it is also said to have helped arm Palestinians by smuggling weapons through Jordan. Although attacks were scaled down following the withdrawal of Israeli troops from Lebanon two years ago, cross-border fighting increased in the past week, fuelling concerns that Hezbollah is preparing for a wider war in the Middle East with backing from Iran.

AL-AQSA MARTYRS BRIGADES

A new group directly linked to Yasser Arafat's Fatah movement through its Tanzim military wing, the brigades are behind the majority of recent shootings and suicide attacks against Israelis. Well-equipped and ruthless in its tactics, its aims are purely secular, hoping to pressure Israel into greater concessions over the creation of a Palestinian state. Tanzim's leader, Marwan Baghouti, tops Sharon's most wanted list.

PFLP

The Popular Front for the Liberation of Palestine was once the prime organisation linked to hijackings and terror attacks against Jewish targets around the world, but its secular Marxist ideals led to dwindling support during recent uprisings. However, it was responsible for the assassination of the Israeli tourist minister last October, after its own leader was killed by an Israeli missile attack on Ramallah. Its followers have recently carried out a number of suicide bombings.

Jenin: the bloody truth

21 April 2002

Was it a massacre? Marie Colvin in the ruins of the refugee camp found cold comfort for propagandists on either side.

The first medical teams allowed into the Jenin refugee camp last week followed the chickens. Human senses were overwhelmed by the devastation and the stench of death, but the birds were not distracted. They were hungry. Two rusty-coloured fowl pecking away at a bundle in the street drew a Red Cross team to the remains of Jamal Sabagh.

He wasn't really recognisable to an untrained eye. His body had been lying there for more than a week. The Israeli army had banned ambulances from the camp for 11 days, and neighbours were too terrified to go to him.

Tank tracks led to his body, over it and onwards through the mud. What had once been a young man was rotting flesh mingled with shredded clothing, mashed into the earth. One foot was all that looked human.

Sabagh was no fighter, his brother and friends say. He was 28 and a father of three. His wife and children had fled on the first day of the Israeli invasion, Wednesday 3 April, but he stayed because he was diabetic and was too ill to run away. He was also afraid he would be mistaken for a fighter.

Two days later, he left his house when the Israelis yelled over megaphones that they were going to blow it up. He walked, directed by soldiers in armoured personnel carriers, with other men to Seha Street at the centre of the camp, carrying his bag of medicines. He joined the crowd. Soldiers yelled at him to take off his shirt, then his trousers. He clung to his bag of medicine as he tried to unbuckle his belt, and he was slow. The soldiers shot him, friends say.

Medical workers shooed away the chickens, wrapped Sabagh's remains in a rug, then lifted them into the back of a small open-bed truck. It drove off, past burned and shell-holed buildings, looking like a medieval plague wagon.

Across the narrow street was a forlorn pile of men's jeans, polyester tracksuit tops and cheap shoes – left by those who had got their clothes off in time, to prove they had no bombs strapped to their bodies, and had been taken to the Israeli army base at the nearby village of Salem.

As the rescue teams spread out over Jenin camp last week, after the Israeli army claimed victory in its battle against several hundred armed Palestinian radicals, it was clear something cataclysmic had occurred.

Instead of the Hawamish neighbourhood – previously a jumble of mismatched cinderblock homes – a vista lay open to the hills beyond.

Stunned and dusty in this new world, returning Palestinians wandered around a moonscape the size of two football pitches. It was littered with the detritus of human life – blankets, a little girl's tartan skirt, a child's orange boxing glove, shoes, a musical keyboard. Women in hijab headscarves dug at the crushed rubble with buckets and bare hands. Five-year-old Ahmed Hindi cried: 'I want to go home.' He didn't know he was standing on it.

Images of this man-made earthquake zone have flashed around the world as evidence that the Israeli prime minister, Ariel Sharon, is responsible for another war crime in Jenin on a par with the massacre of Palestinians in the Chatila and Sabra refugee camps in Beirut 20 years ago.

Israel has responded that the devastation was the consequence of a pitched battle against entrenched terrorists.

What really happened? Tragedy doesn't necessarily breed truth. The propaganda war had begun before the white dust settled over Jenin.

Rafi Laderman, a personable Israeli reserve major, emerged from the battlefield and made the rounds of the media in his rumpled green uniform. His clear plastic spectacles signalled his real job as a marketing consultant.

Laderman insisted that all the buildings in the refugee camp had been destroyed by explosive booby traps set by the terrorists, or levelled by Israeli bulldozers because they 'presented additional engineering difficulties' that could endanger civilians. He himself had stopped the fighting to lead Palestinian civilians to safety.

All that seemed disingenuous. Equally unlikely were Palestinian claims that the Israelis had killed 500 Palestinians in cold blood, most civilians, and buried them in mass graves under the rubble after running them over with tanks. Israel said about 70 had been killed.

Terje Roed-Larsen, the United Nations envoy to the Middle East, cut through the propaganda by stating the obvious: 'No military operation can justify this scale of destruction. Whatever the purpose was, the effect is collective punishment of a whole society.'

He and his family received telephone death threats from Israeli callers for his pains.

Under pressure from many sides – including the United States, Britain, the United Nations and the European Union – Israel has agreed to a UN fact-finding mission. The trouble with such missions, however, is that they become bogged down by obfuscation while evidence goes cold.

To get an objective idea of what happened in Jenin requires an almost forensic investigation, weeding out lies and half-truths and the rumours that a stunned and terrified population has come to believe are true. By doing so, I have come to conclusions that are unlikely to satisfy the propagandists of either side.

Jenin was bound to be a prime target for the Israeli military backlash after a Palestinian suicide bomber killed 28 Israelis as they sat down to dinner in Netanya on Passover eve three weeks ago.

There has been a refugee camp in Jenin since the foundation of Israel in 1948 when Palestinians fled there from the Haifa area. The first residents worried only for their next rations and fretted impotently as their rich orange groves in Haifa were rebranded Jaffa oranges by Israel and exported around the world.

Since then, Jenin has become a stronghold of radical Palestinian nationalism with a population of 11,000 refugees. The Israeli defence force (IDF) believes half the suicide bombers who have struck Israel in the past year were trained in the Jenin refugee camp.

When the Israelis invaded Ramallah on 29 March, in retaliation for the suicide bombings, radicals in Jenin knew they would be next. Sources there said local leaders of Hamas, Islamic Jihad and Fatah, including its militant Tanzim and Al-Aqsa Martyrs Brigades offshoots, organised small fighting cells that included members from each group.

At 2am on Wednesday 3 April, five days after the invasion of Ramallah, Merkava tanks and armoured personnel carriers rumbled through Jenin and headed for the refugee camp on the edge of the city.

The Namal brigade and commandos entered from the west; the Golani brigade from the south; and the Fifth Brigade, a unit of reserve troops called up from their day jobs, went in under the command of Laderman.

The odds were far from equal. The Israelis had tanks, armoured personnel carriers and rocket-firing helicopter gunships. Its soldiers were in full battle gear with bulletproof vests, helmets and M-16s. Against them was a guerrilla force of several hundred men armed with Kalashnikovs and home-made bombs called *kuwa* – Arabic for elbow – manufactured from pieces of plumbing.

The two sides faced each other in a camp about 2½ miles long by ½ mile wide. In this tiny battlefield the radicals not only resisted the might of the Israeli army longer than the combined Arab armies did in the 1967 six-day war, but turned themselves and their militant cause into the stuff of instant Palestinian legend.

'The fighting was the fiercest urban house-to-house fighting Israel has seen in 30 years,' said Laderman.

The narrow dirt alleys provided perfect ambush hides for Palestinians who grew up in this maze. The Israelis tried to keep off the streets, progressing from house to house by breaking through the walls with explosives and hammers.

On the first night of the invasion, Israeli soldiers blew out the yellow metal door of Ismael Khatib's home in the Hawamish district and hauled him out to act as a human shield as they knocked on his neighbours' doors.

As they did so, two gunmen across the alley opened fire. Hugging Khatib in front of him with his left arm, an Israeli soldier balanced his M-16 on Khatib's right shoulder and fired back wildly.

Kuwa bombs were hurled by Palestinians. Khatib threw himself on the ground and crawled away, only to circle around and climb in his back window. 'I felt like I died and came alive again,' he says.

The next day another Israeli patrol crashed through the wall into his living room. They stayed, keeping him, his wife and children hostage in a room.

A far more serious ambush sealed the Hawamish area's fate. By Monday 8 April, most of the surviving gunmen had been forced into this neighbourhood. Early next day, 16 reservists of the Fifth Brigade moved into an alley in Hawamish, searching for a house to use as a lookout post. Their leader, Major Oded Golomb, set charges to blow the door.

As he did so, a Palestinian bomb exploded and gunmen began firing from the opposite roof. Thirteen Israelis were killed.

Israel's retribution was swift. Armoured bulldozers, two-storey behemoths as impregnable as a tank, began knocking down houses in Hawamish. Hurriya Kreini was in her home with her family when an Israeli bulldozer began destroying the house without warning. She and her husband managed to push their children out of a window before the house tumbled down.

By Thursday 11 April, Hawamish had disappeared. That was the day the Israeli operation officially ended, but hours after the Israelis announced that the last 35 fighters had surrendered (they ran out of ammunition) I stood in a village called Borqin looking down into the camp. The sound of heavy machinegun fire still rose from the valley. Helicopter gunships shot bursts of heavy-calibre bullets. Explosions sounded and white puffs rose above the camp.

The Israelis let in the outside world slowly and grudgingly. The camp was finally opened to international aid agencies on 14 April, but journalists were barred. Until only two days ago, Israeli soldiers shot at journalists they spotted trying to slip through the olive groves that slope up from the camp, or along a back dirt road.

The obstruction fuelled speculation that the Israelis were trying to hide something. There were mass graves, some said; bodies had been hauled off in refrigerated trucks; others swore hundreds of bodies were under the bulldozed homes.

Israelis bridled. 'Our mission was to penetrate into Jenin area and dismantle the terrorist infrastructure and we did that,' insisted the ubiquitous Laderman. 'I have a five-year-old daughter and now I feel I can let her out in the playground.'

I eventually gained access last Tuesday, walking in with as open a mind as I could muster.

Late in the day, when all was quiet, I was walking past the Jenin hospital. Nearby, women and children were slowly making their way back to temporary lodgings after a day trying to find their homes and relatives. An armoured personnel carrier pulled up at the end of the street behind us. The Palestinians took no notice – until the soldier in the turret opened fire straight down the street with his machinegun.

I dived for shelter. Children cried in terror. The soldier initially fired over our heads, but now bullets flashed by at chest height. The screams turned to moans as the APC headed towards us down the street.

It rolled into sight, stopped the gunfire and swivelled the huge barrel to point directly at us. Then the soldier waved his hand in anger, yelling: 'Go, go.' I think he just wanted everyone off the streets.

If I was now convinced by claims Israelis opened fire indiscriminately on civilians, weighing up the truth of other allegations would be much more difficult. Even what can seem obvious is not necessarily true.

From a house hit by a missile in the centre of what the Palestinians now call their own Ground Zero, rescue workers pulled human remains that people said were of a small child. They lay on a rug and seemed indeed very small to the eye. But when I found a doctor, he was dubious.

'This person has been reduced; I think in a fire,' the doctor said. 'See that bone?' He poked around and found a large thigh bone. Not a child.

When I tracked down the owner of the house, he said that four fighters had been holed up in his house firing on the Israelis when a missile hit it.

Scores of interviews in the camp did show consistency, however. Story after story – from people who had not yet met one another since they fled – indicated the Israelis had used Palestinians as human shields and had taken families hostage to protect their makeshift posts set up in their houses.

In a house overlooking Hawamish, the Sabagh family were sweeping out after having Israeli soldiers there for eight days. Trying to scrub off Hebrew slogans, Jamili Sabagh, 52, said the family were held in a tiny room upstairs.

'They gave us no food, no water. The room they put us in was too small for 13 people. They fed our dog to torment us, and not the children,' she said. 'Our home was a garbage heap when they left.'

It is one of the few on the block untouched by missile strikes, a sign that it was indeed used as a post by the Israelis.

Ismahan Stati is a pretty, shy university student. Israeli soldiers came to her house on the third day and blew open the door, she said.

'They took me as a hostage,' she said. 'They were afraid.'

They knocked on a nearby house, and when nobody answered they blew open the door with a grenade fired from a gun. In fact, Afaf Dusuqi, 52, had been slow coming to the door and was killed instantly by the shrapnel.

Afaf's mother held her body, covered in blood, and screamed for an ambulance but the soldiers fired into the house to drive her back. 'I was shaking with fear,' Stati recalled.

Outside the Dusuqi house, there is still blood on the concrete stoop, and there is a 6in hole in the yellow door where the lock used to be.

Afaf's body stayed in the house for five days until the family could smuggle it to the cemetery for burial in a hurried mass grave. I found her name scrawled on a stone where she will lie until her family can give her a proper burial. Doctors at the Razi hospital have her death certificate.

There is a bizarre twist to this story. A rumour began that Stati was a suicide bomber. The story started, her family believes, when a neighbour saw her standing in the group of soldiers, heard an explosion and ducked, then looked again to see the body of a woman.

The rumour is still around the camp, illustrating why every fact must be tracked down here.

Stories of cold-blooded executions were told to me in detail but could not be substantiated. A woman said she saw 'with my own eyes' the execution of eight Hamas members and a 16-year-old boy who was the son of one of the men but had nothing to do with politics.

It sounded difficult to believe of the IDF, but she had a name. In the end, I found the true story; an awful tale, but not a cold-blooded assassination.

Fathi Chalabi, a bird-like elderly man, showed me where the Israelis had blown a hole in his door to enter his home at night. About 30 soldiers had forced their way in and separated out Chalabi, his son Wada'a, 32, and another man, Abed Sa'adi, 27, in the courtyard.

'They told us to face the wall and take off our shirts,' Chalabi said. 'They were looking for suicide bombers. But we were not. My son was the caretaker at school. He was one month from getting his university degree.'

It was dark, and as Wada'a picked up his shirt, the Israelis spotted an elastic bandage he wore for back pain. Someone shouted in Hebrew.

Chalabi remembers the officer's name was Gabi. They opened fire, hitting the two younger men, who fell on Chalabi.

The last he remembers is some kind of argument between the soldiers. Then they shone lights on the bodies and he played dead. 'I was covered in Wada'a's blood,' he said. The Israelis left up the alleyway. Dark dried bloodstains still marked the concrete when Chalabi spoke to me.

Equally callous was the shooting of Omar Nayel, a shop owner. 'I was in my house looking out, trying to see what was happening,' said Fathi Abu Aita, a neighbour. 'I saw him walk across his courtyard, I think going to the loo.' Two shots rang out and he fell. Nayel's body lay in the garden for days.

My conclusion after interviewing scores of refugees is that there is no evidence Israeli troops entered the camp aiming to 'massacre' Palestinian civilians. But in many cases they shot first and did not take much care to find out if the target was a civilian or not.

Under the fourth Geneva convention, they are required to protect the civilian population, and wilful killing of a civilian is a potential war crime.

I am also certain that numerous Palestinians were held hostage in their homes while Israeli troops used the building as a base or a firing post, and that others were taken door to door as a human shield, sometimes thrown into rooms ahead of Israeli troops.

Both are violations of international law, which protects civilians in wartime.

As for the bulldozing of the Hawamish area, this seems to have been out of a combination of fear and revenge rather than premeditated.

I asked Laderman how he felt now. He said he was satisfied that the 'nest of snakes' has been snuffed out. As for the new generation of suicide bombers the military operation has probably created, he said: 'They would have become suicide terrorists anyway.'

Two terrible deaths tell story of the Palestinian predicament: last assignment for a local hero

21 July 2002

A young Palestinian man was killed last week in Jenin. Few noticed: he was not that different from ambitious young men anywhere in the world. He wrote, took photographs and ran his own newsletter about the heritage of his city until the mayor closed it down.

His name was Imad Abu Zahra and his greatest challenge was trying to be a journalist in the West Bank under Israeli occupation.

The Committee to Protect Journalists (CPJ), based in New York, has this year listed the West Bank and Gaza as the world's most dangerous places for reporters to work because of Israeli gunfire – all the more so for Palestinian journalists, who lack even the nebulous protection of an international organisation.

On a hot and sunny day last week a gunner on an Israeli tank shot Imad in the leg as he photographed an armoured vehicle that had run into an electricity pole in the central square of Jenin.

According to the Red Crescent charity in Jenin, he bled to death because Israeli soldiers halted the ambulance that was trying to reach him. The Israeli Defence Force (IDF) disputes the account.

Whatever the facts, they do not begin to convey the loss. Imad was my translator earlier this year as I tried to unravel the reality of an Israeli army attack on the Jenin refugee camp in pursuit of armed militants.

The invasion left a neighbourhood flattened by army bulldozers amid charges – unfounded, as it turned out – that there had been a massacre.

Imad – a burly single man of 34 who dressed like a public schoolboy and was self-conscious about his premature balding – was indefatigable in his desire to discover what had happened. He could not bear propaganda. If someone tried to sell him a line, he would listen politely and dismiss the tainted testimony.

He could also be infuriating. Something of a local hero for his independent reporting, he would stop and talk to everyone as we walked through the camp – a handshake here, a hug and condolences for someone in distress there, a conversation with a young man who wanted to know about his video camera. It took an unnervingly long time to get anywhere.

'I know we need to work, but I can't walk past people who have just lost everything,' Imad said.

In an interview with a father who had seen his two sons shot in front of him, Imad gently questioned him over and over again, never losing his patience when the distraught old man kept losing his train of thought. He meticulously photographed and videoed the destruction for his own purposes of documentation; nobody would buy most of his pictures.

Imad belonged to no political group. The mayor had thrown him in prison for criticising him in his newsletter; he called the Palestinian Authority a 'bunch of crooks', although he respected Yasser Arafat; most of the Islamic militants, he said, did not even know their Koran.

He was, above all, an unaffiliated Palestinian nationalist. In 1987 he had been a student leader during the first intifada (uprising), led by teenagers throwing stones. He attended two terms of Bir Zeit University, but had to stop going when the Israelis made travel between West Bank cities impossible and the university was closed for most of the time anyway.

In the new intifada that began 22 months ago, he felt his best role would be to get at the truth of what was happening.

The tragedy of his death is heightened by its senselessness. Israelis feel besieged by suicide bombers – justifiably, since 236 people have been killed in such attacks aimed at civilians. But Imad's friends say that is no excuse for opening fire on an innocent Palestinian journalist, or any other civilian.

The IDF command denies this is happening. I know there is unprovoked firing on civilians because I survived a similar situation with Imad.

We were walking out of the Jenin camp in the late afternoon, on a street filled with women and children returning to temporary shelter in the city after seeing their destroyed homes for the first time.

I heard the grinding gears of a tank pulling around the corner, and then the terrifying sound of the machinegun on its turret firing a fusillade of bullets in our direction. There was no provocation, no attack.

I had a flak jacket marked in yellow tape with foot-high letters 'TV', identifying me as a journalist – in theory in any language – as did Imad. It made no difference. The soldier who was firing was about 20 yards away with a clear line of sight.

There was very little shelter on a street lined with closed shops. We threw ourselves behind a low concrete wall as bullets streamed past at chest height. Women screamed; a little boy sobbing with fear clung to my legs. A man across the street opened the door of his house and yelled for us to run to him for refuge but there was no way of crossing.

That night I realised how brave Imad was. The tank rolled down the street to our hiding place. The turret swivelled to point directly at us. We were silent, except for the little boy, who sobbed more loudly and hid his eyes. Then the turret popped up, and a soldier yelled: 'Go, go.' The women and children huddled around us, hoping the jackets identifying us as journalists would protect them.

Dusk was closing in as I reached the flat where I would sleep. I was shaking and all I could think of was getting inside. The group of about 15 women and children who had been following begged us to walk them home across town. A burst of gunfire and the grinding movement of a tank sounded again on the next street. I could not do it.

I had been hit by a grenade a year earlier, and that day I had seemed to feel what it would be like to be struck by a bullet. Imad, however, walked on with them. He told me the next day that the journey had taken him five hours, and he had been shot at twice.

He knew he was taking too many chances. When I told him he had to be more careful, he said: 'I'm from Jenin. I'm a journalist. I have the right to walk on my streets. Don't worry ...'

The IDF's account of his death is that the armoured vehicle that had run into a pole was attacked by a Palestinian mob throwing fire bombs and firing at the accompanying tank. The tank returned fire in self-defence.

The story is contradicted by eyewitnesses and by pictures taken by Sayeed Dahla, a Palestinian photographer who was with Imad and who was also shot. The photographs show the armoured vehicle marooned on an empty street. There is no mob. There is not even a person in the photograph.

'The Israelis are lying,' Sayeed says. 'Everyone had fled when the tanks came into the centre of Jenin. People were terrified. They left their shops open and their cars on the street and ran.

'Imad and I were alone on the street when the tank opened fire at us. I told him to be careful of that tank, but he just said, "This is a good photo". Then they shot us.'

Sayeed points out that both men were wearing jackets – his said 'Press', Imad's 'TV'. A boy removed Imad's jacket when he was struggling to breathe after being shot.

Btselem, an Israeli human rights group that monitors the actions of the IDF with the help of former Israeli soldiers, claims that hundreds of unlawful killings of Palestinians should be investigated. But few actually are.

Of 25 IDF investigations opened in the past 22 months, six were closed without a result; others have yet to be completed. Only three have resulted in disciplinary action.

'The army hardly ever opens investigations into cases of unlawful killing,' says Lior Yavne, Btselem's spokesman. 'The army is basically conducting a policy of impunity. Soldiers realise they can do anything they want and they will not face problems. They know nobody is monitoring their behaviour.'

Yavne points to what he regards as the important difference between now and his time in the army between 1991 and 1995. 'Before this intifada every shooting death was investigated. The commanders have now decided we are in an armed conflict short of war, but that means they don't have to open an investigation in case of death.'

Even when they do, Yavne claims, the investigators – military police – rely on the word of the soldiers who did the shooting and their unit commander.

Forty Palestinians are reported to have been killed since 20 June, when tanks rolled into West Bank cities. Btselem says that at least 20 of the dead were unarmed civilians.

The CPJ has taken up Imad's case, but is not optimistic. Sixteen journalists have been wounded by Israeli fire, two of them fatally, since September 2000. 'In none of the cases has the IDF taken responsibility,' says Ann Cooper, the CPJ's director.

'I don't think there is a deliberate policy to kill journalists, but certainly this year we did see the IDF using major force to keep journalists out of areas where they did not want that story covered – they didn't want eyewitnesses.'

The last photograph of Imad, taken by his friend Sayeed, shows him sitting in the street pressing his hand into a huge wound in his right thigh.

His trousers are soaked red, and his grey polo shirt is splattered with blood. His sunglasses hang from his neck and his eyes look way too old for his age. He is quiet, perhaps the first time I saw him not talking.

A number of organisations have called, offering help to his dependants. His family have turned them down, saying their boy would rather have had justice.

Guantanamo

Mindless torture? No, smart thinking

27 January 2002

The treatment of captives in Cuba has provoked outrage, but it is sending a powerful message: don't mess with the US. Marie Colvin reports.

It is difficult these days being essentially liberal-minded and American. As someone who has spent years covering insalubrious and ignored parts of the world, trying to illuminate the aspirations of people struggling under poverty and oppression, I have grown used to incomprehension or antagonism.

It's a lot worse this time round. To disagree with the chorus of condemnation of the American detention of 158 Al-Qaeda and Taliban prisoners at Camp X-Ray in Guantanamo Bay is to face a firing squad of criticism, insults and, maybe worse, the disappointment of people one respects. The left, in particular, has cribbed from George Bush Jr: you are with us or against us.

The anger at the American treatment of arguably the most committed terrorists in the world has united many on the left and right in Britain. Columnists wring their wordsmith hands; the Americans have 'lost the moral high ground'. Tony Blair, the prime minister, is a 'poodle' for not condemning the conditions in this tropical prison.

Nobody writing this has been there. Those from the International Red Cross and the British Foreign Office who have inspected the camp reported that the prisoners' main concern was not their harsh conditions but how to contact their families.

It is, then, Osama Bin Laden's second success, after the bombing of the World Trade Center, the Pentagon and the death of almost

3,000 people, to be responsible for this disintegration of the western consensus that we face a common enemy.

In Britain the media used to be filled with moving stories of the 76 Brits who had lost their lives in the attacks. Now, suddenly, we are told it is the Al-Qaeda fighters who deserve our sympathy. So what has changed?

The outpouring of condemnation of American action in Guantanamo Bay comes from photographs released by the Pentagon last weekend of prisoners kneeling in Day-Glo orange suits, bizarre blacked-out ski goggles, ear mufflers and blue masks. Inhumane, the commentators cried; sensory deprivation, torture.

Torture? I have seen the victims of torture. They are crippled because the soles of their feet have been beaten so badly. They have burns all over their bodies. They are missing fingernails, limbs, ears. They are traumatised because their women and children have been raped in front of them.

The prisoners pictured in Guantanamo were in a state that moved the human heart: complete vulnerability. But what was really happening? These were not young naive Pakistanis unwittingly caught up in a war. These, if you believe the Pentagon, were the 'hardest of the hard': Al-Qaeda members who had trained in suicide bombings.

If the Americans were guilty of anything, it was of not making clear the context in which the photographs were taken. Now it has emerged that the captives on view had just got off a transport plane and were waiting to be registered. Their restraints were a temporary measure.

The Americans, worried that the captives could see or hear their colleagues and plot an attack during the flight, cut off those means of communication. They manacled their hands and feet to prevent movement. In the camp, the goggles, mufflers and masks are off. They are manacled only when they are out of their cells to exercise. They spend most of their time in 8 x 6 foot cells under roofs with chain-link walls. Not comfortable, but conditions in a Texan jail are probably worse.

Why the precautions? One prisoner has already vowed to kill an American before he leaves Camp X-Ray.

Yet despite these clarifications, the images continued to provoke outrage. One British newspaper movingly described Taliban prisoners in Afghan jails being tortured under the new regime, including an elderly man who was beaten to death. It added that these abuses 'pale into insignificance before the cynical acrobatics that George W Bush's administration has gone through to strip these prisoners of their most basic rights'.

The *New Statesman* decried the fact that the Americans were 'denying them insect repellent'. This, among other charges, led the magazine to conclude that the Americans had 'dropped all pretensions to be a defender of human rights and a source of moral authority'.

Back in the White House, such protestations were initially brushed aside by Donald Rumsfeld, the defence secretary, as 'the questions, allegations and breathless reports' of people he described as 'either uninformed, misinformed or poorly informed'.

In public he stuck to his verbal guns. For all the liberal simpering, America was playing hardball. The captives were not prisoners of war, they were 'unlawful combatants'; the Geneva convention protecting prisoners' rights would apply only in so far as it suited the American investigators, eager to continue their questioning of the captives that the convention rules would prohibit.

Behind the scenes, though, resolve was wavering. In a leaked document revealed by *The Washington Times* yesterday, it has emerged that for all of Rumsfeld's macho posturing on the media podium, an internal conflict was taking place. Unnerved by the tide of opprobrium against America's treatment of the prisoners, Colin Powell, the secretary of state, has urged the president to reconsider the classification of the captives.

The request, revealed in a memo from White House counsel Alberto Gonzales to the president and forwarded to the most senior figures of his war cabinet, outlines the legal issues involved, reminding the president of Powell's original request. 'Specifically he has asked that you conclude that GPW [Geneva Convention II on the treatment of prisoners of war] does apply to both Al Qaeda and Taliban fighters,' he writes.

Such a stance pits Powell against the vast majority of Bush's national security team, shattering the carefully honed image of a united front in the war council.

Gonzales advises the president that 'the arguments for reconsideration and reversal are unpersuasive', but even so the issues will now be debated at a National Security Council meeting tomorrow. Rumsfeld is also due to visit Guantanamo shortly to witness the conditions first hand and to allay the continuing fears that whatever the circumstances of the captives themselves, the handling of the incident has been a public relations disaster for the White House.

For in Britain and the rest of Europe, the Cuban issue is not just about the 158 prisoners, it is about uneasy feelings over a resurgent America. The Bush administration has declared war on terrorism and shows every sign of following through with what will be a long fight.

The Central Intelligence Agency has been given expanded powers, including the right to assassinate a 'terrorist' on executive order. The Americans are making up the rules as they are confronted with a new world containing new threats, and that makes everyone uneasy. And it should.

Yet how to fight an organisation present in 40 countries, with sleeper cells in most of the West, that abides by none of our rules?

Knee-jerk condemnation may not be the answer, comes the response from some unlikely quarters at home and abroad.

In Britain the vast majority of the public feel little sympathy for the captives. 'The treatment of prisoners in Camp X-Ray is an issue for the liberal elite, of which I confess I am one,' said Chris Huhne, Liberal Democrat MEP. 'Most Europeans relate to the opinions in the US.'

Polls here certainly bear out Huhne's opinion. *The Mirror* has been running an emotive campaign questioning the detentions.

One front page headline read 'Stop it'. Its readers thought differently. Despite the campaign, 91% of readers thought the conditions at Guantanamo were fine. In a poll on Radio 4 last Friday of perhaps a more liberal audience, 61% of those questioned thought the same.

Interestingly, the place where there has been almost no debate is the Middle East, original home to most of the detainees. Reports in the Arab press say there are at least 10 Saudis in Camp X-Ray, yet the Saudi government has made no representations.

'The Arab governments hate these people,' said Bari Atwan, editor of the independent London-based *Al-Quds Al-Arabi*. 'They want the Americans to execute them. Most of them are charged with crimes in their home countries and if they were sent back they would be charged in one day, tried on the second in secret and executed on the third. Try to send them home, they will apply for asylum at that camp.'

There is a dark side to the silence in the Middle East, of course. 'Nobody in the Middle East will complain,' said Khairallah Khairallah, a respected Lebanese commentator based in London. 'They know their own jail cells are even smaller, with no light. What's this about too much light? Nobody wants these people. Nobody wants to admit they are the products of our society.'

Unlike the reaction in America, in the Middle East the response to the offending photograph has been so strong that some have accused the Americans of deliberately leaking it in a 'dark ops' plan to deter terrorists.

Wittingly or not, it has succeeded. 'In the Middle East, people say the picture is the other face of America,' said Khairallah. 'Nobody will stand up to America now. They know if they do they will get a "shower" from Donald Rumsfeld.'

If it was planned, it goes back to the statements of Bin Laden gloating over the weakness of America. In one interview he talked about the lesson he had learnt in Somalia, when the American forces withdrew after 18 soldiers were killed in a debacle dramatised in the new film *Black Hawk Down*.

'Our boys were shocked by the low morale of the American soldier and they realised the American soldier was just a paper tiger,' Bin Laden said.

'After a few blows, America ... rushed out of Somalia in shame and disgrace, dragging the bodies of its soldiers. America stopped calling itself world leader and master of the new world order.'

That statement has been believed across the Middle East since the failed Somalia operation: Americans quailed at the first sign of violence.

If you were a Muslim and died in a martyrdom operation you went directly to paradise and your own 70 virgins. Even if you got caught at least you got your televised day in court and a chance to broadcast your cause to the world. For such men, the images of Guantanamo have been a salutary lesson.

Americans react differently when their country is attacked. The photographs show would-be extremists that there is no glory, just Day-Glo overalls, mosquitoes and anonymity. In the war against terrorism, that is as significant as any victory on the battlefield.

Iraq

One call from the great dictator and another day of designer torture began in prison

4 August 2002

When Saddam took power he stamped out all opposition. Marie Colvin talks to a man who endured his brutality.

It was not just the torture. It was the morning telephone call. Every day the duty officer at Abu Ghreib prison in Baghdad would call for instructions on the 'programme' for the 33 men isolated in one wing. When it was Saddam Hussein on the phone, the officer would stand to attention. Beating on the back today? Yes, sir.

Four times a day, the prisoners were taken from their cells and tortured. The methods varied – whipped with cables, battered with wooden beams, barbecued alive. No questions were ever asked, no information was ever sought. This was sadism Saddam-style – systematic and with extraordinary personal involvement and attention to detail.

The prisoners had started out as a group of 54 senior military men and civilian officials in the leadership of the Iraqi regime alongside Saddam before he seized the presidency more than two decades ago. They were all men who had been close to him, all men who, his spies had told him, were strong enough to oppose his bid for control.

Twenty-one were executed within a week of their arrest, another 14 during 3½ years of imprisonment. Only 19 survived. They went home to their families as living skeletons.

One of these men, who now lives in exile in Europe, has decided to tell their horrific story for the first time in the hope that it will inspire Iraqis to fight Saddam.

This survivor, who wants to be known as Mohammed, has taken 19 years to summon the courage to give the first insider's account of the barbaric methods Saddam used to consolidate absolute power.

In Iraq in the late 1970s, Saddam was vice-president but increasingly became more powerful than Ahmed Hassan al-Bakr, the elderly head of state.

Other members of the ruling Revolutionary Command Council (RCC) whispered to each other that there was 'something fishy' about Saddam, Mohammed remembered. Those close to him and his family were being given powerful positions at home while strong military officers were being sent abroad to far-off diplomatic posts.

Saddam was not too powerful to be criticised to his face. 'In those days we could say to him, "You are wrong", and we did,' Mohammed said. 'But he was a very good actor.

'Once, when I said to him, "You are behaving like a corrupt businessman, accumulating money and palaces", Saddam invited me out to the country.

'We had a barbecue in a small house with two rooms. He was warm and generous. "See," Saddam said, "this is the reality. I am a simple man." Of course, later he built a palace on that same spot.'

On 12 July 1979, Saddam made his move. He called a secret meeting of Ba'ath officials and said there had been a coup plot against him. He also said the president wanted to resign for health reasons.

The charges were false – there had been no conspiracy – but Saddam had an extensive network of spies and security agents to build his case.

The arrests began. Most of the detainees were members of the ruling RCC. Saleh al-Saidi, a powerful colonel who had jokingly referred to Saddam as 'Al Capone', was arrested at his command centre in western Iraq. Shukri Sabri al-Hadithi, ambassador to Morocco, was arrested and his cousin Murtada, a foreign minister, was also seized.

The prisoners did not take their arrests seriously – until all 54 were taken to the offices of the Mukhabarat, the intelligence agency. They were beaten, questioned perfunctorily and taken into a hallway. 'We were put facing the wall,' said Mohammed. 'Then we were told to turn and our sentences were pronounced. There was no trial.'

Twenty-one were sentenced to death. Thirty-three received sentences of one to 15 years.

After a week they were led into the hall again. 'They told Noori Hamoodi Ahmed [a senior government official] to sit on a chair under a spiral staircase. One man shot him with a Kalashnikov. There was blood all over the walls.'

An hour later Ismail al-Najar, another senior bureaucrat, was put on the chair and the others watched as 15 rounds were fired into him.

On 8 August a further 19 were executed. By then, those sentenced to imprisonment had been taken to a wing of Abu Ghreib – where the torture began.

'On day one, I was taken four times to be beaten on the back,' said Mohammed. 'This was 30 to 80 strokes each time. On day two, I was beaten chest and face. You have to realise we were beaten with thick cables with metal in the middle. Every hit you bleed.

'Day three, on the head. Day four, we were told "put your legs out of the cell" and beaten. We weren't taken out of our cells; maybe the guards were tired.

'All of us found the beating on the legs most painful. When they finished, they made us march in our cells with our bleeding legs. I couldn't believe I was still standing. I thought to myself, "God gave humans amazing resilience."' On day five they were told to stick their hands out of their cells, which were hit on both sides. On day six they were beaten on the back again.

Between torture sessions, each prisoner was told to sit on the floor in the corner of his cell in silence. Anyone who disobeyed was beaten. 'There were days when I wanted to die, but there was no means to commit suicide,' said Mohammed.

The military men tapped to each other in Morse code, making futile plans to overwhelm the guards. They asked each other to take care of their families if they died. They lost track of time.

'We only knew if it was hot or cold,' Mohammed said. 'In the summer they would make us lie under four black blankets. In winter we slept on the floor with no cover.'

The torture grew more sadistic. 'Once they asked me, "What are you thinking?", and when I said "I am thinking of a good meal", they said I was lying and beat me.'

Prisoners were forced to pull hair from each other's beards. They were made to bark like dogs. They were told to sing a song, and if they did not know the words they were beaten.

Small things that had brought Mohammed joy now became horrors: 'When I heard the songs of the birds in the morning, I thought only that now the torture will resume.'

He remembers the day when they were all beaten with wooden beams and a blow knocked out a piece of Abdel al-Qubaisi's skull. It bounced off a prison wall.

'It was a triangular piece from the lower right of his skull,' Mohammed said. 'Two of us put it back in, sort of fitted it as best we could, and wrapped his head with a dirty cloth. He lost his mind for two weeks.'

When al-Qubaisi, deputy commander of the Ba'ath party, regained his senses, the guards resumed torturing him.

On another day Ahmed Wahed Maedi, a prominent colonel, was brought a shirt and trousers, cleaned up and taken away. He came back mentally disturbed but later told a horrific story.

He had been taken, all cleaned up, to see Barzan al-Tikriti, Saddam's half-brother and head of the Mukhabarat. Barzan, whom he knew, had asked about his family and given him a glass of orange juice. After 15 minutes he was taken to a room with no furniture, only a carpet in the middle of the room. Guards put cuffs on his hands and legs.

'They brought my fiancée,' he told Mohammed in a monotone. 'A man came in half-naked. By his accent he was from Tikrit [Saddam's home village]. He started tearing off her clothes. She was screaming and naked. I couldn't do anything so I put my face to the wall and started hitting my head on the wall.'

They forced him around to watch his fiancée being raped. 'She was panicking, choking, fighting and then she was speechless.'

After the rape they brought her an orange juice which looked identical to the one Maedi had been given by Barzan. It was poisoned: she died in 15 minutes. The naked man kicked her to make sure she was dead, kicked Maedi and left.

Then the killings started. The prisoners were herded naked into a basement room where the guards chased and beat them with huge beams of wood.

'We were climbing over each other and trying to use our friends' bodies as shields. Everyone had bones broken. My collarbone shattered,' Mohammed said.

A doctor came with a white coat and stethoscope. Anyone who was injured was to put his hand out through the cell doors. Murtada al-Hadithi, who had been a foreign minister, was told: 'You will be treated first out of respect for your position.'

He was taken away.

'When Murtada came back, he told us the doctor had given him a tablet. He knelt to pray, then he started screaming and collapsed. It was late afternoon. He died at midnight. His cellmates yelled to the guards, but they were told to "sleep with him and shut up".

'The rest of us thought, "He is very lucky". We wished we could follow him.'

A month later, two more were killed. 'They were taken downstairs and given tablets that killed them immediately. They left their bodies and we could smell them after some days. It was hot. The guards thought it was funny. They would yell to the bodies, "Hey, why don't you answer me, you think you are so special?"' Hamid al-Dulaimi, a colonel from a powerful tribe who had been exiled to Nigeria as ambassador before he was called home, suffered the worst fate. 'He was aggressive and Saddam disliked him.'

Dulaimi was tied to a ladder in his cell. Guards then lit timbers under his feet and watched while they burnt, making jokes about a barbecue.

'He screamed for 10 minutes, then he stopped. We did not understand why. All his skin and fat and tendons burnt off. They stopped the fire when his legs were half gone.'

One by one they were killed off. Riad al-Qadoo, a lieutenant-colonel, was made to dance in the centre of a circle of guards while they beat him to death. Mohamed Sabri al-Hadithi, who had been ambassador to Kuwait, died the same way. But the torture did not end there.

Al-Saidi, who had joked about Saddam and Al Capone, was the 14th and last to be killed. He was beaten to death in July 1982.

In 1983 the survivors were released to house arrest and discovered that their families had been sent fake confessions of treason. None recovered fully. Their property had been confiscated and their movements were restricted.

Mohammed escaped in 1991 after the Gulf War. He said he wanted to speak now in the hope that decent Iraqis, both in the regime and outside, would hear the story for the first time and would be encouraged to work against Saddam.

Why the great dictator thinks he can still win: Saddam's mind

2 March 2003

To the outside world it seems astounding that Saddam Hussein has not taken the opportunity to survive. The closer war looms, the more it is a racing certainty that the Iraqi leader will die, buried in the rubble of his bunker, shot through the head with the one bullet he says he keeps for himself, or hanged by a vengeful mob while trying to flee.

Why won't he just cough up his weapons of mass destruction, add the documentation the United Nations wants, and in one swoop defuse the American-led campaign to oust him? Or, if he can't bring himself to do that, why not step down, hand over to an ally, and leave a disappointed Washington pretty much forced to call the war off? Why commit suicide?

Because that's not how he sees it. Looking out at the world through Saddam's eyes, the perspective is fairly distorted. Some of that view even Tony Blair might envy.

No one disagrees in cabinet, for example; the last time a minister begged to differ, the Iraqi leader took him next door and shot him. So no one tells him uncomfortable truths.

There appears no shortage of love and loyalty. When Saddam

met a group of civil administrators last week, they chanted with joy and pledged to be a 'sword in his hand'. And these were the men who deal with things such as pensions, not sarin gas.

But in a country ruled by fear the reality is very different. Saddam is a master of manipulation and self-delusion. In a rambling three-hour television interview with the American television star Dan Rather last week, he spoke in lofty terms of Iraq as a beacon of freedom, peace and humanity; this from a man who has invaded two of his neighbours and driven 4m of his countrymen into exile.

He also explained why Iraq had really won the war in 1991 (it was George Bush Sr who asked for a ceasefire, not him), and that he could never go into exile because that would mean betraying the Iraqi people.

If Saddam's view of home is distorted, the perspective gets even further from the truth when he looks beyond his borders. It should be no surprise that international politics are not his forte. This is a man to whom no one speaks anything he doesn't want to hear and who has travelled out of Iraq only once since taking power in 1979.

That trip would not have given him much insight into world diplomacy – it was to Cuba, where he and Fidel Castro spent most of their meeting discussing their bad backs. Castro sent Saddam to his favourite osteopath.

Those who know him say this lack of understanding of international intricacies is the key to his belief that he can survive a confrontation with America. So far, they say, Saddam believes he is winning on the diplomatic front.

From his perspective, just by sitting in Baghdad he has wreaked havoc among his enemies. He looks out and sees an increasingly divided Europe, with Britain taking the lead in supporting an American-led military strike, backed by Spain and Italy, while France and Germany remain opposed to any war, and the smaller countries are torn between.

He can then see Nato facing one of the greatest tests of its unity since it was founded 54 years ago. It has been riven by a dispute in which France, Belgium and Germany blocked the alliance from making preparations to defend Turkey in case it was attacked by Iraq.

Saddam may also smile with satisfaction at the bitter rows between the US and France and Germany. He will have noted the mutiny of Labour MPs against Blair last week, the most serious since Labour took power.

All that before he even looks to the United Nations Security Council, where Britain and America are pushing for a second resolution, against virulent opposition from France, Russia and China, which say weapons inspections in Iraq should continue.

'Saddam is encouraged, he feels he is on stronger ground,' said Abdel Bari Atwan, the editor of *Al-Quds Al-Arabi*, an independent Arabic newspaper based in London.

'He is loving creating divisions in the western world. He feels he is definitely in a better position now.'

Saddam still thinks he can make a deal. He is like a grudging trader in the souk, conceding inch by inch, unembarrassed about reversing himself.

In the interview with Rather, he insisted he would not destroy the Al-Samoud missile system, as ordered by Hans Blix, the chief UN weapons inspector, because it has a range of more than the 150 kilometres limit set by the United Nations. It seemed a showdown was in the making.

A day after the interview was aired, Iraq had announced it would start destroying the missile system by yesterday's deadline. Crisis averted, as ever at the last moment.

That is the other key to Saddam's belief that he can survive as leader of Iraq. He will spin out every deadline, play for time. He believes if he can hold off the American–British invasion long enough, it will be the heat of summer and all will be put off until next year. By then, something else will come up.

It's not a very graceful strategy, but nor is it, yet, a failure. With 200,000 American troops in the Gulf backed by 40,000 British forces, the ultimate outcome should not be in doubt – but Saddam doesn't seem to have learnt from his earlier miscalculations.

Ghassan Charbel, the assistant editor of the newspaper *Al Hayat*, last week recalled the countdown to war in 1991 after Saddam's invasion of Kuwait. The Yemeni foreign minister was in Baghdad on 16 January, trying to persuade Saddam to pull out of Kuwait and avert conflict. 'Saddam told him: "We will eat the Americans", and sent him home,' Charbel recalled. The next day, the American bombing campaign began.

Saddam did finally agree to withdraw, giving his offer to Yevgeny Primakov, the Arabic-speaking former Russian foreign minister who is an old friend from his stint as ambassador to Iraq. Almost at the same time that Primakov conveyed the last-minute offer, allied troops invaded Kuwait from Saudi Arabia.

Beyond misreading international politics, another thing that makes Saddam unlikely to surrender power is his megalomania. He really believes he is heir to Nebuchadnezzar, the king of Babylon who captured Jerusalem in 586BC, and Saladin, who evicted the crusaders from Jerusalem in 1187. 'He has a deep, mystical relation with Iraq,' said Charbel, who has researched the Iraqi leader for years.

Saddam is not completely relying on his gamble that the Americans will not invade, however. Sources in Baghdad said that in the past month, however confident he may appear, Saddam has started preparing for a possible war.

He has already given orders to his generals on what to do in case of invasion, so that he cannot be found by monitoring his communications. Trenches are being dug around Baghdad and the speculation in the intelligence community is that they will be filled with oil and ignited to obscure the view of troops and from planes, although they will not affect smart bombs.

Like Saddam's other hero, Joseph Stalin, the Russian dictator (Saddam has read all his biographies and can recite long passages from Stalin's speeches), he seems to be planning for a siege. Iraqi sources said he knew he could not win outright, but if he could hold out long enough – and enough civilian casualties appeared on television screens around the world – the United Nations might step in to halt the war.

There is one last scenario. He told a friend, now in exile, he would never be taken alive. 'In my pistol, I will guard one bullet,' the friend quoted Saddam as saying. 'It is for me. I will never be in the hands of the Americans.'

Hunt for Saddam & Son, the murderous duo most wanted: Uday the unstable

23 March 2003

In the early days of Saddam Hussein's presidency, Iraqi magazines carried *Hello!*-style profiles of their new ruling family. There were stories about the president working late, then returning home to help the children with their homework. Saddam and his first wife Sajida were pictured in idyllic settings with their brood – Uday, the elder son, his brother Qusay and the girls, Ragda, Rana and Hala – swimming, picnicking or shopping for clothes.

The reality was that already the children, especially the boys, had grown demanding and imperious. With their father as an example, they considered themselves to be above the law.

Saddam was proud of his elder son and one day took the four-year-old Uday, whom he called his 'cub', out for a treat. Some doting fathers take their sons to the office; Saddam took Uday to watch dissidents being tortured in the cells of a Baghdad prison.

While it was clear that Uday had inherited Saddam's brutal tendencies, at first he showed little sign of his father's drive. After university he was content to swan around Baghdad in his collection of smart cars, adding to his reputation as a playboy and dabbling in business. He hired a woman to jump naked out of a mountain of pilau rice at a party; girls he lusted after risked the health of their male relatives if they refused to submit.

In 1984 Saddam went to a school picnic for his youngest daughter, Hala, where he met Samira Shahbandar, the daughter of Hala's teacher. A beautiful woman from an old Baghdad merchant family, she became Saddam's official mistress and later his second wife.

The liaison infuriated Uday, who believed his mother Sajida had been wronged. Uday could not challenge his father, but on a warm October night in 1988 he snapped.

Kamel Hanna Jejjo, Saddam's favourite retainer and his intermediary to Samira, attended a party for Suzanne Mubarak, wife of the Egyptian president, on an island in the Tigris. Jejjo began shooting off volleys from an automatic rifle – nothing out of the ordinary in Baghdad, but the noise annoyed Uday, who was holding his own party nearby.

After Jejjo ignored Uday's message to stop, the president's son muscled his way into the party, hit Jejjo with a stick and stamped on his back until his spine broke. Jejjo died in hospital that night.

Saddam threatened to execute Uday, then jailed him for three days after Sajida intervened. Uday was sent to Geneva, into the care of an uncle, Barzan. The exile lasted a month until he pulled a knife on a Swiss policeman and was deported home.

'Uday was never the same after he killed Jejjo,' said Ahmed Allawi, a civil engineer who was in Uday's university class. 'Before, he was arrogant and did what he wanted, but after that he was out of control. It was like he went mad.'

The next subject of Uday's wrath was Hussein Kamel el-Majeed, husband to Saddam's daughter Ragda. He had organised Iraq's clandestine overseas procurement network for programmes of biological, chemical and nuclear warfare. After the first Gulf war he had also crushed Shi'ite rebel leaders. But in 1995 Hussein Kamel's relationship with Uday, who was once more back in Saddam's favour, reached crisis point.

During an argument with a cousin, Uday shot his uncle Watban in the leg. Hussein Kamel saw the writing on the wall: nobody was safe from this homicidal 'cub'. That night he packed Raghad and their four children into a Mercedes and fled to Jordan.

With him went his brother Saddam Kamel, Rana and their three children. Saddam Hussein was shaken and humiliated and burnt Uday's fleet of luxury cars.

But Hussein Kamel became disillusioned with his exile. Saddam promised him all had been forgiven, but when he was met at the border by a smiling Uday wearing sunglasses and a sharp suit, he must have known that it was all over.

Within four days Hussein and Saddam Kamel were dead, murdered in their home with other family members by Uday and his gunmen.

As Uday's behaviour became more and more unpredictable, Qusay began to emerge as an increasingly powerful figure. Saddam gave him sensitive jobs in the security forces that had never been offered to, or perhaps had never been desired by, the flashier Uday.

Rumours of Uday's extremes seemed impossible to credit until the arrival in exile of Latif Yahia, who had been forced to undergo plastic surgery by Uday because he wanted a double. Yahia described Uday's private world. Torture videos were weekly entertainment and he had his own torture cells in the basement of the Olympic headquarters.

When Uday was shot in an assassination attempt in 1996, Saddam had little sympathy. But he gave him control of a 30,000-strong militia and a place on the National Security Council, a central body of the regime.

Now, however, there are rumours from Baghdad that in the current conflict the notoriously unstable Uday has been placed under house arrest to prevent him revealing any information to the enemy.

Target Saddam: life on the run

21 December 2003

Marie Colvin in Baghdad; Tony Allen-Mills in Washington

When Saddam Hussein was pulled from his tiny bolthole he had with him a briefcase full of papers. Marie Colvin in Baghdad and Tony Allen-Mills in Washington unravel his eight months in hiding.

In the end it all came down to a hole in the ground and a battered green briefcase. The new Nebuchadnezzar, the man who had rebuilt Babylon to his own glory, crouched on a bin bag in the damp earth as his enemies closed in. But he still had his empire. There it was in his briefcase: documents, hand-written reports – the proof he needed that he was still in power, still in control, still killing, still able to make men tremble at the sound of his name.

'I am Saddam Hussein, the president of Iraq,' he insisted as American soldiers pulled him from his rat hole. The smelly, shaggily bearded figure had made the blinkered blunder of a megalomaniac, however.

In the eight months since the collapse of his government, he had successfully commanded a phantom regime from hiding. His briefcase held copious evidence of a resistance movement run on the lines of a Ba'athist totalitarian state with himself at the top. It contained hundreds of key names – and now all of them were in American hands.

Intelligence sources who revealed its contents last week said they were amazed both by the unexpected extent of Saddam's involvement in the resistance and by his folly in keeping this detailed dossier with him. Does Osama Bin Laden walk around with the name and function of his every military commander in his shoulder bag? Did Martin McGuinness?

Saddam's biggest mistake, however, may have been to believe the reports in his green briefcase. As ever, he was being lied to by his acolytes. The 'battle reports' they couriered to him said what he wanted to hear: that the resistance was defeating the American army. Did he dream that he would soon be restored to power?

As the Ba'athist resistance network is now rolled up by the Americans and their Iraqi allies, thanks to the briefcase, it is possible to reconstruct Saddam's life on the run since the tanks entered Baghdad.

This is also the story of how the Americans tracked down the dictator, overcoming their own initial mistakes and finally using logic, deduction and the help of anti-Saddam Iraqis to pinpoint his lair.

The potted palm looked strangely familiar to Nada Yunis, a 36-year-old Iraqi businesswoman. She suddenly realised as she watched Saddam in a television propaganda broadcast that he was sitting in her living room.

It was 6 April. After a fortnight of uncertainty about the Iraqi dictator's whereabouts as American troops closed in on Baghdad, Yunis's sighting provided the first clear evidence that he had survived a 'decapitation strike' at the start of the US invasion.

Yunis's furnished house in the elite Mansur district of Baghdad was rented by a senior member of the Republican Guard.

As she watched the latest pictures of Saddam talking to senior aides, she recognised the orange curtains. They were sitting on her dining room chairs. The palm stood where she had left it.

It was as close as anyone would come to identifying Saddam's precise location.

Next day a CIA informant claimed to have spotted the elusive president entering another Mansur compound only half a mile from Yunis's home. Within 45 minutes a US Air Force B-1 bomber demolished the compound with four precision-guided bunker-busting 'smart' bombs.

'Just in case he didn't die before, let's have him die again,' joked a US intelligence official.

Of course, he did not die at all. It would take eight frustrating months and one of the world's most expensive manhunts to track him down to a hole in the ground.

Having failed to seize Osama Bin Laden in Afghanistan, the American intelligence officials were in little doubt how difficult it would be to find Saddam, however advanced their technology.

They had some of the world's most sophisticated surveillance tools on hand. The pride of the Pentagon's monitoring 'platforms' is the RC-135 Rivet Joint aircraft, a converted Boeing 707 loaded with antennae for picking up electronic communications.

Flying high over Iraq for up to 10 hours, the RC-135 could pick up signals up to 230 miles away and pinpoint the source of the conversation to within one to three nautical miles.

Further data was provided by spy satellites codenamed Micron and Trumpet. Micron is permanently positioned 22,300 miles above the Middle East and transmits signals to a British monitoring base at Menwith in Yorkshire. Trumpet flies in an elliptical orbit and is configured to monitor mobile phone calls.

Suspect intercepts were instantly compared to computerised profiles of Saddam's voice.

To the massive eavesdropping effort were added drones that scanned potential hiding spots with thermal probes, hoping to detect body movement underground; the radar in Apache attack helicopters, originally designed to target moving tanks, was also used to monitor unusual traffic patterns, such as fast-moving convoys.

It was a technically formidable operation that got US forces nowhere.

Time and again special forces were sent into action in the Sunni triangle between Baghdad and Saddam's stronghold, Tikrit. Somehow the fugitive ex-dictator always seemed to have moved on.

When his sons Uday and Qusay were killed in early July there was a surge of fresh leads from local Iraqi informants. But still no sign of Saddam.

Col James Hickey, commander of the US 4th infantry battalion based at an old Iraqi military compound in Tikrit, was in charge of the hunt. Looking out from his terrace over the River Tigris last

August, as a junior officer at his shoulder shot doves at dusk, Hickey said: 'There is a high probability that this old man is in my area of operations. I'm ready. If he's here, he's got a problem.'

He added: 'If he's here we'll get him. I think it will be sooner rather than later.'

It proved to be a long time later, but Hickey was correct. Saddam was on his patch.

Ad Dawr, a village of nondescript concrete homes, palm trees and sunflower fields beside the Tigris, was the scene of one of the great moments in Saddam's mythology. He boasted that after trying to assassinate Iraq's President Abdel Karim Al-Qassem in 1959, he fled by swimming the river to Ad Dawr, where he holed up to recover from a bullet in the leg.

Only minor elements of the story are true, but Ad Dawr – in the heart of the Sunni triangle – resonated with Saddam. He spent his unhappy, violent childhood in another nearby village, Awja, which he is said to hate. Ad Dawr was safer.

Sure enough, this is where he was found skulking in his hole near a squalid hut last weekend. So far, so predictable. Why was he not found earlier? The reason is that for several months his actions – and those of his protectors – were far less predictable.

Appearances are deceptive. His last hiding place looked as if this man of many palaces had hit bottom – the egg shells on the floor of his tin-roofed shanty kitchen, the few T-shirts and socks still in their plastic wraps. If these are all indications of a life with no baggage, they equally indicate a life with a well-organised support system. Somebody brought him those T-shirts and socks and his eggs and Mars bars.

Nor would he necessarily have felt uncomfortable in simple surroundings. As president, he preferred to spend his nights in small, secure houses in the grounds of his palaces. Identical presidential meals were prepared simultaneously at palaces and houses alike. In his world, it was better that no one knew where he ate or spent the night. In effect, he had lived on the run for years before he vanished from view last April.

There is strong evidence that he remained initially in Baghdad as the Americans took over. Those who admit to giving him shelter there live in sumptuous villas with walled gardens. He would have had little hardship.

In one Baghdad house a woman who admitted that her family had sheltered Saddam for a night showed off the butt of a cigar he had smoked under her roof. 'I will always treasure this,' she said.

In another, the owner revealed that Saddam had given him £2,800 for just one night. A high price for a bed and breakfast?

'No, it was a gift,' he said, smiling. Saddam had brought his own breakfast; he refused even to take tea, albeit politely – no doubt a vestige of the days when he had a taster in every home.

Outside Baghdad conditions were less luxurious. Mud-brick huts are the norm for much of the country. It is believed that he rotated between about 20 such huts once he left the capital for the Sunni triangle.

Iraqi and American sources believe that – realising movement itself would attract detection – he lay low at each place for a few weeks, occasionally travelling in a small, battered car to meet resistance commanders.

The documents in his briefcase show that the resistance members were all approved by the military bureau of Saddam's Ba'ath party, an organisation so ruthlessly intrusive that it investigated army officers' fiancées and promoted men who turned in their own brothers for execution.

One of the documents reveals a 'talent spotting' committee of eight senior officers who recommended former officers, all Sunnis, who had skills the resistance needed.

'Someone would [then] come to your door, and say the president sent us and he needs you to co-operate,' revealed an Iraqi working with the Pentagon to translate the documents into actionable information. Nobody declined.

The resistance had a standard hierarchical military structure.

Baghdad was divided into two sectors, each headed by a former top officer. Under each of these men were four senior officers, then 13 cells each also headed by an officer.

The money and authority for operations came from Saddam. At least five men from Baghdad were able to contact him directly for orders and to deliver information and money, but the cell leaders had the authority to make their own decisions on specific attacks.

'Saddam's strategy was to embarrass and humiliate Americans,' said an Iraqi source who has seen the documents.

'The people working for him had choice of target, within the outline of attacking American soldiers, international organisations, the Iraqi police – any target that would embarrass the Americans. That was the goal. If you, as a cell leader, believed you had the capability, you were authorised to go ahead.'

The operational reports submitted to Saddam sound, in the words of an American military source, 'like a son reporting to his parents'.

This was no guerrilla army running on faith, however. All the reports in the briefcase make clear that the resistance leaders were jockeying for favour and expected money for their successful attacks. Their reports were highly exaggerated. In one, a cell leader reported that his group had killed 200 American soldiers, clearly an exaggeration. He was still paid.

As the number of resistance attacks increased and America's post-war death toll surpassed its wartime total, Hickey's senior officers at Tikrit watched the hunt for Saddam unfold on highly detailed digital maps projected onto wall-mounted computer panels.

Using special antennae mounted on every tank, Humvee and Bradley fighting vehicle, commanders had a pinpoint view of all operations under way across the Tikrit region. Unmanned flying drones beamed back video pictures of target locations.

There were 12 raids after tip-offs. In one, troops raced to a farm-house where they found furniture covered with thick dust in the front room. The back bedroom, however, was newly cleaned. There were pristine Italian suits (favoured by Saddam) in a wardrobe. Bottles of men's cologne and shampoo were on the night table. These were not the luxuries of the average farmer, but the suits' owner was nowhere to be found.

Saddam's lifestyle would soon get tougher, however. The US was about to change its tactics.

Until late summer the Americans were preoccupied with rounding up what Hickey called 'high-value targets', the 55 most wanted members of the old regime and their bodyguards. Then they realised Saddam was with lower-level but highly trusted relatives.

The work that led to him through this tribal network was distinctly low-tech. A pair of junior intelligence specialists used coloured pencils and paper to disentangle Saddam's family tree.

Lt Angela Santana, 31, and Corporal Harold Engstrom, 36, compiled a chart that analysed Saddam's links to the six main tribes of the Sunni triangle – the Husseins, al-Douris, Hadouthis, Masliyats, Hassans and Harimyths.

Santana and Engstrom were members of the 104th Military Intelligence Battalion in Tikrit. She was an executive secretary before joining the army; he a schoolteacher.

It took weeks of legwork before the chart began to take shape. From an initial pool of 9,000 names gleaned from military databases, detainee interrogations and Iraqi informers, Santana and Engstrom steadily zeroed in on the inner tribal circles believed to be close to Saddam.

Their work was initially too slow for the Pentagon. The US military occupation was looking increasingly ragged. Infighting broke out between rival intelligence agencies, seriously hampering the flow of data to US special forces.

By early November General John Abizaid, commander of troops in the region, had decided to disband the separate special operations task forces that were hunting for Saddam.

In their place came a new highly classified commando group known as Task Force 121. Assembled from elite special forces such as the US Army's Delta Force, Navy SEALS and CIA paramilitary operatives, the task force was given the mission of 'neutralising' by capture or assassination any remaining Ba'athist leadership figures. Saddam was HVT-1 – High Value Target number one.

A former CIA station chief declared: 'We have to resuscitate Iraqi intelligence, holding our nose, and have Delta and agency shooters break down doors and take [the Saddam loyalists] out.'

This new task force fared little better than its predecessor. Donald Rumsfeld, the US defence secretary, was becoming increasingly perturbed. 'The fact he's alive is unhelpful,' he said last month.

When Rumsfeld travelled to Iraq to pay a pre-Christmas visit to troops, he was openly amazed that so much American time and money had failed to capture Saddam.

'I'm dumbfounded when I think about it,' he told Major General Raymond Odierno, the 4th infantry's commander.

'The chances of us using that kind of money to find somebody – to figure out how to develop a network and produce the information that would do it – I mean, that ought to be do-able.'

The Americans' problem lay in a shortage of intelligence and linguists to sort through the data that poured in from informants. Things began to change after they brought in the Information Collection Programme (ICP), which is run by the Iraqi National Congress in co-operation with the Pentagon.

In exile, the ICP had helped defectors leave Iraq. It is now operating out of headquarters in Baghdad. Its information and analyses proved accurate.

'We passed their information to units on the ground, and it was solid,' said an American military source.

Santana and Engstrom's detective work identified a close associate of Saddam whose name kept popping up in intelligence reports. He was originally believed to be one of the former dictator's bodyguards, but his significance increased as the two intelligence officers added more information to their chart.

Hickey described him last week as a member of a 'very important family' based in Tikrit, and as 'a middle-aged man with a very large waistline'. He has not been named but has been identified as a former senior officer in Saddam's elite Special Security Organisation.

Three times in early December Hickey's troops tried to capture this man. Each time they missed him, but seized relatives and other individuals who added a little more information to Santana and Engstrom's chart.

Finally, on Friday 12 December, a Special Forces raid on a house in Baghdad netted the 'fat man'.

'When I heard this source was captured I knew we were onto something,' Santana said. 'We had someone who was very close to Saddam talking, so there was a great chance we would find him that night.'

It took only four hours for the captive to spill the beans. He revealed that Saddam was on a farm on the Tigris, and that the soldiers should look for 'an underground facility'.

The farm belongs to Qais Naqim, an apparently insignificant former clerk in the presidential office who had retired because of heart disease some years ago. That he had escaped the attention of American or Iraqi investigators, yet provided Saddam's ultimate bolthole, proves how difficult the hunt had been.

At Naqim's farm Hickey's troops had their rendezvous with history. The underground facility turned out to be a T-shaped hole barely wide enough for Saddam to wriggle into, but wide enough for him to put his hands up in surrender.

Saddam had a gun but did not use it. Few of his resistance commanders appear to have been any braver.

The ICP and Americans are now going on nightly raids together to round up Saddam's network in Baghdad. None of the commanders has put up a fight. All have been found with large amounts of money at their disposal, a key indication of involvement in the resistance, because senior army officers' official salaries are blocked. In one house, £38,000 was found, in another £45,000.

'At first they deny everything,' said an Iraqi source involved in the debriefings. 'They say they were just sitting at home, that they only joined the Ba'ath party because they had to under Saddam.

They were angels! Then, in a few days, they start implicating their colleagues.'

An American military source described the joint raids with the ICP as a 'good combination'.

'They blend in to the neighbourhood, and know the people. We have the expertise in interrogation,' said the source.

Saddam's network is being rolled up in a targeted, meticulous manner. There are none of the mass neighbourhood searches that angered Iraqi civilians earlier in the year.

One night last week a senior Iraqi officer – who had been identified from Saddam's briefcase dossier – drove with an ICP and American team to point out the villa of a resistance colleague. He was given a balaclava to hide his face.

Photos of the house were taken, a GPS location punched in, and plans for an arrest began. The following night the target was seized.

Not everyone believes this is really happening, however. Diehards say Saddam is free. Awja, his home town, is gripped by the rumour about a little girl who was walking in the street crying last week.

A black BMW pulled up and the man inside asked: 'Why are you crying?' She said she was crying because her president was captured. He laughed, and she recognised the laugh. It was Saddam. He gave her money for sweets, and said: 'Stop crying, go to school, and be sure I will never be captured.'

Iraq: the mind behind the horror

7 March 2004

Marie Colvin, Mitchell Prothero in Baghdad; Richard Woods,
Tony Allen-Mills and Nick Fielding

More than 200 Shi'ite worshippers were slaughtered by suicide bombers in Iraq last week. America blames an ally of Osama Bin Laden who, it says, is trying to foment civil war.

Inside the administrative Green Zone, the one small area of Baghdad that is comparatively secure and peaceful, officials were preparing on Friday to mark a new dawn for Iraq. An interim constitution leading to democratic elections was ready for signing: good news after a week that had left the country scarred by religious terrorism on an unprecedented scale.

Television cameras and reporters were on hand. A slogan in Arabic – 'We all participate in a new Iraq' – hung over a table on which fountain pens were laid out. But at the last moment the representatives of Iraq's 15 million Shi'ite community, which was still mourning its dead, refused to sign.

Officials played down the debacle but in private Paul Bremer, head of the Coalition Provisional Authority, was furious. Almost one year on from the invasion, Iraq's volatile mix of Shi'ite and Sunni Muslims, Kurds, Turkomen and other factions are refusing to play the parts that Washington has written for them.

Is it all going to blow up in George W Bush's face during this American presidential election year? Is civil war imminent? After last week such fears cannot be dismissed.

On Tuesday, hundreds of thousands of Shi'ites had gathered in Baghdad and the religious city of Karbala for the festival of Ashura when a series of suicide bombs ripped through the crowds, killing and maiming pilgrims on the holiest day of the Shi'ite year. About 200 died and hundreds more were wounded.

The atrocities were part of a pattern of anti-Shi'ite attacks stretching from northern Iraq across to Pakistan, where terrorists machinegunned crowds in Quetta killing at least 40 people.

The Americans immediately blamed Abu Musab al-Zarqawi, a notorious Jordanian-born terrorist with a bounty of $10 million (about £5.4 million) on his head and links to Al-Qaeda. Such foreigners were trying to foment civil war in Iraq, the Americans claimed, adding that Grand Ayatollah Ali al-Sistani, the main Shi'ite leader, was staying commendably calm.

Al-Zarqawi may well have a hand in attacks in Iraq and he is a useful bogeyman for the Americans to target. But he is not the only problem.

In a mosque in Baghdad last week, Sheikh Moyad al-Baydhani warned of Sunni–Shi'ite tensions and anger against the American occupiers. Al-Baydhani is a follower of another Shi'ite leader, Moqtada al-Sadr, who is a radical willing to urge violence.

'We will wait for permission from [al-Sistani] before we go forward with any violence,' said al-Baydhani. 'But we are ready to fight the Americans for failing to protect Iraq and the Shi'ites.'

Another atrocity, or a change of heart by al-Sistani, could tip the balance. The Arab world fears the worst.

'Iraq is now facing a grim future,' said Abdel Bari Atwan, editor of *Al-Quds*, the well-informed Arabic newspaper based in London.

'Most people in the south, the Shi'ites, now believe the United States cannot guarantee even the basic necessities of life, such as electricity and fuel, let alone security.'

The split between Sunni and Shi'ite Muslims goes back 1,300 years to a battle near Karbala between rival claimants to lead the Muslim caliphate. In the bloodshed, Imam Hussein, a grandson of the prophet Muhammad and a Shi'ite leader, was killed.

Sunni and Shi'ite sects diverged and have followed different customs ever since.

For extremists, antipathy runs deep. Like Osama Bin Laden, al-Zarqawi is not just a Sunni but also a Wahhabi, a fervent believer in fundamentalist Islam. Wahhabis hold that Shi'ites are infidels.

Al-Zarqawi is believed to have been jailed in Jordan in the early 1990s for militant activities. After he was released, he was suspected of plotting to blow up bridges and hotels during millennium celebrations.

He fled to Afghanistan where he set up training camps for militants. Although linked to Al-Qaeda, he kept his distance.

When the Taliban regime was collapsing, al-Zarqawi was badly injured in Kabul, losing a leg, but escaped into Iran and moved on to Iraq where he was treated in hospital. He has since been linked to Ansar al-Islam, a fundamentalist group in the north of Iraq, and also to terrorist cells in Europe.

'Al-Zarqawi is developing a global profile similar to that of Osama Bin Laden,' said MJ Gohel, an international terrorism expert at the Asia-Pacific Foundation. 'In our view he is likely to be the catalyst for creating a system in Europe and the Middle East for providing new recruits for global terror attacks.'

According to American intelligence, al-Zarqawi met Mohammed Ibrahim Makawi, an Al-Qaeda commander, in eastern Iran in February last year as America and Britain prepared to invade Iraq.

In early January this year, al-Zarqawi is believed to have met Hassan Ghul, another Bin Laden emissary. Days later Ghul was captured in the Kurdish border area. According to US intelligence, he was carrying a letter from al-Zarqawi outlining his Iraqi operations.

The letter identifies the Shi'ites as the key to destabilising Iraq, because 'targeting their religious, political and military symbols will make them show their rage against the Sunnis and bare their inner vengeance'.

Whether or not the letter is genuine, the anti-Shi'ite strategy ascribed to al-Zarqawi is an obvious one for a Sunni terrorist seeking to create turmoil in Iraq.

The Shi'ites were oppressed under Saddam Hussein. Last year, in the final weeks of his regime, he had 15 Shi'ites executed in Karbala for trying to celebrate Ashura.

The festival falls on the 10th day of the first month of the new Islamic year. This year was the first for decades that Iraqi Shi'ites could freely celebrate.

Hordes poured into Karbala, beating their chests and ritually cutting their heads. The first bomb exploded in the courtyard of the main shrine. As pilgrims ran for their lives, according to some witnesses, two suicide bombers blew themselves up by the exits. 'It was planned to inflict the maximum number of casualties,' said Khalil Shakir, a guard at the main gate.

More bombs followed. Hassan Hadio, a 22-year-old Shi'ite, saw a man run into a throng of pilgrims and explode. The bomber's head flew 25 yards through the air. As the crowds fled in panic there were more explosions.

The local hospital was overwhelmed by the dead as volunteers offered to donate blood. Ali Hussein, its deputy director, said: 'I don't need people to give blood; I need people to carry bodies.'

In Baghdad there was further carnage when bombs exploded at the shrine of Kazimiya and other Shi'ite sites. In Basra, police officers found a car packed with explosives at a petrol station near the path of a Shi'ite procession. Four suspected terrorists, including two wearing explosive belts, were arrested. In Kirkuk, in northern Iraq, another bomb was defused.

What was remarkable, after such bloodshed, was the reaction of the Shi'ites. If this was an attempt to make them 'bare their inner vengeance', it failed. There was anger – much of it targeted at American troops – but no violence. Can this restraint last?

The fact is that most members of Iraq's Shi'ite and Sunni communities rubbed along peaceably enough under Saddam's yoke and are not blood enemies. Iraq's almost daily violence is the work of a minority of Sunni forces – mostly former Ba'ath party members embittered at the overthrow of Saddam – augmented by foreign Arabs pursuing their own 'jihad'.

The Shi'ites have assassinated former Saddam officials whom they blamed for anti-Shi'ite atrocities, but they have left alone the majority of Sunni, who were not part of Saddam's regime. That restraint has been largely down to al-Sistani, who has been the guiding hand behind Shi'ite political strategy and tactics.

He has refused to meet Bremer, but called for co-operation with the Americans as long as they made it clear that they would be leaving Iraq. He has insisted that the future of the country must be decided by elections, calculating that this would lead to the Shi'ites, who make up 60% of the population, commanding the majority share of power.

His influence was clearly at work last week: restraint in the face of brutal terrorist provocation, followed by the politically devastating boycott of Bremer's showpiece constitutional ceremony.

The danger is that more radical elements in al-Sistani's constituency – such as al-Sadr – are advocating violent confrontation. Some observers fear that last week's violence will reduce al-Sistani's influence and promote the power of the radicals.

'The building blocks of civil war are being put into place,' said Gareth Stansfield, an associate fellow at the Royal Institute of International Affairs in London. 'Three big issues are coming together all at once. The Sunni desire to hold on to power, the Shi'ite resurgence and Kurdish nationalism.'

As the bombs caused mayhem in Iraq last Tuesday, Senator John Kerry was clinching the Democratic nomination for the next American presidential election. He is ready to make Iraq a key issue in his coming battle with Bush.

On Wednesday General John Abizaid, America's top military commander in the Middle East, appeared in Washington to give senators and congressmen an unusually candid appraisal of the situation in Iraq. Although Abizaid said he was 'optimistic' that civil war would not break out between Sunni and Shi'ite Muslims, he warned that the Iraqi security forces still lacked the training to replace American troops.

Even if the coalition does manage to hand over sovereignty as planned at the end of June, many American troops will have to stay in the country. Last week Sir Jeremy Greenstock, the senior British representative in Iraq, said that British troops would have to remain for 'at least another two years, maybe more'.

Any big losses of American forces would revive Democratic accusations that Bush blundered into Baghdad without thought for the consequences. On the other hand, Kerry could be badly undermined if coalition moves towards Iraqi democracy make progress.

For all the carnage and failure to find weapons of mass destruction, most Americans still believe that Bush was right to go to war against Saddam. The big question mark is the unquantifiable threat of further violence between Sunnis and Shi'ites or against American forces.

Alarmists play on the Sunni–Shi'ite divide, but it is more complex. In the main cities, Shi'ites and Sunnis intermarry, go into business together and live side by side. In other areas tribal, family and class ties are as important as religion and have so far ensured that neither Sunni nor Shi'ite populations have become unified blocs.

The danger is that more atrocities will cause both communities to retreat into religious allegiances for safety.

In Baghdad yesterday, Bremer was still in intense talks with Iraqi leaders, trying to secure agreement for the interim constitution. Officials hoped that it would be signed this week. But as Greenstock warned, the days in the run-up to the handover of sovereignty in June are likely to be 'bloody'.

THE RELIGIOUS DIVIDE HAMPERING A NATIONAL REBIRTH

Under Saddam Hussein the Sunni Muslim minority dominated the Shi'ite majority for decades. There are about 20 million Arabs in Iraq, of whom about 75% are Shi'ite and 25% are Sunni.

After the first Gulf war, a Shi'ite uprising in the south of the country was brutally suppressed by Saddam. They now see the chance of dominating any freely elected government.

The Sunni minority are concentrated north of Baghdad, along the Tigris and Euphrates rivers. Beyond them in the northeast there are up to 5 million Kurds, who want their own autonomous region.

The dispute over the interim constitution last week centred on a clause that would have given the Kurds considerable power in deciding the long-term future of the country. Though the Shi'ites and Kurds are separated geographically and have no territorial disputes, the Shi'ites refused to allow the minority such power.

Other minorities include Turkomans, Iranians and Arab Christians.

Face to face with death in a 'pacified' Iraqi town

BAGHDAD

29 October 2006

A few months ago Saab al Bour was a showpiece town where Americans were building schools and fixing the water and electricity supplies. Even the Shi'ites and Sunnis rubbed along.

The dusty settlement of sand-coloured brick buildings six miles northwest of Baghdad is now a ghost town, shorn of its residents by Iraq's relentless sectarian wars. They took to the road when mortars, 15–20 a day, started crashing into the town, fired by Sunni extremists targeting the Shi'ites.

Sunni neighbour turned on Shi'ite neighbour in a struggle that eventually drove out 90% of the original population of 30,000.

Before I set out for Saab al Bour yesterday, I had been assured that it had been 'pacified'. Our two UH-60 helicopters flew low out of Baghdad's fortified green zone, swooping over the capital, its once-crowded arteries devoid of traffic.

We banked over flat stretches of baked earth and a few patches of green and came in low to a wasteland in the middle of the town, guided by grey smoke rising from two armoured cars that had been sent ahead to secure the landing. This did not look like a pacified town.

American soldiers in desert camouflage uniforms leapt out of the helicopters to set up a perimeter, 6ft apart, around us. Crouching, M16s perched on their shoulders pointing out in a circle, they eyed the mud and sand brick houses suspiciously. Only a mangy yellow dog moved.

Within half an hour of my arrival Apache helicopter gunships filled the sky, firing on insurgents just the other side of a canal with loud blasts of their cannons.

In the town's police station, sandbagged and covered with camouflage netting, Lieutenant-Colonel Dave Thompson sat with two members of the local council. The police were supposed to be there to brief us, but they had been called to an 'incident'. Later one policeman told me the incident was an attack on their commander's home and they had rushed to help.

This is just a microcosm of the problems besetting Iraq. The town of Saab al Bour had been quiet when the American army, backed up by Iraqi soldiers, was based there. It sits on the edge of Anbar province, a Sunni stronghold. Shortly after the soldiers handed over to the Iraqi police at the end of last month, the fighting began.

Khaled Lateef, a councillor who stayed throughout, said the mortars were fired by Sunni extremists from across the canal, aimed mostly at the Shi'ite areas.

The police were outgunned by the insurgents. The Iraqi and American armies had to move back to pick up where they had left off. Thompson tried to be upbeat: 'We're down to one mortar a day,' he said. 'We're back to rebuilding.'

Every time one tiny corner of Iraq is fixed, another chunk falls apart. Take Yarmouk, a wealthy Baghdad neighbourhood famed for its manicured gardens, fashionable boutiques and spacious villas. Living just a mile from the American troops in the green zone, residents have until recently felt far removed from Iraq's sectarian violence.

They were wrong. A district that for decades was 70% Sunni and 30% Shi'ite, where members of the two different strands of Islam lived side by side, mingled and even married, has been 'cleansed' of 90% of its Shi'ite residents. Their choice was to leave or die.

A doctor forced out of Yarmouk by Sunnis described the thugs' methods. 'They kidnapped my son,' he said. 'They broke his nose, then they raised a pick-up truck on a jack, turned the truck on and put his legs under the spinning tyres. All the skin was torn off.' After payment of £10,500, he got his son back. The 20-year-old university student wore shoes last week for the first time in months.

'I hired security guards but they fired an RPG [rocket-propelled grenade] at my house. I couldn't stand it any more. We left Yarmouk.'

Yarmouk is a shocking example of Iraq's sectarian strife because the Sunni–Shi'ite violence is usually portrayed as a cancer confined to slums run by radical militias. But this area was home to an educated elite who played tennis at the club and went abroad for the summer.

The slaughter consuming Sunni and Shi'ite Muslims in roughly equal measure may appear like anarchy from afar, but a closer look reveals a sinister plot. Starting in the west of the city, Sunni militants have seized district after district, creating their own zone that extends into the heart of Baghdad.

The Shi'ites are not innocent. Since the explosion at a Shi'ite mosque in Samarra in February, their militias have exacted vicious revenge. The morgue classifies victims according to their injuries; if a victim has been beheaded, he is a Shi'ite killed by Sunnis. If he has been killed by a power drill to the head, he is a Sunni murdered by Shi'ites. Most victims have been tortured. Bodies are dumped by the roadside and lie there for hours.

Nouri al-Maliki, the prime minister, vowed last week – not for the first time – to clamp down on the militias. He has made scant progress, partly because he depends on a political party allied to a Shi'ite militia. The US Operation Together Forward launched in August to pacify Baghdad has failed dismally.

While the Shi'ites are fired by blind vengeance, the Sunnis appear to have a plan.

They are trying to split Baghdad in half in advance of a proposal to carve Iraq into three federal regions.

Most of the country divides easily. The north is mainly Kurdish, the south Shi'ite, and the central desert region Sunni. Baghdad, too mixed to divide without a massive population transfer, is the sticking point in this plan.

But look at the changing map of Baghdad today. From the western suburb of Abu Ghraib, neighbourhoods have fallen under the control of Sunni radicals, their Shi'ite residents sent fleeing, their homes abandoned or taken by Sunni families, their businesses bombed, shuttered or reopened under Sunni ownership. Baghdad is on its way to becoming two cities, the west Sunni, the east and north Shi'ite.

The militias conducting this ethnic cleansing have a deadly system, described by an Iraqi intelligence officer and former residents of Yarmouk. First they terrorise the area, shooting children selling ice or black-market petrol on the street. Then they go for the shops and businesses.

It worked in Yarmouk. The Amari bakery was run by three brothers; two were killed and one injured. He fled. The bakery is now the Ahmed bakery, run by a Sunni. Abu Allah, also a Shi'ite, ran the grocery. He was shot and survived, but fled Yarmouk.

In the third stage, the Sunni militants go after the police, attacking checkpoints until they pull out. Then they target Shi'ite residents. 'You wake up to a bullet in your garden. Or a note saying leave this area in 36 hours. After all the killings, you pack up and go,' said another former resident, who knew of eight people killed near his home.

The Shi'ite houses and shops are considered '*ramim*', Arabic for spoils of war, and handed to Sunni families.

There is a police station in Yarmouk but the police are holed up inside, powerless to intervene, because the insurgents are better armed. The best way to bribe a policeman these days is with bullets; they stop expensive cars and where once they demanded money, they now want ammunition. Last week 18 policemen were killed in a Sunni ambush in Khan Bani Sa'ad, 20 miles north of Baghdad, because they had run out of bullets.

Two police officers from the Yarmouk precinct described their predicament. One was a Shi'ite married to a Sunni, the other a Sunni married to a Shi'ite. One had been shot seven times on his doorstep; the other had his car blown up.

When the Sunni officer's in-laws came to stay, he woke to find a note wrapped around a bullet. It read: 'There are Shi'ite in your house. Your future is this bullet if they do not leave.' They left.

There are some signs of social resistance. On Thursday in Mansour, which borders Yarmouk, 3,000 people, mostly families, gathered at the Hunting Club to celebrate Eid, the end of Ramadan. The skirts were low on the girls' hips, there was barely a hijab in sight, and Abir the DJ spun western and Arabic discs.

'This is our way of fighting the terrorists who are trying to destroy life in Iraq,' said Hasanain Mualla, the manager.

And then there is the bravest ice-cream seller in Baghdad, a Sunni. When Sunni militants demanded he close because there had been no ice cream in the time of the prophet Muhammad, he told them: 'I'll stop selling ice cream when you ride up on camels to threaten me. There were no BMWs in the time of prophet Muhammad either.'

The butcher of Baghdad awaits his death sentence

BAGHDAD

5 November 2006

In 24 years of tyrannical rule, Saddam Hussein brought death to millions in three wars, torture to the countless pitiful souls incarcerated in his dungeons and isolation from much of the world to the once-proud country that he cowed.

Today Iraqis expect to see the leader who terrorised them condemned to face a hangman's noose for just one of his many crimes – the execution of 148 Shi'ite men from the village of Dujail, 40 miles north of Baghdad, in retaliation for an attempt on his life there in 1982, when he had been in power for only three years.

The country is braced for the verdict amid fears that the dictator's Sunni supporters will mount revenge attacks on Shi'ite areas.

In a clear echo of the mood of most Iraqis, Nouri al-Maliki, the prime minister, said yesterday that he hoped Saddam would be given 'what he deserves' when the verdict is handed down.

If, as expected, Saddam is convicted of crimes against humanity and stands in the dock to hear his sentence, I will watch with that particular attention that comes from fascination and disgust. I have reported on the misery that he has inflicted on his countrymen for more than 20 years, from the ill-judged invasion of Iran that left more than a million dead, to his equally disastrous foray into Kuwait, which left his nation in ruins.

He has cast a dark shadow of evil over every moment I have spent in Iraq – a man who had personally tortured some of his victims and even walked his young sons through his prisons to witness the barbarity.

Today's case dates back 24 years to an ambush in which 10 gunmen fired at his convoy. In revenge, the surviving villagers testified, Saddam had hundreds of them arrested and tortured. As well as the 148 executed, a further 399 men, women and children were consigned to a desert camp.

The survivors say they relish the prospect of Saddam suffering the same punishment that he meted out to so many others. He ordered myriad death sentences for crimes as petty as insulting him or his sons, Qusay and Uday, sometimes in remarks conveyed to the authorities by teachers overhearing their pupils' accounts of conversations at home. Nowhere was safe in Saddam's Iraq.

The chief judge is due to read out a 200-page verdict on Saddam and seven co-defendants. Also facing possible death sentences will be Barzan al-Tikriti, his half-brother and intelligence chief, and Taha Yassin Ramadan, the former vice-president.

It will be the culmination of a bitterly divisive case that began in October last year in a crowded and chaotic courtroom where Saddam and the others heard shocking testimony from their seats in a heavily guarded 'cage'.

A Dujail woman who was 16 in 1982 testified that she had been hung by her wrists, then by her ankles. She was tortured with electric shocks, beaten with cables and forced to watch her family being killed, she said. The court was told that by the time the hang-man received a list of 148 men to be executed, 46 had already died under torture.

Saddam's cold disregard was emphasised when he intimated that he had no reason to recall Dujail's destruction or the deaths of men, women and children. 'It's not as if Saddam Hussein did not have [other] work to do,' he told the judge.

His contempt for the villagers reflected his attitude to far blood-ier campaigns against the Kurds in the north and Shi'ites in the south. In his 1988 campaign against the Kurds, he unleashed his army on northern Iraq and killed 100,000, including 5,000 in the village of Halabja, where chemical weapons rained down death.

In 1991, after the Americans drove Saddam out of Kuwait, he killed a similar number of Shi'ites in the south, mowing them down with helicopter gunships when they dared to rise up against him.

Saddam and his cousin, Ali Hassan al-Majeed, known as Chemical Ali for his role in the poison gas attack, both face the charge of genocide for the Kurdish campaign in a separate trial.

The dictator's complete lack of remorse is striking. He seemed genuinely puzzled when confronted by testimony of torture and killing. 'Where's the crime?' he asked the judge, arguing that such reprisals were only to be expected against traitors.

The 55-week trial was meant to mark the start of Iraq's Nuremberg – the exposure of an evil regime. Instead, dogged by delays and interruptions, it has veered between tragedy and farce.

Saddam harangued the judges, insisted that he was still the president of Iraq and told the court to 'go to hell'. Two judges were changed: one resigned and a second was forced to step down after saying that Saddam had never been a dictator. Three defence lawyers were murdered.

Amnesty International has been among the strongest critics of the trial, arguing that it was 'a deeply flawed process'. American officials in Baghdad were relieved that it had not collapsed. 'A verdict on Saddam is what we wanted and at last that's what we're getting,' said one.

Saddam's case will automatically go for review to an appellate chamber, Iraq's highest court. If it upholds the outcome, he will face the gallows 30 days later.

Saddam's death could go a long way towards curbing the insurgency that is tearing Iraq apart. Most of the Sunni militants are former members of his Ba'ath party, fighting to win back the power they have lost. They still harbour the faint hope that he will lead them again.

The crime he will never answer for is the ruination of the lives of millions of Iraqis who survived the wars and repression, but are still condemned to lives of chaos and despair.

'I watched Saddam die'

31 December 2006

The knock on the door came just before 6am. Saddam Hussein's executioners were disguised with black balaclavas.

He spent his last minutes yesterday in the sordid bowels of Iraqi military intelligence headquarters, once home to his own torturers and killers.

Just as the dawn call to prayer was beginning over the city, he was led, shambling in leg irons, to the scaffold to pay the price for his crimes against the Iraqi people.

'We took him to the gallows room and he looked like he wondered what was going on,' said Mowaffak al-Rubaie, the Iraqi government's national security adviser, who saw him die. 'He looked at the gallows not believing what was going to happen.'

As the world reacted with mixed jubilation and condemnation to the hanging, Rubaie revealed that the deposed dictator muttered as he was taken to his death: 'Do not be afraid; it is where we all go.'

Rubaie was among the 15 people in the ill-lit room that was Saddam's last sight on earth. The former Iraqi dictator showed no remorse, said Rubaie, speaking by telephone from Baghdad.

'He was respected throughout before and after the execution. We followed rigorously international and Islamic standards.'

After the dramas of Friday night, when Iraqi officials said Saddam's death was imminent but his lawyers tried to stay his execution with an appeal to a United States court, his fate was set early yesterday.

Nouri al-Maliki, the Iraqi prime minister, had signed the death warrant before going to celebrate his son's wedding, and the presidential council had endorsed it.

The American jailers who had custody of Saddam were ordered to surrender him to the Iraqi government. They offered him tranquillisers but Saddam refused. 'We received physical custody of Saddam Hussein around 5.30am from the coalition forces, and we took over and he became ours,' said Rubaie.

As US troops stood guard outside, Saddam was first led to a sparse and unheated holding room in the bowels of the headquarters of Iraqi military intelligence. It would not have been lost on him that his own security forces had tortured and killed many people in the same grim building. Saddam was left for about half an hour to contemplate his fate. Iraqi law provides that a condemned man be allowed a final cigarette and a meal before his execution.

'He was handcuffed and we took him and sat him down,' said Rubaie. 'There was a judge, a deputy general, deputy minister of justice, deputy minister of interior, a couple of other ministers, myself and a doctor.' After formalities they took him through 'a huge file' of documents detailing his trial.

'The judge took him through the conviction. He was silent until he saw a video camera, and then began shouting slogans such as "God is great". He started his rhetoric: "Long live Islam, down with

Persia", down with this and that. He started shouting his head off.' Rubaie made a last gesture of mercy. 'His handcuffs were a little tight, and hurt him, and I instructed the guards to loosen them.'

The formalities over, the four masked executioners stepped forward, taking his hat and scarf. Short, tubby and dressed in leather jackets, they looked more like Al-Qaeda killers in an amateur terrorist video than those responsible for carrying out the sentence of death on a former head of state. Even though Saddam had shrunk in stature since the days of his pomp, he towered over them.

He had dressed for death in clothes sewn by his personal Turkish tailor: black trousers, shined black shoes, a starched white shirt, black pullover and a black wool overcoat that protected him against the deep chill of his remaining minutes in the execution suite. His hair was dyed his signature black, but he had heavy bags under his eyes.

In sight of a new hemp noose hanging from the ceiling of the dank room, the executioners removed his handcuffs to tie his hands behind his back. As he stood close to the trapdoor one wrapped Saddam's black scarf around his neck to shield it from rope burns.

When they went to put the black hood over his head, he mumbled: 'That won't be necessary.' The noose was slipped over his head.

He stood looking almost bewildered, and an executioner awkwardly tightened the knot of the noose on the left side of his neck.

Even on the brink of death Saddam had not forgotten the video camera. Just before he dropped through a trapdoor on a platform surrounded by red railing, he shouted the Muslim profession of faith, 'God is great and Muhammad is his prophet' and 'Palestine is Arab'.

'He was standing with the rope round his neck,' said Rubaie. 'The executioner started reading verses from the Koran, "There is no God but Allah and Muhammad is his messenger". He repeated it twice and [Saddam] went down in no time.' The hangman pulled a lever, and Saddam dropped silently about 3 feet through a metal trapdoor. It was 6.10am. Rubaie said he died instantly. 'It was so, so quick, totally painless and there was no movement after that.'

Sami al-Askari, who represented the prime minister at the hanging, said he 'heard his neck snap'. A video appearing later on Arabic websites showed Saddam dangling on the rope, his neck apparently broken.

Saddam hung from the rope for about 10 minutes, watched by the audience of about 15 people who could see him dangling under the platform. A doctor checked that his heart had stopped, then one of the executioners untied him. There was blood on the rope. The executioners put him in a white body bag and took photographs as proof for diehard loyalists that Saddam was dead. Iraqi television broadcast a still photograph of the last image of the dictator, his neck at an unnatural angle, sticking out of the white shroud.

Munir Haddad, an Iraqi appeals court judge, also witnessed the execution. He said afterwards: 'One of the guards present asked Saddam Hussein whether he was afraid of dying. Saddam said, "Why would I? I spent my whole life fighting the infidels and the intruders."

'Another guard asked him, "Why did you destroy Iraq, and destroy us? You starved us, and you allowed the Americans to occupy us." His reply was, "I destroyed the invaders and … I destroyed the enemies of Iraq, and I turned Iraq from poverty into wealth."

'Saddam was normal and in full control. He said, "This is my end. I started my life as a fighter and as a political militant. So death does not frighten me."

'He said, "We're going to heaven, and our enemies will rot in hell."

'When he was taken to the gallows, the guards tried to put a hood on his head, but he refused. Then he recited verses from the Koran. Some of the guards started to taunt him.'

The guards chanted the name of the Shi'ite firebrand cleric Moqtada al-Sadr. 'Who is Moqtada?' Saddam sneered.

'A cleric who was present asked Saddam to recite some spiritual words,' Haddad said. 'Saddam did so, but with sarcasm. These were his last words, and then the cord tightened around his neck and he dropped to his death.'

Sunni sheikhs turn their sights from US forces to Al-Qaeda

9 September 2007

Former insurgents queue to take money and promise to back the coalition in a military volte-face. Marie Colvin reports from Jurf as Sakhr, Iraq.

Four months ago the scene would have been unthinkable. Captain Henry Moltz of the 501st Parachute Infantry Regiment led a small group of men up the deserted street to a single-storey municipal building of mellow ochre brick that had been cracked by mortar blasts during months of ruinous fighting with Sunni insurgents.

At the entrance he was greeted with a kiss by Sheikh Sabah al-Janabi, a leading member of the tribe that had spearheaded many of the pitiless Sunni attacks on American forces in and around the little town of Jurf as Sakhr, 25 miles south of Baghdad.

As Moltz, 28, ducked out of the sun into the sparsely furnished interior last Thursday, a second sheikh was waiting for him with another kiss and a look of eager expectation. Moltz swiftly put him at his ease. 'Sheikh, we have the first payment,' he declared.

An aide pulled from his knapsack a thick, heavy wad of used notes tied with rubber bands, and placed it on a table. Then came another, and another, until the table was piled high with 19 bundles of 2.5 million dinars – each worth $38,000 (£19,000) in all.

Moltz looked the second sheikh, Taleb al-Janabi, in the eye. 'If you keep to your contract and keep fighting the enemy, we owe you the balance,' he said.

The balance is $189,000 (£93,000), to be paid over three months if the sheikh sticks to his side of the bargain and drives out the largely foreign fighters of Al-Qaeda in Iraq who have set up camp in date palm groves along the banks of the Euphrates in Ruwiya, to the west.

Taleb nodded acknowledgment of the deal. The bricks of cash were bundled into a plastic bag and he sat on a sagging sofa, cradling the money contentedly in the lap of his grey dishdasha.

Now it was the turn of a third sheikh, Hamid al-Janabi, to step up to the battered table, where three documents had been pinned down against the breeze of a fan by a coffee cup, a mobile phone and a handheld radio.

As he signed them in green ink, it was possible to make out three blue dots on the back of his hand – a traditional tattoo denoting membership of a Sunni tribe that had been allied to Al-Qaeda and had helped to make life hell for the Americans in a fertile strip of land that became one of the most perilous in Iraq.

More bricks of dinars worth just over $30,000 (£15,000) were handed over, the downpayment on an agreement worth $181,600 (£90,000). According to the United States government purchase order-invoice voucher that Hamid signed, he had undertaken to supply 'cops' to the quantity of 'one (force)'. His contract required him to provide 160 tribesmen to fight insurgents in Farisiya, to the northwest, and prevent them from attacking American troops.

The 'cops', who will earn the hefty local rate of $370 (£180) a month, have been fingerprinted and retina-scanned and will carry US identity cards. They have already set up checkpoints and clashed with Al-Qaeda fighters whom they supported before switching sides to the Americans.

One of the younger members of Moltz's A Company acknowledged that he found it hard to grasp such a rapid shifting of alliances.

'I'm not sure about this,' he said. 'Two months ago, these guys were shooting at us. Now we're supposed to be friends. It's kind of hard when you know that guy blew up your buddy.'

Moltz, a Texan who has lost three close comrades in the attacks of the past year, said simply: 'They used to want to kill me, now they want to sign a contract with me. It's hard to get your head around but it is working.'

Taleb and Hamid were the latest recruits to a programme that could prove pivotal in some areas to the prospects for the American 'troop surge' under General David Petraeus, the US commander in Iraq.

When Petraeus appears before Congress tomorrow to deliver his report on the progress of the surge since troop numbers rose from 130,000 in February to 160,000 in June, he will be able to point to several startling successes in parts of Iraq where violence has abated.

Although fighting continues to exact a grim toll of American soldiers and Iraqi civilians alike in towns and cities where it is hard to see hope, the recruitment of enemy sheikhs to the coalition cause has made officers such as Moltz optimistic for the first time in four years of brutal insurgency.

The initiative is being run under the euphemistic title of 'concerned citizens programme'. 'We thought of calling it the ex-terrorist programme but that didn't fly,' one officer joked.

In the area where Moltz's A Company operates, the number of improvised explosive devices (IEDs) detonated against American troops fell from 30 in May to none in August. Nobody is saying the problems have gone away. However, the policy of allying US forces with Sunni insurgents to confront Al-Qaeda has proved so effective to the west of Baghdad in Anbar province – where Falluja and Ramadi used to be the terrorist strongholds – that President George W Bush described it as one of the safest parts of Iraq during a flying visit last week.

Four American soldiers nevertheless died in combat operations in Anbar last Thursday – a reminder, if any were needed, that after so much war, any peace remains fragile. American deaths in Iraq have now passed 3,760 and the number of Iraqi civilians killed last month alone was officially put at 1,773. Independent estimates of civilian deaths go as high as 2,800.

Some critics also worry that the deals with Sunni sheikhs might ultimately turn them into warlords, even if the stated aim is for their private armies to be absorbed into the Iraqi security forces as soon as possible.

However, the agreements signed in Jurf as Sakhr, Babil province, after a year of intensive fighting seem to point to a way forward, both in protecting American soldiers from attack and in crushing Al-Qaeda.

In the past year the Americans based in Babil have endured one of the most relentlessly ferocious onslaughts seen by any US forces in Iraq. They found themselves on a Sunni–Shi'ite faultline that runs to the south of Baghdad's suburbs, and became targets for Iraqi militants on both sides of the religious divide even before Al-Qaeda arrived to compound the misery.

The trouble went back to 2003, when the Iraqi army was disbanded after the fall of Saddam Hussein. Members of the Janabi clan, many of whom had been elite soldiers, returned home bitter at their loss of power to the Shi'ite majority.

They formed the backbone of the Sunni insurgency in the province, establishing makeshift bases among the groves of the Euphrates and its canals.

But this predominantly Sunni area also contains the Shi'ite towns of Iskandariya and Musayyib, where the Mahdi Army holds sway.

The Mahdi militias rose up in a bloodthirsty quest for vengeance after the Shi'ite Askariya shrine at Samarra was bombed in February 2006. They attacked seven Sunni mosques in Babil and then turned their anger on American troops.

US losses were heavy – 51 American soldiers have died in Babil in the past 10 months – and Moltz's A Company faced the grinding daily certainty of an attack.

Mortars and rockets rained down on its Jurf as Sakhr compound, little more than a collection of shipping containers with five camp beds each where the men snatched what sleep they could behind concrete walls.

Whenever they left their outpost, they knew there was every chance of coming under attack, whether from snipers or roadside bombs. 'It was crazy,' said Captain Kevin McDaniel, a platoon leader. 'On one patrol in December, we hit three IEDs and an ambush.'

On that particular patrol, McDaniel and his men were driving north up the Euphrates when the lead vehicle was hit by by the first improvised explosive device. 'The second one was really big,' McDaniel said. 'They had dug a tunnel under the road and placed a ridiculous amount of explosive there. It blew the front off a Humvee. The crater was up to my chin and 12 feet wide.'

When he followed the detonating wire into a field to investigate, gunmen opened up from behind the palms. 'We fired off more than 1,000 rounds and called in Apache helicopters,' he said. 'On the way back we hit a third IED. I couldn't believe it.'

A series of disasters befell the men in rapid succession. Staff Sergeant Christopher Brerard, a company favourite, was killed when insurgents detonated explosives hidden beneath a roof where he was keeping watch. 'You felt if it could happen to him, it could happen to anyone,' McDaniel said.

Another member of the company lost both legs to an IED, and a third who was wounded in the head has had nine brain operations and might never recover.

The outpost was mortared on Thanksgiving evening; the company's Christmas dinner was blown up; and at one point a lorry pulled up to the blast wall and gunmen who jumped out started blasting away at a watchtower.

Nobody was hurt in the latter incidents but morale hit rock bottom. The company rarely saw the enemy and there seemed no prospect of a let-up in the cycle of violence. The beginning of the troop surge in February went virtually unremarked in Jurf as

Sakhr. Many in the company were questioning the point of being there.

When Sunni tribesmen started coming to parley, the troops' suspicion was understandable.

Why the sheikhs' sudden change of heart? Several reasons have been given. Al-Qaeda followers who were initially honoured as allies, who led the resistance from the front and paid well, had outstayed their welcome. Many of the foreigners tried to enforce the strict rules of the Wahhabi strand of Islam: locals were tortured for 'un-Islamic' behaviour – punished for smoking, drinking and possessing photographs and films.

The tipping point seems to have come when Al-Qaeda fighters began forcibly taking sheikhs' daughters for their wives, perverting a tribal tradition of forging alliances through marriage.

'It was a harsh, tyrannical regime,' said Lieutenant-Colonel Val Keaveny, a commander who was in Anbar when its Sunni tribes came to the Americans to talk about changing their allegiance. 'Iraqis simply don't want to live like that.'

In the Jurf as Sakhr area, the Sunnis' dissatisfaction coincided with Petraeus's surge strategy.

In Baghdad the surge brought boots on the ground; in the Babil area, it meant more airpower. Fierce air assaults were launched on insurgent hideouts up the Euphrates valley.

Moltz found that he was able to call for helicopter cover. Logistics improved. The objectives were extended from pacifying the area to preventing insurgents from using one of Babil's main roads to transport weapons and car bombs to Baghdad.

The Sunni sheikhs were getting worried. 'They saw we were not going anywhere, and they risked losing everything as the Shi'ites gained power,' said Major Rick Williams, 45, who hosted the first talks. His expertise on tribal politics is derived in part from his Cherokee Indian ancestry. Colleagues call him 'the sheikh dude'.

'They thought they should get some power while it was still possible or they would be hung out to dry,' Williams said. 'They are in the end responsible for the wellbeing of their tribe.'

Williams called both Sunni and Shi'ite leaders to talks, but only the Sunnis turned up. The negotiations started badly. The Sunnis insisted that the Americans remove Nouri al-Maliki, the Shi'ite prime minister. Otherwise, they said, they would stage a coup.

Discussions became serious in July with the involvement of Fadl al-Janabi, an engineer at the local power plant. A colonel came across him carrying the body of his sister, who had been killed by a mortar, down a road and gave him a lift to the hospital. Later he came to the Americans and said: 'I have 300 guys who want to come with you.'

The discussions ended with a vote among the tribe that was orchestrated by Sheikh Sabah al-Janabi, who has become Moltz's point man in persuading others to switch to the Americans' side.

In August, Moltz began signing contracts with the sheikhs lined up by Sabah. The documents set out in detail what the Americans expect for their money, from the deployment of patrols to the elimination of anyone who attacks their soldiers.

US forces will not go on operations with their new Sunni allies but will support them with firepower or helicopters if necessary. The model is spreading. Deals have also been done with insurgents in Diyala province, north of Baghdad, which Al-Qaeda once proclaimed part of the 'Islamic Caliphate of Iraq'. Today, 25 tribes in the area have men on the US payroll and Al-Qaeda is on the run.

In the Amariya district of western Baghdad, a Sunni leader known as Abu Abed has received 50 fighters and weapons from sheikhs in Anbar, and is fighting with a militia to eject Al-Qaeda.

As for Jurf as Sakhr, the town is slowly being restored to life. The Americans are moving quickly to rebuild, reflecting another component of Petraeus's strategy to bring order to war-torn areas wherever possible.

There are plans to remove the piles of concrete rubble that were once shops or homes. Teenagers have been hired to clear the streets of rubbish. Moltz and Sabah walked round with an engineer last week, working out what needs to be done.

'There is no doubt that he [Sabah] was one of the bad guys,' Moltz said. 'It's not easy doing business with someone who may have been responsible for some of the operations against us. But this area is secure now.'

Sabah is circumspect about his former role in attacks on American soldiers and it has never been discussed openly with his new allies. 'I know some people were fighting the coalition forces,' he said cautiously, 'but now is the time for peace.'

Moltz is hoping to build a new police station, start a medical clinic and renovate the municipal offices. 'Every time in the past I've talked about the town, a bomb would follow within 24 hours,' Moltz said. 'This time, nothing. That leads me to one of two conclusions. Either we have killed all of the enemy, or they [Sabah and his friends] were the enemy.'

He shook his head and made for the exit, only to find no fewer than seven sheikhs blocking his way. Nervously fingering their robes, they asked to discuss getting their men into the new American force. 'We're very happy to work with you,' Moltz said. 'Talk to Sheikh Sabah.'

I felt a new terror on Basra's streets

BASRA

16 December 2007

Islamic militias are waging a brutal campaign for control in Iraq's second city as British troops give way to local forces today, reports Marie Colvin in Basra.

There are two photographs in every police file. One is a long shot of a woman's discarded body, the other a close-up of her last expression.

All the women fell foul of the unwritten rules of the new Basra – they dressed wrongly, they left the home to work, or perhaps they were merely rumoured to have a boyfriend.

Forty-eight manila files have been opened in the past six months. Not one case has been solved. The bare number cannot begin to conjure the horror of these deaths at the hands of Islamic extremists who have the port city in a tightening grip of fear.

In one folder at the Basra police station, the young woman in the autopsy photograph seems to be straining upward in agony, her eyes popping in terror. She is 'female unknown identity, found in Hayer Hussein neighbourhood, behind the electric station. 24/8/2007'.

In another, a woman's nose has been crushed. Trails of blood run from her closed right eye like lines of tears. She is 'female unknown identity, found in Al-Mishraq al-Jaid neighbourhood, behind the car dealer. 7/11/2007'.

Their autopsies revealed painful deaths. One woman found in 'a red dress' had a 9mm bullet wound in her left hand, three in her right hand, three in her right upper arm, and three in her back. Two of the women were beheaded, one with a saw.

Residents say police have not been investigating. 'Everyone knows the militias are doing this, but the police live in fear of them. We all do,' said a middle-aged businessman who was too afraid to give his name.

The walls of Basra would be a good place to start looking for the killers. One graffito on a wall bordering the main Al-Dijari road reads: 'We warn all women of Basra, especially those who are not wearing abbaya [a long, loose black cloak worn over everyday clothes], that we will kill you.' It is signed in the name of an offshoot of the Mahdi Army, the strongest militia in Basra.

It is not just women who live in fear. Professionals such as engineers, doctors and scientists have been dragged from their homes and murdered.

Yet last week Gordon Brown responded angrily in the House of Commons when challenged over the security situation in Basra.

'Iraq is now a democracy,' the prime minister said. 'Millions of people have voted. When I went to Basra, only two days ago, I found that there had been a 90% fall in violence over the past few months. We are now able to hand over Basra to provincial Iraqi control ... This is Iraqis taking control over their own security.'

But what kind of security will the British be passing on to local forces in a ceremony at Basra's international airport today? Will David Miliband, the foreign secretary, who is flying in to represent the government at the formalities, genuinely be able to remark upon a job well done? Or are the Basrawis being delivered into the hands of the militias?

The phone rang on the walnut desk of Major-General Jalil Khalaf's office at midnight. He is the new police commander of Basra and had just been telling me about his determination to stop the killing spree.

The call sent him into agitated overdrive. He picked up another receiver and started barking orders: 'Put checkpoints around the area. Seal it. Quickly. Quickly. The car is white model Crown. All checkpoints, arrest all cars of that description.'

Half an hour earlier, a young Christian woman had been kidnapped in the Kharj neighbourhood, and he feared the worst.

Khalaf, a dapper dresser in a sharply tailored black suit with matching waistcoat, arrived in mid-June and appears to be the first commander to start taking any action. Brown's figures suggest it is taking effect.

'I have reopened all 48 women's files and started investigating them,' he said.

'They are also slashing their faces for wearing make-up. These groups declare "We are religious", but this is not religion.'

He believes the true death toll is higher. Families have buried their dead rather than face what is considered a loss of honour, whether the victim is blameless or not.

He has sent a 100-page report back to the national government in Baghdad, detailing Basra's problems. They differ from those in Baghdad, which had descended into fighting between Sunni and

Shi'ite factions before the American 'surge' policy of increasing troop numbers brought some semblance of order this autumn.

Basra's 2m residents are almost all Shi'ite – the fighting is among the main three parties that represent this branch of Islam who are vying for wealth and power.

The stakes are high. Basra, through Umm Qasr just to the east, is the country's only port and the outlet for most of Iraq's oil, of which the province has the country's greatest reserves. Most of the nation's imports come across its docks too.

It should be a wealthy city, but to drive around reveals the extent of its deterioration. The whole place stinks. The governor, a member of Fadila, the region's third most powerful militia, couldn't fix the sewage pipes, so he diverted them into the Ashar river.

The city is mostly low concrete buildings, many crumbling, and whole neighbourhoods are inhabited by squatters who have thrown up illegal and badly built brick or shanty houses. There are daily cuts in electricity and water supplies.

The only civic project that seems to be going well is the provision of new pavements with red tiles. This despite the fact that the city's roads are pitted with potholes. Strange until one learns that the province's governor has just opened a tile factory.

Khalaf's efforts to bring order to the city have given him black bags under his eyes. He describes a world in which the police and the political parties and militias are separate and competing forces. So far the militias are winning.

'The problems are like an interlocking chain,' he said. 'The militias control the ports, which earns them huge sums of money. That money they use to fund their own activities.

'Second, borders,' he continued. 'There is a 280-kilometre border between us [and Iran].

'Smugglers cross the borders with guns and weapons and these go to the militias. We don't have enough guards or the sophisticated equipment you need to stop them. You could smuggle a tank across that border if you wanted.'

The militias are exporting oil products and animals, too, he said.

His efforts to stop them and weed the militias out of his own force have not gone unnoticed. So far he has survived seven assassination attempts. Many of his bodyguards have been killed. He believes most of the attempts came from within his own force.

'I will enter the *Guinness Book of Records* for assassination attempts,' he said.

The root of the problem, Khalaf believes, was the misguided manner in which the British set up the security forces, particularly the police.

'They relied on the political parties and allowed them to nominate people for positions in the police,' he said. 'Of course, the parties nominated their own members.'

Khalaf's personal stock-taking revealed huge quantities of police communications equipment had been delivered directly from police warehouses to the militias, and 1,000 cars had disappeared.

'They were cars with police insignia painted on the side!' he said, exasperated.

Khalaf also found he was paying 3,500 members of the force, at the cost of millions to the Iraqi national treasury, who were actually serving with the militias. They didn't even bother to show up for work.

His report to the government detailed 28 militias or their offshoots. 'All of them have weapons, all are well-trained,' he said. 'They have RPGs [rocket-propelled grenades], many rifles, bombs, mortars. Their weapons are stronger than ours.'

So worried was he for my safety at the end of my interview that he gave me four trucks of soldiers as an escort to the building I was staying in, and his personal Koran for extra safety. I was already forced to travel under cover of traditional abbaya for fear of identification as a westerner.

The level of lawlessness is striking even during a short visit to Basra. On my first day, a male relative of the family I was staying with was kidnapped driving into Basra. A series of desperate calls began to try to find him. It has become a well-established ritual.

The next day, waiting in the anteroom of Major-General Farid Mohan, commander of the army in Basra, I asked the man next to me if he was okay. He had two black eyes and lumps on his bald head.

It turned out he was the leader of the first ministry of finance delegation to visit Basra in five months. He had been kidnapped and tortured. Mohan had negotiated his release hours earlier.

Iyad Ahmed sat slumped forward in the grey dishdasha (robe) and leather sandals that he had on when he was kidnapped from his room at the Qusr Al-Sultan, the best hotel in Basra. He had arrived 20 days earlier to investigate the ports and borders.

'When I was kidnapped, I was investigating the theft of 653 new cars stolen from the international free zone in the middle of the afternoon. The thieves killed the guard at the gate as they drove the cars out.'

Following the trail, the ministry team found that 90 of the cars had been used in assassinations, and 35 in suicide bomb attacks.

Ahmed thinks he was targeted when he started investigating free zone officials for what he believed was their involvement in the car hijacking. The free zone is said to be controlled by the Badr organisation, the Islamic party controlled by Abdul Aziz Hakim, the second most powerful Islamic party in Basra.

'I was threatened,' said Ahmed in an outraged voice. 'A Mr Falah, the senior man, told me, "See what we will do to you today".'

About 11.30 that evening eight new 4x4s full of gunmen stormed into the hotel.

'They dragged me out of my room in just this,' he said slapping his dirty robe. 'I was shouting, "I am a government employee". I thought at first they were after the two women working on my team.'

He was blindfolded, driven to what he believes was a farm because of the noises and tortured for 24 hours. 'They beat me all over, they kicked me, and they hung me by my wrists for three hours.'

Mohan secured his release by promising the kidnappers a 'gift' if they gave him Ahmed. It is a mark of the hypocrisy of some Islamic extremists that because the Koran forbids them from extorting money they pretend that their ransom for a kidnapping is a 'gift'.

Ahmed vowed to keep working, although rather fearfully. 'These militias are bigger than the government,' he said.

The government of Nouri al-Maliki, the prime minister, appears finally to have acknowledged the problem in Basra, but it is unclear if it has the will to wrest the city from the grip of the Islamic parties and their thugs.

'The government is trying to support the forces in Basra,' said Ali Dabbagh, its spokesman. 'We're not trying to hide the fact that there is a threat in Basra, but we think most of the threat is coming from organised criminal gangs who are hiding behind the slogans of JAM [local shorthand for the Mahdi Army].'

He pointed out that 15,000 police had been fired from forces across Iraq because they were engaging in criminal activity or belonged to a militia.

He said that another part of the problem in Basra was that there was a 'political struggle – [Islamic] parties are fighting each other'. He said, however, that he thought today would witness 'a smooth transfer of power to Iraqi security forces.

'They are capable of dealing with Basra and we can ask the Iraqi security forces or multinational forces to intervene if there is a problem.'

Yet it is hard for the Baghdad government to move against the religious militias because it is itself led by Shi'ite religious parties. In the cauldron of Iraqi politics, being seen to attack one's coreligionists is not a good idea.

The Mahdi Army is in theory observing a six-month ceasefire, which it announced in late August. Huge murals of Moqtada and his father Mohammed Sadiq al-Sadr line the main roads, rather like larger-than-life portraits of Saddam Hussein did when he was president.

The Sadr office in Basra is a rival centre of power to the official government. Pick-up trucks, new Toyotas, even two police cars are parked outside the gates of the compound. Inside the activities are not just military. There are departments for welfare and even a tribunal run on sharia principles.

I met Sheikh Ali As-Sayeedi, one of their leaders, in his office, furnished with stuffed faux-Louis XIV furniture, korans and kitsch plastic ivy.

Many leaders used to declaim openly that their ambition was to take power in the city. But now that the British troops are leaving and Iraqis are taking over, they are more cautious in their language.

Sayeedi, however, insisted that the Mahdi Army had driven British forces from Basra and that they would not give up fighting until the US-led coalition left Iraq.

'It is a good next step for Iraqis to take back their sovereignty in Basra,' said Sayeedi. 'We believe all forces should leave the country. We don't respect any agreement with these forces.

'Our people are freedom fighters not militias.

'Our programme is to help the Iraqi people and make everyone happy in Basra.'

Why then, I asked him, is everyone in Basra blaming the Mahdi Army for the violence in the streets?

'People here support us,' he insisted, leaning forward and visibly angering.

'Criminals do crime and then say that they are the Jaish al-Mahdi [the Arabic term for the militia] to appear stronger.'

It is not hard to find the signs of muscle-flexing on the streets, however. On Friday, the Muslim day of prayer, Mahdi checkpoints closed down the city's main roads for their new custom of busing in hundreds of followers to pray in the middle of the main arteries.

Traffic snarled as drivers wove through dirty side roads to get around the jams.

As prayers broke up, men wearing the black turbans of the Mahdi Army strolled away, machineguns slung casually over their shoulders.

The British gave up the battle for control of the streets of Basra months ago. In September they withdrew from Basra Palace, their base for four years, to the airport.

They say they expect the transition to be smooth. The Iraqis have been policing themselves for four months without calling for help. The British insist the handover is no defeat but the next step in the nationwide transition to Iraqi control.

'The formal handover allows them to deliver Iraqi solutions in an Iraqi way,' said Major-General Graham Binns, the commanding officer for British forces in Basra province. 'The way forward is to have the Iraqis take the next step.'

He insisted the British were not cutting and running. They will remain at the airport, reducing to 2,500 by next spring. The Basra government can call on them for support that ranges from surveillance to re-entry.

Binns confessed to regrets. 'I was more of an idealist when I arrived and perhaps too ambitious,' he said. 'I didn't think it would end this way.

'I'm proud of the way we built up the Iraqi security forces, but we were unable to meet the aspirations of the Iraqi people. I would like to have done better.'

Tomorrow the Iraqi police and army will mark their first day of independent control of Basra with a military parade at Basra Palace.

Last Thursday, Iraqi army guards lounged in sociable groups at the massive arch that leads into the compound on the Shatt al-Arab waterway. Three drank tea together, their weapons leaning against the concrete blast wall installed by the departed British.

They seemed unworried, unlike the civilians outside the walls of the new army headquarters. They certainly didn't look like soldiers ready to take on the well-armed militias.

Few in Basra would say that the British have met their goal, 'to establish the security necessary for the development of political institutions and for economic reconstruction'.

An opinion poll published today suggests that 70% of Basrawis believe security will improve after the British have left – mostly because they have been removed as a target – but every one I spoke to said this was their number one worry.

'I must look over my shoulder every minute when I am on the street,' said Rula, a 36-year-old mother of four who has refused to quit journalism despite threats. 'I look hard at the face of my daughter before I leave for work. Someone might cut my throat and I will not come home again.'

Fears that the militias will begin an all-out battle for Basra or that the city will descend into chaos are unlikely to materialise. The factions will no doubt clash as they jockey for power, but they have carved out their lucrative spheres of influence and have too much to lose to go to war.

Iran will play a key role in the future of Basra. Tehran has more influence here than anywhere else in Iraq. The mullahs fund all the Shi'ite groups rather like a wealthy donor hedging his political bets.

Essentially, the political players are happy with their lot. It is the rest of the people in Basra who will suffer, most likely for years to come.

'I went to university because I had dreams for my future,' said 18-year-old Nayla. 'Now I only go to classes twice a week because I am so afraid to leave the house. I have no future.'

Saddam's victims left to suffer as henchmen prosper

HILLA

3 February 2008

Forlorn mounds of sun-bleached clothes stretch across the barren field. Traces of the people who died wearing them – a washed-out vertebra near a small canvas shoe, a jawbone by a faded lavender dress – reveal that they mark the shallow graves of 1,200 of Saddam Hussein's unidentified victims.

Little else except a lingering stench marks the bleak burial site that lies up a muddy track in Mahawil, a farming village just outside the Shi'ite southern Iraqi city of Hilla. Even the weeds have not grown back.

Up to 15,000 men, women and children are believed to have been shot and buried here when Saddam unleashed the elite Republican Guard on his rebellious people in 1991, just days after he promised the United Nations that he would 'end all military action'. He had lost his war in Kuwait; he would win this one.

An estimated 100,000 Shi'ites and Kurds died as the Republican Guard tanks rolled northwards in a murderous onslaught on those who had risen up against him.

The vengeful Iraqi troops struck hard in Hilla which, like most of the Shi'ite south, had been seized by an angry population following encouragement from the first President George Bush to rebel against Saddam. American help never came.

Hilla lists 4,800 families who lost a member.

When American-led troops invaded in 2003, the city was buoyed by the knowledge that President George W Bush and Tony Blair had cited Saddam's massacres as part of their justification for war.

Many were impoverished because they had lost their breadwinner or had suffered as Saddam cracked down on the region. They thought their lives would be transformed when the Americans and a nascent Iraqi government pledged to give them compensation and help.

Paul Bremer, the American diplomat who ruled Iraq as head of the new Coalition Provisional Authority, told a press conference in May 2004 that the CPA would pay $25 million to compensate Saddam's victims. A press release announced the formation of a task force to distribute the money.

Less than a year later, the Iraqi government's assurances of help were enshrined in draft legislation. It promised a monthly pension, cancellation of debts, help with home loans and provision of land to 'the victims of mass graves'.

Yet today, most of the families who uncovered relatives in the Mahawil field are still living in desperate poverty.

Their anger is compounded by the fact that all but the most senior members of Saddam's ruling Ba'ath party, mostly Sunnis who victimised them, have either returned to their jobs after an initial purge, or are collecting government pensions.

Sadiya Saleh, a 67-year-old widow who found her daughter, Halda Aboud, 34, and her grandson, Mohammed Aboud, 12, in the mass grave, was left in a wheelchair after Iraqi soldiers kicked and beat her as she tried to save her son.

Surviving on handouts from relatives and sales of sunflower seeds, she is one of the many still waiting for the promised compensation for appalling suffering at the hands of their own government.

'Soldiers came to my house looking for guns. I told them we are poor, we have no weapons,' said Saleh, dressed in the traditional black abbaya robe, last week. 'My daughter was in my house because she used to visit me once a month. They dragged her out with her son. He was only 12. They were screaming.'

Saleh threw herself on top of her own son Nasir, who was the same age as his cousin. Her voice breaks as she continues. 'They punched me and kicked me in the back until they got me off him and took him away.' The beating left her crippled.

Nasir returned traumatised two days later. He did not speak of what had happened for 12 years. Formerly a bright, happy boy who loved football, he never went back to school or played with his friends again. Only when the news came that Saddam's regime had fallen did he break his silence.

Saleh gathers her abbaya closer as she tells his story. 'Nasir told me that every night a group was taken out and never came back,' she said. One night, Halda, Mohammed and Nasir were driven to the field in Mahawil and shoved into the night, blindfolded and with their wrists tied. The soldiers opened fire.

'Nasir said they all fell and he was covered with blood but not shot,' Saleh said.

'Dirt fell on top of him but not too much. After a while he crawled out and hid in the trees.' After Nasir told his story, Saleh went to the field.

It was a chaotic, desperate scene, as I recall from seeing it myself. I remember walking over the hill to a vision from hell.

In the blazing heat, a yellow mechanical digger was gouging a huge trench, gently dumping dirt and bundles of bones wrapped in cloth.

Men dug with shovels and their bare hands. Others separated the bodies and laid them out gently on blankets, placing recognisable objects on top – a watch here, a small gold necklace on a pile topped by a skull. The smell was overpowering.

A loudspeaker broadcast a name when an identity card was found. Thousands of men and women walked past the rows of bodies, some throwing themselves on a dirty jumble of rags and bones they recognised. Others trudged by with their dead wrapped in plastic bags.

Saleh recognised Halda's body by her clothes, a grey dress over brown trousers and a brown scarf. 'I knew her clothes. I bought them for her,' she said. Next to her daughter were the bones of her grandson.

She now relies on Ayat, a nine-year-old granddaughter, to push her decrepit wheelchair and clean for her. She has not been able to afford heating gas for a fortnight, despite the bitterly cold Iraq winter.

Ayat sits on the arm of her chair, wearing a woolly hat and scarf and embroidered jeans, solemnly listening to the story. Her only smile comes when her grandmother says that 'she is such a help to me'. The 500,000-dinar (£200) monthly payment now being mooted by the government would change everything but there is little sign it will be paid soon.

Saleh's sense of injustice is intensified by the relative comfort enjoyed by former members of the Ba'ath party, which Saddam built into his personal fiefdom during three decades of power. 'The Ba'athists have their land, their houses and their cars,' Saleh said bitterly. 'We have nothing.'

Shalah Jabar, 62, would be one of the targets of her anger should she meet him. He worked as an accountant in the government fabric factory in Hilla and rose through the ranks in the Ba'ath party.

Bremer's first decree expelled all Ba'athists from public jobs. As the insurgency took hold in 2004, fuelled by Sunni bitterness at their treatment, the decree was watered down.

Teachers, who generally held lower ranks in the party, were allowed to return to their jobs. Jabar and others of similar rank could apply for pensions. He now receives £200 a month, along with what he earns from rent on his grandfather's farm. He makes no apologies.

'I joined the Ba'ath party out of a sense of patriotism in 1976,' he said last week. Many of his rank, called district officers, spied on their fellow residents, but he insisted that he had merely given lectures and organised cultural events.

Asked why he had stayed in the party as it turned into an instrument of Saddam's oppression, he replied: 'I wished to continue my studies. I could only do that if I was in the party.'

There is no doubt that it was almost impossible to get ahead in Saddam's Iraq without joining his party. But this is small solace to Saddam's victims.

On a wall outside the government-run Martyrs Memorial Foundation in Hilla, a handwritten sign reads, 'Ba'athists not welcome'. Inside the ramshackle office, there is no electricity. Men in shabby suits and women in black abbayas queue to fill out the forms that the government requires for a job or compensation.

Few have been helped, admits Hussein Jabar, the 32-year-old director, who lost a nephew and two uncles in the mass grave. He is angry with the Americans who, he says, should help since they are the occupying power. He also chides the Shi'ite-led Iraqi government.

'Our young government has forgotten many things and this mass grave is one of them,' said Jabar in his unlit office. He said he had given plots of land to 534 families, although he is aware they have no money to build homes.

'The families have already been caused too much pain by the deaths of their relatives. I hope we can give them something,' he said.

Story after story is told as if it is fresh. Najia Aziz, now in her sixties, saw Iraqi soldiers shove her 20-year-old son Mazen Yousef into a car as he walked to a friend's house. He had just returned from serving in Kuwait.

'I ran to the car, begging and screaming at them to release him. I kept running after the car,' she said.

She never gave up hope, going from prison to prison, asking for him for years. 'I almost didn't go to the grave. I was telling myself, "He didn't do anything. He won't be there",' she recalled. She did not know that Saddam regarded the returning soldiers as suspect because so few fought.

Aziz identified her son's bones through the army leave permit still in the pocket of his jeans. A friend who had been with him in prison told her he had been so badly beaten before he was shot that he couldn't open his eyes. 'My spirit left with him that day,' she said.

There are fears that the desperation and injustice felt in Hilla and among other families who lost relatives to Saddam's brutality could provoke renewed sectarian fighting unless the government acts on its promises.

The Mahdi army, the radical Shi'ite militia responsible for attacks on allied forces, has been boosted by their rage. Many of its recruits from Hilla, who had relatives buried in the mass grave, joined because they felt their plight was being ignored.

The unclaimed bones in the field are as neglected as the living. After a few months of lying exposed, dirt was spread over them and clothes and personal items were left on top of the shallow graves for those still looking for their loved ones. There is little chance of that now.

Every year on the anniversary of the March 1991 uprising, Hilla residents travel to the site and stage a demonstration calling for a memorial to honour the dead.

Even that small plea has been ignored. They will be there again next month.

REBELS CRUSHED

After Saddam Hussein's crushing 1991 defeat in Kuwait, rebellions broke out in Kurdish areas of northern Iraq and among Shi'ites in the south.

The rebels seized 14 of Iraq's 18 provinces. Many expected American support. It never materialised.

Instead, Saddam regrouped and brutally suppressed the uprisings. Up to 100,000 died.

Middle East

Gaza's mourners plan 'spectacular' revenge: War on Terror

GAZA CITY

28 March 2004

The huge kitchens at Hamas's chosen catering company worked non-stop last week.

By tradition, the families of the latest 'martyrs' had to feed the hundreds who sat at new marquees put up for the mourning period. Taxis and battered cars were loaded up at Eastern Catering with foil-covered platters of rice and lamb, and sped off to the vigils of the bereaved.

Last Friday the martyrdom industry was in full swing. Under a green awning in the courtyard of the El-Amrain family home, men sat stoically on white plastic chairs as little boys with green Hamas headbands raced about in play, twirling child-sized Hamas flags bought for the occasion.

A nearby minaret broadcast the sermon of the local imam, who promised that every shaheed, or martyr, would be granted automatic passage to heaven for 70 members of his family as well as his own 72 virgins in paradise.

The preacher thanked God for giving martyrdom to Sheikh Ahmed Yassin, the spiritual leader of Hamas, the militant Islamic group he founded in 1987. It was said that the 67-year-old Yassin had long craved martyrdom, lamenting that because he was paralysed, 'martyrdom had to come to him'.

On Monday it did – in the form of an Israeli missile that struck after bodyguards pushed his wheelchair out of a mosque at the end of early morning prayers. Anger and emotion at his assassination sent support for Hamas, which had already grown during 3½ years of intifada, soaring.

After the imam on the minaret finished his sermon, everyone at the El-Amrain family's mourning tent dug their white plastic spoons into their lamb platters.

They were there for Hamman El-Amrain, 26, who was one of seven brothers, all Hamas members.

Like thousands of boys in Gaza, Hamman had joined Hamas's youth group, aged 12.

Five years later he graduated to Izzedine al-Qassam brigades, its military wing.

He died on Wednesday after being shot by an Israeli tank he was trying to hit with a 'betar', a rocket grenade that Hamas manufactures locally.

There was little doubt among the men at the mourning tent that more martyrs would soon join Hamman. Hamas leaders have vowed vengeance. 'Martyrdom is one of our strongest assets,' said Mohamed El-Amrain, 29, Hamman's brother and a ranking Hamas member who sits on a committee that hands out cheques to the families of verified martyrs.

Bloodthirsty threats are common after Israel kills Hamas officials, but last week in Gaza there was growing evidence to support the Israeli fears that emptied streets and cafés in Jerusalem and Tel Aviv alike.

Mohamed El-Amrain warned that Hamas was planning a 'spectacular' attack. He said he expected the near future would see a continuation of smaller incidents such as a failed Hamas raid on Thursday night on the Gush Katif settlement, where two Hamas gunmen tried to swim ashore. Both were shot dead. The revenge for Yassin, however, would be different.

'We will strike the Israelis in a totally new way, where they will not expect us,' El-Amrain said. 'This will be a revenge that shows them we can hit them anywhere and that we will never stop.'

There was agreement with his words even among Palestinians who oppose such attacks. 'Hamas has to act against the Israelis and avenge Sheikh Yassin, or they will lose respect on the street,' said Saeb al-Ajez, a general in the Palestinian Authority (PA) government forces in Gaza.

He is in the unenviable position of being responsible for stopping Palestinian attacks on Israelis, under the terms of an agreement with Israel. His own population views that agreement as moribund and his efforts as betrayal.

'For Hamas's credibility, their answer has to be in a dramatic and different way,' al-Ajez said.

He believed they might try to assassinate Israeli ministers, a suspicion borne out by the recent appearance on a Hamas website of a 'most wanted' pack of cards depicting the Israeli government, headed by Ariel Sharon, the prime minister, on the joker card.

Al-Ajez, whose hair has gone grey and who dresses in starched khaki uniforms, says Hamas is now far more popular in Gaza than the Palestinian Authority, which is dominated by Yasser Arafat's secular group, Fatah.

'To the population now, Hamas is the valiant resistance,' the general said. 'My soldiers at the checkpoints feel in such a difficult position. They are supposed to prevent Hamas from attacking Israel, but at the same time Israel attacks them. The door is closing on our fingers.'

The assassination of Yassin has left open the possibility that the fundamentalist Hamas could turn in a more radical direction. Yassin, although an implacable foe of Israel, had in recent years moderated Hamas's insistence that it would fight on for a Palestinian state that included Israel proper as well as the West Bank and Gaza.

He had adopted the position that Hamas would settle for a state on the West Bank and Gaza, although not as a final resolution – the next generation would be free to fight on.

Abdel Aziz al-Rantissi, a paediatrician who replaced Yassin as Hamas leader in Gaza last week, has taken a far more radical stand. He has been implacable in insisting that Hamas will settle for nothing less than every inch of former Palestinian land, and that military struggle – not negotiation – is the way forward.

Last week, however, some Palestinian observers said that al-Rantissi might moderate his position now that he had the top job in concert with Khaled Masha'al, Hamas's political leader, based in Damascus.

Strains between the authority and Hamas could come to a head if Sharon goes ahead with a plan to withdraw unilaterally from Gaza. Last week Israeli commentators said the killing of Yassin and promised assassinations of other Hamas leaders indicated that Sharon intended to proceed, but that he wanted to decapitate the group first. This would prevent any possibility of Hamas taking over from the Palestinian Authority in Gaza and turning it into 'Hamas land' on Israel's southern border.

The authority and Hamas are in talks to try to avert civil war. Ziad Abu Amr, an independent member of the Palestinian parliament who is on the committee that negotiates with the Islamic forces, said Hamas was insisting on power-sharing in the event of an Israeli pull-out from Gaza.

'Hamas wants to be a partner. It doesn't want to be excluded after Israeli withdrawal,' Abu Amr said. 'So far Arafat doesn't accept any partnership with Hamas. But if we don't succeed in persuading Arafat to accept power-sharing, we are going to face civil strife.'

More young men lined up for death last week, and most of them seemed far more committed than 16-year-old Hussam Abdu, whose photograph went round the world last week after he was stopped at an Israeli checkpoint with a suicide bomber's vest and decided he wanted to live.

Asked by Israeli interrogators why he had agreed to undertake the mission, he replied: 'It's because people don't like me.' He said he had been teased at school and wanted to be a 'hero'. The services of 72 virgins in paradise had been an additional incentive, he acknowledged.

At another mourning tent in Gaza on Friday, a further line of silent men in white plastic chairs sat with the family of Ishaq Nasar, 19, a Hamas 'frogman' killed trying to swim ashore at the Jewish settlement in Gaza on Thursday.

Abu Osama Nasar, 17, seemed strangely joyful as he described how his brother, now in paradise, had told him he planned to avenge Yassin's death. Abu Osama was raring to join him. He had always wanted to be a suicide bomber, he said, but his parents had told him to wait until he grew up. Now that he was 17, he had put his name down.

Over and over, the teenager acted out, with obscene enthusiasm, the motions of his chest blowing up. There was no way, he said, that Palestinian Authority forces could stop Hamas from continuing to fight.

'If the PA wants to stop the resistance, they will fail,' Abu Osama said. 'They are a failed leadership. If they try to come here, we will cut their necks.'

There is unlikely to be any shortage of business in the foresee-able future for the Eastern Catering company. Yesterday, children at Yassin's grave watered wilting carnations in the rectangle of rocks and cinderblocks that marked the outline of his resting place. All agreed that they would like to be Hamas martyrs when they grew up.

A seven-year-old Palestinian boy was shot and killed as he stood at the window of his home in a refugee camp in the West Bank city of Nablus yesterday. The Israeli military blamed stray Palestinian gunfire.

Into the underworld

17 July 2005

Beneath the Israeli–Egyptian border is a secret world: a network of narrow tunnels, through which Palestinians smuggle weapons – and even wives – into the Gaza Strip. But these 'snake holes' also carry the risk of disaster and death. Marie Colvin enters the subterranean labyrinth.

Nadr Keshta was 18 and his attractive young neighbour had caught his eye. He started hanging about on street corners, trying to catch sight of her as she walked home from school in her blue-and-grey uniform. For weeks she ignored him. When she finally waved back to his wink, it was her signal that she returned his interest. Without ever exchanging a word, they considered themselves 'engaged'. That was where their story, as told by his younger brother Mohamed, led into the subterranean world of the 'tunnel people' of Rafah, the southernmost city in the Gaza Strip. He needed money now, to build a house for his bride and, truth be told, to show off a bit – buying a new gun was first on his list. For young men in Rafah, a gun is street cred; it's cool, like having the latest pair of trainers.

Nadr was earning a pittance on his father's farm. Gaza has been locked down by the Israeli army since the armed Palestinian intifada began in September 2000. There are no jobs for young men, because Gaza can no longer export the fruit and vegetables that were the staples of its economy – tomatoes that used to sell for $20 a crate are down to $3 in the local market. Only a few men have permission to enter Israel for work.

Nadr turned to the only paying job in Rafah: digging tunnels under the Israeli-Egyptian border. I had heard rumours of tunnels for years, but never really believed them, because there is nothing but white sand that runs through your fingers. How could you have a tunnel network in this flimsy sand? My scepticism was buttressed by knowledge of Israel's defences: the army has erected an 8 foot wall that plunges invisibly many more feet underground along the Rafah side of the Philadelphi road – a dirt stretch patrolled by armoured Israeli Jeeps that parallels the Egyptian border – to stop tunnellers. Then there are explosions every night in Rafah, set off arbitrarily by Israeli engineers in the hope that they might collapse an undiscovered tunnel.

But a chance conversation resulted in my living in Rafah for a week with the 'tunnel people'. It was like discovering a lost tribe in a city I had been visiting for 15 years. I found an extraordinary, secret tunnel culture known only to a few Palestinians. The tunnel people told me they originally smuggled in contraband drugs, women, cigarettes (5 shekels in Egypt, 12 shekels in Gaza), and even the python that still slithers around in the Rafah zoo, and the ostrich that escaped during the May 2004 Israeli incursion, to the great glee of Rafah kids, who rode bareback on the big bird until the zookeepers recaptured him. Since the second intifada began five years ago, however, the tunnellers have mostly smuggled weapons.

The profits are huge. A Kalashnikov sells for $200 on the Egyptian side, but fetches $2,000 on the Gaza black market. A good night's delivery is 1,200 Kalashnikovs – a profit of more than $2 million. Bullets – 50 cents in Egypt, $8 wholesale in Gaza – are even more profitable. A standard one-night delivery returns a profit of $750,000. The tunnels are financed by wealthy families – locals call them the 'snakeheads' – who run the tunnels as businesses. They rent the passage to anyone who pays $10,000 for one night's use – a gun dealer, Hamas or Islamic Jihad, the militant Islamic fundamentalist groups, or a man who can't get his wife legally into Gaza. Cash is the currency, not politics, patriotism or sentimentality.

They rent, build or buy a house, even an entire farm, just to disguise a tunnel's 'eye', as they call the entrance. The gun dealers are their biggest clients. 'We call them blood dealers,' said Abu Sibah, 36, the bearded head of a rogue Palestinian militia in Al-Bureij refugee camp north of Rafah, outside a car mechanics' shop where he had stored his latest shipment of Kalashnikovs and a rocket-propelled grenade (RPG). 'But there is nothing to do about them. We depend on the tunnels for guns.' He was particularly proud of the shiny black Belgian revolver in his belt – at $3,000, a special order. It was to this world that Nadr Keshta turned for the money to marry.

His relatives were in the tunnel business and he heard a 'big project' was about to start. He signed on with a group of eight young men, all relatives. In the tunnels there is a hierarchy: those not related to the patron work for $100 a day as diggers, while those who are relatives get a share of the profit in return for their labour, a much better deal. When the tunnel is finished they are entitled to a percentage on every load that passes through it.

Israel has made endless efforts to stop the tunnellers; apart from explosives, bulldozers have chopped away at Rafah's unlovely blocks of concrete houses that used to sprawl right up to the border fence. But all that has done is make the digging longer and more arduous. Tunnels now have to extend about 880 yards to span the bulldozed divide. Keshta expected to make $20,000 as his share of the tunnel's first load, and then a continuing profit as long as it remained undiscovered. In Gaza, that was enough to build a house and have some left over for his new gun and a wedding reception. But disaster struck.

At the start, the new project ran smoothly following well-rehearsed procedures. Keshta and his fellow diggers began excavating a shaft from a back bedroom of a three-storey house. The tunnel was financed by Hisham al-Sha'ir – the al-Sha'irs are known as Gaza's premier tunnelling family.

An al-Sha'ir grandmother had died there and the house was empty. The tunnel 'eye' was concealed by four marble floor tiles. They dug a narrow shaft, barely wider than their bodies, 40 feet down through 'hard sand' – red sand that is impacted and solid – until they reached a layer of soft sand. The tunnellers of Gaza are self-taught geologists; their grandfathers discovered that a 'hard sand' stratum runs under Rafah to varying depths.

They dig through it until they hit the soft sand below – the layer of hard sand becomes their ceiling. They are hunted by both the Israelis and the Palestinian Authority (PA).

Keshta and the other young diggers lived day and night in the house, so that their comings and goings would not arouse suspicion. They hid the telltale sand in other rooms. But unbeknown to them, the explosives that the Israelis periodically set off had weakened the hard-sand ceiling. Three days of unexpected rain weakened it further, and the tunnel collapsed on Keshta and his two cousins, Nidal al-Sha'ir and Sufiyan al-Sha'ir.

The three were trapped. Other diggers heard Nadr yelling over the intercom that goes through every tunnel: 'Help us, help us, help us to live.' The three entombed teenagers began chanting 'There is no God but Allah, and Muhammad is his prophet,' the phrase that Muslims intone in times of crisis.

The tunnel financier raced to the scene and began digging with a bulldozer along the tunnel's path, but nobody knew the boys' location. Friends and relatives gathered at the intercom in the back bedroom.

'There is no air, it is too dark, we are feeling like we are in a grave,' Nadr's brother, Mohamed, heard him shout. 'I was sure then that they would die,' Mohamed said, remembering his sense of helplessness. For nine hours, the cousins were heard praying aloud and pleading for rescue. The Palestinians dug on their side of the Philadelphi wall and the Israelis began digging on theirs after a desperate relative broke the tunnel code of secrecy and drew the Israel Defence Forces (IDF) a map of the tunnel's path.

Nadr Keshta's illicit fiancée heard of the disaster, but she could not come even just to hear his voice: her parents would have been furious if they had known of her relationship with a boy they had not approved. She would have been considered to have dishonoured the family. Juliet, who doesn't want her real name used, was despondent. She had no idea her Nadr had gone down the tunnels. 'Why did he do this? I wanted him, not money!' she cried in secret. But she had to hide her distress from her family. After nine hours of solid digging, an Israeli bulldozer accidentally cut the intercom wire and there was silence on the line that connected the three cousins to the world above.

Keshta and his cousins had made the mistake of young men the world over: succumbing to the lure of the big score. But the price in Rafah's tunnels is higher than elsewhere. However vast the sums to be made in the tunnel business, it is not easy money. Death stalks this subterranean world – the horrific slow death of suffocation below the surface. The day before I arrived in Rafah, a teenager had been electrocuted in a tunnel and his body dumped where he, but not the tunnel 'eye', would be found. Families who receive the bloated bodies of their tunnel dead take a little consolation from the fact that tunnellers who die digging are considered *shaheed* – martyrs to the Palestinian cause – even if they mostly die in the pursuit of profit. In Rafah, the culture of the martyr is as pervasive as guns.

Yousef and Ahmed Keshta, 24 and 31, run the most popular barber's shop in Rafah, the Shaheed Salon – the Martyrs' Salon. The walls are plastered with photographs and posters of late former customers. Instead of shampoos and conditioners, the shelves of mirrored cabinets are lined with keepsakes from the dead: a string of worry beads left by Mahmoud al-Sha'ir the day before he was killed; a toy gun from their youngest customer to die in a tunnel. Their most popular hairstyles are the side-buzzed marine cut – modelled on that of the American marines seen on the news, even though most young Gazans are vaguely anti-American – and the French cut, so called because it resembles a mushroom when done properly. I asked a bearded Martyrs' Salon customer, who sat with a white bib in front of a mirror, if it was not disconcerting to be stared at from all sides by the dead. He looked at me as if I came from a different planet. 'Of course not. I remember them all: most are relatives, neighbours, friends – it is my duty to remember them.' There are more realistic voices, but they don't drown out the siren call of money.

Israeli tanks rolled into Rafah in May 2004 after five Israeli soldiers died when Palestinians fired an RPG at an armoured personnel carrier. IDF tanks and bulldozers destroyed another entire block of homes. Ibrahim Keshta knocked holes through his walls to get his family out. 'It used to be a big neighbourhood here. Now there are only dogs,' he said as he brought a tray of glasses of sweet tea and sat cross-legged on the floor of his half-ruined house to talk. 'You die alone here.'

Looking down through windows emptied of glass by tank shells, Ibrahim's view is of a mound of rubble – all that remains of a small tin-roofed house custom-built to hide the 'eye' of the tunnel where his younger brother Mohamed died. A baby fig tree grows above the barely visible sunken path of sand that is the only trace of the destroyed tunnel beneath.

Ibrahim blames a 'snakehead' for luring his brother underground. 'He told my brother, "Join my crew and you will have nice expensive guns, a nice house, you can marry,"' he says, waving his arms around with lingering outrage, shooing away his three small children, who return moments later to listen and giggle.

After hundreds of yards of digging and one day away from punching through in Egypt, on his first tunnel job, the roof collapsed above Mohamed and his boss. Both died.

In Ibrahim's neighbourhood alone, locals reckon there are about 20 tunnels in various stages of destruction or excavation. Down the street from Ibrahim's ruin is the rubble of a house destroyed because the owner had financed one of the most famous tunnels in Rafah: the one commissioned by Yasser Arafat, then president of the Palestinian Authority, to smuggle in 50 tonnes of weapons from Iran aboard the freighter *Karine A*, which the Israelis captured in the Red Sea. Arafat denied any connection, but the trace was clear: the PA had commissioned the $100 million cargo of rockets, missiles, mortars and sniper rifles. When I went to the site of the destroyed house, a white baby donkey lay basking in the sand at the foot of all that was left: a mound of dirt and concrete slabs. After my visit, the PA found the 'eye' of another tunnel dug to connect to the main one – right underneath where the baby donkey had been tethered by a rope invisible to the casual observer.

More terrifying than the spectre of sudden death is the psychological trauma of spending months underground in a space 2 foot wide by 2 foot 4 inches tall.

A 770-yard tunnel can take six months to finish. When tunnellers lowered me by rope down a shaft that began in a little girl's bedroom with posters of cuddly animals on the walls, I was gripped by panicky claustrophobia. The so-called 'safe' hard-sand walls trickled away on my head as I passed into the depths; the sand crumbled each time I scrabbled for footing on the way down; the walls closed in, and the bare bulbs did little to alleviate the darkness or the fear that the whole thing might cave in on top of me at any moment.

'To do this work, you have to throw your heart away,' says Ayed (not his real name), who at 28 is considered a veteran digger. So comfortable with his work has Ayed become that he sleeps in tunnels. He has a muscular, wiry body and spade-like callused fingers. He brews coffee up top, and takes a flask down with him and thinks nothing of staying underground for days. As I would learn, each tunneller has his own methods. Unlike the tunnel that I went down, where hard sand formed the walls of the shaft, Ayed's entry shaft is lined with metal plates specially welded for the job. As boss, he checks the tunnel's progress with a compass every 10–15 yards; after 20 yards he installs a bespoke engine that hauls back nine 'boats' containing pails of sand. Two tunnellers work at the face, Ayed digging and the other loading the pails. Two work at the foot of the shaft unloading the buckets, then buzz when the buckets are empty, and the forward crew starts the engine to haul them back.

If the sand gets soft on the horizontal he is digging, Ayed either installs supports or just tunnels lower to make sure he has a hard-sand ceiling. He is nostalgic about the time he worked in a well-financed tunnel where the owner installed air conditioning.

At 55 yards, he brings in a vacuum cleaner and hooks it up to a hose to draw in air. It is gospel in Gaza that Israel has banned the import of vacuum cleaners. By the time the tunnel reaches 55 yards there are three systems operating: a specially engineered motor-and-pulley system to get the pails of sand to the mouth of the tunnel; an intercom on a separate wire to connect him to the top; and a third wire that brings in electricity to power the bare bulbs that line the tunnel.

Ayed can judge the distance by experience; nine buckets of sand equals one yard. A typical day is 10–11 hours of digging, 10–15 yards of progress.

Every tunnel is measured meticulously: 2 feet wide, 2 feet 4 inches high. Wider than that, and experience shows collapse is likely.

There is black humour, much as in any other dangerous profession. Ayed laughs as he recalls the time he put up a pipe to see where he was going, and it came up in the living room of a house and he could hear a mother yelling at her child. He traced the location and paid the family for their silence. As in gold-prospecting, all tunnellers dream of the big score.

'Even when we have no tunnel, we meet – and what do we talk about?' said Ayed. 'We talk about houses we have spotted that might be good for a tunnel; if anyone has heard of a tunnel deal going down.'

Their hero is Salman al-Sha'ir, now 85, the grandfather of all the tunnellers. He was called in whenever a tunnel had a problem and could always solve it. Famously (at least in tunnel lore), he once single-handedly dug a tunnel to Egypt when his son was caught on the Egyptian side, and rescued him. Salman' s tunnel career ended when Israeli commandos snatched him from his farm; he now languishes in an Israeli prison.

Ayed's experience on the Egyptian side – punching out the other 'eye' – gives an incredible insight into how this strange underworld connects to a larger network of international arms dealers. Over the years he has been working, he has seen the provenance and quality of weapons change. Guns used to come from Egypt and Yemen; now the great bulk come from Darfur in Sudan, where civil war is raging. The dealers have migrated there and sell weapons by the tonne to the Bedouin who live on the mountainous border and are subject to no law. The Sudan connection is well known in Gaza, but Israel's military intelligence, usually among the best-informed in the world, still lists Egypt and Yemen as the main provenances for the guns used against them.

Ayed told an extraordinary tale of the time he was stranded in Egypt. As tunnel boss, he was responsible for the diggers, all relatives of the tunnel patron, so he could not leave them behind without risking a blood feud. When they punched through on the tunnel into the Egyptian side, the army had been tipped off and started firing. Ayed got everyone and the shipment down into the tunnel but was too late to escape himself. He fled with the Bedouin suppliers into the mountains, then watched them take delivery of tonnes of weapons from dealers in Darfur. 'I stayed with the Bedouin for 12 days until I found a tunnel to go back to Rafah,' Ayed said.

'In the mountains, the Bedouin are heavily armed; they even have anti-aircraft weapons. The Egyptian army can't go there.' Abu Sihab, of the rogue militia in Al-Bureij, says: 'The good guns we are getting now are from Darfur. The bullets from Darfur are shit – I always check them and they are bad.'

There are exceptions, probably as common as the Las Vegas gambler who gives up after his big score. The only tunneller I met who had given up described tunnelling as addictive. 'It takes a special kind of person,' he said. He would only talk to me in secret; we met in the middle of a field of 3 foot-high corn and sat on the ground. Even then, he was nervous. He treated his 10-month digging as a high-risk investment; he got shares in return for labour and earned $45,000. Unlike any other tunneller, he never went back.

He now has a house and is looking for a wife. He is the exception.

Tunnellers such as Ayed live for the next tunnel; he says there are always shipments waiting with the Bedouin in Egypt; anyone who can get a tunnel across is assured of business.

Ayed has been buried three times, but never as disastrously as Keshta and his cousins. 'Only my head was free,' he said. 'It only took me two hours to dig myself out, and then I went back to digging.'

Neither his wife nor his family knew he was working on a tunnel; he told them he was working in construction in Gaza City and that it was difficult to come back at night because of the Israeli checkpoints that cut Palestinian Gaza into three sectors. When he did go home, he showered first and walked a circuitous path back.

Nadr never got to marry his Juliet or buy his 'cool' gun; the Israelis found him, still alive, in the collapsed tunnel. The photo of his miraculous rescue is on the wall of the Martyrs' Salon, but he is now in an Israeli prison with a lengthy sentence to serve; his secret fiancée has vowed to wait, but their life is essentially over.

For Ayed, given the number of tunnels being dug, and the Israeli explosives, his experience may not be enough; the chances are the night will come when he won't be showering and walking home ever again. Ayed and I discuss how many tunnellers have died, and he tells me he will leave the tunnel business for a steady job. But when I ask him what he dreams about, his eyes light up and he says: 'I dream of building a tunnel all for myself. I'll wait for this "hot" time [pressure from Israel and the PA] to pass. Now I have my own connections on the Egyptian side.' I point out the odds are against him. Even after the Israelis withdraw from Gaza soon, the PA's hunt will continue. He says with a big smile: 'No one will stop the tunnels. I'll teach my children.'

Bulldozer Sharon wins through, but bigger battles may lie ahead

NEVE DEKALIM

21 August 2005

Marie Colvin, Aviram Zino, Uzi Mahnaimi and Hala Jaber

Most of the teenagers had been awake all night at the three gates of Neve Dekalim when, just before dawn, they caught the first sight of the Israeli soldiers who had come to evacuate the largest Jewish settlement in Gaza. They roused themselves into a linked-arm barricade and began singing psalms.

By 8am the sun was beating down and the teenagers, mostly infiltrators from Israel and West Bank settlements, were joined by long-time residents who were actually the ones being moved out.

One young couple wheeled a pushcart with twin toddler girls with blonde ponytails to the front line. Teenage boys sporting what have become the settlers' characteristic orange T-shirts darted forward with sharpened screwdrivers to puncture the tyres of the army buses.

Despite such initial signs of youthful bravado, by yesterday Neve Dekalim's 2,500 residents had gone – barring a few left behind to ease the handover – as had some 85% of the 8,500 other people who until last weekend had lived in 21 settlements built in the midst of Gaza's 1.3 million Palestinians.

When the process resumes today after a break for the Sabbath, Israeli forces hope to clear the remaining settlements of Netzarim and Elei Sinai in northern Gaza and Katif, Atzmona and Slav in the Gush Katif bloc, before turning their attention to four isolated settlements in the West Bank. Once the bulldozers have destroyed the houses, the Palestinians are expected to move onto the land by October.

Some of the last settlers may yet put up resistance, however, especially in the Sanur and Homesh settlements, built on territory in the West Bank that religious Jews regard as part of Eretz, or biblical, Israel. And, in a further bizarre twist, youths from Neve Dekalim were last night frantically text messaging each other to gather this morning at the gates of their settlement, which they believed would be lightly guarded, to retake their now empty homes.

Militant Palestinian groups, too, could cause problems despite attempts by Mahmoud Abbas, the Palestinian president, to keep a lid on violence. Yesterday dozens of Hamas gunmen took over Gaza City's central square, threatening further attacks.

I spent the week with the Jashis, a Yemeni Jewish family. Avi, the father who had never lifted a hand in the home, was in charge of the packing. Naomi, his wife, shouted at him not to touch her things because she was not leaving, cooked ever bigger meals, and washed ever more laundry – even though her five children and husband had lived and slept in the same clothes for days.

On the night the army arrived I went out on a resistance operation with one of their sons, Adiel, 21, and other young 'commandos' as they set out to implement a plot they had cooked up since Ariel Sharon, the Israeli prime minister, announced the evacuation. Their plan was to short out the entire electricity grid to stop the soldiers. Rubi Braun, 19, led us down secret shortcuts to pick up fellow plotters.

Our raid swiftly turned to farce. First, Adiel shouted abuse at a passing army patrol – not the best move for undercover saboteurs – and broke down in tears. The 'commando' team retired to the Jashi family's veranda to make him tea to soothe his nerves. Then it turned out nobody had brought any tools, obliging the boys to disperse to their parents' homes to find some.

It was 3am, after another break for tea and hugs, when our group finally reached the electricity box. They poured their parents' barbecue accelerant onto newspaper, stuffed it into the box and lit a match.

The paper flared and fizzled out and that was it. Everyone appeared hugely relieved and went home, but not before swearing a solemn oath that they would return to Gaza.

Walking home in the moonlight, they passed the settler girls who had arrived from the West Bank in support, now sitting on the kerb in their orange T-shirts, no longer shouting abuse at the soldiers but in quiet one-to-one conversations.

When the army surrounded the synagogue at Neve Dekalim at 10am that day, its loudspeakers rang with Sharon's voice. They were playing a recording made six months ago in which the prime minister, once the settlers' champion, had reminded soldiers they had the right to refuse any order that interfered with their personal beliefs. There could have been no more dramatic demonstration of the volte face the pull-out represented for Sharon.

Inside the compound of the main synagogue, the teenage boys and girls finally separated after three days into same-sex groups, the girls into the Sephardic synagogue, the boys across the court-yard to the Ashkenazi synagogue.

The army also split up: male soldiers into the synagogue where the boys had holed up, female soldiers to the synagogue where the girls had gone.

As Neta Balban, an Israeli major, announced they would have to leave, the girls shouted her down with religious songs. They went on for more than 12 hours until the last were finally talked into leaving. Dehydrated and distraught, they were put on a bus to Ashkelon.

Late that night the soldiers came for the Jashi family. Avi cried quietly in the corner. Naomi was hanging up another batch of laundry and had the makings of chocolate cake on the kitchen table. She shouted and cried, was put on the bus out, ran back to kiss her house and was put on the bus again.

But she returned, scampering like a child a quarter her age to give her house a last kiss. Her sons sobbed as they finally corralled her into the bus.

On Friday night, in a hotel in Jerusalem for her first Sabbath outside Neve Dekalim and the first in 20 years that she had not cooked, Naomi sat bewildered at a picnic table, picking like a small bird at the donated fish.

'Where will I live? My boys can be ruined by this city,' she muttered. 'I am not feeling stable; this is not a good life.'

So what really happened last week? What was theatre and what was real? If the army had really wanted – and despite the threats posed by the 8,000 settlers of Gush Katif and 7,000 more infiltrators – it could have evacuated the settlements in 24 hours. Instead the troops listened to lectures from everyone from rabbis to 10-year-old girls on democracy and religion, and stood stone-faced as they were accused of being as bad as the Nazis.

Not one soldier dared to challenge the absurdity of such comparisons and point out to settlers they were being moved three miles, with their families, to inside the borders of a nation ready to receive them sympathetically and compensate them for their monetary, if not spiritual, losses.

For Sharon, like the rest of Israel watching the harrowing scenes on television, there should be cause for quiet satisfaction this weekend. Some 59% of people questioned in a poll for the *Yedioth Ahronoth* newspaper backed the pull-out; 89% said the security forces had handled it well.

For many members of his right-wing Likud party, however, Sharon remains guilty of the worst betrayal. Binyamin Netanyahu, his main rival, has called for an emergency party conference at which he is expected to challenge him for the leadership.

The polls give Netanyahu a 20% lead over Sharon among the 140,000 Likud members, many of whom are angry about the Gaza withdrawal and out for revenge. Sharon's position is complicated by the pressure from America to follow up the withdrawal with other concrete actions, almost all of them anathema to his rank and file.

Abbas, too, who has announced that long-delayed Palestinian elections will be held on 25 January, is under pressure from the militants – as yesterday's show of strength by Hamas demonstrated.

Both Hamas and Islamic Jihad, another militant group, have hailed Israel's withdrawal from the Gaza Strip as the victorious outcome of their military attacks. Although agreeing to maintain a ceasefire to allow an orderly Israeli pull-out, they have vowed to target the 235,000 Jewish settlers still in the West Bank and the 180,000 living in and around Arab east Jerusalem.

'The battle is not over,' said Osama Hamdan, Hamas's representative in Beirut. 'Negotiations alone failed to achieve such results; it was only the second intifada and the armed resistance that made this possible.'

There are other questions, too, linked to the ultimate economic viability of Gaza and its 1.3 million Palestinians, most of them impoverished. Palestinian sources say the crucial issue to be hammered out with the Israelis over the next few weeks is guaranteeing Gaza unfettered access to the outside world.

The Israelis have been insisting they should have a presence at the crossing to Egypt from Gaza. The Palestinians have refused, but say they will accept monitors from a third party, such as the European Union.

With unemployment running at an estimated 70%, the World Bank has warned that the withdrawal from Gaza could go badly wrong unless the Israeli government relaxes border controls to allow imports of necessities and exports of vegetables and fruit.

'Only when the people of Gaza can make stable contracts and import-export controls are relaxed will their economic situation get better,' said a source in the International Crisis Group, 'and that is the only security for Israel.'

Sharon may be loath to give in to any further pressure from the Americans, let alone from the Palestinians. Those who know him say he has now consolidated the boundaries of Israel to what he considers defensible.

The question now will not be how to move Sharon, because historically he moves only how and when he wants, but rather how he wants history to view him. At 77, this old warrior may be as difficult to predict as the people he leads.

MON 15 AUG

8,500 settlers in 21 settlements across Gaza are given leaflets telling them they have to leave by the following night.

TUE 16 AUG

First three settlements – Dugit, Rafiah Yam, and Pe'at Sadeh – are cleared, with little resistance.

WED 17 AUG

Settlers weep amid growing demonstrations in Netzer Hazani and Ganei Tal. A female soldier is stabbed and protesters set up barricades.

THURS 18 AUG

Settlers in Netzer Hazani throw paint and stones at soldiers before hiding in synagogue.

FRI 19 AUG

Bulldozers move in to Kerem Atzmona, while protesters in Kfar Darom try to blind soldiers with mirrors and pour sugar into petrol tanks.

SAT 20 AUG

Operation suspended for the Sabbath.

Five settlements in Gaza – Netzarim, Eli Sinai, Katif, Atzmona and Slav – and four in the West Bank – Ganim, Kadim, Sa-Nur, and Homesh – remain to be cleared.

Fear and defiance in the battered city: Beirut

16 July 2006

Marie Colvin and Uzi Mahnaimi

It was with the first sip of her morning coffee that Kokhi Hatan saw the Israeli tank explode before her eyes. 'The tank had moved only a few metres into a firing position when it was blown to bits by a huge mine,' she said.

The drama she watched from her back garden in the Galilee border village of Shtulah last Wednesday, as Hezbollah gunmen ambushed an Israeli patrol on the road running along the frontier with Lebanon, was the trigger for the worst crisis in the region for two decades.

Sources in Hezbollah, the radical Islamic organisation that runs a state-within-a-state in Lebanon, say the attack was five months in the planning.

The purpose was to seize hostages and hold them to ransom for prisoners in Israel.

The Hezbollah assault unit had clearly done their reconnaissance. After infiltrating overnight they smashed Israeli CCTV cameras that monitor the border and hid in a peach orchard to wait for two Israeli armoured 'Hummers' to begin a daily 9am patrol.

The border area had been mostly quiet since May 2000, when Israeli forces withdrew from southern Lebanon. Now the Hatans, an Israeli Kurdish family, watched in horror.

'They waited in the best location,' said Assaf, Kokhi Hatan's husband, pointing to a curve in the patrol road through his fields.

The two Hummers were hit by rocket-propelled grenades and went up in flames. Three soldiers were killed outright and two taken prisoner by the Hezbollah unit, which crossed back into Lebanon before a nearby Israeli base even knew what was happening.

The attack made clear how well-trained and equipped Hezbollah has become with the help of Iran, its main backer, since the Israeli withdrawal from south Lebanon. It has built outposts along the border, in some places only a hundred yards from the Israelis.

As Israeli reinforcements scrambled, Hezbollah units inside Lebanon began a harassing barrage. Mortars crashed with a sickening sound close to the Hatans' back garden as soldiers with megaphones urged villagers to take cover.

About 500 feet above, two Israeli Cobra assault helicopters fired missiles to stop the Hezbollah mortars. Every five seconds they released a puff of hot metal balloons to divert Hezbollah anti-aircraft rockets.

By the end of the fight, eight Israelis were dead including the tank crew, killed as they came to the rescue.

In the chaos it was 10.30am before the Israeli military realised that two soldiers – Ehud Goldwasser, 31, and Eldad Regev, 26 – had been captured. It was another 15 minutes before the military secretary to Ehud Olmert, the Israeli prime minister, passed him a note: two soldiers were confirmed abducted by Hezbollah.

Olmert could not believe what he was reading, Israeli sources said. He had been in an emotional meeting with the distressed parents of Gilad Shalit, 19, the Israeli soldier abducted in Gaza on 25 June. They had just been pressing him to order an immediate exchange of prisoners to free their son.

Now he was embroiled in a second crisis involving captured soldiers, unheard of in modern Israeli history. He called General Dan Halutz, the chief of staff, and said, 'Danny, try to find the soldiers.'

Then he had to tell Shalit's unhappy parents: 'I'm sorry. I'll do my best to bring back your son, but as you can see I can't give in to the terrorists' demands to release thousands of prisoners.'

Olmert, elected only four months ago, knew that the crisis could decide his fate.

Unlike his predecessor, Ariel Sharon, Olmert has no military career to bolster his authority.

Already two weeks into a massive military assault on Gaza in reaction to Shalit's abduction by Palestinians, Olmert ordered the opening of a second front. By midday Israel had launched a full-scale operation on its northern border.

Israeli sources said that the first air force sorties were aimed at 50 buildings where Hezbollah is thought to hide long-range Iranian-made rockets. Planes attacked 150 targets within 24 hours, dropping hundreds of tonnes of explosives.

As the confrontation grew Hezbollah rockets poured into northern Israel on an unprecedented scale – as many as 200 in the first 48 hours, according to the Israelis – and hitting as far south as Haifa, Israel's third city, for the first time.

The Israeli response rapidly escalated into an all-out attempt to cripple Hezbollah. Israel destroyed bridges across Lebanon, power stations, roads and glass-fronted business centres in Beirut. It bombed the international airport, sent warships to enforce a naval blockade and hit the highway to Damascus, the main overland route out of the country. All the fragile Lebanese government could do was appeal for a ceasefire.

'Our aim is to smash the Hezbollah,' said a military source, 'but if the rocket attacks do not stop, we'll consider sending in ground troops.'

Israel was gripped by the drama. Everyone serves in the army and knows someone in uniform. There is a tradition of 'never leaving a single soldier behind'. As a result, while the Arab world fulminated that the capture of 'only' three soldiers had caused the killing of scores of civilians, and the European Union criticised Israel's 'disproportionate response', no Israeli questioned the military onslaught to rescue three soldiers.

It was a catastrophe for Beirut, which had been in the final stages of recovery from many years of civil war, expecting a bumper crop of tourists. Now it is a city under siege.

By far the heaviest toll from the bombing has been borne by civilians. Most of the dead – 96 according to the latest count yesterday – have been civilians, hospital staff said.

In Bir al-Abed, Hezbollah's south Beirut heartland and home of its leader, Sheikh Hassan Nasrallah, downed wires snaked across streets littered with bomb damage and young men scurried for cover as Israeli planes appeared overhead for the fourth day running.

Usually in Bir al-Abed, a teeming suburb of tenements and shops, a stranger cannot walk the crowded streets more than a few yards without being stopped and questioned threateningly by Hezbollah militants. Now the streets were deserted and the young men asked their questions in a near frenzy.

'Okay, come, see, the Israelis are killing us!' Then, 'Planes, I can see them, hear that!' Bombs or missiles hit targets nearby with three loud crumps.

The ferocity of the Israeli attacks took Hezbollah by surprise. On the front line, its leaders appear nervous but resolute. It may have miscalculated the response to its raid but it was not backing down. 'If you want open war, we will give you open war,' Nasrallah said to Israel in a television address in Beirut on Friday after Israeli missiles struck his house.

Dramatically, he introduced video footage of an attack on an Israeli gunboat, saying, 'Now in the middle of the sea, facing Beirut, the Israeli warship that has attacked the infrastructure, people's homes and civilians – look at it burning.'

Israel confirmed that a ship had been hit. Four Israeli sailors were reported missing.

Celebratory gunfire erupted around the city, including, it appeared, from the Lebanese army as tracer fire from anti-aircraft guns arced overhead.

Although Hezbollah is unpopular in Christian east Beirut, it retains broad support because it is seen as having forced the Israeli withdrawal from southern Lebanon in 2000. The question now is whether this crisis will increase support or eventually rebound against it.

The fragile political situation in Lebanon has become dangerously fluid. Both Iran, Israel's arch-enemy, and Syria – the former occupying power and another Hezbollah sponsor – are manoeuvring for advantage. And Beirutis are dreading the return of their violent past.

'We are so depressed,' said Layal al-Arab, 22, a nurse. 'Two days ago we had everything, shopping and beautiful cafés. Now everything is damaged – including ourselves.'

Birth, death and destruction on Lebanon's road to hell

30 July 2006

Marie Colvin sees the innocents caught up in retreat from besieged village.

Three hours after she gave birth to a boy named Attar, 27-year-old Abir Feras started walking. Her home had been destroyed by an Israeli airstrike and when the next barrage blew in the windows of the hospital where she should have been resting, she feared that all her family would die unless they left.

First she took the intravenous drip out of her arm. Then she wrapped the newborn in a blanket as her husband Mohammed gathered her three other young children together.

With the scream of Israeli jets overhead, they began the nine-mile trek from Bint Jbeil, a southern Lebanese village besieged by the Israeli army, to the town of Tibnin, where 1,600 desperate men, women and children had taken refuge in another hospital.

They had to walk because no cars could be driven on the cratered road.

'I was breathing so hard I was dizzy and in so much pain,' Feras said when she reached the hospital, a stopping place for the poor, the old and the infirm, many of whom had been trapped in their villages under an onslaught for the past two weeks.

The last stretch of the road to Tibnin rises up a steep hill with no shelter from the sun, and families clutching white pieces of cloth to show that they are not fighters are weeping, shaking and barely able to speak by the time they arrive.

Feras carried her baby for four hours until she reached the fragile safety of the hospital as more jets roared down in dives, terrifying everyone inside, and surveillance drones swarmed overhead like angry wasps.

Last Thursday four-day-old Attar lay on a mat in the basement of the hospital, writhing and grimacing, apparently from pains in the stomach.

The basement was lit only by candles on the floor because the electricity had been cut off. The bread and beans that the adults were given every day were of no use to Attar. 'I have no milk for him,' Feras said, gesturing to her breast.

'I think I was too frightened. We are getting milk from every person who can help us, but every day it is different milk. There is no Nido [formula milk for babies].'

The hospital at Tibnin is a milestone on the road from hell. When they reach it, the shattered but relieved villagers look as if they are falling into the safety of a battlefield fox hole. They bring heart-stopping stories from a devastated hinterland.

Sometimes they strain to be heard against the background noise of huge bombs landing nearby. Everyone cringes and children scream.

A little girl called Hibba ran around the hospital courtyard, picking geraniums until her father dragged her inside when the planes came closer. He was feeling guilty. Hibba had a cut under her eye because when an Israeli bomb fell near her family as they were walking to Tibnin, her father threw her to the ground for protection. The family survived but she was wounded by a stone on the ground.

There is only one doctor in the hospital and he is angry. Nabil Harkus earned his degree in Bulgaria, worked in Europe for 10 years and then came home to Tyre, the main southern Lebanese city.

He volunteered to serve at Tibnin hospital and in another time he would have ended a long day with a cold beer. But when I arrived, he pounced on me as the only foreigner, denouncing Israel, the West and what people in Lebanon see as the destruction of their country.

After an argument Harkus apologised, saying: 'I lost my control but who can see this and not scream?'

What Harkus sees is a daily stream of misery. He chainsmokes at night in his bed just off the emergency room, where he gets no sleep and has lived in the same bright blue hospital scrubs for a week.

'I see injured civilians and they're only the poor people who have no money to run away,' he said yesterday. 'Only the poor people die. I am a doctor but I have to wrap the dead people for their coffins.'

Nobody in this hospital refuge sleeps until 6am, when the bombing subsides.

Children run through hallways that are dark in daytime because there is no power.

They are shooed back only when they try to run outside; their parents sit shell-shocked along the walls and others are ready when the drones overhead might target a gathering.

Everyone here knows that two Israeli missiles hit two Red Cross ambulances last week and one precision-guided bomb scored a direct hit on a United Nations post, killing four UN officers. They had been calling headquarters for six hours to liaise with the Israeli army, which was well aware of their co-ordinates.

They were in a border post founded in 1948 and took shelter in the bunker that was constructed to survive the 155mm artillery normally used by the Israelis.

According to the UN, the bomb that hit the officers in their shelter was designed for exactly what it did: it crushed the building on top of them and left no chance that anyone would survive.

The atmosphere at the hospital is febrile. On Friday Arbid Malek, a 38-year-old professor of mathematics who had come to southern Lebanon on holiday to visit his family, arrived at the hospital, having spent 16 days under bombardment.

Beside him was Latifa Baraqat, 45, who has eight children. When I met her she was in the hospital basement, living in a room measuring 10 foot by 5 foot. There, lying on a pallet, were her 10-month-old twins Ali and Mohammed.

Baraqat was dressed in a black robe and gold hijab and this was the first time she had seen a distinct difference in the twins' personalities. Ali, whom she cradled as we spoke, never cried, even though there were huge explosions outside. Mohammed erupted in screams.

This family, like so many others, had come from Bint Jbeil. Baraqat had held out there for 15 days and served a last meal of bread and the slices of cheese that they kept for the other children.

Baraqat said they had fled from house to house until Israeli helicopters hovered above the building next door to them and rocketed it nine times. They then decided to walk to Tibnin.

'We were surrounded by missiles. They were hitting everywhere – we only decided to walk because we were staying for so many days in a basement and we had no more food or water for the children,' she said.

Later in the day a desperate family group of 13 people came from the village of Aitaroun, near Bint Jbeil.

One woman, 7½ months pregnant with her first child, collapsed in the emergency room still wearing her pink pyjamas, the only thing she had managed to leave her house with.

Her husband Mohammed, 27, a labourer, sat next to her, his hands on her belly because they were so worried that the walk had damaged their baby.

'He's kicking and kicking so much – I am in a lot of pain,' she said. It had taken them six hours to walk from Aitaroun because she kept having to sit down and rest.

Her mother wept beside her: they had left a sister behind and nobody knew where she was.

Gaza's deadly guardians

30 September 2007

A radical Islamist state has emerged from the smoking ruins of Gaza, threatening a new war with nearby Israel. Marie Colvin ventures into the lair of the Hamas extremists imposing their hardline doctrine on Palestinians trapped there.

Hamas wants you to believe it has created a benevolent sanctuary where once chaos reigned. At the beginning of the journey into Gaza it's easy to believe that things are better.

There is no longer a Palestinian immigration desk after the long walk from the air-conditioned Erez terminal on the Israeli side, past concrete blast walls, and down a dusty track in the furnace heat. But further down the road, Hamas gunmen have taken over the checkpoints. They are polite and well turned out in blue camouflage trousers, clean black T-shirts, shiny black boots.

Once hostile, they now smile at returning foreigners who fled after the kidnapping of Alan Johnston, the BBC reporter, and the savage bloodletting between the Palestinian National Authority (PNA) forces and Hamas in June that left the fundamentalist party in absolute power.

So does everyone else in Gaza. It's like hearing the first songbird of spring. The welcome starts in the taxi. 'Gaza is safe now. We have security, praise be to God,' says Munir, my driver for years, who always in the past shook his head and moaned about how terrible everything was.

It's the same at the Al Deira hotel, mostly empty, where once aid workers, diplomats, journalists and sophisticated Gazans mixed on the terrace overlooking the Mediterranean. 'Everything is safe now. You are welcome,' says Amir at the front desk.

For the first time on a trip to Gaza, I was stopped going the wrong way down a one-way street, by one of the young Hamas volunteers in yellow vests now standing up to drivers in a culture that considers a red light to be a mere suggestion to slow down.

The rubbish still smells, but now it is piled neatly in the streets. Families stroll late at night. Gone is the gunfire that used to punctuate days and nights and often escalated into street battles that left innocents dead on the pavements.

Then you start talking to people in private.

Young men show you bruised limbs and welts on their feet; every girl wears a hijab head covering and, for the first time, women wear niqab Saudi-style face coverings that reveal only the eyes. And people whisper.

Welcome to Hamastan.

Ahmed Al-Naba'at, 24, sits in his courtyard in an oversized Barcelona shirt. He looks too young to be the father of the three young children who toddle barefoot round the tiny dirt courtyard.

His feet still hurt. Hamas came for him at 2am.

About 30 armed men, their faces masked but wearing the black uniforms and badges of the Izzedine al-Qassam Brigade, the military wing of Hamas, had surrounded the house. They covered his eyes and took him away in a car.

'They took me somewhere, I don't know, a room,' Naba'at says. He has high cheekbones and the near-black skin of his Sudanese ancestry. 'They were screaming and beating me, punching me, slapping me on the face,' he says. 'Then they tied my legs together and started falaka' – a traditional Arabic torture where the soles of the feet are beaten with sticks. 'I relaxed.'

He sees the surprise in my face. 'I thought they were going to kill me,' he explains. 'When I realised it's just falaka, I thought, okay, it's just torture.'

Qassam dumped him near his home, hours later. It took him half an hour to walk what usually takes two minutes. 'You were lucky,' interjects his unsympathetic father, who is sitting against a courtyard wall. 'Most of the people they beat, they throw them unconscious in the street and they are not found until the morning.'

His crime? Earlier that night at a party for a friend's wedding, Naba'at had danced and played a song popular in Gaza – an over-romanticised ballad to Samih al-Madhoun, a Fatah commander executed by Hamas during the fighting. Hamas cameramen had filmed as Madhoun was dragged down the street amid spitting crowds, shot in the stomach, beaten and shot some more. It was shown on Hamas television that night.

The overblown ballad of his death 'Your blood is not for free Samih/You left behind an earthquake/We will not forget you Samih' is such a Gazan hit that many young people have it on their mobile phones. Hamas, predictably, is furious. Three of Al-Naba'at's friends who had danced at the wedding were also beaten.

Al-Naba'at, who left school at 14 and worked as a farm labourer and painter, has little recourse. He is too afraid to sleep at home any more. His father is clearly exasperated like many of the older generation, he thinks his sons should shut up. He points to another son, 17-year-old Mustafa. Hamas came after him when he burnt a Hamas flag: they arrested his father and twin brother until he gave himself up.

Hamas is not just going after the poor. Azil Akhras is a sophisti-cated 24-year-old woman with heavily kohled eyes, thick, flowing black hair and rouged lips, comfortable in her jeans and tight red shirt. Life used to be shopping, going out maybe to Roots, a popu-lar Gaza nightclub even though it now serves only soft drinks and going to the beach. Her life changed dramatically three months ago when Hamas took over Gaza.

'Now, I cover my head when I go in a car. Hamas is at the checkpoints. Last week, they stopped a girl who was not covered and they beat her brother when he tried to protect her.'

She and her sister must be careful; they are alone. Their father, a former government health minister, has fled Gaza to escape Hamas. He has holed up in Ramallah, the West Bank capital, and is unable to return.

It's not just shopping trips she misses. A university graduate, Akhras had wanted to sit her master's degree; she wanted to travel. 'I had an idea, I wanted to be famous in history. Maybe a journalist,' she says. 'Now, there's no chance, I can't even go outside.' She resents Hamas's repression. 'If I decide to cover [my head], it will be for my God, not some Qassam soldier.'

Gazans are living in a climate of fear. The place is eerily serene, not only because of the presence of disciplined Hamas security forces on the streets but, as in all successful police states, because everyone has started policing themselves, afraid of the consequences of stepping over a line not defined in formal law.

Hamas took power after five days of vicious, internecine fighting with the security forces of the PNA, who mostly belong to the rival Fatah organisation co-founded by Yasser Arafat, the late president.

Tension had escalated into clashes between the secular Fatah, who governed for a decade and whose members stack the civil service and security forces, and Hamas, after the religious party won national elections in March 2006.

The differences were exacerbated by Gaza's isolation. The international community cut funds to the Palestinian government after the Hamas election victory. Israel blocked the millions in tax revenue it was supposed to pass on for imports, and closed the borders intermittently. The economy went into freefall.

A national unity government formed in February failed to end the confrontation. But the speed of the coup in Gaza was shocking.

Hamas fielded only about 7,000 members of the Executive Force, its police force, which was backed by the Izzedine al-Qassam Brigade, the military wing of the party, against the 70,000-strong government forces loyal to Mahmoud Abbas, the Palestinian president.

There are many reasons for the swift collapse: the government security forces hadn't been paid for 18 months and were demoralised by the corruption of their own leaders. Their commanders fled, and many foot soldiers found that their guns were locked in storage. Hamas was better armed, better trained, and fought with the single-mindedness of those with a cause.

It was the worst ever clash among Palestinians: 110 died, and the population is still shocked by the brother-on-brother nature of the battle. Today there is a deadlock, and essentially two Palestinian governments. Abbas fired the Hamas-led coalition government and named a new emergency cabinet, but its powers run only in the West Bank. Hamas ministers refused to step down.

By Palestinian law, the government must be renewed by the parliament, but Hamas dominates the legislature and, anyway, it lacks a quorum: about one third of its members are in Israeli jails for belonging to Hamas.

The evidence of the ferocity of the fighting can be seen across Gaza city. The headquarters of the Preventive Security Service, the PNA's main security force, was the last stronghold. Now occupied by the Executive Force, there are gaping holes in the walls from bullets and rockets.

Abbas's presidential house is guarded by Hamas police who brew tea under new posters of Hamas members killed in the fighting. They shake their heads at the marble floors and luxurious furnishings, contrasting it with the home of Ismail Haniya, the Hamas prime minister, who lives in the al-Shati refugee camp.

At the Muntada, the Palestinian version of the White House, Hamas fighters stroll the corridors, and dust gathers on Abbas's rosewood desk, where Arafat once sat.

Hamas is extending its control. Nobody is safe if the example of Ashraf Juma, one of their more articulate opponents, is anything to go by. Juma is a senior member of Fatah, who refused to leave his home or office in Rafah, Gaza's southernmost city on Egypt's border. He is one of the most popular politicians in Gaza: when Hamas won the election, sweeping Gaza, he was one of the few elected from the Fatah list.

He was leader of the al-Aqsa hawks during the first intifada (uprising), and hands out money from his own pocket to the needy of both Fatah and Hamas (these days it's from his brother's, a wealthy businessman). His latest project is to find £5,000 for school uniforms for poor children.

None of it was any protection from Hamas. It began on the internet. Juma was criticised on the official Hamas website for supposedly sending Abbas the names of people whose salaries should be cut because they were Hamas members. Then critical leaflets were distributed in the local mosque. 'Someone called from Hamas and said, "Leave your office. This is a preparation for an attack on you,"' he says, sitting at home in a white short-sleeved shirt, dark trousers and sandals.

The next day, as he and his office staff finished evening prayers, blue police cars pulled up, disgorging men in the uniform of the Executive Force. They also wore black masks.

As he opened the door, he saw his secretary, Osama, trying to fend them off with a table. The gunmen began screaming and shot Osama in the thigh. They started beating him in the hallway before running off. 'You were my sons. I served you,' he shouted after them.

Juma shakes his balding head, and describes how the situation turned almost farcical. As word spread that he had been attacked, hundreds of people poured into Shifa hospital and packed the emergency room and courtyard.

'There were so many people, the doctors couldn't work properly. Look, they put stitches in wrong,' he says, ducking his head to show newly healed scars. The crowds carried him out of the hospital before the doctors had finished, afraid that Hamas would return, and grabbed Osama from the operating room before his broken hand and gunshot wound were treated.

They almost killed their hero. Juma fell unconscious, Osama writhed in pain. Hundreds poured into the streets, denouncing the Executive Force. A doctor finally came and treated both of them at home.

It was a night of terror for many. Ismael, 29, an English teacher for the United Nations Relief and Works Agency, sits in the front room of the house he had just painted for a marriage that now will never happen.

'My last hours before they came were happy,' recalls Ismael, who doesn't want his last name used because Hamas threatened to kill him if he told the story.

'I had just gotten engaged and I spent from 7.30pm to 11pm talking with my friends about what we would do for the celebrations,' he says.

Suddenly, his house was surrounded by armed men in black with Qassam Brigade emblems. 'One tried to hit me with a stick, and I said, "What are you doing? I have done nothing."'

They took him first to the Sayed Sayel Executive Force post. 'They put me against a wall and started shouting, "Have you been to a demonstration?"' he says. 'They became hysterical, shouting, "You have been making riots here," beating me with sticks, metal bars, stones.'

His ordeal had just begun. 'They said, "What about the orphans?"' Ismael supports two orphans, Allah, who is nine and needs an eye operation, and Dina, who is 11, while trying to get them medical help through an American charity. Hamas said he should have no contact with foreigners.

They beat Ismael for an hour and a half, moving him at one point during the night to Idara Madaneh, the civil administration building in Jabaliya camp. He was blindfolded, but two young teenagers who had been taken in ran to him, screaming 'Teacher! Teacher!', probably recognising him from school.

'Then Hamas started beating me on the arm I was using to try to protect the children,' he says.

He was finally released at 4am with a warning not to talk, and not to go to a hospital. A doctor friend came round and treated him secretly.

Photographs from the June beating show welts on his back, ferocious bruises on his left arm, and a swollen right arm and elbow. He won't show me his legs out of modesty, but says they were black, and his knees are still not right.

But that was not the worst. His fiancée's family heard of the incident and believed he was a political activist against Hamas, which would endanger her future. Her father revoked his permission to marry and he has not spoken to his fiancée, a fellow teacher, since then. 'My sister tells me she is crying and crying,' Ismael says.

Can't they marry when things calm down? 'No chance. This is our tradition.' For the first time in a long story, he brushes away a tear.

'Most of the educated people here feel they are living in a country that doesn't belong to them,' he says when he recovers.

Hamas is not triumphalist in its takeover, as was the first prophet of militant Islam, Ayatollah Khomeini, who immediately set himself up against the West and all who didn't want to follow his unforgiving brand of Islam.

But then he had oil, 50 million people, an army, air force and navy, and control of his own borders. Hamas is isolated and depends on international aid, with little but farming, fishing and a hostile neighbour that controls its borders, sea and skies.

This heavily armed statelet is squeezed between Israel's southern border and Egypt's northern border, separated by a chunk of Israel from the West Bank, the bigger, richer other half of the Palestinian 'state'.

The West Bank is still occupied by Israeli soldiers and Jewish settlers: they withdrew from Gaza two years ago, but still control the borders and ban all air and sea traffic, except for tiny wooden fishing boats allowed to go out six miles.

Since the Hamas takeover in June, Israel has not opened the main crossing points for even a day, and the economy has collapsed. The United Nations Relief and Works Agency (UNRWA) estimates unemployment at 80% among the 1.4 million inhabitants. There are no exports; a trickle of food bought by private Palestinian merchants from their Israeli counterparts is allowed across at the tiny Sufa crossing. It must be one of the strangest commercial dealings in the world. The Israeli army moves in pallets from about 100 trucks a day, shooting at anyone who approaches before they withdraw behind the fence; then there is a bizarre Mad Max-style race by forklifts to get the merchandise left in the no-man's-land.

In three months, an estimated 70,000 jobs have been lost in the construction industry alone. UNRWA has had to stop £47 million in projects funded by donors; apartments for those whose homes were destroyed by Israeli fire, oxidation projects for Gaza's overflowing sewage-treatment plants. Everyone is desperate. 'This place is a powder keg waiting to explode,' said John Ging, UNRWA's Gaza director.

Instead of the open defiance of Khomeini's Iran, Hamas has developed a parallel system: show a reasonable face to the world in the hope of ending Gaza's isolation, while enforcing the unforgiving law of the state of Hamastan at home.

Ismail Haniya, the silver-haired Hamas prime minister, could be a poster boy for moderate Islam. When I see him, he is sitting with Arab journalists, and gently lecturing them like the professor he once was. Aware he stands little chance with the West, he is seeking Arab support.

He tells them that negotiations are possible under certain conditions with Mahmoud Abbas, who is welcome to come back to Gaza. No women will be forced to wear the hijab – that is a personal choice. Well, of course there can be no negotiations with Israel, although that could happen if they recognise Palestinian rights.

There is duplicity even in the detail, however: Haniya may say that women are free not to cover their heads, but before I go to his office an aide calls to tell me to be sure to wear a headscarf.

And recognising Palestinian rights is Hamas-speak for 'We want all of the land of mandate Palestine, from the Mediterranean to the Jordan River,' a maximalist position that ignores the fact that most Palestinians have moved on from 1948 to accept the existence of Israel, and would settle for a two-state solution. Negotiations are moribund, but Fatah-led governments have signed agreements with Israel recognising the reality that two states is the only solution.

Haniya may be the smooth-talking Hamas frontman but he lacks real power. A former professor of religion, he was a compromise choice fielded by Khaled Mesha'al, the exiled Hamas leader based in Damascus. 'When we were negotiating, whenever a difficult point came up, Haniya had to leave the room to call Mesha'al,' one of Abbas's top lieutenants said.

The real power lies with Mahmoud Zahar, who is in the strange position of being a foreign minister who can't travel from Gaza (Israel has closed the borders even to government officials).

A militant once expelled by Israel, he was expected to be prime minister after the Hamas victory, but Mesha'al apparently considered him too radical, and more of a threat than Haniya.

Sitting on a couch in the foreign ministry damaged in an Israeli bombing, he is scathing about Abbas. '[He] committed big crimes against the law, against human interest.' Zahar is dressed in a light-grey safari suit, his beard neatly trimmed, his shoes polished. He exudes confidence and scorns any need for Hamas to reach out for a compromise. 'Abbas is acting as an agent of America and Israel.'

The power that stretches beyond his title peeps out. 'We have information that Fatah are organising themselves into cells,' he says. 'We will find them and we will crush them.'

There is no sense of urgency in finding a solution to the desperate need of the average Gazan with a large family and no work.

'We are not in a hurry. Palestinians are used to being under siege. I believe sooner or later the West will change its mind,' he says calmly.

Again, during the interview, his power beyond that of the average diplomat is revealed when he takes a phone call about the siege of the powerful Dagmoush clan, the kidnappers of Alan Johnston, the BBC journalist. Earlier in the week the clan killed two Hamas policemen.

'Tell them that by 10pm we will go in if they have not agreed. We will enter their houses one by one.'

Across town that very siege is under way. Hamas has again surrounded the Dagmoush neighbourhood as they did to get Johnston back. They have cut off the water and electricity.

Few in Gaza have any sympathy for the Dagmoushes. One of the leaders of the clan and Johnston's main kidnapper, Mumtaz Dagmoush spouts extremist Al-Qaeda rhetoric, but his so-called Army of Islam has about 20 members and is better known for theft, gun smuggling and kidnapping. Fatah let Gaza's powerful families run wild, sometimes using them against Hamas.

Hamas has taken them on. Breaking the Dagmoushes is crucial to consolidating power.

The discipline of Hamas on the front line of the siege of the concrete-block houses in the neighbourhood is in contrast to Fatah's members who won't talk until they get word from a commander over the walkie-talkie. Once allowed to talk, Abu Yehia, the local commander, doesn't have much to say. 'We are imposing law and order. This is our duty. Islam tells us that.'

Hamas is demanding that the Dagmoushes surrender the guilty members of the family, and give back stolen weapons.

That night, the family does surrender, led by Mumtaz Dagmoush. He is double the size of the average Gazan, tall, broad-shouldered, with a shaggy dark beard and wild hair. He and his entourage screech their pick-up trucks into the Preventive Security compound, jump out waving guns and, seeing me, starts waving his M16, shouting: 'Get this journalist out of here!' With both sides jostling and shoving, for moments it seems there will be a shoot-out.

Dagmoush finally hands over bags of guns, then marches with his bodyguard into the darkened police headquarters and starts pounding on the commander's door, shouting: 'I gave you my weapons, let me in there.'

The M16 is in the air again, 50 men all shoving with guns and elbows, and shouting.

Eventually, he calms down and half an hour later is talking to Abu Dahab, the Hamas commander.

Dagmoush tells me, 'We've just had an English guest staying with us for a while,' referring to Alan Johnston, the kidnapped journalist. I asked him why he kidnaps, and if his activities other than kidnapping will be affected under Hamas. He shrugs: 'Business is business,' he says.

Now that Hamas has solidified power, they are putting in place their system of keeping it. One part of this is a new 'ladies unit', reminiscent of the one in Iran where fierce, make-up-free women drag other women out of cars and away for re-education. Ominously, Hamas have failed so far to set up a court system, so cases are being heard by an Islamic judge.

The one thriving industry is the arms industry.

I visit a Qassam area leader in Yibne camp in southern Gaza who has been 'cooking' for three days making the explosive mixture that goes in the rockets they fire into Israel.

He takes me to one of the many armouries they have and shows me the extraordinary range of weapons they manufacture locally, mostly in underground factories. What they can't make, they smuggle through tunnels from Egypt.

The armoury is in a small, concrete block house, indistinguishable from its neighbours in the squalid maze of the camp. The home-made weapons I see include foot-wide land mines, tank-busting missiles, guns, rocket-propelled grenades, all stored amid the clutter of a bedroom with flowers on the shelf above the bed and a teddy bear lying belly-up on the floor.

He is nervous while we are there – the Israelis target such places if they get information from collaborators – but he opens up when we go to another house for tea, although he won't give his name. He is unconcerned about his outside image, and this is the true voice of Hamas.

'Of course we will create an Islamic state. This is called for in the Holy Koran,' he says. What would that mean, I ask him.

Well, for one, sharia law. 'For a murder, death, not this life sentence there is now. A thief should have his hand cut off. An adulteress must be stoned,' he says, in a chillingly nonchalant voice.

'There is no possibility of recognising Israel,' he says. 'All the land is ours. We are taught this by our leaders and they will never compromise.'

His certitude comes from how Hamas recruits. It gets them young; my informant started at 14. Only when he proved himself 'mentally and spiritually' was he allowed to join Qassam and receive military training.

And not all girls are like Azil Akhras. Gehad Nehan, 19, is studying law at the Hamas-dominated Islamic University in Gaza. She wears glasses, a hijab, and is covered in a navy-blue robe down to her thick black shoes. 'Hamas has taken over the police stations and now the life is good.'

She insists women are equal, but as she talks, a different reality is revealed. At the university, she says, 'the boys say woman is weak, her work must be in the home. I say this is wrong.'

Even getting to study was a struggle. 'My father hits me and he punishes me and says I should not go to the university. It's difficult.'

But despite having described Hamastan as virtually a perfect state, she has the yearning of all here to leave. 'I want to travel all over the world and see people and how they live.'

Those who have already travelled are the most angry at Hamas.

One restaurant owner begins by extolling Hamas for improving security. He sits at a banquette in his eatery in a yellow polo shirt. Christmas streamers still hang from the ceiling, and Whitney Houston is on the soundtrack.

'And they cancelled all family connections,' he adds. 'Before, if someone was connected to the government, they could eat and just not pay.

'But they are not the future for the Palestinian people,' he insists. 'We need a government that can deal with the international community.' Despite growing dissatisfaction such as his, there is little sign that the green flags of Hamastan will be coming down any time soon.

Iran

Iran split as fun-hungry young spurn rigged poll

TEHRAN

15 February 2004

They call themselves the Third Generation. Twenty-five years after Ayatollah Khomeini returned from exile, the grandchildren of his Islamic revolution are angry that conservatives have blocked their hopes of reform by engineering almost certain victory in elections this week. What they will do about it is probably the most important question for the future of Iran.

They are a powerful force by sheer weight of numbers: an estimated two out of three Iranians are under the age of 30. Most of them are more likely to turn to the internet for guidance than the mosque. They do not agree with Khomeini's edict: 'There is no fun in Islam.'

Perhaps the most prominent of the new generation is Zahra Eshraghi, Khomeini's granddaughter. Despite her credentials, she was among more than 2,000 reformist candidates that the Guardian Council, a 12-man unelected conservative body that vets candidates for their adherence to Islamic law, banned from standing in the elections.

She is soft-spoken but blunt in her outrage. 'There is no defence for their actions,' Eshraghi said yesterday. 'What they did was illegal. Now I cannot defend the government any longer.'

The result of the ban was that half of the parliament resigned. A boycott of the election has been called by the reform parties, including one led by Eshraghi's husband, Muhammad Reza Khatami, a sitting MP who was also barred from standing and who is the brother of Muhammad Khatami, the president.

Eshraghi, 40, could not be further from the image of the stern, turbaned Khomeini.

Like most younger Iranians, she loves fashion and dresses in a thigh-length shaved fur coat with fur cuffs and high-heeled suede boots. She throws a long black chador, the covering for women that is law in Iran, over the ensemble when a man enters her office.

She laughs easily but is stern in her denunciations, calling her famous ancestor into the fray. 'If he was alive, it would never have come to this. I think the conservatives have set us back 300 to 400 years,' she said.

Last Friday, the traditional day for prayers, teenagers out of sight of their elders at the resort village of Darband, in the mountains above Tehran, stretched the concept of the chador beyond recognition.

One teenage girl made do with a hip-length leather jacket and a skirt, her scarf pushed back to reveal blonde streaks in her dark hair. Boys in reflective sunglasses and tracksuits chatted and laughed with girls at open-air restaurants.

Nobody seemed worried about the clerics' mandatory separation of the sexes.

However, this cheery scene concealed confusion, disillusionment and anger. A gaggle of fashionably dressed girls curled up on one banquette, discussing whether to boycott the parliamentary election this Friday. One had taken an informal poll at her university; nine out of 10 were planning to stay away from the polls.

'I'm not going to vote,' said Somayeh, a 23-year-old business administration university student. 'How can we vote when there is no choice? This is not a democratic vote.'

It is a far cry from the parliamentary election in 2000, when 80% of Iran's 22 million voters selected the reformists. During their four-year term they tried and failed to loosen the strict Islamic guidelines and to rein in the power of the unelected conservatives who control the judiciary, intelligence and security and discipline the press.

The reformists did not get a single piece of important legislation into law. The Guardian Council, which checks whether proposed legislation complies with sharia (Islamic law), vetoed them all. In this election the conservatives ended any pretence of democracy.

Campaigning began on Thursday, a day after celebrations of the 25th anniversary of Khomeini taking power. These were far more muted than in previous years, with pamphlets being handed out on the streets. The government's biggest challenge will be getting enough people to the polls; a low turnout would be an embarrassment in a country where more than 50% routinely vote.

Predicting what will happen after Friday's ballot is difficult. There are two Irans. On the day when the teenagers were enjoying spring temperatures in the mountains, hundreds attended prayers at the University of Tehran led by Ayatollah Khamenei, the supreme religious leader and Khomeini's successor. He told a crowd of women in all-enveloping chadors and men in baggy suits that their enemies were trying to undermine the elections. It was clear he meant the reform candidates.

Watching was 25-year-old Hamide Mostafavi, a computer student with three children.

'He [Khamenei] is perfect,' she said. 'I can't see any problem with him.'

Asked what he thought about the banned MPs, Ali Rabbani

Nejad, a hefty cleric in robes and a white turban, said: 'They are spies.'

So far there is no sign that the majority of the Third Generation will do more than boycott the elections, undermining the legitimacy of the expected conservative government.

Active resistance will certainly not come from the 'first generation' – the peers of Khomeini – nor from the fathers and mothers who lived through the revolution and fear a return of the violence of the early years of the regime.

After the banning of the elected reformists, however, there is a nascent movement among the young for what is being called phase two of the reform movement. They are taking an increasingly vocal stand, a risky business in a country that jails outspoken journalists and writers.

Most had been committed to reconciling Islam and democracy, but now say the fact that unelected conservatives could overrule majority opinion has shown that to be impossible.

'We believed we could achieve change gradually, within the democratic institutions. Now we have lost all hope of that,' said Omid Memarian, a 26-year-old journalist who moved to a non-governmental organisation after the youth magazine that employed him was closed down for being un-Islamic.

'I couldn't believe it when I heard that they banned all the reform people,' Memarian said. 'I have voted in every election since I was 16, but I'm not going to vote in this one. I'm not going to take part in their theatre.'

He added: 'You can use my name – I don't care if I go to prison.'

Memarian said the conservatives had allowed a small measure of social freedom to depoliticise the younger generation so that it would be easier for them to hang on to power.

Many students are loath to take to the streets – partly because when they last did so they were attacked by regime thugs; and partly because they believe that the reform party failed to live up to their expectations. Disillusionment has bred apathy among many.

'President Khatami says the right things, but he is no hero,' Memarian said.

He and others who support change in Iran believe that the reform movement must go back to basics and organise grassroots opposition among students, non-governmental and women's organisations.

'The strategy of the reform people was to reform from inside, through law building,' said Hamid Jalaiepour, a professor at the University of Tehran and former editor of several closed reformist newspapers. He was banned from standing in the last election and served a prison sentence. He has another court date three days after the election. 'Now we want an Islamic republic without special rights for the clergy.'

There are fears among more liberal Iranians about what will happen next. 'It is possible the conservatives will try to ban everything after the election,' said Eshraghi – strange words from the granddaughter of the man who founded the Islamic Republic of Iran.

Despair and fear among the Tehran dancing classes

26 June 2005

At a dinner last week I sat with a young Iranian friend who was weeping openly by the end of our Indian tandoori, writes Marie Colvin.

He faced an impossible choice: he loved his country and wanted to stay to work within the system but had just spent two months in prison without charge, apparently over something carried on his mildly critical internet website. He had been beaten for hours each day.

He was crying at the memory of his head being smashed against the concrete wall of a prison cell for four hours one day and because he felt a coward. Mostly he was crying because, as he put it: 'I just can't take even one more minute in prison,' and he felt he should be stronger and stand up for his belief in reform.

All he could think was that if Mahmoud Ahmadinejad were elected they would come for him the next day.

I told him to go. At the time, I thought he was being paranoid. Ahmadinejad, the mayor who looks and sounds like a throwback to bygone revolutionary days, seemed such a long shot.

In fact my young friend was prescient. At the age of 28 he foresaw better than I who would be the next president.

At noon the next day he boarded a bus to Turkey. He was not even sure whether he would be allowed to cross.

Others had tried, only to find themselves listed at the border as 'people not allowed to leave the country'.

Unlike most of his generation, he had dedicated his few adult years to trying to build what he called civic society – trying to reach out to the less educated, the less privileged. He held workshops about 'understanding democracy' and 'women's rights in Islam'. 'They didn't want to hear about human rights,' he complained. 'We never reached them. It's our big failure.'

It was impossible to underestimate the depth of fear, panic and incomprehension among Iran's wealthier and more liberal youth yesterday. One young woman told me: 'I fainted when I woke up and heard the news.'

The young had pushed the boundaries of earlier restrictions to the point that they didn't seem especially harsh any more. They drank alcohol at weekend parties, danced at ecstasy raves in underground car parks and had serial relationships in a country where, officially, contact between the sexes is illegal unless you are married or brother and sister.

Girls wore make-up that in the early days of the revolution would have earned them an 'acid facial', and hijab scarves were pushed so far back they would be fashionable in Paris.

A member of Iran's most successful rapper band – illegal, of course – had confidently told me: 'It's not as bad as it seems. We have got so many fans they'll never stop us.' When I called him yesterday the bravado was gone. He said he was going to keep his head down and 'see what happens'.

Some ripples of concern were already felt by a rich young crowd, few of whom had bothered to vote, at a glitzy party in northern Tehran on Friday.

Roxanne, standing by her pool in a clinging white mini-dress said: 'I'm going to have to leave this country. It's not going to be a place I want to live any more. Our country has been hijacked.'

A young disillusioned reform party researcher said: 'We are still going to get where we want. It's inevitable. The only difference is that whereas under [Ali Akbar Hashemi] Rafsanjani we would have got there slowly and peacefully, now there will be bloodshed.'

When I said goodbye to my idealistic friend on the eve of his bus ride, he made a simple but proud gesture: he solemnly shook my hand in full view of everyone in the restaurant. He could have been arrested. 'You are no coward,' I thought.

He made it across the border.

Egypt

Mubarak lights a democratic flame

CAIRO

4 September 2005

There could not have been more of a contrast on the campaign trail last week.

Hosni Mubarak, who after four terms is facing his first multi-candidate presidential election, read his speech to a partisan crowd from behind a cordon of twitchy security men. At an opposition rally, his main rival called for change and was hoisted on the shoulders of ecstatic young men.

The 77-year-old Mubarak, wearing a light grey suit and a white shirt open at the collar – his one concession to the young technocrats on his campaign who are trying to soften his image – arrived in the town of Zagaziq hours late for 10,000 supporters sitting in the stifling heat of a huge tent.

He promised reform, 4.5 million jobs and land redistribution, all music to the ears of the audience, mostly peasants. But it was unclear how much they understood of the promised new era of democracy.

They interrupted his speech with chants of 'Nam, Mubarak' (Yes, Mubarak), recalling the system by which presidents have been elected since King Farouk was overthrown by a revolution in 1952. Parliament nominates a president, always the incumbent, and he submits to a yes-or-no referendum. Mubarak has won four of those.

This year is different. After an unprecedented wave of dissent in the past year, and pressure from America, Mubarak agreed to a constitutional amendment allowing opposition parties to contest the presidency.

Nine candidates, all but two of them obscure – including an elderly fortune teller – are running against the Egyptian president.

Mubarak allowed only 19 days of campaigning, ending today. Egyptians go to the polls on Wednesday when Mubarak will seek to extend his 24 years in the presidency by another six-year term. He is almost certain to win.

Earlier this year Egypt's conversion to multi-party democracy, elections in Iraq and the mass protests that drove Syrian forces out of Lebanon appeared to herald profound change across the Middle East. There was talk of an 'Arab spring'.

However, democracy seems to be having some teething troubles in Egypt: eligible Egyptians who did not have a voter's card when the election was announced in January have not been allowed to sign up; the estimated 4 million Egyptians living abroad cannot vote; a demand by President George W Bush for international monitors has been rejected, and local groups which had asked to observe the polls have been refused.

Nor does Mubarak's praetorian guard appear to have been briefed on press freedom.

Confronted by a press corps making its way to collar officials before his speech, one nervous guard complained: 'Do you all have to go? Can't you just send one person and he will tell you the important things?'

The election coverage of the state-owned media has been heavily weighted in favour of Mubarak, although the independent newspapers have been anything but sycophantic – they have called the president corrupt, decrepit and dictatorial and attacked Gamal, his son and political heir.

Egypt's strongest opposition movement, the Muslim Brotherhood, is banned and does not even appear on the ballot. That said, the election has stirred those in Egypt who have been able to follow it. For the first time in a country ruled by emergency law since Mubarak came to power after the assassination of Anwar Sadat in 1981, they have been able to listen to criticism of the president without being imprisoned for it.

Many have seen Mubarak – his hair dyed black but looking surprisingly vigorous for his years – in the flesh for the first time. He used to remain aloof in his office. When candidates such as Ayman Nour, head of the liberal El-Ghad party, started touring the country, Mubarak's advisers said that he had better get out there as well.

It has not been the most comfortable experience for the former fighter pilot.

After a few trips to face sweating citizens, Mubarak is said to have told a friend: 'It is as if I own my house and now I have to bid for it at auction.'

Mubarak has some formidable supporters, however. Yousef Boutros-Ghali, his finance minister and nephew of the former United Nations secretary-general, does not mince words. Educated in America and with a doctorate in economics, he traces the main issues of the campaign – poverty and corruption – back to the economy he is trying to reform.

'We had a medieval tax system. It's taken four years but I've reformed it, top tax 20%, lowest 10%. We've had a surge in tax receipts. Our customs law was the most obscure and confusing in the world – I went at it with an axe.'

Boutros-Ghali believes the groundwork has been laid for democracy and that international intervention has nothing to do with it. 'Democratic elections do not come from the foreign press or foreign intervention,' he said in an interview.

'If democracy is not home-grown, it will not last. The test is not if this is a perfect democratic election – it is: have we let the genie out of the bottle? I think we have. Irreversibly.'

Nour boldly challenges the gradual approach of Mubarak and Boutros-Ghali. At 41, he is of a less patient generation and by nature a grandstander. His campaign has been chaotic. A bus was scheduled to take journalists to a rally in Port Said at 4pm on Thursday. At 5pm Nour was still sitting in his apartment in a bedraggled suit and a bright orange tie that is the symbol of his campaign, in tribute to the Ukrainian people's revolution.

'People are thirsty for change,' he said. 'We've found that one of the problems is that they can't quite believe it will happen. But I believe we've broken the barrier of silence.'

Nour finally left Cairo at 8pm, arriving just before 11pm. An enthusiastic crowd was waiting and there were no security guards. People pushed up to the podium, rapt and sweating.

He has his finger on the pulse of the dissatisfaction in Egypt, where 25% unemployment has decimated the hopes of the younger generation. Young men cheered when he focused on the lack of jobs. When he talked about the desperate conditions of a nearby slum, nobody stopped a young woman who jumped on stage to bare an arm, shouting that mice had bitten it in her slum house.

Many had come just for the show of free speech. 'Arab spring? I haven't seen enough democracy to know which season we are in,' Nour said. He will not win and fears what will happen after the election.

Mubarak is expected to name a vice-president, perhaps two. More controversially, there are indications he could manoeuvre Gamal into the leadership of the NDP ruling party, which would set him up for the succession.

While this is a far from perfect democratic election, the genie may well be out of the bottle.

Kosovo

How one careless phone call ended Radovan Karadzic's liberty

27 July 2008

Marie Colvin and Andrew Wander

A careless phone call brought Radovan Karadzic's colourful life on the run to an abrupt end, write Marie Colvin and Andrew Wander in Belgrade.

As the long-haired, bearded man who had become known as the local eccentric walked out of the Leotar supermarket in a suburb of Belgrade nine days ago, he unexpectedly turned back to the checkout girls.

'I want to say goodbye,' he said. 'I'm going on vacation. I need a rest, I've been working a lot.' He could not know how prescient his words were.

Radovan Karadzic, 63, wartime leader of the Bosnian Serbs and one of the most wanted men in the world, had only a few hours of freedom left after almost 13 years on the run.

Sofia Kaluderovic, 44, at the checkout, rang up the usual purchases for the man she believed was Dragan Dabic, a new age doctor: yoghurt, specially ordered cherries, the nationalist newspaper *Pravda* and a bottle of Bear's Blood, a cheap Serbian red wine.

As he left the shop, he cut his usual distinctive figure, dressed in a black T-shirt and trousers, sandals, his long white hair bound with an elastic band into a top knot and his face buried beneath an enormous white beard and oversize glasses.

In retrospect, Uros, the shop's owner, realised that his customer may have found comfort in the shop's name, Leotar – a famous mountain in the Serbian part of Bosnia that Karadzic ran as president of the self-styled Srpska Republic.

'He was a real gentleman,' Uros said, remembering his jokes and generous tips. 'If I'd known who he really was, I would never have charged for anything. I will die sorry that I didn't recognise him.'

Karadzic's disguise was effective right up until the moment he was caught. He boarded the 73 bus from the stop around the corner, carrying a bag containing a laptop, two mobile phones, clothes including swimming trunks, and Euro 600 (£472) in cash.

His plan to leave Belgrade apparently spurred Serbia's security services into action. They had been watching him for a month and did not want to take the chance of him slipping away.

As the bus passed the Teloptic factory in an industrial part of town, a group of men in civilian clothes boarded and asked if they could talk to Karadzic. He refused. They showed him their badges, told him that they knew who he was, blindfolded and handcuffed him. He went quietly. It was a surprisingly pedestrian end to an extraordinary life on the run.

Karadzic had been a wanted man since 1996, when international arrest warrants were issued for him and Ratko Mladic, the army general who was his partner in the slaughter and 'ethnic cleansing' in the 1992–5 Bosnian war that left an estimated 200,000 dead.

Karadzic's lawyer filed an appeal against his extradition from Serbia just before the deadline at 8pm on Friday, but the former leader is expected to be flown this week to the United Nations tribunal at the Hague to stand trial on charges including genocide. He faces life imprisonment.

In Belgrade there was a muted reaction to the arrest of the one-time Serbian hero. Had he been arrested a decade ago, nationalist Serbs would have poured onto the streets in violent fury, but last week the protests came mainly in the form of disgruntled youths.

Serbs attributed the lack of an outcry to the length of time that had elapsed since the end of the war. Equally, it may just have been that everyone was stunned at the revelation of Karadzic's life on the run. They had expected something more like a dramatic shootout on a mountain.

No one knew quite how to react when it emerged that he had been selling 'human quantum energy' diviners on the internet from a flat in surburban Belgrade, speaking at conferences for alternative health and maintaining an intimate friendship with a rather good-looking younger woman.

The breakthrough in the hunt for Karadzic came last month from a single telephone call. A Serbian security source said that the call, from Karadzic's mobile phone, was his 'fatal error'.

For years, Serbian and international security services, including Britain's GCHQ eavesdropping centre, had tapped the telephones of his family, relatives and friends and routinely raided their homes and took them in for questioning as part of a campaign to locate Europe's most wanted man. That would have been no secret to Karadzic, who had a $5 million bounty on his head.

He appears, however, to have become complacent after years in his new skin. At some time in June, according to two Serbian security sources, a telephone call from a mobile number in Belgrade was monitored on the tapped line of one of his relatives. The number was traced to a Dr Dragan David Dabic, living in a small rented apartment in New Belgrade.

Serbian security agents monitored Dabic, following him on his walks in downtown Belgrade and stops at coffee shops and cinemas, visits to his favourite local, the Madhouse, where he would pick up and play the gusle, the traditional Serbian string instrument, and monitoring his telephone calls. It is unclear when they realised that Dabic was in fact Karadzic. 'I think he started to believe himself that he was not Radovan Karadzic,' said Bruno Vekaric, the senior adviser of the war crimes prosecutor in Belgrade. 'We've been following him for a long time.' Pressed, he agreed it was 'about a month'.

Having decided that he could be arrested without posing a security threat and sure he was their man, they decided to act.

'We believed he was moving home,' Vekaric said.

Bozo Prelevic is the former Serbian police minister who served in the first government after the fall of Slobodan Milosevic, the Serbian president who died in prison during his trial at the Hague. Prelevic believes that Karadzic's success was his downfall.

'He started to believe that he would never be arrested,' said Prelevic, who is still close to Serbian security forces. 'He had become overconfident, speaking at conferences. Karadzic could not live without an audience. Calling that relative was his fatal error.'

It may not have proved so had there not been a change in the Serbian government three weeks ago. After elections in May, Boris Tadic, the president, was able to form a new pro-western government with its sights set on membership of the European Union. Key to that prospect was the EU's insistence that war criminals would have to be apprehended. It can be no coincidence also that Karadzic's arrest came the day after an ally of Tadic's was installed as head of the state security service.

Indeed, in a more favourable political climate in Bosnia, near the ski resort of Pale above Sarajevo which is still a stronghold of

Bosnian Serb nationalism, Karadzic had been able to live openly even after his international arrest warrant had been issued.

Last week, friends and former supporters in the picturesque town said that everyone in Pale knew where Karadzic lived until the beginning of 2000 – except Nato it seems. Its green jeeps carrying troops who were searching for him routinely drove by his not-so-secret safe house, where he was often joined by his wife Ljiljana.

'In the early days there were 40 security people around him,' recalled Milovan Bjelica, a leader in Karadzic's Serbian Democratic party, last week. 'Up until late 1999 it was normal to see him. If I wanted to talk to him about something, he would send a car to pick me up. We would sit and discuss things. We would eat dried fruit and nuts and drink coffee.'

Karadzic's former house, a three-storey, wood-fronted chalet set back from a dirt road behind tall pine trees, was deserted last week. Broken windows let in the slanting rain and pine cones littered the stairs to the french windows on the ground floor, but it must once have been a luxurious residence. Karadzic and Ljiljana also spent time in a small white house outside Pale that they still own.

Bjelica does not think Nato was really interested in capturing Karadzic. 'They believed it would endanger their own forces,' he said, a view endorsed by regional experts at the time.

He insists that he did not see Karadzic after he left Pale in early 2000. He said the rumours were that the former Serbian leader was hiding in remote mountain villages, monasteries or even caves.

'But Radovan was not a country man,' Bjelica said. 'He needed the city, so I never believed these stories. I thought he was in Russia, or maybe Argentina.'

It was a renewed initiative by international forces that forced Karadzic to abandon Pale. Yet he still managed to see his family. Letters seized by Nato forces during a raid on the marital home as late as December 2002 reveal clandestine visits from Ljiljana while he was on the run. 'Now summer is practically here, everybody is going somewhere, so it would not be a problem [to meet],' said one missive.

Later, presumably after they had met and done more than hold
hands, he jokes about his wife feeling unwell: 'If I was younger, I
would hope you were pregnant.'

It is not certain precisely when he moved to Serbia, but it was
after Vojislav Kostunica, the hardline president, was elected. It soon
became clear that the government was opposed to returning
alleged Serbian war criminals to the Hague.

'Karadzic realised he had a better chance of hiding in a forest of
people in the big city than in a forest of trees,' said Goran Petrovic,
former head of the Serbian intelligence agency. 'He said goodbye
to the people he knew and came to Belgrade alone. In Belgrade
there were people who knew who he was, but they were less than
five [in number].'

The first time he showed up as Dabic, the full-blown new age
character, was in 2005. Mina Minic, an alternative healer from
Belgrade, recalled last week an unusual visitor to the large house
he shares with three generations of his family.

'He [Karadzic] came to my house and brought flowers to my
wife,' Minic said. 'He kissed her hand and asked for me to become
his teacher. I remember he was so tall, dressed like he was from a
monastery.'

Minic explains that after taking a five-day course in 'human
quantum energy', a student is awarded a military-style 'rank' based
on their talent for the subject. Karadzic was given the rank of
general.

He threw himself into the role. His articles in *Healthy Life*, a
Serbian alternative medicine magazine, show a man who was
fluent in new age thinking. 'It is widely believed our senses and
mind can recognise only 1% of whatever exists around us. Three
per cent we understand with our hearts. All that remains is
shrouded in secrecy, out of the reach of our five senses; however, it
is within our reach in the extrasensory manner,' he wrote in one
article.

Minic's teaching helped to form the cornerstone of Karadzic's
new identity. 'Dragan Dabic' rented a small flat on the third floor

of a block in Belgrade, decorated with a gaudy glass lampshade and a vase of dried flowers by the window.

Last week Karadzic's books were still piled on shelves and papers were strewn across a desk next to a fax machine and office desk lamp. On a rail in front of the door hung coats and suits.

Karadzic was a regular customer in the Madhouse bar, where he drank red wine and listened to traditional Serbian music, sitting at a banquette where he could look at the portraits above the bar – of himself and Mladic.

He ate at the Arkidiye, a smart café-restaurant nearby. He always sat at the same table, in a screened booth in the corner of the restaurant, where he would eat cheap, simple meals of *prebranac* (dried beans) or *topli obrok* (a fish meal).

'He had great charisma,' said the restaurant manager Ziza Stevo. 'He was always alone and was not a man you could chat with. I had the impression that he was always fasting. He seemed much taller than Karadzic.'

The revelation that has transfixed Serbia is that while supposedly on the run he enjoyed a close bond with Mila Cicak, an attractive 53-year-old divorcee who lives in an apartment with her university-age son in the Zemun neighbourhood of Belgrade.

Certainly her association with alternative medicine is working; she looks a decade younger than her years. Cicak is coy about how they met and denies allegations in Serbian newspapers that they were having an affair. Kosa Maksimovic, a neighbour who knows Cicak well enough to have lent her money in the past, said Cicak had told her that she went to Dabic for treatment for migraines.

Last week, sitting on a stool in her tiny flat, Cicak looked exhausted from the week's events. 'Of course I didn't know who he was. Who could know that?' she said. 'You can't imagine how I feel.'

She admits she bought into the strange world of alternative therapy. 'I had read about quantum energy, so I knew that Dr Dabic was a great expert. He told me he was working with an autistic child, so I asked to meet the child and work with him. That's how our co-operation began.'

She says she last saw him on the Friday morning before he was arrested: 'We went together to visit the autistic child. He said he needed to travel, that he was going away for two weeks.'

Cicak denies having an affair with Karadzic, but their relationship was clearly close. 'They always came together and they would hold hands,' said Tanya, a secretary at *Healthy Life*. 'I thought they were husband and wife.'

Whatever the truth of their relationship, there was no contact last week as the family of Karadzic took over.

Dragan Karadzic arrived at the empty apartment in Belgrade on Thursday to collect his uncle's belongings. Accompanied by two thick-set men wearing baseball caps and leather jackets, he was intercepted by police as he entered the flat.

They demanded to see written permission but, after a heated discussion, they accompanied Dragan into the apartment, allowing him to leave with a pair of battered trainers, a black tracksuit, two dictionaries and some vitamins.

After an angry tirade and threats against journalists, Dragan revealed that his uncle was fasting and needed the vitamins, before racing off in a muddy black Mercedes estate car.

This weekend Karadzic was in a Belgrade prison cell with a barred window in the door. He was refusing prison food, but eating hazelnuts and walnuts brought by Luca, his brother, and reading newspapers that all pictured him on their front pages. It is already an outdated image – he has yet again changed his appearance, demanding to be allowed to shave and cut his hair.

This week will be one of recovery from shock in Serbia and legal manoeuvres that will most likely see Karadzic in a new role: that of prisoner in the Hague.

The UN high representative in Sarajevo has denied permission for Ljiljana or his children, Sasa and Sonja, to travel to Belgrade to visit him.

Intelligence agencies are now engaged in the process of piecing together Karadzic's movements. Attention will turn to Dragan Karadzic, who this weekend told a Serbian newspaper that he had been the only person helping his uncle over the past six years as he hid from justice.

There were clearly some near-misses with the authorities along the way. Yesterday Austrian police said anti-terror units had found a man who looked exactly like Dabic while searching an apartment in Vienna for a murder suspect last year. The man was not connected to the killing and was released without being finger-printed. Meanwhile, an Austrian newspaper reported that Karadzic had worked in Vienna as a 'miracle healer' in 2006, seeing patients in the homes of Serbians living there.

In Serbia, the government has vowed to move on and focus on capturing Mladic, the next most wanted man in Europe. Serbian sources say that will be a different odyssey. The general behind the Srebrenica massacre is never alone and is surrounded by armed bodyguards willing to fight to the death rather than give up their leader.

Rumours that Mladic had given up Karadzic to save himself were just that.

Petrovic said: 'Arresting Karadzic was not a big risk. To catch Mladic would be different. Mladic's bodyguards have orders to kill him rather than let him be captured. Karadzic was a doctor. Mladic is a crazy military man.'

Karadzic's home for the foreseeable future is already waiting. At the detention centre at the Hague they have prepared an en-suite cell, about 18 metres square, with a television, facilities to cook Balkan specialities with fellow war criminals and a ping-pong table.

If he is to represent himself in court, as he has promised to do, Karadzic will also need one more thing: the bearded guru of human quantum theory could soon be swapping his tomes on alternative health for law books.

PART THREE

Marie with Billy Smith, the cat she rescued
from the streets of Jerusalem.

Middle East

Bloodied Gaza set for the endgame

11 January 2009

Marie Colvin, Sara Hashash; Uzi Mahnaimi in Tel Aviv;
Sarah Baxter in Washington

In the emergency room of Al Shifa hospital in Gaza City, Dr Raed al-Arayni was entering his twelfth day of nonstop work and was preparing for yet another operation when his worst nightmare came true.

The bloodied little boy being carried into the room by a neighbour was screaming at him. 'Baba, baba [daddy, daddy],' the child cried.

'I did not recognise my own child because of his injuries,' recalled Arayni. 'For a few seconds I couldn't move, my knees became weak. I could barely stand at the sight of my child halfway between life and death.'

Running over he realised that both his sons – Hathifa, 7, and Abdul Rahman, 5 – were lying in his emergency room, severely wounded.

Tears streaming down his face, Arayni began working feverishly on Hathifa, who had the worst injuries. A chunk of shrapnel had pierced his chest, his right leg was broken and blood poured from his wounds.

A colleague began treating Abdul Rahman. The nerves in his broken left arm had been severed and he had no feeling in his hand. They were able to stabilise the two boys.

'I just thank God my children didn't arrive to me in bits and pieces, missing body parts as the women and children I see arriving daily,' said Arayni, standing by Hathifa's bedside, his face showing the exhaustion of almost two weeks of back-to-back operations. The slight, bearded surgeon had not returned home for 12 days, grabbing a nap or a meal at the hospital when he could.

When the Israelis launched a massive attack against Hamas, the Islamic extremist group that rules Gaza, to stop it launching rockets against Israel's southern cities, he had moved his family from their home in Jabaliya, a crowded refugee camp just north of Gaza City. They took refuge with a relative in the more central Fakhura district, believing they would be safer.

The surgeon pushed aside the thought of his own children as the wounded poured in, sometimes so many that the operating floors were slick with blood. Injured men, women and children were piled in the corridors and surgeons commandeered the recovery room.

On Tuesday Um Mustafa, his wife, and their boys had gone up on the roof of the building, desperate for some fresh air after almost a week inside while Israeli jets screamed overhead and missiles, tank and artillery rounds pounded the coastal strip day and night.

The boys had been playing for about an hour when Um Mustafa sent them downstairs for a bottle of water. Moments later a huge explosion rocked the building, followed by a second. Two missiles had slammed into the girls' primary school next door run by the United Nations Relief and Works Agency, where Gazans fleeing the fighting had been given refuge. Some 40 people, many of them women and children, were killed.

A controversy still rages over the strike on the school, one of three bombed by the Israelis within 24 hours. Israel claimed militants had fired mortars from near the school. UN officials insisted their security guards kept militants out of their compounds and that they had even given the Israeli military the GPS coordinates for their 23 schools, refuge for some 15,000 Gazans, to avert such a tragedy.

As soon as Hathifa and Abdul Rahman were stabilised, Arayni went back to operating on the casualties from the school bombing. As he left their room on Friday, leaving the boys in the care of their weeping mother, Abdul Rahman woke from a feverish sleep and began calling out for his father.

'I want my daddy. Where is he? Is he hurt?' he cried. His older brother, the shrapnel still in his chest because it is too dangerous to remove, reassured him. 'No, he's treating other kids who got hurt like us,' Hathifa said.

By the standards of the past fortnight in Gaza, the Arayni boys were lucky. At the last count 830 Palestinians had been killed and some 3,000 wounded, according to health officials in Gaza. The Hamas-run health ministry said at least a third were children.

Israeli troops were dug in on the outskirts of Gaza City and hunkered down in Palestinian homes they had seized. Hamas's security forces had been driven from the streets, but struck back in hit-and-run attacks from tunnels, sniped from rooftops and continued to launch rockets into Israel.

Northern Gaza was a wasteland. Whole blocks of the concrete apartment buildings and small homes of the refugee camps of Jabaliya, Beit Hanoun and Beit Lahiya were devastated, hit by missiles or demolished by military bulldozers.

Aid officials warned of a humanitarian disaster. The UN said two thirds of Gazans were without electricity and half had no water. Food and medical supplies were running low.

On Wednesday Israel relented slightly, announcing it would stop firing between the hours of 1pm and 4pm to allow aid agencies to deliver supplies.

Nevertheless, it showed no sign of ending its operations any time soon. From Israel's perspective it is fighting a crucial battle, backed by near-unanimous popular support, against an enemy committed to its ultimate destruction and which has continued to target its citizens in the south.

There was more evidence of that yesterday as at least 10 Hamas rockets were fired at Israeli targets. One hit a block of flats in the city of Ashkelon, wounding two people.

'Israel has acted, is acting and will act only according to its considerations, the security needs of its citizens and its right to self-defence,' Tzipi Livni, the foreign minister and the ruling Kadima party's candidate for prime minister, said on Friday.

How close is Israel to achieving its goals? What has the bloodshed achieved and is there any sign of it stopping? Israel launched Operation Cast Lead on 27 December, little more than a week after Hamas refused to renew a six-month truce that had largely held and resumed its rocket attacks on southern Israel.

The operation's aims were to stop Hamas's rocket launches into southern Israeli cities and end the smuggling of weapons through tunnels under Gaza's southern border with Egypt.

Israeli intelligence repeatedly warned that Hamas was stockpiling increasingly sophisticated long-range Grad rockets, manufactured in China but passed to Hamas by Iran, along with its homemade Qassam rockets. Israel believed that unless it acted soon, Hamas's ability to strike would present a grave danger.

That prediction proved accurate. As soon as the Israeli missiles began landing in Gaza, Hamas launched rockets that reached further than before, hitting the cities of Ashkelon, Ashdod and Beersheba.

Last week a Grad rocket landed on Gedera, a town 28 miles from Gaza and less than a mile from the Israeli air force base at Tel Nof, where nuclear weapons are believed to be stored.

The wider strategic aim of the operation is the need to confront Iranian-sponsored bellicosity. The supply of Grad rockets to Hamas followed Tehran's sponsorship of Hezbollah, the Lebanese-based Shi'ite militant group which had fired rockets at Israel's northern cities and fought a war with Israel in the summer of 2006.

The threat of a nuclear-armed Iran, the rising power in the region, is foremost in Israel's thoughts. Last week in Washington, Sallai Meridor, Israel's ambassador to the United States, warned in an interview that Iran would have enough enriched uranium this year to manufacture a nuclear bomb.

If Israel is to address such a threat militarily in the future, it will need to have subdued the immediate threats on its borders. The timing of the attack on Gaza was also influenced by the Israeli general election, due on 10 February. As rockets terrorised southern Israel, the ruling coalition, led by Kadima, was increasingly open to accusations of being soft on defence and trailed the right-wing Likud party, led by Binyamin Netanyahu, in the polls.

The arithmetic of Israeli politics is fiendishly complicated, but the effect of the Gaza operation is revealed in the fortunes of the Labour party headed by Ehud Barak, the defence minister. Two weeks ago, before the attack, it was struggling in third or fourth place in the polls with only nine or 10 expected parliamentary seats (out of 120) after the elections. After a week of operations that figure had risen to 16 seats.

Likud is still leading the race with an expected 32 seats and Kadima is likely to win 27 or so seats, but the centre-left block is closing fast.

A decisive victory over Hamas may pull the rug from under the right-wing bloc and possibly allow a Barak–Livni coalition. But if Hamas can claim victory, it will strengthen Likud and its allies and Israel will probably get Netanyahu as its next prime minister.

There could be no doubt that Israel had the upper hand after two weeks of fighting, but the operation, which Barak described as one of 'shock and awe', had reached a difficult point by this weekend.

Israeli pundits all agreed that the government needed a 'clear win', such as an assurance of quiet on the southern front, to withdraw with any semblance of victory and to justify the high price of international opprobrium.

That was not even on the horizon. On Friday, Palestinian sources said Hamas's weapons caches had been decimated and scores of the tunnels it used to import weapons had been destroyed in the bombings. But with its leadership hiding in underground bunkers or holding talks in Egypt, and only about 400 of its 15,000 officers and foot soldiers killed, the organisation was largely intact.

For Israelis this provided two starkly different choices. One was to declare victory and withdraw, either unilaterally or with a semblance of a ceasefire brokered by the international community.

The other was to implement 'stage three' of Operation Cast Lead, following the initial bombing and subsequent ground assault, and continue into the crowded neighbourhoods of Gaza City and refugee camps. Here Hamas has created a virtual underground city of tunnels and the warren of alleys and narrow streets make it far more difficult for Israeli forces to manoeuvre.

Ehud Olmert, the outgoing prime minister, was said to be advocating going even further and aiming to topple Hamas. The organisation had won elections in 2006 and 18 months ago ousted Fatah, led by Mahmoud Abbas, the moderate president who runs the rival Palestinian Authority, from Gaza.

Avigdor Ben-Gal, a decorated and influential retired Israeli general, said this weekend: 'We need to conquer the Gaza Strip and put the Hamas military and political leaders on a French ship to leave Gaza for good, just as we did with [the former Palestinian leader Yasser] Arafat in Beirut 1982. We've already conquered a bigger Arab city than Gaza [namely, Beirut], our army is trained and fit for the mission. The politicians should give the order.'

Some Fatah officials have even privately expressed the hope that Israel would rout Hamas, so stung were they by being forced out of Gaza.

Expanding the incursion would carry high risks. So far the Israeli population has supported the operation: a poll on Friday showed 91% of Israelis in favour. But that could change dramatically if casualties start piling up, as they did when an operation was launched against Hezbollah in Lebanon in 2006 to stem the flow of missiles on Israel's northern cities. Israel did not then secure the crushing victory to which its people were accustomed.

For Hamas, however battered, the equation is far simpler. All it has to do to declare victory is survive. The leadership is certain to reap the kudos from having stood up to the most powerful army in the Middle East without jets, tanks or sophisticated weaponry.

Hamas appeared to be regrouping after, incredibly, being shocked at the original Israeli attack. This was despite the tanks that had been massing on its borders for days and Israel's public warnings that it would not tolerate rockets being launched on its soil.

'Hamas actually believed that firing rockets into Israel would force it to open the Rafah crossing [into Egypt],' said a senior Palestinian who has negotiated with them.

'They were shocked at the massive Israeli response. They are very naive.'

However, Izzedine al-Qassam, Hamas's military wing, was said still to have high morale and other extremist groups in Gaza were fighting side by side with Hamas.

Whatever the Israelis decide to do – and there were reports that leaflets had been dropped on Gaza yesterday warning the residents to expect a dramatic escalation in hostilities – they have to do it quickly.

Israeli soldiers stationed on lines at the edge of Gaza City were increasingly becoming sitting targets. The thousands of reservists who had been called up finished a week's training on Friday and could not be kept in the camps indefinitely; they have civilian jobs and families at home.

In addition, the Israeli government was well aware that international pressure was building, fuelled by horrific images that have emerged from Gaza despite Israel's refusal to allow foreign journalists to enter the coastal strip.

International diplomatic efforts to end the conflict were grinding slowly forward. Both Israel and Hamas rejected a UN security council resolution that had called for an 'immediate ceasefire'. Olmert called the resolution 'unworkable' and Hamas rejected the resolution on the grounds that it had not been consulted.

Crucially, the Americans, Israel's superpower sponsor, abstained from the vote, preferring to back an Egyptian-brokered ceasefire. These efforts appeared to be moving ahead. General Amos Gilad, a senior Israeli official, visited Cairo last week and will do so again today, and a Hamas delegation, both from Gaza and its Damascus-based politburo, travelled to Cairo yesterday.

A senior Palestinian source who had seen the proposal said it contained four points and put Egypt as the sole broker between the two sides.

The first point, he said, called for an agreement between both 'factions' on an immediate ceasefire; the second point was the opening of the Gaza border crossings to allow humanitarian aid and 'Egypt to continue its efforts'; the third point was a vague provision for an international element, presumably to monitor the border; and the fourth point provided for Egypt to oversee talks between Hamas and Fatah to end their bitter dispute and form a united leadership.

Despite fighting talk from Hamas members, those dealing with them say that although they are still insisting they will not stop fighting until the Rafah crossing into Egypt is open – their key demand and their own litmus test of a real victory – they want a ceasefire.

In the longer term, both Israelis and moderate Palestinians realise that the only way forward is a political solution. Israel would love to see Abbas retake power in Gaza. Should he replace Hamas on the back of an Israeli invasion, however, he would be perceived as an Israeli stooge.

'There is no eliminating Hamas. They are part of the Palestinian people whether we like it or not,' said Ghassan Shaqa'a, a senior Palestinian politician and an adviser to Abbas. 'You have to talk to them.'

Everyone is waiting for the US presidency of Barack Obama, who will be sworn in on 20 January. Despite the economic crisis, sources in his administration said that he knew he would have to engage in the Middle East crisis, although he was hoping that there would be a ceasefire by the time he took office.

'God knows he will have enough on his plate, but he has to work from day one on this or the only options left will be bad ones,' said Martin Indyk, a Middle East adviser to Hillary Clinton, the incoming secretary of state.

Indyk, the author of a new book, *Innocent Abroad*, based on his experience as an American ambassador to Israel, reiterated the US policy that the only solution was a two-state solution, with some special provision for Jerusalem, the city holy to Jews, Muslims and Christians.

Obama indicated last week that he could open contacts with Hamas, a first for an American president.

He is likely to begin a complicated three-way chess game involving talks with Syria and contacts of some sort with Iran. A diplomatic breakthrough with Syria could isolate Iran, a bonus in the campaign to stop it from going nuclear, and encourage other Arab states to come to the negotiating table.

'Obama won't be able to do it alone,' Indyk said. 'He'll need leaders in the region like Anwar Sadat [the late Egyptian president and the first Arab leader to make peace with Israel in the 1970s]. The president will need to be ready to grab the moment when it arises.'

For the citizens of Gaza it cannot come too soon. Of all the suffering among Gazan civilians, few endured worse than the Samouni clan. Last week four young boys from the extended family were rescued after three days of being trapped in a home with the bodies of their mothers and relatives.

Their emaciated condition horrified aid workers who had spent days trying to get permission from the Israelis to rescue them.

Their ordeal began last Sunday, shortly after Israel invaded. Troops ordered families to gather in one large house while they searched the Zeitoun neighbourhood. On Monday morning, with about 90 men, women and children inside, three Israeli missiles slammed into the house, according to the survivors.

Sixteen were killed in the strike – seven women, six children including a baby found curled up under its dead mother's arm, and three men. Ahmed Samouni, 15, told his tale from his hospital bed, a tube snaking out of his nose and his hands still black with blood and grime.

'Some of their heads were exploded,' he said, still shaking from the experience. 'The door was open. A chicken came in and started to eat the brains from their heads. I pulled off the chicken, crawled to the door and closed it with my feet.'

Down the hall are his brother Yaqub, 10, and cousin Abdullah, 8, so badly wounded that they can barely speak. Another cousin is in intensive care.

Yesterday more horrors visited Gaza. Eight members of a family, including two women and two children, were killed in Jabaliya when an Israeli tank shell hit them as they sat out in their garden to bask in the unseasonable winter sun.

The neighbour who took them to hospital did so in the boot of his car because their bodies were mangled together.

Amid all the uncertainty about Israel's intentions and the search for a ceasefire, human tragedy seems to be the only thing guaranteed.

Beyond the violence, a solution is on the table

11 January 2009

The ferocious fighting in Gaza between Israel and Hamas, the militant group, might seem to make the prospect of peace between Israelis and Palestinians more distant than ever. Stand back from the spasm of violence, however, and the two sides are closer than the fighting might suggest.

Polls show consistently that the majority on both sides agree that the solution to their conflict must be two states side by side: an Israeli state with a Jewish majority and a Palestinian state. No doubt they would be edgy, suspicious neighbours and any agreement would be grudging on both sides but the acceptance of the concept has taken root.

On the main issues there is now more agreement than division on how these states could look and function.

TERRITORY

The Palestinians have long insisted that Israel must withdraw to the borders recognised by the United Nations before the 1967 war when Israel seized the West Bank from Jordan and Gaza from Egypt.

The negotiations are now down to detail that might seem pedantic elsewhere.

The latest idea is of a 'land swap', whereby Israel would keep the four main settlements in the West Bank that have been built over the 1967 line and have grown into virtual cities, such as Ma'ale Adumim, essentially a suburb of Jerusalem.

In return for recognising that reality on the ground, the Palestinians would be compensated with land from within the borders of Israel proper. Maps have been drawn which would cede areas of the southern Negev desert to a Palestinian state.

The two sides are now only percentage points apart. Ehud Olmert, the outgoing Israeli prime minister, has offered the Palestinians 93% of the area of the West Bank. Mahmoud Abbas, the Palestinian president, has said he could cede 2% but no more, according to Palestinian sources.

Israel has said that it would uproot 70 of the 120 settlements on the West Bank, home to about 60,000 settlers. But 440,000 people would stay.

JERUSALEM

Both sides claim the city as their capital and it remains a hugely contentious issue. However, the Israelis have accepted that no deal can be made that does not offer the Palestinians some part of Arab East Jerusalem. There are various ideas for an international component for the sites holy to Jews, Muslims and Christians in the Old City.

LINKING PALESTINIAN LANDS

The Palestinians insist their state must be contiguous, so there are various solutions that would connect Gaza on the Mediterranean in the south to the West Bank, which lies to the north. They range from a tunnel that would cost billions of dollars (preferred by Israeli security), to a bridge, to a heavily guarded road that would go from Gaza to the West Bank city of Hebron.

REFUGEES

Millions of Palestinian refugees, who left what was then the British mandate of Palestine during the 1948 war, are scattered far and wide.

They want to come home, but most of those homes are in what is now Israel and their return would overwhelm and end the idea of a Jewish state. The outlines of a solution would be to allow refugees the right to return only to the West Bank and Gaza. Those relinquishing claims to their ancestral homes would be given compensation.

SECURITY

Israel wants to be sure that once it cedes control of territory, rockets will not start coming over the border, as they have from Hamas in Gaza. One proposal is for an international force in the West

Bank. The Palestinians have requested a multinational force led by the Americans.

It is also worth noting that the Israeli use of Gaza as proof that rockets would come from the West Bank is somewhat disingenuous. While Israeli soldiers did pull out of Gaza in 2005, Israel retained control of the borders, air and sea; and for the past 18 months, since Hamas took power, it has maintained a virtual siege which destroyed the economy and radicalised many living in the coastal strip.

ELECTIONS

There is no doubt that the violence, now in its third week, has set back the chances of any peace negotiations. And getting them onto a track that could realistically result in a settlement is made more difficult by the weakness of both governments.

In Israel, Olmert faces corruption charges and stepped down as his party's candidate for leadership, leaving Tzipi Livni, the foreign minister, as the candidate for the centrist Kadima party which is now in power. Lacking military credentials, she is vulnerable to a challenge from Binyamin Netanyahu, the hardline Likud candidate, who was ahead in the polls last week for the 10 February election.

Abbas is also weakened by the fact that his writ runs only in the West Bank since Hamas's violent coup in Gaza in 2007.

For any settlement with the Palestinians to succeed, there would first have to be unity between Fatah and Hamas, which rejects the existence of Israel, or the election of a Fatah-dominated government. Elections are due next year.

Netanyahu stokes fears to take poll lead

JERUSALEM

8 February 2009

Israel's right-wing hawk is striking a chord with election voters who mistrust peace with Palestinians.

His silver hair blowing in a chill wind, Binyamin Netanyahu, the right-wing front-runner in Israel's general election, was eager to reassure a crowd of Jewish settlers in the West Bank last Friday: victory this week for his Likud party would mean no Palestinian state on their land.

'The election on Tuesday will be about one issue – whether this place will remain in our hands or will be handed over to Hamas [the Islamic extremist group] and Iran,' he roared to adoring supporters in Beit Aryeh, a small settlement.

If Palestinian militants were in control, rockets would rain down on Israel's international airport only 15 miles away, he warned.

Netanyahu, 59, has won his lead in the opinion polls by repeatedly articulating the anxieties of voters like the inhabitants of Beit Aryeh, whose settlement is built on land won by Israel in the 1967 war. It would therefore be returned to Palestinian rule under the peace agreement envisaged by the United States.

Despite the global financial crisis, Israel's politicians have largely ignored the economy on the campaign trail. This election is about how to deal with the Palestinians.

Coming just six weeks after Israel's invasion of Gaza to stop Hamas rocket attacks, it has seen the right making large gains as a result of Israeli fears of the Palestinian threat.

The latest poll in the *Haaretz* newspaper predicts that right-wing parties led by the hawkish Likud will win 66 seats in the

120-member Knesset, Israel's parliament, with 54 going to Kadima, the governing centrist party, and smaller parties on the left.

Kadima, led by Tzipi Livni, 50, the foreign minister, is closing the gap with a predicted 25 seats to Likud's 27, but commentators say the trend is clear. 'A wind from the right is blowing through the country,' said Shlomo Yerushalmi, an analyst on Israeli television.

Netanyahu, who was prime minister from 1996 to 1999, was not spelling out the details of his plans publicly and refused Livni's challenge to a debate. In briefings, however, the Likud leader – who grew up partly in America – has disclosed that he would spurn any US attempt to negotiate the creation of a Palestinian state in the West Bank and Gaza.

'We will not withdraw from one inch. Every inch we leave would go to Iran,' Netanyahu said, referring to the financial and military support that the Tehran regime gives Hamas. The Islamic extremist group controls Gaza and has a growing presence in the West Bank.

Under Netanyahu's plan, Palestinians would not have a sovereign state but self-governing, non-contiguous 'population centres'. He also proposes an 'economic peace' that would improve living conditions for Palestinians in the hope that this would help moderate opinion to prevail.

Gideon Levy, a *Haaretz* columnist, expressed a common view when he called the plan 'a mix of condescension and dehumanisation', but it strikes a chord with those voters who distrust the idea of making peace in the face of a growing Palestinian radicalism.

A Likud government would annihilate Hamas, Netanyahu claimed, a goal seen as unrealistic even by the Israeli intelligence establishment.

Netanyahu's election would be a setback for the administration of President Barack Obama, who vowed to push for Middle East peace 'from day one' and appointed George Mitchell, the former Northern Ireland envoy, as his representative in the region.

The resurgence of the right is exemplified by the startling rise of Avigdor Lieberman, 50, the Russian-born leader of Yisrael Beiteinu (Israel Our Home), once considered to be a fringe party.

The one-time Moldovan nightclub bouncer and former aide to Netanyahu rose to third place in the polls last week and is predicted to gain 18 seats, more than the Labour party.

Lieberman, who relishes his hardline reputation, has called for all Israeli Arab citizens to swear a loyalty oath to the Jewish state or lose their citizenship. He also proposes to transfer many Arab Israelis to Palestinian rule by redrawing Israel's borders.

'I think Lieberman will be the big kingmaker in this election,' said Michael Barak, an Israeli pollster.

In the complex world of Israeli politics, Lieberman's surge has helped the centrist Livni by siphoning votes away from Netanyahu.

Their supporters could hardly be more different. While Netanyahu stood on that West Bank hill surrounded by dour men in suits, Livni held a rally at which she belted out, karaoke-style, 'Non, je ne regrette rien' (No regrets), the signature tune of Edith Piaf, the French singer. The show starred Dana International, Israel's trans-gender Eurovision winner.

Livni's speech echoed the themes of Obama's campaign in the United States.

'We are going to do it,' she told the ecstatic crowd of women in tight, low-slung jeans and men in T-shirts. 'Don't vote from fear or despair. The easiest thing to do is to paint the future as black.'

Livni, a lawyer and former agent for Mossad, Israel's overseas intelligence agency, entered the Knesset only 10 years ago. As foreign minister she has led negotiations with the Palestinians for the past year, but she has also been short on details during her campaign, fearing that her backing for a separate Palestinian state would alienate many voters.

Whoever wins the popular vote on Tuesday will still have to form a coalition government. The smaller parties seem certain to hold the larger parties to ransom in pursuit of their special interests. Alliances in Israel can be bizarre and by Friday Livni was saying she would consider taking Lieberman into a coalition led by her.

Netanyahu's dream coalition would include Labour, once Israel's leading party but now in fourth place despite being led by Ehud

Barak, Israel's most decorated soldier and the present defence minister.

All the pollsters were making cautionary noises last week, with up to a third of the 5.2 million voters still undecided. Few people were prepared to predict which of the two starkly opposing options for bringing peace to Israel and its neighbours would win the day.

Israel's secret war

15 January 2012

Marie Colvin and Uzi Mahnaimi

In the desperate race to stop Iran developing nuclear weapons, shadowy forces are assassinating its top scientists.

Early in Tehran's grey wintry morning last Wednesday, Mustafa Ahmadi Roshan, a young scientist in Iran's controversial nuclear programme, got dressed at his home in the northern suburbs. The events of this last hour of his life could have come out of a spy film.

Small groups of Israeli agents were watching key points in the Iranian capital. Their target was Roshan. They would be dead themselves if they were caught.

For Israel it was a classic assassination mission. 'What is seen in espionage films as a simple operation is a result of hard work, many months of intelligence gathering and a well trained team,' said a source who released details, impossible to verify, to *The Sunday Times*.

'There is zero tolerance for mistakes. By nature, every failure not only risks the neck of the agents but also risks turning into an international scandal.'

Since its foundation in 1948, Israel has used assassination as a national weapon, striking targets abroad ranging from Palestinians who killed Israeli athletes at the 1972 Olympic Games in Munich, to enemies on the streets of Amman and a Hamas leader in a Dubai hotel room in 2010.

Now Iran is the target. In the past two years assassins have attacked five scientists in the state nuclear programme, killing four of them. Mossad, the Israeli external intelligence agency, is widely believed to be responsible.

The murder of civilians divides Iran's critics – and Israel's. Some find it repugnant, others see them as casualties in an undeclared war that is greatly preferable to the alternative of full-scale conflict.

One Israeli source claimed the killings were a precursor to a military strike, not merely an alternative, to make it more difficult for Iran to rebuild facilities if they are bombed.

Last week Iran defiantly announced it was enriching uranium at a new site, Fordow, built under a mountain near the holy city of Qom to protect it from aerial attack. The assassins were ready. As Roshan, 32, prepared to leave home, he was monitored from a makeshift control room in a safe house nearby.

Israeli agents were also watching the entrance to Iranian intelligence headquarters in the city centre. Suddenly they noticed a number of cars and people running; then they saw police rushing into the nearby streets. Another agent monitoring radio traffic between the Tehran police and security forces confirmed unusual activity. Had the operation been exposed?

In 1997 two agents of Caesarea, Mossad's top hit squad, had bungled an attempt to kill a Palestinian leader in Jordan and were arrested before they could flee, triggering a diplomatic crisis.

Jordan is relatively friendly to Israel. Iran is its bitterest enemy. There was no point in hesitation. If the agents had been rumbled, they would never escape anyway. The mission commander decided to go ahead.

Just before 8am on Wednesday, Reza Qashqai, Roshan's bodyguard and driver, arrived. Qashqai knew the risks. He checked under the silver Peugeot 405, a state-issue car, and looked beneath the bonnet before slipping into the driver's seat to wait for the scientist.

The house was in the Cheezar neighbourhood of northern Tehran, a village overtaken by the sprawl of the capital but still home to quiet traditional families who supported the regime.

Roshan got into the car, ready for a long day as deputy head of the Natanz uranium enrichment site, where he supervised procurement.

It was two years almost to the day since the murder of Masud Ali Mohammadi, an expert in quantum physics at Tehran University, who had been one of Roshan's mentors at the Iranian nuclear programme. Mohammadi, 50, was the first victim of the wave of assassinations.

Iran claims that its nuclear programme is for peaceful purposes, but the West accuses Tehran of working to develop a nuclear bomb.

Europe and America have led an unsuccessful diplomatic effort, based on sanctions, to try to stop the research. Israeli hawks, knowing their nation would be the target of an Iranian bomb, talk of a bold pre-emptive strike from the air that, Washington fears, would lead to war. So the reality is a secret campaign against soft targets such as the Mohammadis and Roshans fulfilling the mullahs' ambition for an Islamic nuclear weapon.

Roshan, a chemist, was one of the young scientists in the programme. He was not the most brilliant but was trusted by an increasingly paranoid regime because he came from a traditional religious family and had remained loyal while many of his fellow students had objected to the restraints of the Islamic regime. He had been talent-spotted at the Sharif technical university, where he joined the Basij, a fearsome militia controlled by the Iranian Revolutionary Guards.

Soon after graduation he married and was recruited to the Iranian nuclear programme to work at Natanz, Iran's main uranium enrichment complex. Colleagues said that like any new father he was transformed when he talked about his young son.

As the clock ticked towards 8am, an Israeli spotter reported via a secure text that Roshan was being driven from his home. Qashqai was at the wheel, a crucial detail because the bodyguard would be slower to respond if he was driving.

The assassins' commander took the final decision. 'Go,' he told agents who were standing by with a motorcycle in a hidden garage. They left immediately, weaving through the gridlocked streets of rush-hour Tehran.

In the five attacks on nuclear scientists, the hit squad has used a motorbike every time. The motorcyclist is ubiquitous in the capital's traffic jams, often wearing a surgical mask for protection against the heavy pollution and able to move close to the target between the lines of stationary cars without attracting attention.

Wednesday's team were familiar with the streets, the hallmark of a successful operation. They speeded up to reach Gol Nabi Street, which Roshan always passed on his way to work.

At 8.20am they spotted the Peugeot. The masked figure on the pillion seat made a quick check that Roshan was the passenger, then attached a magnetic bomb to the car. The motorbike sped away. The plastic explosive had been shaped to deliver its full force at the passenger. Nine seconds later it exploded. The scientist was killed instantly. Qashqai, badly injured, died in hospital.

After the bombing, onlookers milled about watching Roshan's car being hauled away under a cover of blue plastic and taking photographs on their mobile phones. At his funeral on Friday hundreds of regime supporters swore revenge.

'Two targets were always in Mustafa's mind,' Reza Najafi, a friend, said. 'To fight Israel and to become a shaheed [martyr]. He achieved both his targets.'

America denied having any connection with the assassinations last week.

'We were not involved in any way with regards to the assassination that took place there,' said Leon Panetta, the defence secretary. But he did say enigmatically that he had 'some idea' of who was.

The Foreign Office also said Britain had 'no involvement whatsoever' in the deaths of the scientists.

Most experts in the field have few doubts: the assassinations have all the hallmarks of Israeli operations.

Israel did not comment but Lieutenant-General Benny Gantz, chief of the general staff, told a parliamentary committee that this year would be 'critical' for Iran because of 'things that happen to it unnaturally'. Certainly the events of the past two years have been 'unnatural'.

The first assassination victim, Mohammadi, one of the leading lights of the nuclear programme, was killed by a bomb on a parked motorcycle as he walked from his house to his car. Then came more deaths.

In November 2010 motorcycles pulled alongside two cars in different parts of Tehran and then sped away. Bombs attached to the cars killed Majid Shahriari and injured Fereydoun Abbasi-Davani, both nuclear scientists. Davani was named head of the Iranian atomic programme when he recovered.

Target number four was Dariush Rezaeinejad, an electronics expert responsible for high-voltage switches, a dual-use item that can be used in nuclear warheads. He was shot in Tehran by gunmen on motorcycles.

There has also been a series of mysterious explosions. Last November a blast hit a military base used by the Revolutionary Guards, killing General Hassan Tehrani Moghaddam, head of Iran's ballistic missile programme.

The most effective strike, however, was not deadly. The Stuxnet worm, a cyberweapon, attacked and disabled the centrifuges crucial to Iran's programme of enriching uranium. It has been speculated that both Israel and the United States were involved.

The nuclear programme has also suffered from a CIA operation that infiltrated sabotaged parts into some of Iran's black market supply lines.

In December the United States made it illegal for an American company to deal with a foreign bank used by the Iranian petrochemical industry. The European Union has advanced a scheduled meeting to 23 January to consider further sanctions.

The worry now is how Iran will react. The regime may begin to feel as if it cannot protect its own. Sanctions are beginning to bite and the economy is in freefall.

Tehran has threatened to close the Strait of Hormuz, the narrow mouth of the Gulf through which 17 million barrels of oil pass daily; Washington has made it clear this is a 'red line' that would result in military action, western diplomats said last week.

President Barack Obama telephoned Binyamin Netanyahu, the Israeli prime minister, after the latest killing; according to one Israeli source, Obama urged restraint but Netanyahu refused. The United States is thought to have stepped up safeguards at American facilities in the region.

Diplomats believe there is still a chance of luring Tehran back into nuclear talks that could avert a showdown. 'We don't consider an escalation to war an inevitability and we are pursuing a strategy of actions designed to avert conflict. We still think they can succeed,' a western diplomat said.

Iraq

War-weary Iraqi voters catch election fever despite attacks

BAGHDAD

6 March 2010

A country brought to the brink of anarchy by sectarian violence is emerging as a vibrant democracy, despite Al-Qaeda's suicide bombings.

The purple ink on his right index finger was important to Ali Obeid. He held up a shaking hand from his hospital bed to show he had voted before a suicide bomber stepped on to the bus taking his army unit back to base on the eve of today's parliamentary elections.

Obeid, 50, a father of four, was supposed to be on duty today with 200,000 of Iraq's security forces to protect the polling stations. That is why he was voting on Thursday. At least 17 people died when suicide bombers struck two army units and a market.

'They haven't said yet whether they'll have to amputate,' Obeid said, his large brown eyes welling as he stared down at feet wrapped in bloodied gauze.

Still wearing his camouflage uniform, Obeid insisted his enthusiasm for the election was undimmed. He wanted his three daughters and son to have chances he never had.

'The government we need is one that will give us that security to live in peace,' he said. Obeid's ordeal began as a sandstorm obscured the Baghdad sun. A badly dressed man described by the soldiers as 'ugly' blew himself up when the soldiers tried to stop him.

Al-Qaeda in Iraq had vowed to do all it could to stop the election. The bombings seemed to be an attempt to frighten would-be voters into staying at home. But in the emergency room at the Al-Kharkh hospital, the soldiers' eyes flashed with anger and pride, mingled with tears for those who had lost lives or limbs.

'The message we want to give to this bomber, and to the people who sent him, is that we are challenging you,' said Shaheed Salem, 36, who had four gauze patches on his back to cover shrapnel wounds. As he was wheeled into X-ray, Salem, a father of six with a pregnant wife, said he saw the election as a watershed. 'I will protect all the Iraqis who want to vote in this election,' he insisted. 'This determines our fate.'

The theme was repeated fervently last week. While Iraq has been slipping from the headlines amid a diminishing body count, most Iraqis have quietly embraced democracy.

Even the followers of Moqtada al-Sadr, the founder of the Shi'ite Mahdi army, who once vowed not to lay down arms until foreign troops had left Iraq, took to the airwaves to deliver rhetoric, not rounds.

Some 19m Iraqis are going to the polls to choose from among 6,200 candidates vying for 325 seats in parliament in the second general election since the American-led invasion ousted Saddam Hussein in 2003. Turnout is expected to be up to 60%.

The campaign has been a rollicking free-for-all. There are no laws to restrict how much parties spend or where they get their money from. Money for some Shi'ite candidates is said to have come from Iran, while Saudis are supposed to have funnelled cash to hardline Sunnis.

Every street is festooned with placards. In one, a female candidate glows beatifically in a pink suit; in another, an elderly cleric kisses a skull symbolising Saddam's victims. Many are shaking fists.

'They look like maniacs to westerners, but we Iraqis see them as passionate about their ideas,' an earnest university linguist tried to explain.

Every night on the myriad television channels, candidates have shouted, hectored and lectured. Channel-hopping Iraqis have watched them all, mesmerised by this new phenomenon. I met a cleric who turned up smoking a Cohiba cigar, and another candidate who gave a telephone interview to a Tehran station with a glass of whisky in his hand. Every campaign must feed the crowds who attend rallies. There have been so many that the price of lamb has soared from $11 (£7) to $15 per kilo.

One of the main differences compared with the 2005 election is a relative lack of sectarian rhetoric. Among those driven from their homes during the violence of 2006–7, which left tens of thousands dead, the desire is not for revenge, but for security.

'I'm voting for a secular candidate,' said Hekmet Jawad, 42, a Shi'ite engineer from a northern village who now lives as a squatter in an abandoned building in Baghdad, home to 16 refugees including nine children. His brother Qadhum was taken off a bus in 2006 and shot by gunmen who spared Sunni and Christians.

Yet despite his grievances, he insists that a secular candidate can serve the country best.

'We don't need more religion. We need jobs. Families need food for their children.' Three main groups are competing for the vote today. Favoured to win most seats is Nouri al-Maliki, the prime minister, who leads the State of Law coalition, comprised of secular Shi'ite and Sunni groups.

Maliki is running on his record of improving security. Following a series of Al-Qaeda bombs, his lead has slipped. The election appears to be closer than expected.

In second place is Ayad Allawi, a secular Shi'ite politician and former prime minister who heads the Iraqiya bloc.

Allawi, a one-time favourite of British security forces, has locked up a good chunk of the Sunni vote as well as attracting Shi'ite support. He has benefited from controversy over the banning of hundreds of Sunni candidates because they had once been members of Saddam's Ba'ath party.

The third bloc is the Iraqi National Alliance. This includes the Islamic Supreme Council of Iraq (ISCI), led by Ammar al-Hakim, and other well-known politicians such as Ibrahim al-Jaafari, the former prime minister, and Ahmed Chalabi, a former minister.

Although they are running under a religious banner, they have also set out a nationalistic agenda. 'The next government of Iraq will be a coalition,' said Humam Hamoudi, a senior ISCI cleric. 'We need all the main components of the political spectrum.' It is an acceptance that Iraqis went to the brink, and do not want to go back. 'Moderate Shi'ism sells well in this climate,' said one diplomat.

The election is seen in America as a test of President Barack Obama, who campaigned on his opposition to the Iraq war. Obama has promised to withdraw all combat troops this summer, with a complete exit by the end of 2011.

Some fear wrangling over the formation of the new government could lead to further violence, putting this timetable in doubt. The resolve of Obeid and his fellow soldiers may be tested sooner than they wish.

US departure from Iraq opens the door for Al-Qaeda

22 August 2010

Wrangling Iraqi politicians have left the fragile Middle East state with no leadership. As America leaves, terrorists are ready to pounce.

The Stryker vehicles trundled across the border in the dark, lumbering under the weight of their armour like giant armadillos. Jubilant young Americans shouted out to camera crews, overjoyed to be leaving Iraq alive.

'We're going home! We won. It's over, America,' one soldier yelled, incoherent with emotion as he crossed the border into Kuwait in the last combat brigade to leave Iraq after seven and a half years of war.

They had travelled 360 miles, moving only at night to avoid attacks and the 50°C daytime temperatures. They left behind a country frustrated at its lack of a government nearly six months after elections, and shaken by almost daily attacks, including a huge suicide bomb in central Baghdad last week, that many fear could presage a resumption of insurgency.

The Stryker brigade, officially 4th Infantry, 2nd Brigade, is nick-named after its ungainly vehicles, developed during the war to counter lethal roadside attacks by improvised explosive devices (IEDs). It passed clusters of shuttered shops, endless vistas of hard yellow desert and the odd rusted skeleton of a bombed truck, a landscape almost the same as when it came up the highway as a conquering army in March 2003.

Officially, Stryker soldiers were the last brigade combat team to leave Iraq as part of the US withdrawal from 170,000 troops to 50,000 by 1 September, a deadline set by President Barack Obama.

Major-General Terry Wolff, commander of the Baghdad and Anbar provinces and on his third tour of Iraq, last week remembered his own drive in the opposite direction as a young colonel leading the 2nd Armored Cavalry Regiment to destroy Saddam Hussein's regime.

'In 2003 we could not even have imagined where we are today,' said Wolff, 53, sitting in an office surrounded by maps and charts of tribal leaders of Anbar, in the sprawling Camp Liberty outside Baghdad. Mistakes were made, Wolff admits, which meant the removal of the tyrannical Saddam turned into a seven-year occupation, but he has no time for what he believes should be left to the historians. He has a job to do: get the Iraqi army ready for the real withdrawal next year.

The 50,000 American soldiers that are remaining behind will be rebranded as 'advise and assist brigades'. When they cross the border on New Year's Eve next year, the Iraqis will be on their own. 'That's when we kick off the training wheels,' said one US officer.

Wolff says he believes the training wheels are already off. He is, metaphorically, in the position of every worried dad, hovering protectively over a determined and pedalling youngster, murmuring encouragement, sometimes shouting in worry.

Unlike on his first tour, he has learnt an 'amazing' amount about the country, liaises daily with his Iraqi counterpart in Baghdad Operations Centre, and believes the Iraqi military can 'step up to the plate'.

'We've built an Iraq "good enough",' Wolff said. 'I could have built them an American system, but then they're not going to use that.'

Yesterday, the American army stood at 52,000, with 2,000 scheduled to leave by 31 August. The cost of the war so far: $736 billion from the American treasury, with billions more to come this year;

4,416 American lives; 179 British lives; and the lives of at least 100,000 Iraqi civilians and security forces.

The efficiency of that force was not on display in Baghdad last week. On Tuesday 1,000 young men, mostly Shi'ites from poor families, were waiting in Maidan Square in Baghdad to sign up for the army. Unemployment is at 30%, and as high as 75% for young, uneducated men from poorer families. Some had been queuing for days.

Just after 7am, an officer came out. 'The officer started taking our identity cards, and suddenly I was hurled into the air,' said Marwan Ramthan, 18, from New Baghdad, a poor Shi'ite neighbourhood.

He lay on his back in Medical City hospital, four tubes coming out of his battered body. His mother, Ghazia Farhan, 52, wept at his bedside as she said she had to send him for work because, with seven children and a disabled husband, the family needed the money.

'Other places you have to pay bribes to get a job, but we heard the army was giving jobs for free,' she said.

In all, the bomber killed 61 young men and injured more than 100. The explosive, packed with nails, had been tied to his legs so that he could pass a 'pat down' inspection. Security officials said they believed the young bomber was sent by Iraqi insurgents, a mixture of Al-Qaeda and the mostly Sunni Ba'athists embittered that they lost power with Saddam's overthrow. They want to undermine the government, hoping – in a dream that seems increasingly quixotic – to return to power.

Iraqis placed the blame on their politicians, who five months after the March election have yet to form a government. 'The politicians are bickering while we are dying,' screamed one man, sweat and blood mingling on his shirt as he shouldered a coffin on to a taxi.

'Curses on the father of [Nouri] Maliki!' shrieked an elderly woman in an abbaya, a black robe worn by traditional women, denouncing the serving prime minister, a Shi'ite who should have

been her natural political ally. 'Curses on the father of Dawa
[Maliki's original party]!'

The anger at politicians was widespread. The bomb and a wave
of assassinations of police, municipal officials and judges last week
has created an air of apprehension.

Iraqis take it personally because they have individually stood up
to the terrorist threat. In March they braved Al-Qaeda warnings to
vote in their second parliamentary election. But no party won
enough seats to form a government.

Abu Ahmed, 39, who works at Baghdad's ancient book market,
said: 'People are shocked. They were so happy to vote, but they
found that the politicians did nothing. Nothing!'

Iraqis fear a return of the sectarian violence that erupted in a
similar political vacuum in 2006–7 after it took five months to
form a government after June 2005 elections.

The current wrangling is Byzantine. Until last week, Ayad Allawi,
a former prime minister whose Iraqiya party won 91 seats, was negotiating with Maliki's State of Law party, lying second with 89 seats.

It was to be a marriage of convenience between Allawi, a Shi'ite
whose party won by attracting the votes of Sunnis who felt disen-
franchised by the Shi'ite government, and Maliki, the increasingly
authoritarian Shi'ite prime minister who has clung to power with
American support.

Both Maliki and Allawi insist they should be prime minister.
Allawi upped the stakes at the weekend, saying he would no longer
consider Maliki a partner and turning to negotiations with his
Shi'ite rivals.

In an interview, Allawi threw down the gauntlet, offering to
negotiate with the leaders of the insurgency. 'We need to get the
insurgents back into the system,' Allawi told me, echoing a strategy
being considered in Afghanistan. 'I would negotiate with the top-
level leaders as long as they lay down their arms and say they will
obey the rules of this country.'

His remarks will infuriate Maliki's camp, who see the insurgents
as remnants of the Saddam regime.

The Islamic Supreme Council of Iraq, one of the main Shi'ite parties, refused to enter any coalition headed by Maliki, despite threats from Iran to withdraw funding. 'We believe in the rule of law,' said Hamam al-Hamoudi, a senior council official and key negotiator. 'If Maliki returns as prime minister, we risk returning to the one-party rule and intimidation we experienced under Saddam.'

Hoshyar Zebari, the foreign minister, said meddling by regional powers had been a huge problem. Iran, he said, had been manoeuvring for a Shi'ite government, while Turkey and the Sunni Arab states had lined up behind Allawi.

Leila Khafaji, 59, a two-term member of parliament who is involved in the council's political negotiations, said leading Iraqi politicians had let down their voters in their refusal to find a compromise.

Khafaji is a vivid reminder of the need for a democratic solution. As a 23-year-old with a degree in engineering, Khafaji was imprisoned and tortured by Saddam's intelligence service after refusing to join the Ba'ath party. She was arrested, blindfolded, thrown down stairs, kicked and slapped in prison. 'I found myself hanging from the ceiling,' she said last week of her months of torture.

Eventually sentenced to death, she served 10 years for being a threat to national security, before escaping into exile in Canada. She returned when Saddam fell, and her anger is now turned on her fellow politicians.

'We the politicians are helping the insurgents,' she said last week. 'The politicians are acting in their own interests, not the interests of the people we should be serving. People are now saying it was better under Saddam!'

For the Iraqis, the crisis may be just beginning; for the Americans, the sense of relief at the draw-down is palpable. Outside the concrete blast walls of Camp Liberty, the enemy is gathering for a final push. The Iraqi army is in its cross hairs.

Terror returns to stricken Fallujah

29 August 2010

In the Iraqi city, Marie Colvin finds Al-Qaeda are striking back with a renewed intensity and recruiting a younger generation.

Just down the street from Faisal's Takeaway in Fallujah, an explosion shattered the sweltering morning heat last week, igniting an Iraqi army Humvee on the corner and a police car.

A suicide bomber had driven into the stationary vehicles, killing a policeman. His colleagues heaved bloodied and burnt victims into cars and rushed them to hospital.

Within the hour another police officer had been killed by a 'sticky bomb' attached to his car and detonated as he set off for work. A third bomb blew up at a policeman's house but he was not at home.

The attacks were part of a ferocious onslaught by Al-Qaeda in Iraq on 13 cities, just 24 hours after the departure of the last American combat troops from the country they had occupied since 2003. More than 60 died in the bombings and hundreds were injured.

As I drove through Fallujah the next day, shopkeepers were sweeping glass from the pavement to restore some semblance of normality. But there was no hiding the fact that the insurgents had returned in force to the former Al-Qaeda stronghold and scene of the most devastating American attack of the seven-year war.

'Everyone is worried,' said Sami Sultan, 23, clearing debris from the front of his perfume shop. 'Security has been deteriorating for the last three months.'

Despite the US blitz that destroyed 60% of the city's buildings in 2004, Al-Qaeda was not driven out until 2006, when Sunni tribes formed the Sons of Iraq militia. Its members fought with the Americans and turned the war in Washington's favour.

Last week members of the Sons of Iraq huddled in hot little rooms, lamenting the miserable turn their fortunes had taken since they joined forces with the 'surge' troops of General David Petraeus, the US commander.

Angry and disillusioned, they claimed they had been all but discarded by the Iraqi and American governments, which had promised them jobs and a place in the country's future.

Many had not been paid for two months, they said. They believed their job prospects in the security forces and ministries had diminished because they were out of favour with the Shi'ite dominated government of Nouri al-Maliki, the prime minister.

Major General Mudhir al-Mawla, the official responsible for integrating the 52,000 Sons of Iraq, confirmed yesterday that the process had been frozen for a year. Worse still, the militia has been increasingly targeted by a resurgent Al-Qaeda, particularly in the towns and cities of Anbar province, including Fallujah. Here Al-Qaeda is offering young men $200 (£129) a time to take part in attacks – a huge sum in a city with few jobs.

Leaders of the Sons of Iraq believe some of their members are so desperate that they are accepting cash to turn a blind eye to Al-Qaeda's activities, or even to join the insurgency that they had risked their lives to put down. They can earn about $400 a month to do so, compared with their militia salary of $250.

'When we were fighting Al-Qaeda in 2006, the majority were foreigners,' said Sheikh Hamid al-Hashim, head of the city council. 'Now we are finding 70% are Fallujah natives.'

The return of Al-Qaeda to Fallujah and the degree of support it is attracting from young men enraged by the devastation that still surrounds them have disturbing implications for Iraq as a whole.

The situation highlights not only the divisions between Sunnis and Shi'ites but also the dangers of the politicians' failure on both sides to form a government almost six months after a keenly fought general election.

All eyes will be on President Barack Obama this Tuesday, when he marks the combat troops' withdrawal with a speech. It will no doubt avoid the triumphalism of President George W Bush's ill-judged declaration of 'mission accomplished' in 2003.

Rightly so. The latest surge in violence has intensified concerns that Iraq's forces are not up to securing the country, with less than 18 months to go before the departure of the final 50,000 US troops who have stayed on to assist and advise. Last week's bombings were seen by many in Fallujah as a sign of more trouble to come.

'There is a clear message,' said Sheikh Hamid al-Hayes, a local leader of the Sons of Iraq who knows his enemy well: assassination attempts have left him with a scar from a bullet that passed through the left of his chest, and a missing finger on his right hand.

'They are saying: we exist, and we can strike where we want, when we want. Imagine what we can do when the Americans leave.'

My journey to Fallujah was fraught with anxiety. Until 20 months ago only residents carrying a biometric card were allowed into the city. Now a visitor can enter if a Fallujah resident vouches for them but I had been told of arbitrary exclusions. I pulled on a black hijab (headscarf) and abaya (black robe); women dressed traditionally are rarely searched.

The four-lane highway from Baghdad to Fallujah and on to the Jordanian border was once the best in Iraq. During last week's 30-mile drive I had to cross to the opposite carriageway in six places where the road had been blown up.

A member of the Sons of Iraq met me just outside Fallujah and arranged for a police escort past a long queue of vehicles at a checkpoint into the city.

Soon we were driving at nerve-jangling speed down the main street – to reduce the risk of kidnap, my escorts said. As far as we knew I was the only westerner in town.

Every building flying by seemed to be marked by the fighting: heavy weapons had pierced walls and missile-sized holes deformed apartment buildings where people had hung out blankets to shield themselves from the searing sun. There was little visible evidence of the $190m in reconstruction money that the Americans have poured in.

The police station was protected by two tiers of blast walls. About 20 cars that had been mangled in explosions were heaped in a courtyard.

Brigadier General Mahmoud al-Essawi, the police commander, sat behind his walnut desk, gold damask curtains blocking out the light. He looked exhausted.

'It is true. We are experiencing an increase in violence,' said Essawi, dressed in a camouflage uniform; he received his 10th death threat last week. 'We attribute it to the political negotiations that have been going on so long and we have no government.'

Essawi has been in charge of 4,000 officers since 2008, when he won reinstatement after being purged as a former colonel in Saddam's security apparatus. He has posts available for Sons of Iraq but the government will not approve them.

The militia's resentment of both the US and the Iraqi governments over the failure to integrate them into the security forces was a growing concern, he confirmed.

Hayes keeps a photograph of his brother with Bush on his mantelpiece but says his men have been betrayed. 'We have accomplished what the Americans and the Iraqi army failed to do,' he said, a wide leather belt with a Beretta pistol strapped over his green polo shirt. 'We defeated Al-Qaeda, but the leaders who fought them are sitting in cafés with no jobs and they aren't being paid a penny.'

Al-Qaeda's new tactics have made the position more complex. The group has alternated between brutal attacks and offers of forgiveness as well as wages if the militiamen switch sides and take up arms against the US and Baghdad.

'I'm not sure that many are being paid to join Al-Qaeda, but I am sure they are accepting money to turn the other way when there is an Al-Qaeda operation,' said Hashim, resplendent in a white dishdasha, white flowing headdress and black robe.

'They are saying: why should I fight when I am receiving nothing, despite all the promises?'

Battered Kurds attempt to cling on to city of oil

5 September 2010

Insurgents are trying to drive out Kurdish families before a census that could transform their future by deciding who will profit from oil wealth.

The desperate call came through to the mobile phone of Brigadier Sarhed Qadr, Kirkuk central's police commander, at midday last week. One of his officers was under fire in his own home in the centre of this disputed city in northern Iraq.

Qadr, a former Kurdish resistance fighter, mimicked firing an AK-47 assault rifle as he recalled what happened. 'In al-Riyadh district just two days ago, four of these insurgents attacked the home of one of my men,' said the 40-year-old commander, dressed in an impeccable navy blue uniform with three silver stars and an eagle on his shoulder.

'He was fighting back with his gun, but by the time we reached him his three-year-old son was dead and his wife was injured.'

The onslaught was the latest in an escalating series of attacks as tensions increase between Kirkuk's Kurdish, Arab and Turkoman populations in the run-up to a census on 24 October.

The census will determine whether the Kurds make up the largest ethnic bloc in the city. It is important because the Kirkuk region possesses 13% of Iraq's gigantic oil reserves and generates $27 million a day in revenues. If Kurds prove to be in the majority, this will boost the efforts of the semi-autonomous Kurdish region's government to claim the oil for its own treasury.

Qadr believes security in Kirkuk will deteriorate as Sunni Arab insurgent groups, including Al-Qaeda, intensify attacks on Kurds before the census. He recently fought a pitched battle against an Al-Qaeda unit, killing two and arresting two others.

The captives admitted 30 attacks in the city and said they had been told to speed up operations in the past six months. 'They told us the police are working for the infidels so they are fair targets,' Qadr said.

The commander has survived several assassination attempts. A few months ago insurgents fired a 120mm rocket at his convoy, wounding two of his bodyguards with shrapnel.

Seven improvised explosive devices have exploded on the road as he was passing. 'These are the sacrifices we have to make,' he said. Since the fall of Saddam Hussein in 2003, 280 police had been killed in Kirkuk, he said.

The census, the first to be held in Kurdish regions of Iraq since 1987, has reopened bitter divisions created when Saddam strengthened his grip on the city with a campaign of ethnic cleansing, driving out Kurds and trucking in Arabs.

A sign of how vicious the fight over the city has become is that Izzat Ibrahim al-Douri, Saddam's former vice-president and the last wanted member of his regime still at large, is financing a new insurgent group, Nakshabandiya, active only in the Kirkuk area. Police say it aims to frighten away Kurds and ensure Kirkuk stays in the Arab-ruled part of Iraq.

Iraqi security forces have dismissed recent reports that Douri is dead or incapacitated. They say he is well funded and is thought to have moved from his former base in Syria to a Gulf country from which he masterminds his campaign.

'The coming census is not the only problem,' Qadr said. 'The violence is increased because the Americans are withdrawing and we don't have a government yet that can make decisions.'

Iraq's politics have been paralysed since elections in March failed to give any party a decisive victory. American combat troops withdrew last week, leaving fewer than 50,000 behind to assist and advise Iraqi forces. Because of the ethnic tensions, Kirkuk is one area where they are expected to stay until the final withdrawal on 31 December 2011.

The census is so controversial that local councillors are insisting three census takers call at every door – one Kurd, one Arab and one Turkoman. Given that every Iraqi will be required to stay at home for the one or two days of the census, the operation appears to be hugely unwieldy.

No one knows how many Kurds or Arabs live in the city. Many Kurds who were displaced by Saddam have returned.

'Saddam flattened our area in 1988,' said Hussein Sharif, 38. 'We lived for the summer in a valley; then we had to go to Irbil when it got so cold. We left behind all our sheep and cows.'

After years working as a labourer in Irbil, he dismantled his house and rebuilt it in a barren area that is officially part of Kirkuk's cemetery. Thousands of Kurds have joined him.

Sharif, who runs a small shop that sells everything from soap to carrots, says he cannot take his wife and four children back to the district Saddam levelled. 'There are no services, no water, no electricity,' he said.

Officials in Kirkuk insist the census will not be derailed by the violence. 'We will do all we can to make it a success, because it is important for the future planning of the city,' said Abdul Rahman Mustafa, Kirkuk's governor. The armed guards and blast walls protecting his office are testimony to just how difficult that may be.

Afghanistan

Corrupt, untrained, underpaid, illiterate: the forces waiting to take over

KABUL

6 December 2009

The Afghan police chief sat shivering at his desk, his hands in the pockets of his wool coat, as he tried to answer questions about his men. Police station three is in one of central Kabul's better districts but it had had no electricity for days. It was colder inside than out.

Lieutenant-Colonel Amanullah, the acting chief, was having a tough time satisfying his American 'mentors', young soldiers from Camp Phoenix. They were, in fact, being quite gentle, but the facts about his station kept eluding him.

How many of his men had been trained, asked Staff Sergeant Jimmie Stokely, 30. 'Ninety per cent studied, but I don't know how many passed,' replied Amanullah, sinking a bit in his chair.

He answered a question about staffing by saying he had 105 men on active duty. His personnel manager interjected. The station had '16 officers, 44 sergeants and 98 soldiers'. Were they all on duty? That was unclear. Amanullah slumped further down.

Did he still have 13 checkpoints? At that point Amanullah took a mobile phone call and practically ran out of the room, saying a fight had broken out. He turned the meeting over to Shamsullah Habibzani, the deputy, who sat rigidly erect.

Did police district three still have 13 checkpoints? He would get back to the Americans on that.

Not a piece of paper appeared during the meeting, and the ancient computer on the desk remained dark without power. 'I have to go to the internet café to file my reports,' Habibzani, 25, said sadly.

The Afghan police and army are at the forefront of the strategy announced by President Barack Obama last week, which called for a 'surge' of 30,000 new US troops in the country.

Nearly a brigade of the newcomers – 3,000–4,000 troops – would be trainers, and much of the rest would work with or mentor Afghan security forces. Obama proclaimed that the surge would mean that 'more Afghans can get into the fight'.

Within 18 months, the Afghan army is scheduled to grow from 97,000 to 134,000, and the police force to double. From July 2011, Afghan forces will take gradual control of their own territory and the Americans will begin withdrawing.

At least that is the theory. Last week, however, in visits to the Afghan security forces, a woeful picture emerged of the reality on the ground. The model endorsed by Obama could well work, but to do so, there will have to be an acknowledgement of just how threadbare the forces are, and measures taken to reverse the neglect and ignorance that has caused the problem.

Lieutenant-Colonel Todd Goehler is the head of a 12-man training team that since July has been mentoring Charlie kandak – Afghan for battalion – in Kabul's capital division.

Goehler, a 24-year veteran of the special forces, described a disastrous situation that differed dramatically from the official projections. 'They have been putting Band-Aids on this for a while,' he said.

On paper, Charlie kandak is one of six battalions in the brigade covering the 14 districts of Kabul and outlying areas. In reality, he revealed, only one other exists. Two kandaks are only at 30% capacity and are consequently not deployable. The final two are still 'in the training pipeline'.

Decrepit Russian barracks at Kabul international airport have been earmarked for their arrival. The buildings lack running water and all the electrical fittings have been stripped. At any given moment, 20% to 30% of the 600 soldiers on Charlie kandak's roster are absent without leave. In the Afghan army, a soldier can be missing for up to 60 days before any action – other than the suspension of his pay – is taken.

Illiteracy is high: 70% of inventory receipts are signed with a thumbprint. This engenders corruption because a soldier who cannot read has no idea what he has just confirmed receipt of.

Compounding the difficulties, senior commanders had so little understanding of the mentoring process that they were undermining the programme by breaking up teams that worked well together to plug holes elsewhere. 'They're ripping apart our teams,' said Goehler. 'They [the Afghans] would be much further ahead if they had solid mentoring teams, the right people with the right experience.'

Nevertheless, Charlie kandak has started to fall into some kind of shape. When Goehler's team took over, its colonel refused to leave the base; officers had no idea of logistics, the need to brief for missions, or the inventory and supply process.

On a trip last week to Farzeh, a tiny village in the mountains northwest of Kabul, the difficulties of the transfer to Afghan control were obvious – and so was an image of how it could succeed.

The Americans are anxious that Afghans accept their national security forces, which is felt to be as much a part of the transition process as getting them up to speed technically. So Goehler's team put together humanitarian aid parcels, planned the trip to impoverished Farzeh, then put Charlie kandak in the lead to make the delivery while they followed.

The Afghans were enthusiastic, revving their Humvees like drag racers. 'They drive like a 14-year-old boy joyriding in the spare family car he grabbed when the parents went out,' said one American mentor in exasperation.

Once they reached Farzeh, Colonel Rahmatsha Qimati, commander of Charlie kandak, took the lead. He told the gathered elders: 'You can call us any time, day or night. We know Farzeh is very poor, so we have brought 50 parcels of food and clothing.' Afghan soldiers handed them out to the elders, who complained a bit about the paucity of supplies but seemed happy to have been remembered.

While offering the prospect of hope, this was an isolated example: the army remains in poor shape. However, it is a well-oiled machine compared with what could be seen of the Afghan police force last week. Station three should have had some of the best policemen in the city. The neighbourhood is home to more than 30 foreign companies, a university and two ministries.

Habibzani, the deputy, spelt out the problems. He had graduated from the Kabul police academy, but he could barely support his family of five on an officer's salary of $200 (£120) a month.

The $120 paid to the lowest ranks meant the force attracted those who had no other possibilities – and needed the three meals a day that come with the job – but also meant they felt no guilt about demanding bribes.

A key aspect of the US strategy is to make working for the state more attractive than taking the Taliban's shilling. Yet there was no sign of the wage increase to $165 that the government had announced. Meanwhile, the Taliban pay $220 a month.

Habibzani said 90% of the police could not read or write. Abdullah Fattah, a police trainer standing with him in the gloom of the hallway as black cables dangled uselessly from the ceiling, said police received five months' training. 'They start from such a low level. I need five years,' he said. 'With all the attention of the international community, maybe three years minimum.'

Corruption is rife, and many police are addicted to drugs. There is some evidence that Hamid Karzai, the president inaugurated last month amid allegations of fraud in the election and corruption in his government, has got the message.

'I can confirm we have this cancer of corruption in the police but very soon we will start cleaning it out,' said General Haider Basir, deputy at the interior ministry, which is responsible for the police. Biometric prints have been taken of 25,000 police so that if they moonlight for the Taliban, they might be caught.

But Basir set official standards fairly low. 'To be a policeman, it is necessary to be healthy and not addicted to drugs,' he said. 'They don't need to read and write.'

Hamid Karzai fails Taliban who gave up arms

PUL-I-ALAM, LOGAR PROVINCE

31 January 2010

Marie Colvin and Miles Amoore

The room the Taliban commander Mullah Mohammad now calls home, after bringing his 21 fighters to join the Afghan government's reintegration programme earlier this month, is barely more comfortable than the mountain redoubt he left.

He sits on a thin mat and leans against the wall, his skin dark and weathered, facing the battered Kalashnikovs and a vintage Russian mortar launcher he surrendered in return for promises of money, jobs and land for him and his men.

Instead, the peace and reconciliation commission (known as PTS, its acronym in Dari), set up by the president, Hamid Karzai, in 2005, handed them letters guaranteeing free passage. And nothing else. Mohammad, 48, is stunned and speaks slowly.

'We were fighting all day, and we had nothing to show for it,' he said. 'I began thinking, "Why are we killing our Afghan brothers?"'

Like many mid-level Taliban commanders, he is a conservative tribal Pashtun, not an extremist ideologue. He is the perfect candidate for the government's reintegration programme, which will be absorbed into the bigger and better-funded reintegration council announced by Karzai at last week's London conference. Donors there pledged $140 million (£90 million) towards a $500 million fund to pay the Taliban to lay down their arms.

'They [the PTS] told us they'll protect us, and that we would have the chance to have jobs. Now we have nothing,' Mohammad says.

The drive to Pul-i-Alam, the capital of Logar province, most of which is controlled by the Taliban, was fraught.

The former Taliban commanders I went to meet there had fought in the Haqqani organisation, led by Jalaluddin Haqqani, a 60-year-old warlord who battled the Soviets.

He is said to be ailing and has ceded control of his military wing to his son Sirajuddin Haqqani, a militant in his early forties responsible for a deadly escalation in the Afghan war.

Haqqani is based in north Waziristan, just across the Pakistani border, but most of his attacks are inside Afghanistan. He has boasted that he sent down this same highway the suicide bombers and gunmen who attacked Kabul ministries, shops and a hotel earlier this month, on the day Karzai swore in his new cabinet.

His other great coup was to prime a Jordanian double agent to kill seven CIA agents inside an American base last month.

Last year, Haqqani set up flying checkpoints on this highway to Logar, which is hated by American troops because the Taliban constantly seed the route with improvised explosive devices.

Huddled in the back seat of a car, I was swathed in a brown wool blanket, and instructed to pretend I was asleep if we were stopped at a checkpoint. I was happy it was snowing and the windows were steamed up. Nobody could see inside.

An hour outside town, I called the PTS and it sent an armed escort. Several of its officials have been killed on this road. In Pul-i-Alam, I was bundled into its compound by armed men, keen that nobody should see a foreigner.

The Taliban commanders in Logar gave an insight into the gulf between the promises at last week's conference and the harsh reality on the ground.

Few in London appeared to recall that Karzai set up the PTS five years ago, although it has been poorly funded so far.

Two former Taliban commanders joined Mullah Mohammad. Moulana Saheb Said Ajan, a senior Taliban figure, was angry. 'I brought 40 fighters to the PTS,' he said. 'I told my men: "Other countries are making planes and computers. Why are we freezing in the mountains? We should be building our country."'

Ajan changed sides after falling out with Haqqani's 'Pakistan Taliban', so called because they allegedly receive money from Pakistan's intelligence service, the ISI. He said many more would join if the money was there and they felt safe.

As a commander, Ajan was not paid a salary, although foot soldiers are paid about $200 a month, considerably more than the Afghan police.

'I told the leaders what I needed, and they sent it,' Ajan said. 'They always paid immediately.' He said he received 200,000–500,000 Pakistani rupees (£1,500–£3,700) every month, either smuggled from Dubai, or in bags of cash that would fill the back of pick-up trucks from Pakistan. Ajan decided to take the PTS offer after he was ordered to carry out a raid he disagreed with. 'We were on top of the mountain and Haqqani's people ordered us to the district office here in Pul-i-Alam, to destroy a United Nations vehicle to make them leave,' he said. 'I'm 28 years old. I just didn't want to do this any more.'

He sent tribal elders to check out the PTS and they came back with assurances of money, jobs and security for his family and fighters. 'I'm now living on the floor of this office,' Ajan said dejectedly. 'The Taliban are now dropping letters through our doors, saying if we don't return they'll kill us.'

The success of the reintegration programme is crucial to any transition to Afghan rule. It would take hardened fighters off the battlefield and into the army and police force, which Nato wants to increase to 400,000 men by 2015. But for the system to work, the money must reach the fighters and not be siphoned off.

Ajan's story also illustrates the differences between commanders on the ground and the Taliban leadership, which will have to be part of a political solution if there is to be any lasting peace. 'I strongly believe we need to reach the Taliban leaders,' said Najibullah Mojadidi, the elder son of the PTS chairman and a member of Karzai's national security committee.

'As long as they're not convinced, they'll always have people in Afghanistan prepared to continue the fighting.'

Swift and bloody: the Taliban's revenge

9 May 2010

Marie Colvin, Christina Lamb, Washington

Rebels have returned to terrorise a former stronghold with shootings and beatings, raising doubts about America's ability to secure Kandahar.

The sniper's aim was merciless. Lieutenant Brandon Barrett was shovelling sand into bags to fortify his post in the Helmand town of Marjah when a Taliban gunman slotted a bullet between armoured vehicles pulled around for protection, hitting him in the chest.

Although the sun was setting and the fierce heat of the day had softened, it was still hot and Barrett and Lance-Corporal Marcus Lounello had taken off their flak jackets as they worked.

The sniper's second bullet hit Lounello in the chest.

The call came in to the US marines' forward operating base (FOB) Marjah at 6pm last Wednesday: 'Two down, gunshot wounds to the chest, non-responsive.'

Barrett, 27 and unmarried, from Indiana, was dead before the medical team reached them. Lounello, 21, lost a kidney, his spleen and part of his diaphragm but will survive.

'It's surreal,' Captain Tony Zinni, Barrett's commanding officer in the 1st Battalion, 6th Marine Regiment, said yesterday outside his tented office on a barren base. 'I keep expecting him to walk around the corner, big smile on his face.'

Barrett had been running a post that checked traffic coming in and out of Marjah, a former Taliban stronghold that was taken by the marines and their Afghan allies with an overwhelming show of force in February. A small, wiry officer, he was a favourite at FOB Marjah at the centre of the market town.

Zinni held his emotions in check as he described his last visit to Barrett's post. 'It was a really boring duty but he was good about it,' Zinni said, smiling at the memory.

Some elders arrived and Barrett had chatted to them. 'I said where the hell did you learn Pashto,' Zinni recalled. Barrett had been visiting the neighbourhood's elders, trying to win them round, learning words and phrases.

Zinni thinks the lieutenant was targeted and it makes him angry. 'Everyone in the block knew him, knew he was the officer,' the captain said. Barrett had 60 days left in Afghanistan. His was the first death in Marjah for the battalion's weapons company.

That night Zinni gathered Barrett's platoon for what he said had been one of his toughest moments in his 10 years in the Marine Corps. One of the men still had blood on his trousers.

The 41 soldiers had been together since they were at Camp Lejeune in North Carolina, where Barrett held weekend parties at his beach house. He would dress up as a penguin with aviator sunglasses and a cigar to make people laugh. There were only tears last week. 'I don't even know what to say to you. Our loss is so great,' Zinni said. 'But I do know that Barrett would have wanted us to make a success of this mission.'

Last week was the worst in living memory for weapons company, the first unit to enter Marjah on D-Day, 13 February.

Hours before the sniper killed Barrett, another 13-man squad in the company had been walking down a dusty street in the fierce morning heat, spread out on either side of the road so that only one of them would die if anyone stepped on an improvised explosive device (IED), when an insurgent jumped out from behind a building 40 yards ahead and fired three shots.

One bullet hit Lance-Corporal Matthew Hunter, the point man, in the stomach, just below his flak jacket. The second skidded around the armoured vest of a lucky Lance-Corporal Kyle Schneider, leaving him uninjured. Hunter, known in the squad for his 60 socks, which he would wear for two days and then discard, was seriously injured but survived.

On Thursday a member of the elite Afghan National Civil Order Police, which works side by side with the marines, was also shot and killed. The unidentified officer had arrived at FOB Marjah only two days earlier, determined to get his men out of the check-points and onto the streets.

Marjah was supposed to be safe. When 5,000 marines and their Afghan national army partners rolled in to oust the Taliban who had ruled the town for almost three years, the fighting lasted just two weeks.

'If you go to Marjah today, you will find a city that is free of the Taliban, that has schools that are open, a marketplace, a bazaar,' Major-General Richard Mills, commander of the US Marine Corps in Afghanistan, said just last month.

Marjah has indeed improved. The idea was to set up 'security bubbles', to get the economy and normal life going inside them in the hope that at some point the locals would throw in their lot with the government. Major David Fennell, a civil affairs officer for the marines, explained that his men had moved as soon as the fighting eased.

'We decided to get in there immediately and spend money. To use money as a weapon system,' Fennell said. He started a project paying $5 (£3.40) a day to clean the canals. Only a few nervous locals turned up on the first day, but when cash started to flow, 1,000 workers soon came on board, defying Taliban threats.

Contractors are now engaged in what the marines call 'quick impact projects' – bridges, wells, mosque restorations, anything that shows tangible improvement.

Last week hundreds flocked to the unpainted concrete villa that is the district government's headquarters, a building said to have been commandeered from a local drug lord.

Some farmers received cash in hand for destroying their poppy crop. Others pushed new wheelbarrows full of cheaply purchased mung beans, alfalfa seeds and huge 50-kilo (110-pound) bags of fertiliser. Further down, the stalls of the once shuttered Loy Chareh bazaar lined the street with wooden crates spilling okra, tomatoes, chilli peppers, mint, watermelon.

All that progress is threatened by the Taliban 'surge'. There were always fears that they would re-emerge, bolstered by poppy taxes levied from farmers. But nobody expected their return to be so swift and bloody.

My first night in Marjah had left little doubt that the Taliban were back. On Tuesday I walked out of FOB Marjah with a weapons company squad charged with 'rolling up' an IED-maker called Izra, or 'signature' in Pashto, probably a nom de guerre.

Izra was thought to be sleeping in a small local mosque. There was no moon and it was pitch black. After 20 minutes a light glowed on a rooftop, a suspicious sight in an area where there is no electricity and everyone sleeps during the hours of darkness.

The flashlight followed our progress. Corporal Josh Hurst, the squad leader, realised we had been spotted by the Taliban when his point man saw four men slipping through the tree line. Hurst motioned the squad down a path to a field of dry furrows and mud channels. I realised why I was slipping and sliding while the marines remained sure-footed – they all had night-vision goggles.

I slid noisily into a canal that I had not noticed. Lance-Corporal Tim Ryan hauled me out by the scruff of my flak jacket. Dogs barked. I was terrified that we were walking into an ambush.

After three hours we found the mosque, but Hurst decided to move on because of the danger. 'It just kept getting worse and worse and worse,' Hurst said with good humour when we were back on base.

The strength of the Taliban's presence is gradually becoming clearer. One of their targets is Wafa Aghasheran, a contractor for the marines who builds bridges and wells. He sat cross-legged in his cream-coloured shalwar kameez and dark wool vest last week recalling how Hazrat Gull, 19, his young business partner, had been killed by the Taliban several weeks ago.

'They pulled up on a motorcycle at our project, asked who is the contractor and shot him in the head,' Aghasheran said. 'I ran to the bridge and found him. His head was in the canal. All our workers had run away.'

More recently two motorcycles carrying four Taliban converged on Aghasheran's truck and pointed Kalashnikovs at the driver. They broke both the driver's arms with the butts of their guns and set fire to the vehicle. Their aim was to stop anyone from working with the Afghan government and marines.

They then put up a letter to Aghasheran in the local mosque saying: 'Stop your business or we will kill you and your family.' He smiled and said that he could not afford to stop: at 42, he has three wives and 18 children.

The Taliban are growing bolder. A man in his early twenties known only as Sharitulla was at home about two weeks ago when the Taliban came knocking in broad daylight. When he refused their demand for taxes, they took him out to the desert and beat him to death. His body was left on the doorstep of his elderly father.

While they may not want the Taliban back, many of Marjah's people are reluctant to commit themselves to the administration that has replaced them. 'The local residents don't trust we will provide security,' said Naimatullah, the acting district governor of Marjah, in a late-night interview.

'They are taking a wait-and-see attitude to the government,' he said, fingering black worry beads. 'The people are worried that the Taliban will return and punish them for supporting the government.'

The offensive in which Marjah was captured was the largest in Afghanistan since 2001, when the Taliban regime was driven out by US-supported Afghan warlords after the September 11 attacks on America.

After that victory, Afghanistan was largely neglected as America and Britain became bogged down in the war in Iraq. Only last year did attention shift back. Heavy-handed military operations that killed civilians helped the Taliban to re-establish support and organise a virulent insurgency.

General David Petraeus, who came up with the idea of the 'surge' that quelled the violence in Iraq, has tailored his theory to Afghanistan at a pivotal moment in the nine-year war. The Obama administration is deploying 30,000 new troops to Afghanistan as part of a shift to a counter-insurgency strategy.

Until recently Marjah was seen as a success story that could serve as a template for an expected operation against the Taliban in Kandahar, the birthplace of the Taliban.

'In many ways [the Marjah operation] is a model for the future: an Afghan-led operation supported by the coalition, deeply engaged with the people,' General Stanley McChrystal, leader of Nato and American forces, said.

Yet worries are growing in the Pentagon that if thousands of marines and Afghan security forces cannot entirely defeat the Taliban in Marjah, a town of only 50,000, securing the far larger prize of Kandahar may be an even greater struggle than has been foreseen.

This week Hamid Karzai, the Afghan president, flies to Washington for a meeting with President Barack Obama. The two men know that success in Kandahar will be crucial both to persuading the Taliban to the negotiating table and to enabling Nato forces to leave.

Yet after Marjah, McChrystal is playing down expectations. Last week he warned that it could be the end of the year before any progress is seen.

Afghans find pride in hunt for Taliban

LASHKAR GAH

4 July 2010

Recent raids have shown that well-trained and motivated local troops in Afghanistan are backing Nato's new counter-insurgency plan.

It was the Afghan soldiers who uncovered the cache. Squatting on the dirt floor of a mud-walled house, they found a plastic bag filled with black gunpowder, two yards of detonator cord and a detonator beneath a pile of carpets.

The find was the culmination of a joint raid by a squad of soldiers from the Queen's Royal Lancers and their Afghan partners. As they had suspected, this was a Taliban safe house.

To reach the compound had required a long, slow walk across sun-baked fields behind Lieutenant Will Pope as he swept a Vallon mine detector back and forth, looking for buried improvised explosive devices. Twice he identified suspicious metal and we crouched with our backs turned in case there was an explosion.

By the time we arrived at the compound across the river from Lashkar Gah, Helmand's provincial capital, the soldiers were sweating but determined to be polite. Troops have stopped kicking in doors under the counter-insurgency strategy put in place by Nato's American commanders.

The Afghan soldiers knocked on the huge wooden door and asked to see the elder of the household. They had received reports that a Taliban commander was leaving weapons there overnight.

Inside, women shrieked. An elderly man who came to the door tried to bar the soldiers, saying the women and children were too upset. 'Well, I'm sorry for that,' said Lieutenant Rob Campbell, 28. 'Please put your women in a separate room and we will wait. But we are here to search the compound and we will do so.'

As we waited, Ahmed, the unit's interpreter, started talking to some sullen teenagers watching us across an alley. There were no smiles.

'These two say they will not shake the hand of Isaf [the American-led Nato force in Afghanistan],' Ahmed said. 'They won't give me their father's name. I think we should search their compound.'

Accompanying the squad was Captain Malcolm Dalzel-Job, who was there to map 'human terrain'. He carries a gun, but in the new world of counter-insurgency it is more important to know who lives where, and where their sympathies lie.

Campbell and 'DJ', as Dalzel-Job is known, decided to follow the Afghan's advice and diverted the unit to the next-door compound where the teenagers lived. This was where the gunpowder and detonator were found.

Every patrol by British soldiers now takes members of the Afghan security forces. 'We've stepped beyond the fight against the Taliban,' said Lieutenant-Colonel Lincoln Jopp, commander of Task Force Lashkar Gah. 'We're partnering the Afghan security forces. Any patrol without them, we are 50 per cent less effective.'

In Lashkar Gah there is growing hope that the new emphasis on 'partnering' brings a prospect of turning the country over to the Afghans.

British officials acknowledge that training the army and police is not enough, however: there must also be a parallel track that includes negotiations with the Taliban.

In Lashkar Gah the British Army no longer focuses on chasing Taliban suspects and killing them, thereby creating even more enemies.

In a show of confidence, Jopp walked through a farmers' bazaar, removing his helmet and body armour. The moment might have been staged but the local merchants clearly knew him. The interaction was real.

Rather than ask about the Taliban, he concentrated on everyday concerns, asking how many hours of electricity they had, how much rent they were paying and what the new police were like. Men crowded in to listen and chat, nodding when a bystander said the police had got much better recently. 'They are not robbing us any more,' said one.

Police training has made an enormous advance. A patrol with the Afghan National Police in Kabul last year was dispiriting and dangerous. Few could read, recruits were high on drugs and they demanded bribes at checkpoints.

The change was evident at a recent graduation ceremony at the police academy in Helmand. Graduates stood to attention in clean blue-grey uniforms and polished black boots.

Mohammad Daoud, 26, a former member of the Taliban, could not stop smiling. He had worked for the insurgents in Uruzgan province before fleeing to Lashkar Gah with his family. 'I'm comfortable in myself now,' he said. 'When I came here, I couldn't read. Now, I can write my name and my father's name.'

Lieutenant-Colonel Andy Hadfield, who mentors the police at the Helmand Training Academy, admitted that when he was assigned he was disappointed: he would have preferred to be out commanding his battalion. Like Jopp and the other British officers, he has since been converted to the idea that partnering the Afghan security forces is the way ahead.

'Go back to your communities and be their guardians. Be courageous and honest and proud to say, "I serve Afghanistan",' he said at the graduation ceremony for 94 new officers.

Fears persist that the new strategy may be too little too late. But as the men marched forward to receive their certificates, their pride was evident. One could almost believe they might be the vanguard of an Afghanistan that, while not a democracy as we know it, could achieve the new, more realistic goal of sustainable stability.

'For Afghanistan!' each man cried, as he held up his certificate in the sun.

Iran

Anger at Mahmoud Ahmadinejad's election

14 June 2009

The motorcycle police came from behind. They fired stun grenades that exploded as I was walking among thousands of demonstrators on Tehran's central boulevard, talking to two young women about their anger at what they called the 'theft' of the Iranian election.

Tempers ran high. Protesters jostling shoulder to shoulder filled the road and pavements, punching the air with their fists and shouting, 'Down with the dictator,' and, 'Be ashamed and give us back Iran.'

They were convinced their candidate in the presidential election, Mir Hossein Mousavi, a former prime minister, had been cheated of victory by the government of President Mahmoud Ahmadinejad.

The election had been hard fought – Mousavi and Ahmadinejad were the frontrunners in a field of four – and an evidently tight race had been predicted to go to a second round this Friday.

It was an emotionally charged campaign. Mousavi's supporters, many of them young men and women, nearly shut down the city last week with all-night street campaigning, dancing until dawn as they handed out campaign leaflets.

Such a spectacle had never been seen in a conservative city where women are legally obliged to wear the hijab (headscarf) and an overcoat, and the sexes are not allowed to mix unless married or related.

Rallies for both candidates drew tens of thousands of fervent supporters.

Just as they had all week, yesterday's demonstrators waved green ribbons and banners and wore green T-shirts signalling their support for Mousavi.

'The election was stolen,' Safoor Nayafi, 26, shouted over the din of the march, clutching her black hijab at her chin. 'We are marching to the ministry of interior to get our stolen votes back.' She was just telling me she had a master's degree in science when her voice was drowned out by the roar of motorcycles from behind us and along the sides of the road.

They were riot police, dressed in camouflage uniforms, wearing black flak jackets and black helmets with their menacing visors pulled down.

They fired several grenades, scattering the crowd. Women screamed and fell to the ground; men leapt onto the pavements, then ran back to drag the fallen out of the road. Shop owners pulled scared bystanders inside and slammed down their metal grates.

It took only seconds to realise they were stun grenades, fired into the air to scatter the marchers, but they were terrifying seconds.

An acrid smell hung in the air as young men started shouting and running forward after the riot police. They were from a special unit trained to put down protests and named after Hassan Nasrallah, the Lebanese Hezbollah leader. Confronting them seemed a brave, but foolish, gesture.

About 50 yards ahead of us, at the junction of Vali-asr Street and a square called Saei Park, there was a skirmish, with motorcycles roaring and fired-up young men yelling, 'Allahu akbar' (God is great).

Smoke rose from the scene as the crowd cleared. Two riot police motorcycles lay burning in the middle of the junction, flames leaping from their metal carcasses and smoke rising into the overcast sky. A loud cheer went up from the crowd.

The demonstrators were not seasoned fighters. Tehran residents told me they had never seen such a crowd – young men and women, intellectuals, workers.

One elderly woman came up to me, screaming: 'We hate this government. It's my generation's fault to have let them come in 1979 [when the shah was ousted]. These children are doing what we were not brave enough to do.'

The riot police returned with much roaring of engines and more wielding of stun grenades, but the marchers stubbornly regrouped and the stand-off continued.

Walking back to my hotel, I saw burning dustbins surrounded by riot police swinging their batons at bystanders – they had clearly been set alight by protesters. A colleague said he had counted four more burnt-out police motorcycles and seen dozens of riot police beating people in the street.

Clashes continued into the night and there were reports of one person being killed.

No one knew what to expect next. I asked one of the march's leaders, sweating in his black T-shirt and green wristband, if the protests would turn into a fully fledged revolution.

'I don't know,' he said. 'This is new to us.'

The first protest had begun at about 4am, as Mousavi supporters, who had stayed up all night to wait for the results, converged on the ministry of interior, the department in charge of the poll, in the centre of the city. They were beaten back by riot police, who seemed to have been expecting them.

Later in the morning, I visited Mousavi's headquarters in a five-storey building on a residential street. The riot police had already been there.

A guard in the lobby of the building told me they had stormed in about three hours earlier, firing tear-gas canisters and shouting that they had seen a suspect flee into the building. They beat people with batons, the guard said, and Mousavi had ordered the headquarters to be closed to stop any more violence.

The disappointment at Mousavi's defeat quickly turned to anger as people absorbed the scale of Ahmadinejad's victory.

Polls in Iran are unreliable, but every unofficial sampling had indicated a close race. The outpouring of support for Mousavi in

Tehran could have been deceptive as Ahmadinejad's supporters are mostly the rural poor and urban working class, but the gap between the two candidates caused Iranian analysts and voters alike to suspect that something was amiss.

Mousavi was ensconced with advisers last night, but said he would challenge the result: 'I will not surrender to this dangerous charade.'

He called on his supporters to remain calm until he decided his course of action. Few seemed to be listening, however. Another demonstration was planned in central Tehran for late last night.

Ayatollah Ali Khamenei, Iran's supreme leader, said the election result should stand. 'Other honourable candidates must refrain from any kind of provocative and distrustful words or deeds,' he said on state radio.

News of the clashes travelled only by word of mouth; state-run television was still showing film of queues of voters on Friday. The texting network that Mousavi's supporters had used to organise their campaign was blocked.

Even before yesterday's riots, it was clear many ordinary people felt they had been cheated. 'Almost everybody I know voted for Mousavi but Ahmadinejad is being declared the winner. The government announcement is nothing but widespread fraud. It is very, very disappointing. I'll never again vote in Iran,' said Nasser Amiri, a Tehran hospital clerk.

Clashes show depth of fury

TEHRAN

21 June 2009

Yesterday's open defiance of the supreme leader was astonishing and shows how fast events are moving in Iran.

The two men cradled the woman as she collapsed backwards onto the street, a pool of blood at her feet. The men pressed their hands onto a bullet wound in her neck as her hands fell limp above her shoulders.

Within seconds, her eyes rolled sideways and her pale features were obscured by haemorrhaging from her nose and mouth. Her would-be rescuers shrieked in panic. There was nothing they could do to save her.

The scene, captured on a number of mobile phones, unfolded yesterday in Tehran as protesters fought running battles with riot police and militia on the streets of the Iranian capital.

Another video showed hundreds of people milling about in a street with fires burning in the road. Some were collecting rocks. A helicopter buzzed overhead.

At least five shots were heard and soon after a group of men raced through the crowd carrying a man by his arms and legs. His head was lolling. He was laid on the ground and a crowd gathered. A large bloodstain filled the centre of his white shirt. He lay still and appeared to be dead.

Yet more footage emerged of young men throwing stones at riot police. A number shouted 'Death to Khamenei!', underlining the seriousness of the protests. As supreme leader, Ayatollah Ali Khamenei traditionally occupies an untouchable position in Iranian society.

There was also video of a member of the security forces who had been knocked off his motorbike. A black-clad woman tried to protect him as a number of people, many of them wearing suits, kicked and punched him. A motorbike was on fire a few feet away.

Last night these videos revealed the extent of the defiance of the regime that has sprung from last week's disputed presidential election. Yesterday tens of thousands of supporters of Mir Hossein Mousavi, who claim Mahmoud Ahmadinejad, the incumbent, stole victory in the election, poured on to the streets again. They were confronted with water cannon, tear gas and targeted gunfire.

The largest crowd gathered near the University of Tehran, after evading a riot police cordon which had tried to disperse them. Soon a volley of 20–30 shots rang out – which state television later claimed were warning shots – and the group broke up into roaming knots of protesters. Street battles then erupted as they took the fight to police with rocks.

As night fell it was unclear how many people had been killed or injured in the clashes. What was certain was that Iran was entering uncharted territory.

On Friday, Khamenei had said opposition leaders would 'be held accountable for all the violence, bloodshed and looting' if they encouraged more rallies. It was a clear threat to Mousavi and his supporters.

'It must be determined at the ballot box what the people want and what they don't want, not on the streets,' Khamenei told the thousands gathered for Friday prayers at the University of Tehran. He threw down the gauntlet. 'If the things I have said now are not observed, I will be back here talking in a far more serious tone.'

His seriousness was apparent yesterday with the crackdown on the protesters. Nevertheless, the popular will, represented by the crowds' willingness to risk their safety by taking to the streets yesterday, appeared undimmed. The Islamic Republic of Iran was facing the worst crisis in its 30-year history.

What gave so many ordinary citizens the courage to take to the streets in numbers not seen since Ayatollah Khomeini overthrew the Shah in 1979? Where was this heading? Will yesterday's events presage a brutal crackdown, or are they just a pause in an extraordinary display of 'people power'?

Artemis, a 41-year-old Tehrani woman, is the proud holder of a law degree, but one who has never been allowed to work. She was clear about why she joined the million-plus men, women and children who took to the streets of Tehran last Monday.

'People want freedom and justice,' she said. 'They stole the vote. No one in his right mind believes this result.'

She said she had been afraid to voice criticism before. 'The neighbours listen to you, and people go to prison just for what they say, or what they write. But this is contagious. What you are seeing, all these people, this comes from 30 years of oppression and now we have had enough.'

Gathering in Revolution Square in the summer sun, they walked miles to Freedom Square. Nobody believed the election result, which gave Ahmadinejad more than 60% of the vote in what was expected to be a knife-edge contest, and the sense of anger and betrayal was palpable. 'Where is my vote?' asked placards held aloft. People walked with determination, emboldened by their sense of injustice.

Shouts of 'Down with the dictator!' and 'Death to the Taliban in Kabul and Tehran!' – echoes of the 1979 chant 'Death to the Shah!' – filled the air. Green ribbons, banners and wristbands adorned the marchers.

Mousavi's supporters had been ridiculed by supporters of the regime as merely the wealthy young crowd from the northern, tree-shaded neighbourhoods of Tehran. Last Monday, however, saw the old and the young, designer-clad groups of young women side by side with workers in worn clothes and government clerks in suits.

A young woman with a matching Burberry scarf and handbag walked between an elderly man and woman, a hand in each of theirs as they stared in wonderment. A middle-aged man in a suit walked carrying his briefcase, grey balding head held high.

'Look at all the white hairs here,' pointed out Siamak, a 28-year-old mechanical engineer. 'All of Tehran is here. I think Khamenei will not sleep tonight.'

They passed down the boulevard for hours.

'I was afraid to speak at all before. I thought we were a tiny minority,' said Mona, a 24-year-old software designer in the over-sized designer sunglasses favoured by Tehran's fashionable young women, and a tight red 'manteau', the overcoat that gives a scant nod to the law that women must cover their heads and bodies in public. 'But now I feel we are the majority. I am not afraid any more. For me, fear is over.'

That afternoon Mousavi appeared in Freedom Square for the first time since he had heard in the early hours of last Saturday that Ahmadinejad had won the presidency.

He had been a grey, uncharismatic figure during the campaign, buoyed in the polls mostly by his wife, Zahra Rahna-vard, a scholar and artist with a mischievous sense of humour. She set the tone by holding his hand in public on the campaign trail, endearing the couple to the younger generation.

Now he stood in Freedom Square on the top of a car, dressed in a blue-and-white striped shirt, shouting defiance over a handheld loudspeaker. 'We want respect. We will reclaim our rights,' he promised a cheering crowd. 'We fight on!'

There was tragedy to come that night. As the demonstration wound down, youths wandered home in the darkened streets. The riot police and Basiji volunteer militia had disappeared in the face of such numbers during the day, but they returned with a vengeance.

A swarm of Basiji riding two to a motorcycle attacked one group of youths walking back to the university. 'We tried to run, but they caught us,' said Shabab, 24, a computer science student in jeans and a T-shirt, a green ribbon on his wrist and a huge bandage on the back of his head.

'They were bastards,' he said, pulling a bloodied sweatshirt out of his rucksack. 'When they saw I was bleeding they beat me even more.'

Other students attacked a Basiji headquarters north of Freedom Square with Molotov cocktails and stones. The reply was devastating – gunmen from inside the building fired a fusillade of bullets, killing seven and wounding 26.

They were not the first deaths of the new era in Iran. The students had attacked the Basiji building because their dormitories had been raided before dawn that morning. Basiji crashed through the doors of sleeping undergraduates, ransacking bedrooms and destroying the books in the library. Five students died in the raid.

The violence was not all on one side. During Thursday's protest, I saw a crowd of men and women descend on a Basiji who tore down a poster of Mousavi. They beat and kicked him viciously while others on the march yelled: 'Don't hit him! Don't beat the Basiji!' He was eventually allowed to limp away.

The sight of hijab-wearing teenage girls walking away sweating from punching him as hard as they could was just as disconcerting as the sight of the girls partying all night in the heady days before the vote.

The parallels with 1979 cannot have been lost on the regime, nor Mousavi, who served as prime minister under Khomeini from 1981 to 1989.

The uprising against the Shah spiralled ever higher on a cycle of funerals and deaths.

Demonstrators would take to the streets to mourn fellow protesters shot by the Shah's security forces, suffer losses themselves, and take to the streets again for the new victims.

By Thursday last week, the cycle appeared to be repeating itself. As news of the deaths filtered out slowly on Tuesday and Wednesday, anger grew.

Even members of the national football team, including the captain, Mehdi Mahdavikia, wore green wristbands during a World Cup qualifying match against South Korea, which was shown on state-run television, to signal their support of the protests.

Impromptu shrines were set up around the city. A new march was planned for Thursday: this time the mood was different.

Earlier in the week the rallies had been rumbustious affairs; now they were silent in commemoration of the dead so as not to give the authorities any excuse to attack. Any marchers trying to start a chorus of 'Down with the dictator!' were quickly shushed.

Shunning the bright colours of earlier protests, most women now wore black hijabs and black clothing. One marcher said black had a deep emotional effect as well.

'The colour black is changing the mood,' he said. 'People are preparing for more militant confrontations.'

As much as the millions of people on Tehran's streets last week appeared to be a revolution in the making, aimed at overthrowing the government, in reality they had been allowed to continue because they were playing out a struggle for the future of the Islamic Republic, not its overthrow.

Behind the unprecedented scenes in public, a vicious internecine political battle was unfolding. Khamenei, who has almost unlimited power as supreme leader, with control of the armed forces, media and foreign relations, has abandoned the traditional role of the office, which is to remain above the fray. He has openly taken the side of Ahmadinejad in wanting to retain the unyielding regime of social restrictions and uncompromising international policies.

On the other side, Mousavi is backed by Hashemi Rafsanjani, the wealthy former president who is regarded as the second-most powerful man in Iran. He was defeated by Ahmadinejad in 2005 in an election that was also clouded by allegations of fraud, but heads the Assembly of Experts, a clerical body that is responsible for supervising the supreme leader.

In many ways, Ahmadinejad and Mousavi are the face of the struggle between Rafsanjani and Khamenei.

Rafsanjani's antagonism towards Ahmadinejad was inflamed when the president accused his two sons of corruption during a national television debate. He funded Mousavi's campaign from behind the scenes.

The support of Rafsanjani, whose reputation is of a wily, shrewd diplomat, for Mousavi comes from a shared view of Iran's future. Both believe that the days of Iran's unforgiving revolution are over and that the regime should relax the strict Islamic rules on social behaviour and moderate foreign policy to end Iran's isolation in the world.

'Mousavi believes in evolution, not revolution,' said Sadegh Kharazi, a senior Mousavi adviser.

He described Mousavi's potential foreign policy. 'Mousavi believes in reducing the tension internationally and

confidence-building that could result in a normalisation of relations,' Kharazi said.

He spoke openly of the most sensitive areas in Iranian international policy, relations with the United States and Iran's nuclear
programme. 'If President Obama understands Iran policy and Iran
society, there is a good chance that Mr Mousavi can make a bridge
between the US and Iran.'

On the contentious nuclear issue, neither Mousavi nor
Ahmadinejad would survive politically if they abandoned Iran's
uranium enrichment programme, which the West fears is aimed at
manufacturing a nuclear bomb despite Iran's denials. Mousavi has,
however, made clear he would be open to negotiations to find a
solution.

The reformist view of the world differs markedly from the one
Khamenei made clear in his Friday speech. Both he and
Ahmadinejad have blamed the street protests on 'foreign
intervention'.

'The aggressive powers of the western world showed their true
faces finally, and they are the faces of wolves,' said Khamenei.

'Not only in the United States, but in "dark-hearted" England.'
The hall resounded with chants of 'Death to America! Death to
England! Death to Israel!'

Khamenei also made no secret of whom he supported on Friday.
Praising Rafsanjani for his role in the Islamic revolution, he
concluded: 'There have been differences of opinion between Mr
Ahmadinejad and Mr Hashemi about issues related to foreign
policy, the nuclear issue and some cultural issues. This is natural,
but I personally approve Mr Ahmadinejad's decisions more.'

By putting himself so firmly behind Ahmadinejad, Khamenei is
taking a gamble. Pitting the authority of the state against the
marchers, rather than acknowledging their complaints, forces
them to make a stand on the authority of the revolutionary government. This could have dangerous consequences for the regime,
something that not even Rafsanjani and Mousavi would happily
countenance.

Yesterday's bloodshed will polarise the situation.

One of the placards at a demonstration by Basiji and Ahmadinejad supporters after prayers on Friday read: 'O leader, point the direction and we will run that way,' suggesting they will do whatever the authorities tell them to do.

There are questions, however, about whether the Revolutionary Guard, who were not involved in yesterday's shootings but are waiting in the wings, would fire on the protesters. They are charged with defending the revolution, not the supreme leader, and some guards are loyal to Rafsanjani.

'I will not be able to fire on these people,' said a young off-duty Revolutionary Guard as he watched a march pass by last week. 'Maybe some of us will, but I won't.'

The simple fact of yesterday's demonstrations was remarkable. The protesters had directly disobeyed the supreme leader – which just last week would have been an unthinkable act.

Mousavi himself yesterday further upped the ante, saying that he was 'ready for martyrdom'. In a letter to the country's legislative body he insisted that the election result be annulled, claiming that it that been 'rigged' months in advance. He also called for a national strike if he were to be arrested.

'We will only accept new elections,' a senior adviser to Mousavi said. 'Our representatives are the people on the street.

'Mousavi himself has told me he has had a good life and it is coming to an end. He is willing to fight to the death for justice in this election.

'What you see today is like a medieval confrontation. We are witnessing what happened in Europe with the emergence of John Calvin versus the Catholic Church. At the moment his supporters believe he can continue the reformation.'

How strong their faith will be in the face of a crackdown by the regime will become apparent in the coming days and weeks.

Egypt

Flames and fighting flood along the Nile

CAIRO

30 January 2011

Even after Tunisia's revolt, the rage engulfing Egypt has taken the world by surprise, leaving it trembling at the outcome.

It all began, ironically, on the annual Police Day, when the Egyptian regime calls on its people to honour its widely despised police force.

For the third year running, a group of young Egyptians had posted a notice on Facebook calling for a protest to mark the day. They wanted to highlight police abuse.

Little had happened on the previous two occasions. But this year, Police Day fell just 11 days after street protests in Tunis forced Zine Ben Ali, the Tunisian president, to flee to Saudi Arabia.

The chain of events that led to his exile had started with the suicide of Mohamed Bouazizi, a young fruit vendor who set himself alight in protest at police seizing his cart. Now the Middle East was trembling with anticipation – who would fall next?

In macabre emulation of Bouazizi, several young Egyptian men had already set themselves on fire to protest against poverty, unemployment and the humiliation that comes from not having enough money to get married.

Besides, Egypt already had its own martyr – Khalid Saeed, 28, whose fate has come to symbolise state injustice. Last year he was hauled out of an internet café in Alexandria and beaten to death by the police in full view of people on the street after he accused officers of taking part in a drugs deal.

To begin with, the calls for protest came from Egypt's disaffected youth. One of the internet sites calling for a mass turnout on Police Day was called 'We are all Khalid Saeed'. It had a huge number of hits.

If Saeed was the martyr, Tunisia was the catalyst. The Facebook call to arms struck a chord.

'Without Tunisia, there would have been the same 100 to 200 protesters, tops, surrounded by twice as many police,' a western diplomat in Cairo said last week. 'Tunisia charged the atmosphere with the sense of possibility.'

The Jasmine Revolution in Tunisia convulsed just one small country but it echoed across the Arab world – and nowhere louder than in Egypt.

It is hard to grasp the sheer size and weight of Egypt in the Arab identity: with 80m people, it is the most populous nation, the fount of classical Arabic, an ancient centre of Sunni Muslim learning and a fertile source of newspapers, books, music, films and soap operas adored from Casablanca to the Gulf.

Yet an undercurrent of terrorism lurks on the fringes of Egyptian civilisation. Ayman al-Zawahiri, Osama Bin Laden's right-hand man who helped to plan the September 11 attacks, was born in Cairo. Terrorists killed 58 western tourists at Luxor in 1997 and at least 88 people died, including 11 British tourists, in a bomb attack at the Sharm el Sheikh resort in 2005.

Egypt embodies the woes of other Arab nations – economic deprivation, an oppressive political system, a super-wealthy elite and a family that has ruled for decades.

Its armed forces, once the most powerful in the region, consume billions in American aid but 30 years of peace with Israel have left them indolent and riddled with corruption. They do, however, command patriotic prestige, an asset that could now become crucial.

So the warning signs were there. But none of President Hosni Mubarak's generals or secret policemen seems to have expected the torrent of events last week.

On Tuesday thousands of mostly young men poured into the streets, taking the government by surprise and overwhelming the security forces, who broke ranks and ran.

On Wednesday the authorities outlawed public gatherings and detained hundreds of demonstrators and political activists. The protesters held their nerve. Skirmishes ignited in the afternoon, with riot police chasing people to clear streets, beating some with bamboo staves and lengths of rubber hose.

In the northern city of Suez protesters set fire to a provincial government office and a fire station. Satellite television relayed images to a restive Arab world. At that point, governments and markets around the globe took notice, because Suez commands the strategic canal that carries trade between Europe and the booming economies of the Far East.

Thursday was tense but quiet, except for a bizarre protest in Cairo by lawyers who started throwing rocks from inside the neo-classical building of their union at riot police on the streets outside.

In fact, the eerie calm of Thursday was just the sound of people regrouping, via Facebook, Twitter and mobile phone messages. They called for a Day of Rage on Friday, the Muslim holy day.

After prayers, the word went out to head for Tahrir Square at the heart of old Cairo, which had become the centre of the protests.

Few details were on Facebook, as it had become clear the authorities were monitoring the site. But, as it turned out, few details were needed.

As crowds spilled out of the mosques they scorned the anodyne sermons they had heard as proof that the clerics were in the pay of the government. 'We must express our opinion as individual human beings without bloodshed or destruction of property,' the speaker at the Fat'h mosque said, telling the faithful that the leader should 'be your guide'.

The time had passed for that. The anger of the crowds was directed at Mubarak personally – his rigged elections, the corruption of his circle and his ceaseless grip on power.

'Mubarak must go!' they chanted. Rasha El Sayed, 36, said: 'There are no jobs, and the prices are so high we cannot afford bread. The women are becoming spinsters and the men are sitting at home doing nothing.'

Within half an hour the police started firing tear gas. Only a few brave young men stood their ground, throwing rocks and at one point hurling a tear-gas grenade back towards the police.

After that, protests swelled like the Nile in flood.

Buildings burned, cars were set ablaze, clouds of tear gas hung in the air and gunshots punctuated the chants of protest in towns and cities across the country.

By midnight on Friday, when a haggard Mubarak went on television to say he had listened to his people and sacked his government, pledging to make things better, Egypt was in flames.

The wind of change in the Arab world – long predicted by both Bin Laden and George W Bush – had come. So important is Egypt in the region that the future of the whole Middle East could now be forged on the streets of Cairo and Suez.

Western governments and Islamic revolutionaries from Tehran to Peshawar are holding their breath this weekend. There appear to be three possible outcomes: a transition to democracy; a new dictatorship, perhaps led by a general around whom the old guard would coalesce; or an Islamic state.

However, nowhere has technology combined with peaceful protest beaten a truly ruthless regime, as the Burmese could testify.

From Tehran there came predictions that Muslim fundamentalists would triumph in Tunis and Cairo, as they did over the liberal and leftist factions in the Iranian revolution.

As Washington hopes for an acceptable strongman to emerge, foreboding in Israel may be mixed with a feeling that it might have been better to make peace with a moderate Palestinian state, as Mubarak urged, before the deluge.

Seen from Cairo, it may not be as bad as that. The rich seam of Egyptian political life has included Muslim activists for a century or more.

The government tried last week to portray the demonstrations as the work of the Muslim Brotherhood. It arrested senior Brotherhood members, including Essam Elaryan, the public face of the movement.

In reality, a new political force has emerged: tens of thousands of mostly young people, joined by middle-aged housewives and government clerks. Islam is part of it – but not all of it.

The tide of protest has come so fast that even potential leaders such as Mohamed ElBaradei, the former head of the International Atomic Energy Agency who returned home last week, were caught by surprise.

'Frankly, I didn't think the people were ready,' he said last week in a telephone interview. But they were – and now the world must be ready, too.

Raging mob bays for Mubarak's head

CAIRO

30 January 2011

Demonstrators and police clash in Cairo as officers fire rubber bullets and tear gas while youths attack party HQ and ministries.

The young man was distraught. Ahmed Yassin thought he had proved his mettle by protesting against the government he works for even though he knew it would endanger his job. Then he found himself carrying a dying woman to an ambulance.

'It was a peaceful demonstration,' said Yassin, 28, who works in the oil ministry and felt strongly enough to defy his ministry's ban on joining the protests. 'The police started shooting tear gas. There was a young woman. She fell and I was helping her up, trying to carry her, when a tear-gas canister hit her in the head,' he added, still shocked. 'Her brain came out.'

Yassin, dressed in the black designer jeans and sports jacket of Egypt's middle class, said he and others hauled her to an ambulance. The medics said she was severely injured, but Yassin knew she had died in his arms.

As he spoke, other young men ran past, their faces flushed, their eyes and noses streaming with tears and mucus. 'Mubarak must go! The people want the regime to fall!' others chanted, calling for the end of Hosni Mubarak, the Egyptian president.

Yassin's shock and anger were reflected across Cairo on Friday at the height of a 'Day of Rage' that cast Egypt into confrontation and uncertainty.

'I am a member of the NDP [the ruling National Democratic party],' said Yassin, pulling out his party card. 'But I cannot be quiet. I feel the injustice in my country. We feel humiliated every day.'

Across Cairo there were scenes not seen in living memory. At the October 6 bridge that spans the Nile, young men stumbled down the stairs, their eyes and noses streaming. They had been battling riot police dressed in black who had helmets and riot shields and batons. The police had lined up on the bridge to stop them from exiting onto the road that passed the headquarters of the NDP.

The fighting erupted after midday prayers, with the youths building up numbers and charging the police, only to retreat when officers regrouped and fired tear gas, or charged with their batons and lengths of yellow rubber hose.

The tear gas hit the young men but one canister landed in a passing boat. A soldier aimed so badly that his commanding officer came up from behind and smashed him over the head with a baton.

Thuggish men in jeans and leather jackets – probably secret police, as they passed through the riot police lines – lined up with batons, one with an iron bar. They launched into the crowd, beating everyone they could reach.

The crowd cheered as other protesters toppled a hut used by traffic police and set it ablaze.

In retaliation, the tear gas came in salvos, one after another – choking fumes that stung eyes, nose and throat.

As the crowd threatened to overwhelm the police, there came a barrage of rubber bullets. A police boat launched tear gas canisters from the river that, leaving graceful arcs of acrid grey smoke, sped into the ranks of protesters.

Similar clashes occurred across the capital and were reported in Alexandria, Suez and other Egyptian cities.

The numbers of protesters grew, and the police became increasingly beleaguered. At one point, on a street off Tahrir Square in central Cairo, they appeared to run out of tear gas and started throwing stones at the demonstrators.

By evening, the feared police had fled the streets, routed by the sheer numbers pouring off Qasar al-Nil bridge to seize their goal, Tahrir Square.

But then a strange dynamic developed as the army roared onto the streets for the first time in armoured personnel carriers. They were welcomed with cheers by the demonstrators, who consider the police an arm of the regime, while the soldiers are seen as the 'sons of the nation'.

By midnight, the headquarters of the NDP party were burning, the information ministry was surrounded and fires blazed across Cairo, mostly cars that had been set alight.

The thump of tear gas rounds continued until well past midnight, as did the intermittent crack of live bullets. The big question was whether the army would fire on the crowds. By yesterday, they appeared to have fired into the air instead of at protesters.

The demonstrators ignored the curfews declared by the government and a televised address in which Mubarak announced that he was sacking his cabinet. As they returned to the streets again yesterday, central Cairo resounded to the crump of tear gas rounds being fired.

A huge pillar of black and grey smoke was still rising from the NDP headquarters when dawn broke. The square – tahrir means 'freedom' in Arabic – was littered with rocks, shattered glass, iron bars and charred police cars.

In another day of chaos, two mummies were destroyed in an attack on the Egyptian Museum, which has the world's largest collection of Pharaonic antiquities. Thousands of protesters gathered to storm the interior ministry, the hated co-ordinator of the police, and shots were fired. In the mayhem, it was claimed that at least three people had been killed and their bodies carried through the crowd. It was not clear whether live ammunition or rubber bullets had been fired.

Two police stations were later set on fire, in addition to 17 that had been torched in the capital the previous night.

The army, however, continued to be greeted warmly. In the winter sunshine two tanks were parked on each road entering Tahrir Square. At one, a crowd gathered around the soldiers. 'We are so proud of you. You stopped those sons of bitches of the police from attacking us,' said Ahmed Hussein, a businessman, to a young lieutenant.

Another man said: 'You have finally come to save us from police, we need you to save us from the regime. We do not want just the cabinet to go – we want Mubarak out.'

It seemed that Mubarak's party could soon suffer the same fate as its burnt-out headquarters.

I ran for my life from a crazed, cursing mob

6 February 2011

While speaking to a family whose son had been shot, Marie Colvin found herself in one of the most threatening situations in her career.

The mob had gathered in the alley below the apartment as I spoke to a family whose son had been shot during the anti-government demonstrations.

I had no idea I would soon be running for my life.

Mohamed Salah's father broke into tears, weeping silently, as he told me that friends had carried his body to the door of the house.

It was a heartrending interview. It is always difficult to intrude on a family's grief, but I had been invited by his brother because the family were angry that Mohamed had been killed by the police and they had no recourse to justice.

As I talked to Mohamed's mother and wife, the men in the family grew agitated. They asked for my press card and the national identity card of Madiha Qassem, my translator. They ran up and down the stairs, talking in worried tones.

'People' downstairs in the alley needed to see our identity documents, they said. No problem, don't worry, they said. What we didn't know was that word had gone out through the poor neighbourhood of Embaba in Cairo that a foreigner was in its midst.

It would soon become clear how dangerous was this new Egypt. I am used to threats in Afghanistan, Iraq and other countries in the Middle East, but Egypt has always been a country populated by people friendly to foreigners. Madiha, who has worked in journalism for decades, had no qualms about visiting the Embaba neighbourhood.

But the country has changed. State-owned television has broadcast the poisonous and constant theme that foreigners in Egypt are behind the political unrest that has caused the country to grind to a halt.

I was isolated. My car had been guided to the apartment by a family friend on a motorcycle, and then I had walked the rest of the way because Mohamed's family lived in a ramshackle building on a dirt-floored alley.

By the time I had finished my interviews, the mob below the apartment were beyond reasoning. Even though I was wearing a hijab, or headscarf, I had been spotted and, unknown to me, the word had gone through the alleys that a 'foreign woman' was in the neighbourhood.

I walked down the narrow, unlit stairway to a frightening scene. About 100 men had gathered, shoving each other, shouting that I was a spy, or maybe worked for the hated Al-Jazeera television station. Some had knives shoved in the waists of their trousers.

The men of the family formed a circle around Madiha and me to protect us and try to get us out of the alley.

It was a terrifying moment. In a mob, there is no individual responsibility and these people were working themselves into a frenzy. The men shouted and cursed. The few women in the crowd spat in anger.

Mohamed's brothers and father panicked. They threw us in to the tiny shop of a friend, who locked the metal grille gates against the crowd that was now baying for blood.

The young wife of the store owner spoke no English, but she held my arm and pulled me to the shadows at the back of the shop. There was no back door.

Men came in and out of the darkened shop, allowed one by one through the metal gate, hearing our case and shouting, as Madiha bravely and calmly explained that we were journalists.

A tall, burly young man in a striped sweater took away my press card and Madiha's identity card. The crowd outside pressed against the metal grille.

I called *The Sunday Times* foreign desk to say I was besieged in a neighbourhood called Embaba, but there was little more I could do. In Egypt these days, you cannot call the police; they are either confined to barracks or too frightened or corrupt to be of any use.

Mohamed's brothers had gone to get my driver to move the car as close as he could to the shop; he could not get to the door because the alley was too narrow.

As the anger of the crowd ebbed and flowed, they decided we should make a break for safety. It was a wise decision. Any push by the crowd would have broken through the metal door. A Molotov cocktail tossed in there would have been impossible to escape.

They bustled us through the crowd to the car, and then jumped in on top of us. The crowd pounded on the car, and the windows.

At one point, the angry young man in the striped sweater hauled a policeman into the car. He wanted to arrest us.

Mohamed's family kicked the policeman out of the car, refusing his demand to arrest us. He cursed me and Madiha as 'you bitches'.

My luck was that nobody knew what to do with us – chaos reigned outside and within the car. The first sign of authority was an army checkpoint.

The crazed men, and Mohamed's brothers, agreed to turn me over to the soldiers. A calm, articulate officer shooed everyone away, checked my press card, and said: 'Go to your hotel. It is very dangerous on the streets now.'

Egypt's bloody road to reform

CAIRO

6 February 2011

Marie Colvin and Uzi Mahnaimi

Change seems certain, but while President Hosni Mubarak clings to power there are many innocent victims of the tumult along the Nile.

Mohamed Salah did everything he could to make a success of his life. Despite coming from a Cairo slum, he managed to graduate from high school – a success normally confined to children of the wealthy and members of Egypt's ruling party.

He won a job at the Conrad hotel as a housekeeper, an enviable achievement in a country where 40% of the people live on less than £1 a day. When tourism waned because of the world economic depression and he was fired, he took out a loan to buy a rickshaw and worked late every night, earning a few pence on each trip. He toiled all the harder after his first child was born three months ago.

Like many in Cairo, however, Salah had had enough by the time anti-government protests broke out nearly two weeks ago. Unfortunately for him, so had the police.

Last Wednesday, as pitched battles broke out in Tahrir Square, the centre of the rebellion, Salah was in a crowd that gathered outside the police station in the Imbaba district, a few miles north down the Nile.

A police officer named Mohamed Mktar climbed on top of the building and, in full view, shot an automatic weapon into the crowd. Salah, 25, was struck in the chest.

'They brought his body to my door,' his father said a few hours later. 'I laid him on this bed. I sent for a doctor because I would not believe he was dead.'

The government of President Hosni Mubarak is trying to portray the protests as provoked by foreigners and the middle classes. Salah, however, came from the poorest of the poor. His parents' home is on a dirt alley that smells of sewage. Live chickens lie around, tethered by their ankles. Daylight barely filters through the dilapidated buildings.

Hayam, Salah's 25-year-old wife, sat in her in-laws' house, distraught in a black hijab and abaya. Her infant son, dressed in a lime-green bodysuit, jiggled on her lap.

'Our last conversation was at breakfast,' she said. 'Mohamed said we had to be serious now, and find a way to educate our son. He wanted our boy to have a future that we did not have.'

Salah embodied a popular revolution unlike anything Egypt's class-restricted society has seen. In Tahrir Square, well-dressed doctors mixed last week with bearded members of the Muslim Brotherhood, and women in full-length robes were side by side with glamorous figures in Gucci sunglasses and miniskirts.

Death was indiscriminate. Dr Ahmed Kamal, who was in the square again yesterday, said his room mate at Al-Azhar University, a famous centre of Islamic learning in Cairo, had been shot dead on Thursday morning. 'We are too tired of lies, poverty, corruption and dictatorship,' said Kamal. 'We are here for our principles. We will not go home until Mubarak leaves.'

Yesterday, the 12th day of the demonstrations, was quiet although protesters still chanted: 'Go now, go now.'

The army had reinforced the perimeters of the square. Soldiers wore flak jackets for the first time and stopped supporters of Mubarak from approaching. After the high drama and vicious fighting of the week, however, there was a feeling of stalemate in the square. Who could force Mubarak to quit if he refused to relinquish office?

Holed up with his family in the heavily guarded presidential palace at Heliopolis, eight miles from the square, Mubarak just seemed to become more stubborn each time a foreign leader – led by Barack Obama and David Cameron – publicly urged him to begin the process of surrendering power. At 82, he was fed up and would love to quit, he told an American television interviewer, but not yet. That would have to wait until elections in September.

America, his paymaster, seemed to have lost all influence. Mubarak sent away his old friend Frank Wisner – dispatched to Cairo by Obama with a message that it was time to let go – with a flea in his ear.

Admiral Mike Mullen, chairman of the US joint chiefs of staff, said on Friday: 'There is a lot of uncertainty out there, and I would just caution against doing anything until we really understand what's going on.'

Wisner muddied the waters further yesterday by saying Mubarak should stay on to steer political changes.

Effectively, however, Mubarak has already quit. Although the demonstrators have not achieved their aim of throwing him from office, the way Egypt is being run now is very different from the way it was only 10 days ago. Behind the scenes, a military triumvirate has taken over – reflecting the army's long-standing role as the true power in Egypt.

The new vice-president, Omar Suleiman, a retired general, stands at the apex of a pyramid with the prime minister, Ahmed

Shafiq, also a retired general, and the defence minister, Field Marshal Mohamed Tantawi, operating below him. They are already known as 'the junta' by some Egyptians.

Yesterday, Mubarak attended a meeting with the finance minister to discuss the grim economic situation, which has deteriorated because of the riots – more than 1 million tourists have fled.

However, a source close to him said: 'This is one big show. The president is now a figurehead, not by any means in a position to take decisions, which are being taken by the triumvirate. The three meet every night, taking decisions and then, updating the president.'

Their public posture has been non-confrontational. Suleiman has been on television, saying political transition takes time and urging the opposition to negotiate. Shafiq publicly apologised for the violence; and Tantawi went to Tahrir Square to see things for himself. The army stepped up security for the anti-government demonstrators soon afterwards.

Tantawi was in the square again yesterday with Amr Moussa, the secretary-general of the Arab League, and was greeted with applause and whistles of support.

Suleiman became vice-president last weekend, as the government was overhauled after the interior ministry's riot police had clashed murderously with protesters. However, he has long been close to the apex of power as Mubarak's 'brain' – his intelligence chief, fixer and strategist.

Diplomats saw him as the perfect foil for the president, who is a non-intellectual former fighter pilot. Mubarak regards himself as 'tough, strong and fair', according to a US diplomatic cable released by WikiLeaks, while Suleiman shows the feline political skills of an Egyptian Peter Mandelson.

Suleiman prefers to work from his old intelligence services HQ, arriving every day at 8am sharp for a briefing. He is in control of the intelligence apparatus, although a new intelligence minister has stepped in. Hundreds of his men have been mixed up among the demonstrators in Cairo, Alexandria and Suez, and they have sometimes been beaten up if exposed.

Their main role, however, has not been to act as *agents provocateurs* but to report back to headquarters so that Suleiman stays up to date with the public mood.

His strategy last week was to let the anger in Tahrir Square wear itself out while a number of sacked ministers – including the former head of the interior ministry – were placed under judicial investigation and the military stood by to intervene if the trouble spread really dangerously.

At 10am every day, a giant Russian-made Mi-8 helicopter painted in creamy desert colours started circling around central Cairo. According to an officer on the ground, it was not on a reconnaissance mission but carrying a force of 20 elite commandos, waiting for instructions to land if events got out of control. The flights are set to continue.

'So far what we've seen was a stroll along the Nile river bank,' said the officer. 'If things go out of control, special forces with more choppers are standing by in a nearby airbase.'

While the defence minister, Tantawi, and his chief of staff, General Sami Enan, look after security, the prime minister, Shafiq, is busy with running the non-emergency parts of the state.

'Of Egypt's 84 million people, less than 10% are being directly involved in the demonstrations,' said a local politician. 'People still need to be taken care of.'

Banks and shops have been closed, and long lines of cars were waiting outside petrol stations yesterday. 'I'm not interested with Mubarak or not Mubarak,' said Saide, a taxi driver. 'I have 13 children to feed and the government should make sure there is enough fuel.'

All operations are coordinated to maintain a crisis 'road map', as Suleiman calls it. The timeline extends seven months into the future, with Mubarak nominally remaining in charge. 'It will take two months to alter the constitution,' Suleiman said on television, and then 'five months to prepare for general elections'.

Will this road map survive? The Egyptian army has bolstered its good standing among the population by its handling of the crisis, so a peaceful resolution to the street rebellion is not impossible.

Mubarak signalled last week that he would lift the emergency law, in place for 30 years, that bans opposition parties from running for presidency or parliament. The opposition was yesterday organising a committee for talks with the government that would have been unprecedented just a week ago.

The president remains the stumbling block to formal negotiations, however, as so many lives have been lost by demonstrators demanding that he should go.

The members of the triumvirate, who consider him a father figure, are personally reluctant to humiliate him by forcing him out – as well as arguing that it would be politically destabilising – but they are looking for a way of putting him more obviously in the back seat.

'He is stubborn and wants to keep the [presidential] chair for his own legacy,' said one source close to the regime. 'But he is also afraid that he could lose everything.'

He and his family are said to fear that if he stepped down he could be prosecuted, either for the corruption that has meant he and his family have amassed a fortune, or by victims of his repressive police and army.

Egyptian sources said they believed that Mubarak could save face by agreeing to an internal exile in Sharm el-Sheikh, the resort on the Sinai peninsula where he has a villa on the sea.

One of the leading members of the opposition, Mohamed ElBaradei, the former head of the International Atomic Energy Agency, signalled that there might be room for compromise. He said: 'I'm for a safe exit for President Mubarak. We're going to turn the page; we can pardon the past.'

Who will take over?

The man tipped to succeed Hosni Mubarak, if only in the short term, is his new vice-president, Omar Suleiman, 74. Born into a poor family, Suleiman rose through the army and fought in the 1967 and 1973 wars against Israel. He joined military intelligence and Mubarak made him its head in 1993, with the organisation earning a reputation for the brutal suppression of Mubarak's political opponents, including the use of torture. On a 1995 visit to Ethiopia Suleiman insisted he and Mubarak take an armoured car, which saved them in an assassination attempt.

The kids triumph with Facebook and flyers

13 February 2011

Marie Colvin and Hala Jaber

Egypt's inspirational youth were galvanised when their leader wept on TV. Then they had to reach the low-tech masses by any means necessary.

Tahrir Square, the focus of the world, resembled a city fair. Hundreds of thousands of Egyptians chanted and danced; men with 'dignity' painted on their foreheads pounded drums; young women handed out sweets; children bounced on their parents' shoulders.

They had all come to witness the final act of Egypt's 'people power' revolution. President Hosni Mubarak, 82, was scheduled to speak, and television and radio were reporting that he was stepping down. They thought it was all over.

Finally, at 10.45pm, nearly three hours late, the old man's basso tones boomed through loudspeakers. The crowd began muttering in disbelief. Mubarak wasn't quitting. He was 'adamant to continue to shoulder my responsibility to protect the constitution and safeguard the interests of the people'.

'Donkey,' someone shouted as the square erupted in fury.

That was Thursday. On Friday, it really would be all over, but the crowds didn't know it yet. Perhaps a million spilt out of Tahrir Square into the streets and onto the steps of parliament, demanding Mubarak's resignation. Thousands marched to the television centre and the presidential palace.

Marie in Tahrir Square, Egypt.
Photograph by Ivor Prickett.

At midday, the faithful in the square – including soldiers who had dismounted from their tanks and armoured cars – knelt for noon prayers. At the same moment, Mubarak and his family secretly boarded a helicopter from his palace to the airport, where the presidential plane waited to take them into internal exile at the Sinai resort of Sharm el-Sheikh.

Only a few figures in the highest reaches of his regime knew that one of the most momentous events in modern Middle Eastern history was taking place. As the afternoon drew on, the demonstrators in the square grew shriller in their demands.

Shortly after dusk fell, the long and inscrutable face of Vice-President Omar Suleiman, Egypt's Mr Fix-it, appeared on television screens. Because of the 'very difficult circumstances Egypt is going through', he announced, Hosni Mubarak had resigned.

Power had been handed to the armed forces. 'May God help everyone,' the retired general added briskly.

Tahrir Square exploded. Weeping soldiers standing on their tanks grasped hands with demonstrators. The whole city came out to celebrate. Alexandria, Suez and other towns stayed up all night.

Far away in Washington, a relieved President Barack Obama, who had been tripped up repeatedly in his attempts to manage the Egyptian crisis, compared it to the fall of the Berlin Wall.

The manner of Mubarak's departure raised many questions. What happened last week to bring Egypt's 18-day revolt to such a bumpy ending?

The catalyst was a young man called Wael Ghonim, a local Google executive who had set up the Facebook site that attracted demonstrators to the first anti-government rally on 25 January. He had then been arrested by the secret police.

At the beginning of last week, after days of tumultuous demonstrations, Cairo seemed to be slipping back into routine. There were still large crowds in Tahrir Square, but people were answering the government's calls to return to work while it started negotiations with opposition groups. Had Mubarak regained the initiative?

Then Ghonim emerged from detention. On an independent Egyptian television station – in an interview that illustrated how far the regime's grip over the news media had collapsed – he spoke of his ordeal at being grabbed off the street and held incommunicado for 12 days.

When the interviewer flashed images of young men who had died in the protests, most of them wearing T-shirts and jeans, Ghonim was visibly struck by how similar they looked to himself. They were his tribe. He broke down in tears, watched by a nation that no longer tuned into pro-Mubarak state television.

'I am telling all the mothers and fathers who lost their kids, it was not us who killed them, it was all the people hanging on to their power,' Ghonim said, weeping. The crowds in Tahrir Square swelled and talked of little else.

Ghonim had become the voice of the revolution. He represented the element in the revolt that Mubarak found so hard to grapple with, intellectually or physically: the social media generation.

Mohamed Taman, 34, one of the organisers of the protests, explained: 'We started with a Facebook invitation on a site set up by Ghonim.'

The site was named in honour of a young man beaten to death by police on a street, in plain view of passers-by, because he refused to show his identity card. The Facebook crowd chose national Police Day, 25 January, for their first – illegal – demonstration against abuse of power.

'We didn't have a plan other than to protest,' said Taman. 'We started with 300, and step by step we thought on our feet, and by the end of the day our 300 was 15,000.'

Another of the organisers, Ahmed Maher, 30, had been at a conference in Doha with Ghonim. 'We used the internet to co-ordinate, and also to study revolutions around the world,' said Maher. Knowing that Facebook would not reach Cairo's working class, they also distributed leaflets in poor neighbourhoods.

On the day, he was surprised by their success: 'The police were shocked. Actually, we were shocked.'

The Tahrir Square protesters refused to attend the talks early last week between Suleiman and other opposition groups, including the outlawed Muslim Brotherhood – the first meeting of the government and 'brothers' in almost 60 years.

Mubarak seemed to believe that if he could talk round his long-time opponents, they could talk some sense into the 'kids'. What the regime should have noticed was that – unlike Egypt's 30% illiterate minority – most of the 'kids' running the show were in their late twenties or early thirties, and connected to a cybercommunity whose freedoms they wanted to share.

The protest leaders remained firm: they would not negotiate until Mubarak had left office. Until then, they would remain in the square – where, behind a huge screen made of sewn-together sheets, they gathered to discuss tactics in the office of the Safir

Travel agency, which had been smashed and destroyed in an attack by Mubarak's thugs. Next door, the wrecked Pizza Express was the food bank.

As they plotted, support for the revolution grew wider, reaching into all levels of Egyptian society.

'What our youth have done is a dream,' said Abdel Hakim Nasser, 56, the youngest son of Egypt's late, still revered, President Nasser, who overthrew the monarchy in 1952.

Sitting in the plush office of his construction company in Heliopolis, not far from the presidential palace, he looked the model of upper-class Egypt, but he spoke words unimaginable just two weeks ago.

'Under Mubarak, people have lived in fear, and the establishment has no values except for bribery, favouritism and corruption. This is not what my father risked his life for. Mubarak should resign.'

The same sentiment had reached the highest levels of the military, who see themselves as the guardians of Nasser's revolution. The army had notably fraternised with protesters on the streets, and – urged on by Washington – it moved reluctantly towards the logical consequence of this behaviour: the ousting of the president. But how?

For nearly three weeks the military leadership had been torn between the regime and the protesters, without giving a hint as to whether they would dump Mubarak – one of their own, a former air force commander and hero of the 1973 Arab–Israeli war – and seize control for the first time in nearly 60 years.

As the protests increased in mid-week, however, and Mubarak alienated himself through his 'stubbornness and arrogance' from the one institution that any leader needs to lead or run a country – the military – the mood in the high command finally turned against him, said a senior Egyptian source with first-hand knowledge of the developments.

'The rage and mood in the country dramatically changed as of [Wednesday], when the protests spread not only to main cities across the country but to small towns, villages and nearly every part of Egypt,' the source said. 'Egypt was boiling. The situation on the ground was dangerous and would have erupted in a bad way for everyone concerned.'

As the demonstrators turned out in ever greater numbers and Mubarak made one minor concession after another, growing ever weaker but refusing to go, the Supreme Council of the Armed Forces announced that it was in 'permanent session' – meaning it was on a war footing.

Senior military officials told Mubarak that if he did not leave, the country would enter a state of civil uprising that could eventually split the army itself, according to the source.

It is reported that late on Wednesday, CIA and Pentagon officials – in close touch with the Egyptian generals, who rely on $1.3 billion (£800 million) a year in US military aid – learnt that Mubarak was to be deprived of most of his powers and reduced to a figurehead or step down altogether.

The White House shied from publicly demanding the departure of its former ally, but after Mubarak failed to announce his resignation on Thursday, Obama finally acknowledged that the balancing act was over, and that the protesters had to win. 'The Egyptian people have been told that there was a transition of authority,' Obama said, 'but it is not yet clear that this transition is immediate, meaningful or sufficient.'

When, a day later, Mubarak stepped down, the White House was able to congratulate itself that it had at least ended up on the right side of history. Yet Washington was also faced with the cruel reality that its influence was minimal. For, in the end, it was the Egyptians who applied the coup de grâce.

After his defiant speech on Thursday, a series of senior army and intelligence officers pressed Mubarak to go throughout the night and into the morning. The entire leadership of the military, security services, general intelligence and military intelligence painted a stark picture for him of the reality on the ground.

He was told that Egypt was on the verge of entering a civil insurrection that would bring it to a complete standstill. The entire country would stop functioning and be on the streets. Transport, education, finance, day-to-day business – the whole nation would come to a standstill, plunging it into extremely dangerous waters.

'The picture was depressing and stark, and worsened by the warning that such an eventuality could split the army or force it to confront the people,' said the senior source familiar with the transition of power.

'Even Suleiman explained the dangers to Mubarak,' the source said, adding that the former vice-president and head of intelligence was still working closely with the armed forces and was involved in all the decisions and preparations from behind the scenes.

In the strange hours between Mubarak's flight from Cairo at noon on Friday and the announcement of his resignation, there were clues that the fin de régime had come. Demonstrators who reached his Cairo palace were confronted by razor wire, tanks and armed soldiers. The crowds shouted, sang and waved banners, calling on the army to join them. The soldiers, members of the presidential guard, threw sweets and biscuits to the crowd. The crowd threw them back.

As dusk drew in, the military's resolve weakened. They reached through the razor wire and grasped posters of demonstrators killed in earlier protests and with great reverence laid them on their tanks.

State television was disintegrating, too. The shouts from the crowd demonstrating outside its headquarters became so loud they could be heard on air.

A young woman presenter collapsed on screen, practically weeping. 'We are in chaos here,' she said. 'I am so sorry. We have been telling you things that are not true. Now we can tell the truth.'

A state television reporter went down to the crowd and stuck a microphone through the barbed wire barricade to broadcast – for the first time – what the protests were all about.

Yesterday, the elation of the moment continued. But reality was beginning to set in. The psychological victory was clear. Egypt was no longer a rusting old machine. Overnight it had regained the role of the most important country in the Middle East, its revolution being watched by other Arab populations and their authoritarian governments.

The crowds occupied Tahrir Square late into the night, vowing to return next Friday, if necessary. The young opposition leaders had not received an answer to their demands for the lifting of the state of emergency and the introduction of an electoral programme – although since they had sent it by email, they joked, they were unsure the military had received it.

Feral mobs and fanatics rule Terror Square

CAIRO

27 November 2011

The mood in Egypt's divided 'second revolution' is far darker as brutal police crackdowns put looming elections in jeopardy.

There was a painful sting in the air from lingering tear gas as dusk fell on Tahrir Square and the crowd became more menacing. Once a scene of altruism, idealism and hope, the square that had become the symbol of Egypt's revolution was now divided and unforgiving in the run-up to the parliamentary elections scheduled to begin tomorrow.

Protesters had returned to Tahrir Square in their tens of thousands last week to demand that the ruling military leadership step down, reviving the mass protests of the revolution that forced President Hosni Mubarak to resign in February.

Back then the atmosphere had been festive and communal. Doctors and nurses worked round the clock as volunteers and

everyone who came to join the crowds brought food or handed out
sweets. Foreigners, especially journalists, were welcomed into the
makeshift tent camps and musicians played newly written revolutionary songs to entertain the crowds.

Last week, in what Egyptians were calling the 'second revolution', the atmosphere was darker and violence seethed beneath the
surface. Unlike the earlier Tahrir occupation, this time the square
– actually a roundabout in central Cairo just off the Nile corniche
– had been divided into encampments according to political
affiliation.

There were suspicious glances at strangers. It was frightening,
especially for a lone woman. I was caught in a tidal wave of young
men running from tear gas and shotgun pellets launched from one
side of the square. I was already feeling vulnerable, having been
gassed in an earlier attack by military police against people throwing stones at the interior ministry in anger at the killing of at least
42 protesters.

Tear gas had often been used in the early days of the revolution.
But whereas last time the crowds in the square had gone out of
their way to help, journalists have now become targets. I was
groped by men who were supposed to be fleeing in fear, unable to
see even who was grabbing me and unable to flee because I was
hemmed in by a leaderless mob.

In my mind was the attack the day before on Caroline Sinz, a
reporter for French television, who was covering the events in
Tahrir Square when she was surrounded by teenagers, beaten and
assaulted, and then dragged off by adults, stripped and sexually
assaulted for almost an hour, an experience, she said, that
'amounted to a rape'.

There is nowhere to turn. During the January 25 revolution the
activists had organised the volunteers into groups who divided the
tasks, from cleaning to distributing food to keeping order.

Last week men who tried to help Sinz were beaten back. The
police were no help. Mona Eltahawy, an Egyptian-American blog-
ger and columnist, was grabbed by riot police, dragged by her hair,

beaten so badly that they broke both her arms and sexually assaulted by the military police. 'I lost track of how many hands went down my pants,' she said.

The riot police arrested thousands of protesters and held them without charge. One of the main complaints fuelling the violence was that the interim military government had gradually returned to the ways of the Mubarak regime, arresting awkward civilians on trumped-up charges.

Hossam Bahgat, of the Egyptian Initiative for Personal Rights, said 12,000 civilians had been brought before military courts since February.

'It is terrible but they are doing our work,' said Bahgat, a lawyer. 'The more they abuse the rights of people, the more they reveal their true face.' Tahrir Square is now a political minefield. I escaped the melee of fleeing young men, only to tumble into the area of tents dubbed 'Tahriristan', where the banner of the extreme Salafist movement flew from a lamppost.

Men with the thick black beards that denote pious Muslims sat on blankets engaged in intense conversations about Islam. One handed out pamphlets entitled *How to be a Good Muslim*.

They all eyed me suspiciously and started gathering around me, muttering 'she's a spy' and insisting I showed them my passport. An interrogation began. 'Where are you from? What are you doing here?' If they had not been so menacing it would have been comical. Spying on what – on who is donating the sweet potatoes to be roasted?

Liberals are still to be found in the square, although in lesser numbers, roughing it in tents with Facebook addresses stencilled on their sides. Their discussions last week were still about how to install democracy in a country that has experienced only military rule since 1952 and debates raged about the endless new parties emerging on the liberal end of the political spectrum.

They were heavily outnumbered by the Islamic groups, who were organised and disciplined, and the thousands of poor, uneducated Egyptians and thugs, some remnants of the Mubarak regime's semi-official muscle, who had come for no reason other than that they relished heaving stones at the police.

Pickpockets were rife in the crowd and even patients who lay overcome by tear gas in the square's makeshift clinics woke up missing their wallets, watches and jewellery.

The change in mood reflected a fundamental darkening of the revolution that had been founded 10 months ago on a wave of bravery and hope for the future, of young men and women standing up to a dictatorship and, against impossible odds, overthrowing the despot. The revolutionaries, having decapitated the monster, did what they thought was best for Egypt and deferred to the military, which was supposed to stay in power for six months before handing over to a civilian government.

Now, with parliamentary elections due to begin, the protesters are demanding that the Supreme Council of the Armed Forces step down immediately. They want the resignation of Field Marshal Mohamed Hussein Tantawi, the council's head and a former defence minister under Mubarak.

Their resolve was deepened last week when Tantawi appointed, as a political concession, Kamal Ganzouri, a 78-year-old former prime minister, to lead the transition to civilian power. The young who had created the revolution felt they were being betrayed.

'We will not let them hijack our revolution,' said Ali Sultan, a 28-year-old lawyer who had been arrested by the military. 'I am staying in the square for as long as it takes for them [the military] to leave. The Egyptian revolution will continue until Egypt is under civilian rule.'

The violence ebbed yesterday, partly as a result of a 7 foot wall erected between the protest camp and the interior ministry, which had been a target all week because of the brutality of the police crackdown.

Volunteers distributed free food and donated medicines were brought in to makeshift tent clinics which last week were overwhelmed by the victims of tear gas, rubber bullets and live ammunition. Much of the anger at the ruling military came because they were seen as allowing the interior police to act so brutally against a peaceful protest.

No one had predicted such a violent and sudden 'second revolution'. Instead, the country had been gearing up for peaceful elections. But there was growing anger at the ruling military council, particularly when it published a draft of what it envisioned as a new constitution that put the military above the civilian government and proclaimed there would be no oversight of its budget. The document was withdrawn after protests but the damage had been done.

Ironically, it was a crackdown by the military police last weekend against about 100 protesters who were camped out in Tahrir Square that had re-energised the protesters.

Egyptians from all walks of life rushed to the square in solidarity with those attacked. Every time police and soldiers attacked the protesters their numbers grew, until on Friday more than 100,000 had reclaimed the square.

Anger at the military rulers came pouring out. Critics noted that the military was growing comfortable with its expanding power and attributed that to its desire to maintain its immunity from scrutiny and a status that has for decades given it membership of special clubs, access to exclusive seaside resorts and control over billions of dollars in assets and the levers of political power.

Tantawi used a televised speech last week to dismiss the protesters calling for his resignation but it was unclear if he could cling on to office.

'We are the ones who should be appointing a prime minister, not Tantawi,' said Ahmed Naguib, one of the activists who organised the January 25 revolution via Facebook and is now an independent candidate for a Cairo district.

The elections will still go ahead, although yesterday there was a growing move to boycott them. Naguib, who was staying in a tent, said he no longer wanted to participate in an election that, under this military regime, appeared to have reverted to Mubarak's ways and would result only in a 'sick parliament'. Naguib said he would not leave the square until Tantawi resigned.

The Muslim Brotherhood was the unheard voice in the melee, mainly because it wants the elections to go ahead. The Freedom and Justice party, the brotherhood's political wing, is the most organised party and is expected to garner a substantial slice of the parliamentary vote, which will take place in three stages over the next six weeks. The brotherhood has kept its members out of Tahrir Square, although some are there unofficially.

The protesters received a boost from Washington as the White House called on Friday for 'the full transfer of power to a civilian government … as soon as possible'. The Americans have a good deal of leverage as they donate an annual $1.3 billion in aid to Egypt, money that is even more important now that the economy is in freefall.

By Friday night fevered meetings of the leaders of a loosely organised coalition of political parties, protest leaders and charismatic stars of the January 25 revolution had called for an interim civilian government, which they termed the National Salvation Front, to take over immediately from the military.

To head the new civilian leadership they nominated Mohamed ElBaradei, former head of the International Atomic Energy Agency, Abdel Moneim Abul Fatouh, a former leader of the Muslim Brotherhood, and Hamdeen Sabahy, a left-wing politician. All three are presidential candidates.

'Tantawi should step down and the military should go back to the barracks,' Fatouh told me yesterday. He added, however, that he was opposed to postponing the vote.

'We need immediate elections and the drafting of a new constitution,' he said. 'In fact, I would move the presidential election forward. The future of Egypt can only be secured by a civilian government.'

Amid all the political manoeuvring there was nostalgia in the square for what had seemed to be a revolution, paid for at the price of 800 lives, that could only lead to a better future.

'This is our fault,' said Naguib, meaning the fault of Egypt, as he helped me out of the Islamic encampment but into the path of scampering feral boys he had to chase away. 'We failed to educate them.'

Libya

'I'll still be running Libya when my foes have retired,' insists Gadaffi

6 March 2011

Under-fire Libyan leader sends strong message of defiance to world leaders after managing to cling to power against the odds last week.

The more confidence that Muammar Gadaffi radiated in his ability to hold on to power last week, the more his opponents had to fear.

Scores of young men who felt able to protest a few days earlier when he had looked vulnerable found themselves arrested in night-time raids by the Libyan leader's secret police. Parents have not been told where their sons are held.

'We were all in our beds sleeping when the secret police broke through our door,' said Ali, a mechanical engineer, whose sons, aged 17 and 19, were taken at night with other young men from the Tajura district in eastern Tripoli.

He described how a convoy of dozens of pick-up trucks and 4x4s had swarmed into his street at 1am. His teenagers had been blindfolded and led into the darkness.

'We do not know what prison they are in,' he said. 'We hear they are probably with the intelligence force.'

Secret police raided homes in Tajura and Fashloom almost nightly last week, residents said. Both working-class areas have been hotbeds of rebellion. After Friday prayers nine days ago, five people were shot and killed in Tajura and two in Fashloom.

'There is a great feeling of terror,' said another Tajura resident, a 57-year-old builder. 'Anyone speaking up knows that he will be carted off to prison or worse.' He said police appeared to be using photographs and videos, some from YouTube, to identify men involved in earlier protests.

Last week's arrests appeared to be aimed at stopping another violent demonstration after Friday prayers. If so, the clampdown partially succeeded. There were far fewer protesters – only about 300 – but they still took to the streets. After prayers at the Murad Agha mosque, where men spilled out on to the courtyard to pray, demonstrators marched to a nearby roundabout and chanted 'down, down, Gadaffi', and 'the people want the regime to go'.

Half an hour later black vehicles pulled up and police began firing tear gas into the crowd. Acrid fumes filled the street. Some protesters fled, while others tried to throw the tear gas canisters back at the police.

When protesters began throwing rocks the police fired salvo after salvo of rubber bullets into the crowd and everyone scattered, believing they were being attacked with live rounds as they had been before. The last few were chased off with bullets which police appeared to fire into the air. Residents reported about 40 arrests afterwards.

There is little doubt that Gadaffi's writ still runs in Tripoli, as he went to great pains to demonstrate last week. He exuded bullish optimism in spite of the rebels controlling almost half his cities and world leaders calling on him to step down. A belly laugh burst from him when I asked if he would leave his country. 'Does anybody leave his own homeland?' he said. 'Why should I leave Libya?' He retained the veneer of self-assurance throughout an interview with *The Sunday Times*, BBC and America's ABC.

More laughter punctuated his answers, reinforcing the image that he was still very much in control, despite a rebellion that began last month when his security forces fired on a funeral procession.

Gadaffi, 70, his hair dyed jet black, was speaking as Libya's revolt began to look dramatically different from earlier rebellions in Tunisia and Egypt, where the regimes' leaders stepped down in the face of largely peaceful protests. The rebels who now control eastern Libya seized machineguns, rocket-propelled grenade launchers and even anti-aircraft guns from arms depots.

Gadaffi's message that he was determined to fight on began with his choice of venue for our interview. We met in a fish restaurant with floor-to-ceiling windows that looked out over the sparkling blue water of Tripoli harbour.

It was chosen to put paid to rumours that he had fled Libya and to show that he had no fears about travelling anywhere in his capital.

It was a stunning departure from his usual routine. Gadaffi lives hidden behind the walls of the Bab al-Aziziya army barracks in Tripoli and rarely sits in a room with an outside view, unless it is his desert tent.

His choice of transport conveyed the same message. He arrived dressed in a brown turban and flowing ankle-length robe in a white BMW and walked up the steps to the restaurant. Again it was a far cry from his usual tight security. Normally, his guards race ahead of him, tripping over each other in their zeal.

His show of being in control of the city continued throughout the week. On Thursday he delivered a two-hour speech to the faithful before driving away in a vehicle that looked like a Noddy car.

There were indications that Tripoli is nowhere near as relaxed as Gadaffi made out. Along the main corniche, only smashed glass remains in the frames that once held pictures of the Libyan leader.

In the poorer suburbs of Tajura and Fashloom, graffiti saying 'Down, down, Gadaffi' had been painted over with black paint.

Tajura police station was a burnt-out shell. Sporadic shots rang out at night.

Gadaffi's clampdown appeared to have terrified many Tripoli residents. In Tajura, where little more than a week ago men waiting for the funeral of a demonstrator had openly denounced Gadaffi, people were too afraid to speak.

'I'm sorry, we're afraid. I apologise,' said a man who last week was happy to give reporters his name.

Gadaffi seemed coherent when I spoke to him. He denied that his forces had bombed civilian areas, the chief reason for a United Nations security council resolution that warned of crimes against humanity and imposed sanctions.

'It was media agencies that said such things,' Gadaffi claimed. 'The UN should send a fact-finding mission and then they can take such a decision.'

He insisted that the rebellion was fomented by Al-Qaeda, which had drugged Libyan youths to make them enlist.

He grew emotional when I asked what he thought of David Cameron's move to freeze his family's assets and strip them of their diplomatic immunity.

'I challenge Cameron and everybody else if he can bring one dinar that belongs to me in any foreign bank,' he said, raising his voice. 'I have a tent. I don't like money like him. I'll put my two fingers in their eyes if I have any accounts, whether it is inside or outside Libya,' he added, making a stabbing motion with his fingers.

He had one final message for western leaders: 'Today's presidents who say I should go, I say to you that you will serve out your terms and then you will retire – but I will still be leader of the revolution.'

Siege falters as loyalists defect to side of rebel 'rats'

MISRATA

15 May 2011

Deserters from Gadaffi's army say they were tricked or forced into fighting and are now siding with the rebels.

Two months ago, Naji Mabrouk went proudly to war in the belief that he was fighting for his country. Six weeks later, disillusioned, angry and depressed, he waved down a rebel pick-up truck and defected to his former opponents defending the besieged city of Misrata.

Mabrouk, 29, who had served 10 years in the marines, had believed his commanding officers when they told him that Al-Qaeda and foreign troops had seized Libyan cities.

Why wouldn't he? He had watched Colonel Muammar Gadaffi, the Libyan leader, say the same thing on state television and call for his armed forces to defeat the 'rats'.

But after the fall of Benghazi and the east to the rebels, his faith was destroyed. His naval unit was sent to join loyalist forces that had recaptured Zawiya, a city to the west of Tripoli, the capital.

'There was no Al-Qaeda there,' said Mabrouk, one of 102 prisoners of war being held in a school in Misrata last week, awaiting a decision on whether he could be trusted sufficiently to join the rebels' ranks.

'One of us recognised the body of a man we killed in Zawiya as his friend. Another was a marine. He's now buried in the square, as a martyr.' Mabrouk said he had carried on fighting because prison or worse awaited deserters.

On the eve of his last mission, an attack on Misrata from the sea, Khamis Gadaffi, the leader's son and commander of his own elite brigade, addressed the troops on the beach. 'You're fighting for the freedom of Libya,' Gadaffi said. 'Go into Misrata and push the rats out,' he boomed, before driving off with an escort of 200 soldiers in pick-up trucks armed with anti-aircraft guns.

As Mabrouk's unit waited to launch its skiffs, he told his commanding officer: 'Those rats had better not be Libyans.' Mabrouk said his officer replied: 'Anyone who refuses to fight, I will kill.'

After Grad rockets rained down on the port for an hour, Mabrouk said, a 12-boat attack was launched. His boat steered towards a beach, where he and his comrades hid for the night. In the morning, he flagged down the rebels' truck and surrendered his Kalashnikov assault rifle and four hand grenades.

He does not consider himself a traitor. Like many rank and file troops in Gadaffi's army, he symbolises its weakness in the face of determined revolt. He joined the armed forces straight from school because his family needed the money. Now he wants to take on the regime. 'Gadaffi has taken our money and given us nothing but lies,' he said bitterly.

Many loyalist soldiers who have fought in earlier battles no longer have any faith in the party line. They now know the rebels are fellow Libyans, not drugged Al-Qaeda fighters or foreigners, and the cities, far from being abandoned, are home to families like their own.

A series of interviews last week with soldiers who had deserted or surrendered revealed a deeply demoralised force. One battle group of 40 men surrendered en masse rather than battle on. Many men said they had been tricked or bribed to come to the front line in Misrata, where the fighting has been intense for the past month as Gadaffi has attempted to crush the only rebel-held city in the west of the country.

The former loyalists are being held in a disused school, where they cook their own meals. Omar Shariani, 29, had left the army years ago but was recalled when the rebellion erupted in February. He was sceptical of the regime's claims about Al-Qaeda and had seen police attack unarmed protesters in Tripoli's Tajura district.

He said he had no choice but to obey orders and was sent to Misrata with 30 other men. He was given a Kalashnikov and a pick-up truck armed with a 14.5mm anti-aircraft gun mounted on the back, a weapon favoured by both sides.

As soon as he spotted an opportunity, he said, he escaped and surrendered, taking with him Ali Masoud, 18. 'I took Ali with me because he had no shoes, no weapon and he was so scared of all the gunfire that he couldn't move,' he said.

'I want to tell all of the soldiers who are still fighting for Gadaffi that this man is destroying our country,' he added. 'Do not fight for this man.'

Other members of Gadaffi's forces were also pressed into battle. Mohamed al-Hawat, 25, was in his fourth year at university when he was ordered to take part in a pro-Gadaffi demonstration or he would not be allowed to graduate. He said he was taken by bus to Dafniya on the western outskirts of Misrata. He was issued with a gun and given 45 minutes' instruction. There was no need to worry, he was told: the weapon was just for his protection.

When he was issued with a uniform, it was explained this was so that government soldiers could tell him apart from the rebels. By the time he was put on a lorry to Misrata, the penny had dropped. 'We were all upset,' he said. 'I came for a civilian demonstration, and I found myself in this miserable situation. And I'd told my family I'd be gone a day or two.'

He finally heeded the call of rebels who yelled to him: 'Come to us! We're from Misrata; we're Libyan just like you.'

Last week Gadaffi's forces suffered setbacks in Misrata that far exceeded the impact of deserters leaving their ranks. On the western front, rebels fought desperately to drive his forces back so that their Grad rockets and artillery could no longer reach the city centre.

It was a front that changed hour by hour. When on Thursday I drove from the coastal road towards what had been a relatively secure area the day before, bullets whizzed past and mortars landed in the next field. I jumped out of the car to seek the safety of a low sandbank. The bullets whipped by, sounding like angry hornets. The road had turned into a free fire zone.

At the front, 500 yards ahead, about 100 rebels held a line to which they had fallen back overnight. They called for support and ammunition over a radio. It could have been a scene from the First World War. Rebels lined up, squatting with their backs to a sand berm, the butts of their Kalashnikovs in the sand, ready to go over the top.

Reinforcements roared to the scene in pick-up trucks with metal plates welded to them as makeshift armour. My translator grabbed a Kalashnikov and raced forward, joining rebel troops who advanced shouting, 'Allahu akbar' (God is greatest), only to be beaten back by the loyalists' barrages. Yet late in the day the government forces simply gave up and retreated.

'We're attacking them from three sides,' said Abdel Latif Soweili, the rebels' commander and grandson of a hero of the fight against the pre-war Italian occupation of Libya. 'Yesterday we couldn't get to them. They had families in front of them. They were using the women and children as a human shield.'

By the weekend Gadaffi's lines had been pushed back in the west, yard by yard, out of range of the city.

The biggest rebel victory of the week came on the city's southern border. Loyalists had dug in at the airport and the air academy next door for almost two months, lobbing rockets and tank shells into the city.

Finally last week the rebels tried a plan that had been successful last month on Tripoli Street, the city's main boulevard, where Gadaffi's troops had hidden in high buildings, using them for snipers and as vantage points from which to mortar the city. Unable to force them out by frontal attacks, the rebels cut their supply lines by building barricades of sand and blocking roads.

At the airport they used the same tactics. Gadaffi's forces finally broke under intense fire, leaving behind tanks, cars and lorries and abandoning their dead. The rebels buried them in graves with numbers on the headstones.

Last week loyalist forces attempted another seaborne assault on the port. It failed after HMS *Liverpool*, a Royal Navy Type 42 destroyer, silenced Gadaffi's shore batteries with its 4.5-inch gun.

Yesterday in Misrata, shortages of food and medical supplies were growing. Cooking gas was nowhere to be found, and electricity was cut as generators ran out of diesel because shelling had set the port's storage tanks on fire. Petrol queues were half a mile long.

Families are living on tinned tuna; no fresh vegetables or fruit have crossed the siege lines. There are long queues for bread. Morale among the rebel fighters and civilians remains high, though.

Mabrouk, the marine deserter, said he would continue agitating to join their ranks despite the daily losses and deprivations of the siege. 'We've had enough,' he said. 'We all want to be rats now.'

'We had our orders: rape all the sisters'

MISRATA

22 May 2011

Colonel Gadaffi's forces are accused of violating at least 1,000 women trapped by fighting in the front-line city of Misrata.

The young Libyan soldier showed almost no emotion as he described how his unit had raped four sisters, the youngest about 16, after breaking into a home in the besieged port of Misrata.

'My officer sent three of us up to the roof to guard the house while they tied up the father and mother and took the girls to two rooms, two each to a room,' said Walid Abu Bakr, 17.

'My two officers and the others raped the girls first,' he recalled in a monotone, still dressed in the camouflage uniform he was wearing when he surrendered 12 days ago.

'They were playing music. They called me down and ordered me to rape one of the girls.'

Abu Bakr, from Traghen, a poor southern town, claimed he had been given hashish and was not responsible.

'She did not move much when I raped her,' he said, admitting the girl had already been gang-raped. 'She said in a low voice, "There is Allah. He is watching you." I said, "Yes, Allah is watching me."'

Abu Bakr seemed to regard himself as a victim, however. He said he had become his family's breadwinner after his father left his sick mother and his siblings.

He joined the army when he was offered 200,000 dinars (£100,000), payable on victory for Colonel Muammar Gadaffi, the Libyan leader, he said.

But he had received only a week's training at Yarmouk camp in Tripoli before being sent to Misrata as part of a militia attached to the elite Khamis brigade, named after Gadaffi's youngest son. Their mission was simple. 'We were just told to kill,' Abu Bakr said.

The teenager said he did not keep track of how many times the four girls in the house had been raped. The soldiers in his unit had stolen 12,000 dinars and jewellery from the family, but he had not received a penny, he said.

When rebel forces began closing in on the airport road, the officers sent the family to Zlitan, the next town controlled by Gadaffi's troops, and left, ordering Abu Bakr and eight others to guard the house. They never returned.

'The rebels surrounded us, and we threw away our guns and surrendered.'

Abu Bakr, who is now held in a Misrata school with other former Gadaffi soldiers while the rebels decide what to do with them, said he had decided to speak about the rapes after talking to an Islamic cleric.

Misrata officials said the ruthless assaults by Abu Bakr and his unit had been repeated across the city. Gadaffi's soldiers, they said, had engaged in an orgy of rapes that mirrored their destruction of the city's homes and buildings.

Nothing would have prepared the women of Misrata, or their families, for the ferocity of the onslaught that occurred when they were trapped amid the fighting, mostly in districts that were controlled by Gadaffi's forces for two months.

The brutality emerged only when the rebels broke through loyalist lines and chased Gadaffi's troops beyond the city limits. In their wake, they found horror stories.

Doctors at Hekma hospital found that some of Gadaffi's soldiers had recorded video footage of rapes on their mobile phones. 'They made the girls identify themselves to the camera and show their faces. Then they raped them,' one doctor said. The phones were found on loyalists who had been wounded or killed.

'In one of the videos, there's a woman. She's moaning, "Oh no, no, the sixth one, God help me,"' said one doctor.

A video seen by *The Sunday Times* showed a group of Gadaffi's soldiers in camouflage uniform breaking down a door and confronting a frightened family – a man, a woman, five girls whose ages ranged from about five to early 20s, and a boy aged about 7. The soldiers, shouting and waving their guns, stripped the four older girls in front of the family and took them into the next room, where they raped them. The girls cried for mercy, calling on Allah. A soldier at one point yells: 'Gadaffi is our Allah.' The video was found on the phone of a loyalist soldier.

A Filipina nurse said her best friends had fled to Tunisia after their four daughters and 13-year-old son were raped repeatedly after the family was trapped in their flat on Tripoli Street, the scene of some of the heaviest fighting in Misrata.

'I spoke to their mother,' the nurse said. 'She said the boy was terrible. She said, "Don't even ask about my girls."'

The stories emerging from Misrata mirrored the earlier charges of Iman al-Obeidi, 28, who burst into a Tripoli hotel in March claiming to have been gang-raped by Gadaffi loyalists.

So horrified is Misrata by its rapes that young rebel soldiers have offered to marry the victims, who face ostracism in this deeply traditional society.

'The rebels feel guilty that they did not arrive in time to save these families from Gadaffi's men,' said Dr Ismael Fortia, an obstetrician who estimates that up to 1,000 women may have been raped.

Hardly any of those attacked have come forward because a raped woman is regarded as virtually unmarriageable if she is single, or a shame to her family if she is married.

Doctors and psychologists in Misrata have banded together to help. They will check victims for sexually transmitted diseases and offer abortions.

One of their concerns is that unless they are treated, the women may commit suicide rather than live with their memories.

'The images of their rape will go around and around in their heads, like an endless nightmare, unless they receive counselling and help,' said Dr Mustafa Shigmani.

The terrible revelation comes as Misrata's rebels fight on three fronts around the city, loyalists try almost daily to mine the port and explosions reverberate day and night.

Last week there were faint signs that the regime might be faltering under increased Nato bombing and political pressure.

Safia Gadaffi, the Libyan leader's wife, and Aisha, 35, his daughter, were said to have left the country for Tunisia, although his spokesman denied it. Shukri Ghanem, the oil minister, was reported to have defected.

Gadaffi's regime proffered a Russian-brokered deal under which they would withdraw their troops from the cities if the rebels did the same, and if Nato stopped bombing. The rebels refused, but the mere existence of such an offer from Tripoli suggested that the regime might be apprehensive.

'Time is working against Gadaffi,' said Barack Obama last week in a speech on the Middle East. 'The opposition has organised a legitimate and credible interim council.'

Although Obama's statement stopped short of official recognition, it was the furthest Washington has gone towards acknowledging the council as the country's leadership.

The people of Misrata have suffered the greatest toll in the Libyan conflict, largely because their city has been so bitterly contested by Gadaffi. It is the only population centre in the west of the country that is under rebel control.

In districts newly liberated by the rebels, residents described a reign of terror under Gadaffi's soldiers.

'The soldiers ordered our family out of the house while they searched,' said Fatima, 47, of the Zreig neighbourhood. 'They said they were looking for weapons, but they took our money, our jewellery, everything they could carry while we waited for three hours.'

Families were forced to fly the green flag of the regime. Foot patrols raided homes at all hours. 'They would shoot up the television if you were watching anything other than the state channel,' said Fawzi Damir, 21.

Men disappeared. 'They caught my husband and two of my sons,' said Fatima. The men would usually flee if they spotted loyalists on their street, but two weeks ago they had been taken unawares early in the morning. One son escaped by hiding under her bed.

City officials have said more than 1,000 men, women and children have disappeared.

Some residents took to the streets last week to celebrate an end to the shelling of the city centre. They waved flags and shouted with joy.

They were the lucky ones. One of the unforgivable legacies of Gadaffi is that many of the women of Misrata will never again emerge from their homes and think only of the beautiful sunshine.

Professor leads adopted sons into battle

29 May 2011

A university dean and his loyal students are battling to hold the rebel front line as Gadaffi's shells rain down daily.

A university professor turned rebel commander on Misrata's most fiercely contested front line was wrestling last week with a dilemma far beyond that of most military leaders. He felt a deep personal responsibility for his fighters because most were students who had followed him into battle.

'It is difficult for me because I believe we must fight for our country and I know freedom comes at a price,' said Ali Kerzab, 42, who, until three months ago, was Dean of the Department of Education at Misrata University.

'But most of these boys are students, and I want them to have a future,' said Kerzab, a slim, wiry figure in a makeshift uniform of khaki shirt and dark green jacket and trousers, as he walked behind a sand berm protecting the company from loyalist guns.

'They are enthusiastic and they don't think.'

Kerzab and his 150-strong Abu Bakr Sadiq katiba, or militia company, yesterday marked their second week in Dafniya on the western front, 19 miles from the centre of the besieged port of Misrata. The city is the only rebel-held enclave in the government-controlled west.

The rebels have pushed back the forces of Muammar Gadaffi, the Libyan leader, far enough for his rockets to be out of range of the city centre but their new lines are being pounded daily.

The open farmland of the new front is very different terrain from the buildings and alleyways of the city where they used their local knowledge to drive out Gadaffi's troops.

Last week, Grad rockets whistled malevolently as they arced over the concrete farmhouse and row of small shops Kerzab had chosen as a temporary camp on the road to Tripoli, the rebels' ultimate goal.

One Grad landed in a nearby field, setting fire to dried wheat and filling the air with an acrid scent. A salvo of Grads fired in quick succession from a multiple rocket-launcher landed on the tree line, sending up six columns of black smoke.

Kerzab's katiba has seen six men killed in two months and 30 injured in the past two weeks, a huge cost for a close-knit company. The last death, on 2 May, was of Kerzab's brother, Hussain, 46.

Kerzab was one of just 10 local men who launched an initial assault on Gadaffi's forces on 23 February. His students later joined in, along with drivers, shopkeepers and engineers from his neighbourhood.

'He is like a father to me,' said Salem Shavish, 23, who studied English with Kerzab.

'We all feel Gadaffi took our lives,' said Shavish. 'We see America, the UK and the Emirates and we say, "We have oil, why are we always suffering?"'

So close are members of the katiba that Rabia Mustafa al-Gneidi, 19, another student, has written in careful calligraphy on his Toyota the names of the six men killed since the rebellion against Gadaffi began on 18 February, sparked by troops firing on peaceful protesters.

Gneidi said he and other students felt they had a new life ahead of them.

'I can say what I want,' he said. 'Before, the secret police were always present, and you could go to prison just for saying something bad about Gadaffi, even just to your friends.'

Kerzab is focused largely on the students' survival. 'I worry for each one of them,' he said before racing off in a pick-up truck through an olive grove to retrieve a wayward group who had surged ahead and seemed about to be surrounded by loyalists.

But as the carnage mounted last week, the rebel soldiers in Kerzab's company and their comrades on the front line began to chafe at the high command in Misrata, which ordered them to remain in the same positions on the road to Zlitan, the next town, 100 miles east of Tripoli.

The military council decided the rebel force should halt its advance until Zlitan, a town of 110,000 inhabitants where 1,000 of Gadaffi's troops hold sway, rises up of its own volition.

According to Ibraham Bet-Almal, a member of the city's military council, Misrata's rebels have supplied Kalashnikovs and FN assault rifles to Zlitan's rebel representatives. They meet secretly at night in olive groves, and last week 70 Zlitan rebels came for training with the men of Misrata.

'Our target is Tripoli, not Zlitan,' said Kerzab, who attends military meetings in Misrata when he can leave the front. 'If we impose our will on Zlitan, they will fight us. So we tell them, "We are going to Tripoli, let us go together".'

Mad Dog and me

28 August 2011

Marie Colvin, who has known Gadaffi for 25 years, offers an insight into the mind of Libya's fallen tyrant.

When I saw the looted chaos of the Bab al-Aziziya compound in the centre of Tripoli after its capture by rebels last week, I had a flashback to a night quarter of a century ago – the first time I met Muammar Gadaffi.

In April 1986 I was driven through the empty, dark streets of the city to what was then his stronghold. The tall gates of Bab al-Aziziya swung open and I passed several tanks hidden in the shadows. I remember thinking I would not be leaving without the permission of the Libyan leader.

I was nervous. Gadaffi was in a tense stand-off with Ronald Reagan, the American president, who had called him 'the mad dog of the Middle East' for sponsoring anti-western terrorism, including a nightclub bomb attack that month against American military personnel in Berlin. The US Sixth Fleet was off the coast. Superpower vengeance was expected at any moment.

Gadaffi had given no interviews to the scores of journalists in Tripoli. I was an American citizen, working at the time for United Press International, a US news agency. Why had I, a young female reporter, been awakened at 3am and told that 'the leader' had summoned me?

I didn't know it at the time, but this was classic Gadaffi. He kept no set hours and summoned people. His whim had to be implemented immediately. You had only to see how quickly his aides scurried when he issued a command to know that his rule was based on fear.

My car was met by several beautiful young women in tight camouflage uniforms, high heels and make-up with pistols at their hips. They glared at me, led me underground down several staircases and left me alone in a room with a large desk and a sofa.

The door opened. In walked Gadaffi, dressed in a red silk collarless shirt, white silk pyjama trousers and lizard skin slip-ons. Over it all he wore a gold cape. He turned, locked the door, put the key in his pocket and said, 'I am Gadaffi.'

I remember saying to myself, 'No kidding.' But I think I was just stunned.

It was a weird interview. I kept turning on the tape recorder and he kept turning it off, putting his hand on my knee and saying he was tired and wanted to talk about something else. He seemed isolated. At one point I asked a not particularly clever question, something like, 'How are you feeling now that President Reagan is about to bomb you?'

'Who told you that?' he demanded. Missing my chance to be considered a journalist with highly placed sources, I said: 'I heard it on the BBC.' Gadaffi leapt up, crossed the room and switched on a radio tuned to the World Service.

It was clear that he lived in a bubble of his own making. Libya was at the centre of an international crisis, yet he was sitting alone in his bunker, relying on the radio for news. The isolation could only have been enhanced by his obsession with the security he found underground.

We now know that the tunnels under the compound were more than just a secret way in and out. There was a whole world of living quarters where I must have interviewed him years ago, never knowing I was in a tiny corner of a secret complex.

The famous bedouin tent where he met dignitaries, including Tony Blair for the 2004 handshake, was one of the many props of his personal theatre. He played the bedouin sheikh but he never really lived there. He felt safe only in his burrow.

His paranoid obsession with safety underground became even more clear last week when I entered the house of Moatassim Gadaffi, one of his sons and the national security adviser. Neighbours in the Ben Ashour district said Gadaffi senior had built the house about nine years ago, then given it to Moatassim.

Inside it was decorated in terrible taste, with mud-coloured leather furniture, dark brown modern paintings and an ostentatious, black-and-white swirled marble floor. But down three staircases was an underground world. Much larger living quarters sprawled beneath the manicured gardens, complete with a fully-equipped operating theatre, an x-ray machine and a medical clinic. Armoured doors, painted green, punctuated the wide hallways, with instructions on how to release the lock if trapped by rubble.

'For four years workers were sending out trucks of dirt and no building appeared,' said Dr Ashraf al-Khadeiri, who lived across from the compound's 30 foot walls. 'For four years, an enigma. We thought, maybe he is walking in the ground under us. Now we know.' Khadeiri was the first outsider to enter the underground home after Moatassim fled last week.

During the crisis of April 1986 I interviewed Gadaffi several times, always summoned at the last moment in the early hours, always meeting him underground. I never saw anyone besides drivers and guards. There was no sound from outside.

The interviews were increasingly strange. I arrived for one to find that a bodyguard had laid out petite green shoes for me to wear. It was Gadaffi's favourite colour: he had changed Libya's flag to a flat green banner and he had renamed Tripoli's central square Green Square. But green shoes for an interviewer?

Late on Friday 11 April, he summoned me again and seemed in a more serious mood. He told me he had decided to 'include all of southern Europe in a Libyan counterattack plan'.

Gadaffi painstakingly went over a communiqué with me, changing several words in a statement typed by his office and explaining exactly what he meant. He was anxious to hear what I thought the Reagan administration might do, and he pressed me for information from Washington. He told me: 'I think Reagan must be mad.'

On the night of 15 April the Americans attacked. The use of Stealth F-117 aircraft was vetoed at the last minute – it would have been the first time the top-secret planes were used in anger – and a squadron of F-111s flew from American bases in Britain to hit the compound and other targets.

I called the private number Gadaffi had given me to find out whether he had survived. An aide answered and hung up.

Several weeks later Gadaffi ended a long period of speculation that he had been killed by emerging to make one of his characteristic rambling speeches. He said Reagan was the problem, the American people loved Gadaffi, and to prove it he distorted the content of my phone call – which had been to find out if he was alive – to say that 'an American woman had called and tried to warn me'. I was grateful he did not use my name.

Three years later I was in Tripoli again. It was a month after the Lockerbie bombing, which had not yet been definitively pinned on Libya.

American and British intelligence had identified a chemical weapons plant at Rabta, 60 miles south of the capital. US fighters patrolling the Mediterranean shot down two Libyan planes that had intercepted them. Gadaffi put human shields into Rabta, but this time no bombers came.

I saw him from a different perspective when I accompanied Yasser Arafat, the Palestinian leader, on a visit to Libya. On the plane, Arafat worked through a mass of papers, always with his green pen. Without a break in stride after landing, he climbed into the limousine that whisked him to the hotel Gadaffi had assigned to him. When Gadaffi had still not seen him after 12 hours, Arafat took it as an insult.

He sent me in his convoy back to the airport. It was a feint. The call immediately came that the Libyan leader wanted to see Arafat, so my driver drove me at 100mph to join him at Gadaffi's headquarters.

Gadaffi, in his finest robes, greeted Arafat then turned and noticed me. 'Mary,' he asked (he has never been able to pronounce my name), 'what are you doing here?' It was as if I had wandered in off the street.

'She's with me,' Arafat said proudly, as though we were at a London film premiere. He then went on to lie outrageously about the state of my nose, which at the time was on the wrong side of my face.

Arafat told Gadaffi the Israelis had broken it. The truth was that Palestinian demonstrators had thrown a rock through the window of my car when I was posing as a Jewish settler on a reporting assignment.

Sometimes our encounters were even more surreal. When Madeleine Albright was Bill Clinton's secretary of state, more than a decade after the bombing of Bab al-Aziziya, Gadaffi asked me at the end of an interview if I could get a message to her.

I thought I had a journalistic coup: the mad dog of the Middle East bidding for peace with Washington. Instead, he told me he loved 'Madeleine'. He watched her every appearance on television, and he was annoyed that sometimes the cameras did not show her full face. The fact that, in her sixties, she was five years older than him and no longer a beauty seemed of no importance. Could I get her special phone number for him, preferably for the phone next to her bed? Would I also communicate to her that if she felt the same as he did, she should wear green in her next television appearance?

Albright appears to have been replaced since by a younger edition. An album of cut-out photographs of Condoleezza Rice, George W Bush's national security adviser and secretary of state, was found in one of Gadaffi's underground salons last week. In 2007 he told an interviewer on Al Jazeera television how much he liked her: 'Leezza, Leezza, Leezza – I love her very much. I admire her and am proud of her because she's a black woman of African origin.'

For years, he seemed to be starring in his own movie. I never saw him in the same outfit twice. He was a bedouin tribesman, a colonel and a self-styled revolutionary. He was an Arab and an African, a nationalist and a socialist, a Muslim, a poet and a would-be 'philosopher king' and he had outfits for every role. His military uniforms had more medals than a Latin American generalissimo, and yet he had never fought a war until this year.

Beneath the ludicrous military caps his eyes were dark; they never revealed any emotion other than a canniness, as if a reptile within was always plotting. For his own people he was, in their words, 'the leader'. He preferred 'supreme guide' and fancied himself their mentor, patriarch and uncle.

It was the people, though, who felt the vicious side of his character, and where the lack of pity in those eyes mattered most. He was feared and hated. He would stop at nothing to maintain power.

Gadaffi made much of his birth in 1942 into an illiterate bedouin family in the desert near Sirte, the coastal town where his diehard supporters have been fighting their final battle. But his world view seems to have been shaped during his schooldays by revolutionary upheavals in the Arab world, principally Colonel Gamal Abdel Nasser's seizure of power in Egypt.

He joined the army as the path out of poverty and seized power in 1969 in a coup similar to Nasser's: the virtually bloodless unseating of a weak king by young officers from whom Gadaffi emerged as the most prominent and then dictator.

For a while he was fairly normal. I once thumbed through an old photo album put together by one of his former confidants, which showed Gadaffi on a building site in a pork-pie hat and shorts, looking at an architect's drawing. 'He was always a little strange, but he was easy with us, like a normal person. He changed greatly,' the friend said.

He posed as a tribesman who wanted only the simple life, but Libya under Gadaffi degenerated into a corrupt state that enriched his family and hangers on. He made himself colonel, then abolished all military ranks above that. Despite all his talk of rule by the people for the people, it soon became clear there was only one colonel in Libya – and only one voice, among 6m, that really mattered.

Increasingly unchallenged, he gradually created an unreal world in Libya that mirrored his own fascinations. Grandiose projects never worked. All that remains of his $20 billion man-made river are oversized pipes scattered by the sides of roads or standing bizarrely at the centre of roundabouts in mute testimony to his folly.

He could afford it. Libya had valuable oil on the doorstep of European markets. Until the events of this year it was earning about $47 billion a year from exports – and Gadaffi used the wealth and influence it brought to keep potential enemies at bay and the country under firm control.

Much of the oil wealth was squandered, stolen or embezzled. Gadaffi and his six sons, increasingly important props for his one-man regime, became immensely rich.

He was an impossible interviewee in many ways. When I last talked to him during this year's uprising, I asked who was giving the army orders. He looked puzzled and said, 'But there is no army in Libya!' This at a time that Libyan soldiers were shooting unarmed demonstrators in the streets of Benghazi, Misrata and Tripoli.

He said he would not have to step down as he held no government position, and chided me for not understanding the Libyan system of rule. In 1977, he had invented the 'jamahiriya' or state of the masses, in which the nation is supposedly governed by the people through local councils. In reality, it was a parallel power base that he, his relatives and tribal allies controlled.

His ego knew no bounds. He fancied himself a philosopher, setting out his ideas in a 'green book' filled with banalities such as, 'A man is male, and a woman is female'. Every Libyan school child had to study the pocket-sized tome.

The green book was based on his 'third universal theory', which, an aide once told me admiringly, Gadaffi came up with after lying in a darkened room for weeks with a blanket over his head. When Tony Blair's new Labour announced the 'third way', Gadaffi claimed it vindicated his theory and even threatened to sue for plagiarism.

Libya's population was small in comparison with countries such as Egypt, but despite its riches its people struggled and infrastructure fell apart. It was impossible to imagine Libya as a wealthy oil country. Streets were potholed, cheap brick housing lined the highways.

Libyans went abroad for good healthcare, the wealthy to Europe or America, the middle class next door to Tunisia and only the poor attended Libyan hospitals. Education was among the worst in the Arab world. Gadaffi banned the study of English, pointedly keeping his people isolated from the wider world.

For Gadaffi, the great disappointment was that he never graduated to the bigger stage. He was desperate for international recognition. No matter how much he jumped up and down like a child, the great powers did not consider Libya important enough – strategically or militarily – to worry too much about him, at least at first. So he took to violence to get attention. He made Libya into an isolated, pariah state by spending millions backing anti-western terrorist groups, part of his revolutionary mission to change the world.

His support was as indiscriminate as it was lavish. He funded and armed the Provisional IRA, but when Ulster Protestant paramilitaries came begging, he gave them money too. His largesse went to the Red Brigades in Italy, and Eta in Spain, to Shining Path in Peru and the Sword of Islam in the Philippines.

European capitals were bombed. Assassination squads were sent around the world, targeting Libyan dissidents whom Gadaffi labelled 'stray dogs'. There was no escape; one exile was gunned down at his grocery store in west London.

But it was when Gadaffi turned his murderous attentions directly to the United States, sending agents to bomb the nightclub in Berlin packed with American servicemen in 1986, that Washington and its allies drew the line.

He was not even very good with his few misguided supporters. He put on an Alice in Wonderland 'victory party' after the 1986 US bombing of Libya. Western peaceniks watched from stands erected in the ruins of Bab al-Aziziya as cute children marched by with examples of their hobbies. Then came the Libyan boy scouts carrying live chickens and a few live rabbits.

They appeared to be showing how well they cared for animals – until they suddenly threw them to the ground, disembowelled them with their bare hands and ate chunks of the still-quivering flesh. The peaceniks ran from the stands, screaming.

Gadaffi seemed ever more eccentric. After another interview, I went back to my hotel to be awakened in the middle of the night by a knock at the door. Standing in the doorway were a tall woman and a short Libyan man. She was wearing a full nurse's uniform, complete with hat. Her little companion came up to her hip.

He announced that Gadaffi had thought I looked tired in the interview and had sent his personal nurse. She pulled out what looked to my sleepy eyes like the largest hypodermic needle I had ever seen, and said: 'I Bulgarian. I take blood?'

I said no, I was exhausted, she could do that tomorrow. It was never healthy to give an outright refusal in Gadaffi's Libya. She insisted – 'Just a little blood' – obviously under strict orders. I said:

'Okay, but I know myself and if you take my blood I will definitely be too tired to interview the leader tomorrow.' They conferred, and we agreed she could come by in the afternoon.

I decided to catch the first plane out of Tripoli – to anywhere. But when I went downstairs to check out, I found that reception was under orders to keep my passport.

Luckily, Arafat was in town again and was seeing Gadaffi. Members of Force 17, Arafat's elite bodyguard, had decided to have a coffee in the hotel while they waited for him. When they walked into the lobby, they saw me in distress.

They asked what was the matter, and wrested my passport back after a fierce argument. Driving me to the airport, they saw me safely on to the plane.

The next time I went to Libya I was nervous; but Gadaffi started the interview by practically slapping his leg and laughing: 'Remember the time I tried to take your blood?'

The Lockerbie bombing in 1988 succeeded in winning the attention Gadaffi craved, but it led to tougher international sanctions and ostracism.

Libya was cast into outer darkness for more than a decade. Then came the 9/11 attacks in 2001 and with them, an opportunity. The Americans' subsequent overthrow of Saddam Hussein in 2003 spooked Gadaffi.

In a spectacular volte-face, the Libyan leader came over to the West. Oil companies returned to the desert. His comeback was crowned in 2009 by his first address to the UN general assembly.

He admitted no fault for the terrors of the past, and oppression at home continued. The Libyans were never fooled. As younger generations across the Arab world rose in search of their rights this year, young Libyans decided to fight too.

His rehabilitation has, with hindsight, been rescinded by Europe and America over the past six months as his army has ruthlessly killed civilians to defend his regime. If captured he will now face an international indictment for war crimes. Or will the Libyans mete out their own justice?

'My people love me,' he said in the last interview I had with him this year.

Did he really believe that? I looked into his eyes, trying to read him, and saw not a spark of duplicity showing. Yet he must have known his world was crumbling.

He chose the site of the interview cannily, appearing for the only time I met him above ground – in a fish restaurant of all places. It was puzzling until I realised the backdrop to the huge windows was Tripoli's distinctive port, which would counter rumours that he had fled the country.

Where is he now? The streets I drove through to Bab al-Aziziya 25 years ago are littered with spent bullet cases, broken glass and burnt cars. The walls are daubed with cartoon caricatures of Gadaffi with exaggerated permed hair. The Libyan leader is on the run, with a bounty of $2 million on his head. But he remains a showman. Will his exit be as dramatic as his entrance that night when he told me: 'I am Gadaffi'?

Killing rooms plot bloody retreat of troops loyal to Tyrant Jr

4 September 2011

Libya's civilian death toll rises as Khamis Gadaffi's withdrawing forces continue their murderous brutality in makeshift prisons.

The four men murdered in a trailer must have felt they were on the verge of freedom after months in a makeshift prison on an abandoned construction site. Instead, troops led by Khamis Gadaffi, the Libyan leader's youngest son, shot them in a final act of revenge before fleeing as rebel forces rolled in to Tripoli.

The men, one of them a doctor from Misrata, had been held with about 80 other prisoners in the southern suburb of Qasr al-Ghashir.

Local residents only learnt of their plight on 24 August when they found emaciated strangers wandering around their farms.

They had no idea that Bab al-Aziziya, the Tripoli headquarters of Muammar Gadaffi, had fallen the day before after a fierce battle with rebel troops.

'The poor guys – some of them were injured, some had bare feet,' said Amr Ghinewa, 42, a farmer. 'I shouted at them, "Who are you?" We knew the soldiers were living there, but we did not know about the prisoners.'

The men begged for help for two prisoners who had been shot but were still alive. Ghinewa said an ambulance raced the wounded men to hospital, but they died.

He found a harrowing scene at the construction site, which had been used by the Khamis brigade as an unofficial barracks. The men had been imprisoned in cinderblock cells in a metal-sided storage hangar that was stiflingly hot and had no electricity or water. Last week, tangled blankets and discarded jeans were all that remained in the 10 x 4 foot cells.

In the killing room, a small bedroom with two single beds in a temporary building, dried blood remained on the carpet and floor. A mobile phone video taken by the resident who found them documented the full horror. A balding man, said to be Dr Ali Durati, from Misrata, lay in a grey T-shirt slumped against one bed, blood dripping down the side of his head. His family said he had been driving an ambulance with an emergency case when he was captured at a Gadaffi checkpoint. Another body lay in a corner at the end of the bed.

Two more men, one in a red Puma T-shirt and a second in a T-shirt and navy blue tracksuit bottoms, lay together, slumped against a mattress upended by the wall, both shot in the chest. Thirteen spent casings from AK-47 bullets littered the floor.

The identity of their killers was clear. Stacks of badges from the 32nd Brigade, run by Khamis, along with receipts documenting the delivery of 10 flak jackets, other military hardware and food, were abandoned.

Scenes such as this, showing the murderous brutality of withdrawing Gadaffi forces, brought home the ordeal the Libyan revolution has become for many civilians and rebel fighters.

At the Khamis brigade's Yarmouk barracks, huge craters and burnt, flattened buildings mark the Nato bombings that began in February. The troops seem to have retreated to civilian buildings and left behind a small warehouse littered with the charred corpses of at least 50 prisoners.

Construction sites, abandoned when the war began, seem to have been their preferred next stop. They were perfect places to hide, with ready-made living quarters, office equipment, coffee makers and a civilian veneer to fool Nato planes.

At the New Palace Construction Company in southern Tripoli, stores of weapons have been left behind, some burnt by the Khamis brigade as they retreated. Last week, rebels picked through the barrels of 106mm cannon and Kalashnikovs, loading what they salvaged on to pick-up trucks heading for Sirte, Gadaffi's home town.

They left to local residents their more gruesome finds. The body of one man lay on the floor of a cramped office in a temporary building, shot several times in the chest and stashed under a mattress.

Another four men who had been executed were lined up along the wall of a warehouse, blindfolded. 'It was horrible,' said Mohammed Haddar, a 42-year-old neighbour. 'The bodies had been raked by bullets.'

All four were from Misrata, he said. He recognised one: a doctor aged about 60 who had made a forced television confession. The others were younger.

Other prisons were scenes of inhumanity.

'I cannot show you my body,' said Ibrahim al-Aghi, 46, an engineer thrown in to the infamous Abu Salim jail for organising a network of opposition cells in Tripoli.

His face still swollen and his eyes red, he said he was beaten daily and, when he refused to talk, hung from a tree and beaten with cables and pipes by passing prison guards. They threw sea water into his wounds to revive him when he passed out.

In Ain Zahra, jail to hundreds of political prisoners liberated last week, rebel soldiers still paced the narrow, dark corridors, singing 'Allahu akbar' (God is greatest), trying to persuade prisoners they believed were held in underground cells that they were saviours, not Gadaffi's men.

'We were beaten from the moment we were arrested at the border crossing,' said Alla'a Abdullah, 40, who had been held there with his two brothers since February. 'I was hit on the head with a gun, wood and cables.'

He said guards would come on shift drunk and take prisoners out of their cells to beat them. Others dressed prisoners as women and raped them. It was difficult to doubt his story; on one walkway four new bras lay abandoned, two purple and two red. Abdullah lost 3½ stone in prison.

As the rebel forces liberated more neighbourhoods, the National Transitional Council (NTC), the acting government, sought to bring security to the capital. Tripoli is awash with guns, and much of the city is still without water or reliable electricity. The euphoria of victory is fragile, as so far the only security is enforced by neighbourhood watch checkpoints manned by untrained youths, some as young as 12.

The NTC said it would move to Tripoli this week.

Toxic tyrant's chemical cavern

AL-AJAYLAT

11 September 2011

Chilling new evidence of the brutality of Colonel Gadaffi has emerged among the trampled uniforms at a military base in Libya.

At first sight, the abandoned military base in western Libya appeared to be empty. Army trucks had been left with their doors gaping open in a flat wasteland of red sand and sparse desert grasses.

There were no bodies to be seen in the camp outside Al-Ajaylat, 50 miles west of Tripoli – just uniforms that lay crumpled by the sides of the dirt roadways, as if the soldiers who were stationed here had stripped and fled.

The first warehouse we came to, however, was full – crammed with thousands of wooden crates and boxes piled up to the tin ceiling of a football-pitch-sized cavern. And the contents spilling on to the concrete floor revealed that this was a chemical and biological warfare facility.

I opened some green metal tins in the crates to find black rubber-rimmed gas masks, wrapped in clear plastic. Other crates contained yellow rubber 'NBC' suits with grey boots attached – protection against nuclear, biological and chemical weapons. Cardboard boxes of spare filters marked 'Made in Iran' rose to the roof.

In another warehouse were hundreds of flame-throwers with spare fuel canisters, napalm, detonators for explosives, crates of assault rifles, thousands of anti-personnel and anti-tank mines and countless boxed vials of atropine, an antidote to nerve gas.

The most worrying discovery was in a corner of a third warehouse. A dark, malodorous liquid leaked out of metal barrels. I held my breath, then tentatively snatched a mouthful of air, thinking of the gas masks in the first warehouse – should I get one? There was no telling what was in the barrels other than that it was corrosive; one was holed from inside. Cleared of dust, the label revealed only a skull and crossbones and the word 'poisonous' in Cyrillic script.

Outside, ambulances had been left at skewed angles, including one that seemed to have crashed into a eucalyptus tree. Their interiors were observation chambers designed to test victims of exposure to radiation or chemicals.

Military experts who viewed the contents of the warehouses said they believed that the equipment had defensive and offensive purposes. 'An army uses this stuff to protect its troops from an attack by the enemy, or to protect its troops when they are launching an attack,' a British military expert said.

'The equipment would be imperative in both defensive actions and offensive actions.'

Much of the material in the warehouses was outdated but there was evidence that Colonel Muammar Gadaffi, the fugitive Libyan leader ousted by the rebels last month, had not forgotten his stash.

Documents found in a single-storey office building near the camp entrance revealed that the Libyan defence ministry ordered that 2,000 Czech gas masks and 2,000 chemical protection suits be sent on 26 July from the base to Al-Jufrah, a town in the south still under Gadaffi's control.

Another document recorded shipments to Sirte – Gadaffi's home town on the coast, which was besieged last week by rebel forces – between April and June, including 7,500 gas masks, decontamination powder and liquid, napalm and flame-throwers.

The discovery increased fears that a cornered Gadaffi might be tempted to resort to unconventional weapons, although most observers believe he no longer has the capability to launch them.

From the start of its military intervention in Libya, Nato has set up early warning systems against such a contingency, according to Noman Benotman, a senior analyst at the Quilliam Foundation, a London think tank.

Benotman, the former head of an anti-Gadaffi Islamist insurgent group, said the dictator's next move, as the rebel forces close in, was hard to predict. 'Now there are no rules, no red lines,' he said.

The Pentagon and an international monitoring organisation have indicated that Gadaffi's remaining stockpiles are secure, but it is known that more than nine tons of mustard gas remains in Libya. Some of it may be in bases still controlled by Gadaffi loyalists.

There is less of it than there would have been just a few years ago. Gadaffi agreed to dismantle his weapons of mass destruction in 2003 in return for a rapprochement with the West. To demonstrate his commitment, he ordered that 3,300 bombs that could have been used to drop chemical weapons be bulldozed. But the stockpiles of mustard gas have taken longer to eliminate.

An American embassy cable in November 2009, released by WikiLeaks, suggested that Libya was acting more slowly than it had agreed in the hope of securing greater rewards for its co-operation. As a result, 9½ tons of the poison gas was still in Libya when the uprising against Gadaffi began in February, according to the Organisation for the Prohibition of Chemical Weapons, a body that works closely with the United Nations.

The spread of weapons through Libya has become a significant concern. Mortar shells, mines and even missiles have been abandoned by Gadaffi's fleeing forces at sites the rebels have failed to secure.

Desert storm flushes Gadaffi from oasis of dictator chic

JUFRA

25 September 2011

Our reporter joins a convoy rolling south in search of the colonel – and drives into a ferocious ambush from Gadaffi's protectors.

The shattering of the calm of an empty road in the desert of southern Libya was astonishingly quick. An explosion burst on the rocks near a convoy of anti-Gadaffi forces, sending up a spray of sand with a deafening boom that echoed off the mountains around us.

Bullets zipped by with the buzz of hornets, making tiny puffs in the dust when they hit.

Flashes of light bursting in the red bluffs rising 100 yards from the road revealed the gunmen's positions, but the only sound I could hear was the roar of return fire.

We had left Tripoli in pursuit of Muammar Gadaffi, the fugitive Libyan leader. Now, despite an agreement with the elders of the desert town of Sukna, we were being ambushed by Gadaffi's protectors just outside the town.

Another rocket-propelled grenade (RPG) hit the side of the road and my car skewed to a halt. Abduladiem Majdub, one of the convoy's commanders, thrust a Beretta pistol at me from the front seat and shouted: 'Take this. If they overrun us, can you use it?'

I nodded and jumped out, running doubled-over to avoid bullets, and threw myself down behind a sand dune. Then I decided it was too low and crawled to a rock. I had a pistol, a notebook and a pen.

My main goal was to avoid distracting the fighters who might think they had to protect me. This was a fight for survival. They regrouped and fired 14.5mm anti-aircraft shells horizontally into the mountains, then launched four Grad missiles.

One fighter was hit in the arm and carried off by his comrades before I could see his face. Then the firing from across a moon-scape of rocks stopped and the anti-Gadaffi forces raced towards the source.

I followed them to a small camp under a thorn tree. A green army jacket lay abandoned next to tin tea pots, cans of sardines and tomato paste, seven onions and two packs of pasta. About 50 yards further on, new RPGs lay glinting in the sun at the rim of a gulley. A large machinegun stood on its spindly legs with a rope of heavy-calibre bullets threaded through its barrel. Kalashnikov rifles lay nearby in neat stacks.

Our attackers had evidently dropped everything and run for their lives from the 150 fighters in our convoy.

The men, from Tripoli and Gharyan, in northwest Libya, had been thrown together at the last minute from four 'katibas', or brigades, when a tip came into the capital that Gadaffi was holed up in one of his farmhouses in the south.

These men had driven into enemy territory – the Sahara, where tribes and towns stood loyal to the dictator born to a Bedouin herder. Three ambulances joined the convoy.

At 10am on Tuesday we stopped at a sign saying 'Welcome to Jufra', the central region south of Sirte. The rebels fired off guns to make sure they were working, or just to entertain themselves, and a falling bullet struck me on the shoulder, stinging like a bee.

Later that day we headed up a narrow road through an oasis where a spotter claimed to have seen Gadaffi at a farmhouse. The Gadaffi hunters, pointing Kalashnikovs out of the car windows, twitched at the only sign of movement, a gazelle leaping away among the trees.

This place was a far cry from the dusty roads and cinderblock homes we had passed on the 500-mile journey south from Tripoli. We passed a man-made lake, then came to a long drive leading to a walled compound. The men erupted out of their trucks, guns at the ready, and raced through a gate in the wall, fanning out to search low, modern buildings gleaming white in the setting sun.

The huge swimming pool was empty. 'He is not here,' said Majdub, the 39-year-old organiser of the convoy, before collapsing exhausted on one of the dictator's comfortable beds. 'He is running every day. This is his home. Choose a bedroom.'

The compound contained twin houses – one for Gadaffi, the other for Safia, his wife – each with buttermilk-coloured sofas and prints of desert scenes on the walls. Smaller houses in the compound were for guards and workers.

Abubudellah Hamruni, a second commander of the convoy, drove off without even getting out of his car. He was still nursing a leg shattered during the uprising by a large-calibre bullet and now pinned by an external steel frame.

Frustrated to find Gadaffi not at home, Hamruni began another hunt, for the gazelles he had seen in the date palms. He shot five for dinner, a minor but satisfying victory: the dictator allowed no one but family to hunt his game.

I slept under the stars on an Oriental carpet dragged out of the house. Documents found in one of the outbuildings showed that Gadaffi spent a small fortune on these homes and gardens, although he visited only a few times a year.

A rebel who had never seen a flush lavatory marvelled at a huge marble bathroom. 'Look at this five-star place,' said Ibrahim Gashir, 26, a dental assistant turned fighter. 'He had everything and we had nothing.'

By morning, new intelligence had arrived that Gadaffi was in a second house, one they had not known about, 50 miles to the south.

The route took us through Sukna, the first big town in the Jufra region. The convoy stopped at a checkpoint as four of the town's elders emerged. Elsewhere in Libya, at Bani Walid and Sirte – where heavy fighting was reported yesterday – the anti-Gadaffi forces had tried to negotiate their way in. But this convoy, hot on their quarry's trail, was in a hurry.

The elders, dressed in white robes, listened nervously to guarantees that if Sukna surrendered, nobody would be hurt. Hamruni and Majdub, the convoy's leaders, assured them that water and electricity, which had been cut off three months earlier, would be restored.

'I think it will be OK,' Hamruni said as he watched them return down the road to Sukna. 'I made it clear if they break their word, their city is finished.'

Meanwhile, the rebels took prisoners from cars coming out of the town. A former soldier who would not speak was driven into the desert and made to run at speed in the hot sun, guns trained on his back. He suddenly became helpful.

It was late afternoon when the elders returned and sat in a tent with the convoy's leaders.

'I have brought the message to Sukna and we have an agreement that you can enter peacefully,' said Mohamed Bashir Ibrahim, 67. 'We can guarantee our families will stay in their homes, but we cannot guarantee any of the Gadaffi forces will not attack you.'

Hamruni replied: 'You take care of your families, we will take care of the [military].'

It soon became clear that the agreement had not been unanimous. The convoy ventured down a dirt road just outside town to check the flanks and drove right into the ambush.

Moving on afterwards, the rebels discovered Sukna's secret. Green-painted crates, some of them 20ft long and piled 6ft high, lined a so-called 'valley of the dam' for mile after mile close by. It was the most extensive weapons store anyone had seen.

There were rocket launchers and missiles, anti-aircraft guns, rocket-propelled grenades and innumerable assault rifles and machineguns. Gadaffi's forces had apparently gambled that Nato would not risk bombing this place for fear of fracturing the large concrete dam looming over the valley.

Suddenly word came through that Sukna had surrendered. In the central square, men were celebrating, sweating in the heat and waving red, black and green flags. Gadaffi posters and flags were scattered on the ground.

'Freedom! We can taste it! Finally, we are with the rest of our Libya,' shouted a man who reached into the car to shake everyone's hand. Was he genuine? Was anyone?

Night fell as we drove down another deserted road from which we could see huge fires burning in the hills. Gadaffi's army had launched missiles on the next town, called Hun, razing houses on the outskirts. Nonetheless, the convoy was driving into a final spasm of resistance.

In the end, only a few hardliners were prepared to fight the men Hamruni and Majdub sent in to free the town. We found the inhabitants tired after months of deprivation.

Atik Mohamed, 62, who described himself as a retired army

officer, met the convoy in Hun's central square, where men were firing off guns and waving flags.

'We are happy to see you,' Mohamed said. 'We have been cooking with wood, like our grandparents.'

Young men described more arduous ordeals. Hamza Taweela, 26, said the security forces had ruled with impunity in the last month. He had been arrested returning from a meal during Ramadan, the holy month.

'They fired in the air over us, then threw us on the ground and handcuffed us and blindfolded us,' said Taweela, an engineer. 'They took us to the station and beat us on our backs.'

He never knew what he was accused of. 'They kept telling me I was a rat [Gadaffi's word for rebel]', he said. 'They made us chant, 'God, Muammar [Gadaffi], Libya, it's enough'.'

Another captive, General Sa'ad Suweidi, from Sebha, who had been second-in-command in Hun, said: 'At first, we did not believe that the rebels had captured the towns on the coast.

'My forces here were huge. I had 40,000 men. We didn't think they could ever defeat us,' he said, still wearing his uniform as he sat in the back seat of a Toyota from the convoy. 'But my men – they began slipping away ... I thought the rebels would cut my throat.'

The taking of the two towns meant that the road was now clear to the second Gadaffi house – a white villa with a marble fountain. This was far more ostentatious than the oasis farmhouse, reflecting the 'dictator chic' of the Gadaffi family's homes in Tripoli, with gold-framed mirrors and faux Louis XVI furniture on plush carpets and an enormous king-sized bed in an ornate bedroom.

The house had been used recently: in the kitchen, a box of dates had been chopped open. Cold tea stood in tin pots. But Gadaffi was not in residence and the steam was going out of the chase. The consolation was the capture of tons of weapons and the chance to fire into the sky for hours.

The taking of Sukna and Hun was also celebrated in Tripoli by the new government. With the Jufra region taken, Gadaffi's possible hiding places had diminished. This weekend fresh intelligence came that he might be heading for a second country, en route to a third.

'I am disappointed, of course I wanted to catch him,' said Majdub. 'Maybe someone else will. The point is, we will find him and he will face justice.'

Brutal retribution

23 October 2011

Marie Colvin, John Cantlie, John Follain, Michael Smith,
James Foley, Hala Jaber and Sara Hashash

He called his enemies rats. Yet it was Muammar Gadaffi who was cornered in a sewer pipe, his cruel dictatorship of Libya ending in ignominy and death.

There was always something weird about Sirte, a slice of faux Beverly Hills in the middle of nowhere. Many houses were opulent, with 60-inch plasma television sets on the walls and multi-car garages. The roads were neat and the hedgerows perfectly trimmed, walls whitewashed and the shopfronts new. Everything was clean, almost sterile, unlike the rest of Libya with its crazy old cars, dirt, corner shops and cafés.

Hated by his own people, Colonel Muammar Gadaffi had turned to Africans to inhabit this city of his dreams. Posters around the ring road proclaimed that 'Arab space and African space are one' and 'Africa is progress'. Gadaffi hosted an Organisation of African Unity summit there and proposed it as the capital of a pan-African union.

It was just a grimy coastal village when he was born nearby in 1942; and it is now once again a ruin, destroyed street by white-washed street in the dictator's last stand, which culminated on

Thursday in the world's first YouTube lynching of a tyrant, a lethal happy-slapping of global significance.

The many mobile phone videos posted on the internet tell the final story: the groggy, bleeding despot about to succumb to the howling mob around him. So do the bodies – nearly 100 of them scattered among the debris of his escape convoy on the western highway out of Sirte and in surrounding fields. Burnt, blown up, chopped up by gunfire, shot in the head, most are black Africans. One was decapitated, his dreadlocked head next to his body. They were loyal in extremis to Sirte's notorious son.

The frustrating paradox of the grisly filmed images is that they are inconclusive. Who fired the fatal shot that left Gadaffi with a bullet in his brain? Journalists have flooded into Sirte and other coastal cities to try to winnow truth from the many contradictory claims made by the men caught up in that last moment of frenzy – and by rival factions within the rebel forces.

None accepts the official version that the deposed Libyan leader was shot in crossfire as he was taken alive from the scene by ambulance – any more than they bothered even to register the Nato bromide that the air attack that halted Gadaffi's escape was ordered because his convoy threatened the civilian population. But what did happen?

One clue came yesterday from a rebel commander who confessed anonymously to a Reuters news agency reporter: 'We wanted to keep him alive, but the young guys – things went out of control.'

Though few knew it at the time, the net began closing on Gadaffi on 16 September when rebels pushed into Sirte from the west of the city. For three days they met fierce resistance as regime loyalists massed against them.

Venturing up to the front line, John Cantlie, a photo-journalist who contributes to *The Sunday Times*, found a nightmarish scene. The rebels would reverse up the main street in their gun trucks and let rip, but at about 5pm each day the loyalists moved their best men to the front and the rebel casualties would soar.

Foreign photographers and reporters took to calling that time 'death o'clock'. After three days, with 60 dead and 500 wounded, the rebels pulled back to tend their wounds and reconsider.

Despite the fierceness of the resistance, none thought Gadaffi himself was hiding in the city. Everyone suspected that his fifth son, Mutassim, was leading the resistance in Sirte. His name was heard on radio transmissions.

'We hear them on the radio saying Mutassim this, Mutassim that,' said Mustafa Jalil, the commander of the rebel katiba (brigade), at the time. 'I am sure he is inside. But as for Gadaffi? Who knows. He is like a mouse, a rat. He has run and hidden underground somewhere far away.'

When rebels twice raided the western outskirts of Sirte they arrested groups of Mauritanian immigrants, young men with no passports and no ID.

'These are fighters for Gadaffi!' said one rebel as they conducted basic questioning. 'These men all say they work on the same farm, yet they know nothing about farming and three of them admit to owning a Kalashnikov.'

Yet British military sources said the colonel was believed to have fled to a third country after the fall of Tripoli in August. Western diplomats thought he was on the run in the vast desert of southern Libya, bribing locals to give him refuge. Fierce armed resistance in Bani Walid, a desert town that is home to tribes loyal to Gadaffi, strengthened suspicions that he was hiding there. Sirte, by contrast, seemed too obvious a place to hide.

Two weeks ago, Cantlie was again caught up in the chaos of Sirte at the end of a day's fighting. He had hitched a ride in a pick-up truck inching through a jam of cars and gun-laden vehicles when a rebel clinging to the side yelled: 'Gadaffi! Big hair! Here!'

The rebel gestured to illustrate Gadaffi's long hair – but suddenly the truck hit the splintered casing of a missile, bursting two tyres. 'We need new car. Please get out,' said one of the rebels. What about Gadaffi? 'It is our mistake, he is not here.'

But he was. It is now known that Gadaffi had made Sirte a fortress over the years and stockpiled weapons and ammunition in houses in the city and in the desert outside – where the rebels found some of them.

'Gadaffi knows Nato will hit his bunkers, so he tells his soldiers to empty the bunkers and spread the weapons across the desert so they are safe,' one rebel said. 'It makes life easier for us!'

Details of Gadaffi's weeks in Sirte came from Mansour Daou, one of his top aides, who was caught with him on Thursday but survived thanks to the intervention of Taieb Mohammed Imbais, a rebel brigade leader. Imbais told *Le Figaro*, the French newspaper: 'Daou told me that Gadaffi had sought refuge in Sirte when Tripoli fell, in August.

'He thought he was safe in his tribe. Then when the siege started, it got harder. Gadaffi lived in private homes which had been abandoned. He changed house every day to avoid betrayals and the Nato bombings. He was very discreet. Gadaffi didn't command the battles.

'It was Mutassim who gave the orders. On Wednesday it became untenable. The rebels were very close and Mutassim was hit by a bullet in the foot. He told me he had then taken all the petrol there was left and that they had tried to flee.'

The endgame had come quickly. At the beginning of October, Mutassim's defences were still secure despite suicidal onslaughts by rebel brigades from Misrata, the city between Sirte and Tripoli that took the heaviest pounding from Gadaffi's forces in the early months of the civil war.

From the top of the Sirte hotel, held by rebels, the brave or foolhardy could look out as sniper bullets and rockets whistled all around. The rebels to the east were pinned down. So were rebels to the south. It seemed like a stalemate could last until the end of the year. And still nobody had a clue that Gadaffi was in the city.

It all changed after a Nato bombing assault on 8 October, when the ground did not stop shaking all night. Next morning the rebels pushed forwards expecting the usual fierce resistance. There was none.

In the space of 36 hours rebels surged into the city from the south and east and met at an intersection just south of District Two, a middle-class neighbourhood of spacious houses in the western part of Sirte. District Two was flooded in knee-deep water, perhaps from a bomb or perhaps deliberately. It was to become Sirte's final stand.

For four days the Misratan rebels flattened the area with everything they had, bringing their tanks and heavy guns into the city and blazing away at every building standing between their own positions and the sea.

More and more Gadaffi fighters surrendered, finally conceding the hopelessness of the situation as their city was demolished around them.

Gadaffi, who sometimes styled himself 'king of kings', appears to have spent his final nights in the one-storey home of a loyalist. Hanging on one of the walls inside yesterday was a signed photograph of the dictator in naval uniform. A neighbour said: 'We knew he stayed there. His guards would sleep outside.'

Piles of new army green uniforms littered the floor of one sitting room, along with mattresses for about a dozen men.

Early on Thursday at another house in District Two, Jibril Abu Sharaf, one of the surviving defenders, was preparing breakfast. 'I was cooking for the other guys when all of a sudden they came in and said, "Come on, we're leaving", he told Reuters later while in custody. 'I got in a civilian car and joined the end of the convoy. We tried to escape along the coast road. But we came under heavy fire so we tried another way.'

Nato planes, including RAF Tornados, had spotted the breakout. Colonel Thierry Burkhard, a spokesman for the French defence ministry, takes up the story: 'There was a presence over Sirte. We were notified about a convoy with heavy armament.'

An American Predator drone fired the first missile. 'Then a patrol made up of one Mirage 2000D and one Mirage F1CR attacked the convoy. Both were from the base at La Sude in Crete. I believe they left the base at dawn,' Burkhard said.

'The Mirage 2000D dropped a 250 kilogramme, laser-guided GBU bomb on the convoy. The F1CR monitored the situation. We were not aiming at Gadaffi's vehicle because we didn't even know he was in the convoy. We only found out afterwards that he was there. We don't know whether he was injured by the Nato strikes.'

According to Nato sources, the convoy contained at least 75 vehicles, suggesting it was about half a mile long. It is a mystery how so many had been hidden in District Two, an area only about 1,000 yards by 500, and had survived the rebel shelling.

The huge convoy – with Gadaffi was at its centre – dashed west out of the city at about 8am and tried to break through rebel lines. The Predator strike destroyed 11 vehicles, burning many of the occupants alive. Jibril recalled: 'Then the only thing I saw was dead bodies all around, dust and debris. It went dark.'

The convoy split up and Gadaffi's core group of about 20 vehicles was heading southwest at high speed on the main highway. There are few roads in the area; they were easily spotted and hit by the Mirage's bomb. Gadaffi survived the huge blast with Mansour Daou and Abu-Bakr Yunis Jabr, minister of defence in the old regime, and a handful of others. They appear to have staggered through a line of trees beside the highway and taken refuge in a concrete drainage culvert beneath it.

'I was with Gadaffi and Yunis and about four volunteer soldiers,' Daou said. Wounded in the back by the shell blast, he passed out and did not witness the final scenes of the 42-year dictatorship.

At first. Ahmed Al-Ghazal and his rebel team drove right by. 'We didn't see anyone under the road, so we drove past them,' Ghazal said. 'We only stopped when someone from a sand berm that was next to the culvert started shooting at us.'

Ghazal, a slight 21-year-old who ran a kitchen supply shop in Misrata before the war, was with other members of the Gheran brigade in a 'technical', a pick-up truck with an anti-aircraft gun in the back. They leapt out and – unable to bear down with their heavy gun – fought back with Kalashnikovs. The fighting was suddenly fierce.

One of the enemy fighters dressed in civilian clothes began screaming, 'My leg is broken, I can't help "sayeedi". I can't help the leader.'

Sayeedi is an Arabic word for the respected one. Ghazal and his men thought it must be a senior military officer or one of Gadaffi's regime officials. 'It didn't even occur to us that there would be any Gadaffi there, much less Muammar Gadaffi,' he said.

'Suddenly, Gadaffi was in front of me, half in the tunnel, half out of the tunnel,' Ghazal said. 'I threw away my Kalashnikov and jumped on him. I thought maybe he will disappear or something. I was so shocked I was looking at Gadaffi in person for the first time in my life.'

Omar Shaibani, the 37-year-old businessman turned soldier who leads the Ghiran militia, said that although Gadaffi was heavily armed when his militiamen dragged him out of the culvert, he did not fire a shot despite his calls for Libyans to fight to the death for their leader.

The most striking of his guns was a gold pistol. 'This gold pistol, his private weapon, was in his waistband, fully loaded,' Shaibani said last night. It was inscribed 'Muammar Gadaffi', and on one side had an engraving of his green flag, and in Arabic script the saying, 'The sun never sets on the revolution.'

Shaibani said: 'The fact that Gadaffi had all these weapons, and he didn't shoot means to me that Gadaffi was scared.' He did not know who had killed him: 'Everyone was firing. Our young men were hysterical. I don't know who killed him, but I am not sorry.'

The Libyan peacock, renowned around the world for his colourful and bizarre uniforms, had been transformed into a ragged and bloodied wreck, mumbling incoherently.

The rebels surrounded Gadaffi, and men started slapping him. They were joined by crowds of other rebel fighters, some of them nearly hysterical. Many took out their mobile phones and, as they had done so often in their peaceful lives before this war, began to record what was happening.

This jumbled footage and the confused recollections of those who were present form the raw evidence of what happened next. It is plain that the rebels immediately divided between those who wanted to shoot him on the spot and those who wanted to save him for interrogation.

Shouts of 'Keep him alive! Keep him alive' and 'ya kalb' [you dog!] can be heard through the commotion as Gadaffi is jostled by a throng of men, six or seven holding his arms either side of him.

He has blood on his head and appears to fall to the ground; the men drag him up. Some shout: 'Misrata, Misrata, Allahu akbar [God is greatest], ya kalb!' Gunshots and machinegun fire are heard ringing out in the background.

Even in his confused state, Gadaffi must have realised there was no real likelihood of mercy. One of the rebels put Gadaffi on the bonnet of a yellow Toyota pick-up and started driving it around to show the fighters who they had captured. Gadaffi slid forward, off the bonnet.

A video shows him in a blood-soaked shirt and bloodied face leaning up against it, restrained by fighters. Then he is lying on it in his bloodied khaki uniform, with three men around him holding him down.

They then push him off the bonnet towards another car, as he shouts and struggles against them, waving his arms about and clearly alive. In another video, men make barking noises at him and call him 'shafshoofa' [frizzy-haired one]. Some start pulling the locks of curly black hair, which shows an inch of white at the roots as he has been unable to dye it on the run.

He looks around him confused and disorientated. He wipes his forehead with his hand, looks at his hand and sees blood and extends the bloody palm out to the men surrounding him as if to say: 'Look what you've done to me.' He is wearing his gold wedding ring. A young rebel holding up a heeled black boot with a zip to the camera shouts 'Muammar's boot! His boot! Victory! This is victory!'

Gadaffi himself appears to be saying: 'What is going on? What is going on? What are you doing?' And then he says: 'Haram alay-kum, haram alaykum!' This translates as: 'You should be ashamed of yourselves!' He then adds: 'Don't you know what is haram [forbidden by Islam]?'

In the fourth video that can be deciphered, he is dead. Fighters roll his body over on the pavement. He is naked to the waist with a pool of blood under his head, his arms raised above his head. The body is then paraded through the streets on top of a vehicle surrounded by a large crowd chanting: 'The blood of the martyrs will not go in vain.' What was not clear was how he had been killed.

In Benghazi, the eastern city where the revolt began in February, a young fighter called Sanad Sadek al-Ouraybi was being hailed as a hero yesterday for firing the fatal shot.

Sanad, who said he was in Sirte searching for his missing brother, claimed he was with Misratan rebels when they stumbled on Gadaffi by mistake. He insisted that the colonel was not hauled out of a drainhole but was found walking incognito among a group of women and children.

'I called out his name not believing it could be him,' Sanad said, 'and Gadaffi turned on hearing his name. As he tried to reach for a pistol from his pocket we jumped him and I started slapping and beating him.'

According to Sanad, he managed to get Gadaffi into an ambulance to take him to Benghazi. The Misratan militia intervened, and a firefight broke out for possession of the prisoner. When the Misratans got the upper hand, Sanad said, he shot Gadaffi in the head rather than surrender him alive.

While this account did not ring true to reporters who had investigated Gadaffi's death – not least because there were no women or children in any of the video images of Gadaffi's capture – it illustrates the deadly tensions between eastern and western Libya, and it gives some plausibility to the official Libyan account that Gadaffi died in crossfire during a firefight while being transported in the ambulance.

What seems to have happened, according to another video, is that after Gadaffi had been pulled off the bonnet of the pick-up truck, he was dragged towards a car and then pulled down by his hair.

There are shouts of 'Keep him alive!' and then a man gives out a high-pitched hysterical scream. Gadaffi then goes out of view and gunshots ring out. Some accounts say Gadaffi died in the ambulance. But its driver, Ali Jaghdoun, told Reuters that Gadaffi was dead when he picked him up and drove him to Misrata. 'I didn't try to revive him because he was already dead,' he said.

The dictator's body – and the corpse of his son Mutassim, who was filmed smoking in captivity before apparently being executed – were on show in Misrata yesterday.

In a macabre scene, thousands of people lined up to view the remains of their former leader laid out in a refrigerated room in a market on the outskirts of the city.

The line stretched, several deep, for at least half a mile. Some brought their children.

As evening shadows drew in, two little girls, dressed in their finest dresses and holding their father's hand, skipped as they left.

Gadaffi lay on a single flowered mattress, a plastic sheet under his head where there was a pool of blood. In death, he was still distinctive.

He had clearly shaved on the morning of his flight from Sirte, preserving his strange preference for a moustache, small line of beard under his lower lip.

His face was bent towards the left, covering the bullet hole in his left temple, and his nose had clearly been broken.

His chest was bare, marred by blood smears and holes that might have been bullet wounds; his left side was misshapen with a strange lop-sided swelling.

The scene was surreal. Young men knelt down by his head in the bright light, making the V for victory sign, and smiling, as if he was a big game trophy brought down in the wild.

Somehow, in death he looked smaller, shrunken. His thin shanks and feet stretched below khaki trousers pushed up to just below the knee, their stretch waist bloodied by his wounds.

The fear he had inspired seemed far away from this pale, inert figure.

Many had come to see just that. 'I drove from Tripoli to see him,' said Ahmed al-Nuda. 'I wanted to make sure it was Gadaffi. The man who has made our life hell for 42 years. It is him. Thank you God.'

Libya keeps silence over vampire dictator's grave

MISRATA

30 October 2011

The fighters who ritually buried the dictator in an unmarked grave have sworn to keep the site secret – but are there clues to the whereabouts?

The spectre of Muammar Gadaffi still looms large over the country he terrorised for four decades. Last week a handful of rebels drove into the desert in the dark of the night and lowered his cheap pine coffin into a waist-deep grave they had dug themselves. Then they went silent.

No one would reveal the grave's location. The representatives of Libya's new government had scattered stones to keep wild dogs from digging up his body, but otherwise left unmarked the desolate site in the scrub desert that rolls south of Misrata for hundreds of miles.

Gadaffi's body may have been buried, but Libyans have not yet exorcised the larger-than-life power he wielded and the fear he inspired.

Several of the grave diggers were commanders with whom I had endured missile and mortar fire during the months of Misrata's siege. We had become comrades in the way that the extremes of war create intimate bonds. I had seen their brothers die; they had seen I would not run. They had vowed: 'Anything you need. Anything.'

Last week that changed. 'You were with us in our dark hours,' said Salahdine Badi, the commander of Misrata's katibas, or militias, who was twice wounded in the war. 'I will do anything for you, but I cannot talk about the grave. I cannot betray my country.'

Everyone at the grave, he said, had sworn on the Koran not to reveal its location. Badi explained they did not want supporters to turn it into a shrine or those who reviled Gadaffi to desecrate the site.

Their hushed tones revealed that the reason went far deeper. The way they buried him resonated with ritualistic practice that might suit a vampire. Reports said he was buried at dawn, but everyone there said it was during the early hours of Tuesday, next to Mutassim, his 35-year-old son, and Abu-Bakr Yunis Jabr, 59, his defence chief.

As with all Muslims, Gadaffi's body was washed and wrapped in a white sheet. Then they accompanied him into the desert. 'We each shovelled the dirt ourselves,' said Badi. He could even count the shovels – seven.

Ibrahim Beitelmal, the head of Misrata's military council, who held briefings during the siege in the dark because there was no electricity, also refused to disclose the grave's location. 'Nobody should ever know where we buried him,' he said.

Everyone in Misrata knows everyone else's business and rumours are a favourite pastime. 'My father said it is the first time in memory that Misrata keeps a secret,' said Faruq Ben Ahmeida, 36, a rebel fighter.

At one point a commander considered blindfolding me and taking me to the grave, but then reneged. 'No, the experts will recognise the soil. Maybe in a year, when he is just bones,' he said.

Abdel Rahman Abdel Hamid, the dictator's 43-year-old nephew, now a prisoner, read a Koranic verse over the grave that night while Huneish Nasr, 58, his driver of 30 years, stood quietly. The burns on his bandaged hands had been sustained when Nato missiles ripped through the dictator's convoy as he tried to escape Sirte, his birthplace.

The two men had been forced to keep their heads down during the drive from their cells so they would be unable to identify the location. 'We couldn't see anything,' said Abdel Hamid. 'It was too dark.'

There were sufficient hints, however, that I could narrow down the location to the south of Misrata, in the scrub desert where rebels battled Gadaffi's soldiers.

Libyans have many names for the 'desert' and last week I discovered why when I resolved to follow the clues and try to find the graves.

The desert I wanted was the *hammada*, which translates as 'the stony desert with the red soil and scrubby grass'.

The hammada of Misrata stretches for hundreds of square miles. I consulted a hunter, rented a 4x4 and spent hours travelling over rock, scrub and rolling sand berms, into natural wadis and walking the likeliest locations.

The search yielded tyre tracks that turned out to belong to hunters, stones balanced on top of each other in formations that were obscure markers to all but their builders and beautiful empty vistas. Gazelle and rabbit tracks meandered everywhere; no one moved except for the rare shepherd tending a flock of sheep. The hammada kept the secret of the graves.

The burial was the final indignity for Gadaffi. He died brutalised, stabbed and shot by a mob of blood-crazed rebels he had called 'rats'.

The marks of his sordid death were visible to all as he lay bare-chested in a meat refrigerator on the edge of Misrata. Several onlookers said they had come to see 'that he was really just a man'.

Libya's new government last week began trying to unravel the secrets taken to the grave by Gadaffi, who gave almost all his orders verbally, leaving behind few documents. The interrogators' main goal is to find the billions that he stole from the country he treated 'like a family farm', said one official.

Efforts this week will focus on interrogating members of Gadaffi's inner circle who had been caught when fleeing Sirte, their last stand.

Officials said Abdel Hamid was 'still acting like a Gadaffi' despite having attended his uncle's funeral.

'He doesn't seem to realise the seriousness of his situation,' said Beitelmal, who is questioning him.

'He is a spoilt young man,' said Beitelmal, who defected from Gadaffi's forces to join the rebels and is disdainful that Abdel Hamid, a captain, had no military training but gained his rank because of his uncle. 'He asks for grape juice or milk. He wants his "top-of-the-line Audi" back. Tonight he asked me for the key to his cell!'

Abdel Hamid, when interviewed in the military headquarters, was sallow but healthy and complained about his prison clothes – a navy blue uniform from the local electric company. He said he believed his uncle 'went down fighting to the last'.

Claiming he was against the war, he spoke of Gadaffi admiringly but said he had no idea where the money went, despite living far beyond the means of an army officer.

The death of the dictator triggered rapid changes last week. Nato is to end its seven-month mission tomorrow. At its height, Nato fielded more than 200 aircraft over Libya and some 20 ships off the coast.

Their reach was devastating. Britain flew more than 3,000 out of 26,000 sorties; nearly 6,000 targets were bombed, including 1,600 military facilities, bases and bunkers. By this weekend British forces were already heading home.

The most dramatic immediate result was the 'declaration of liberation', which began a week of celebrations and a political process to lead to elections in 20 months.

Politicians in the national transitional council are in negotiations over the new government. It will be formed within two weeks and will move to Tripoli from Benghazi, where the rebellion began on 17 February.

While it begins to look to its future, the nascent country is still nervous about threats from beyond its borders. Saif al-Islam Gadaffi, the dictator's son who was once seen as a reformer but who adopted his father's fight-to-the-death attitude, is still at large. He was said to be trying to negotiate a surrender to the International Criminal Court, the war crimes tribunal in the Hague.

His lawyer, reached in Algeria by *The Sunday Times*, said he believed he would win his case and wanted a guarantee that if he was acquitted of charges of killing unarmed protesters he would be freed and not deported to Libya. 'He believes he is innocent and has been organising his case for months,' the lawyer said, asking to remain anonymous.

The former rebels fear his supporters could still wreak havoc. Last week Badi said he planned to head south with his men to defend the southern border. 'We have to organise safety for the country,' he said.

Syria

'Bombs fell like rain. You could only pray'

5 February 2012

Marie Colvin, Peter Kellier and Annasofie Flamand in Beirut;
Hugh Macleod and Sara Hashash

As the Syrian opposition steps up its attacks on the regime, a stand-off in the city of Homs claims more than 200 lives.

The fighting in Syria spiralled yesterday into the worst violence since protesters began their uprising against the regime of President Bashar al-Assad almost a year ago. More than 200 men, women and children were killed in Homs, a northern city that has become the centre of the opposition, rebel sources said.

Wounded civilians sprawled bleeding in a makeshift clinic at a mosque in the Khalidiya district, which appeared to have borne the brunt of mortars and tank shells fired by government forces.

Independent journalists have been banned from the area but desperate inhabitants got the information out in brief, fearful telephone calls. 'We have just buried 50 martyrs,' said Abu Jihad, an opposition activist. 'We've had to build a new graveyard for them because the old one was full.'

He said the residents had named the new burial site Maqebrat Al-Shohadaa, or 'graveyard of the martyrs'.

The attack on Homs came at a critical moment, hours before the United Nations security council met in New York to consider endorsing Arab League demands for Assad to step down and transfer power to his vice-president. Thirteen countries including Britain and the United States supported the resolution but it was vetoed by Russia and China.

An anti-government activist from Homs who asked to be identified only as Muhammad gave a graphic account of the build-up to the onslaught.

He said an armed opposition group, which he thought was a unit of the rebels' Free Syrian Army (FSA), attacked a checkpoint in Khalidiya and kidnapped 17 soldiers. At roughly the same time, he said, another armed opposition group struck at a Syrian air force security base in the area. Shortly after that, the army responded by attacking the opposition in Khalidiya.

'The sudden escalation was on both sides,' he said. 'There were victims on both sides, but the bombing was indiscriminate.'

Separate accounts spoke of four apartment blocks being largely destroyed in the bombardment and dozens of bodies being pulled from the rubble.

Residents of Homs described a night of terror. 'It was like a machinegun shooting randomly, only much, much heavier,' said Omar Shakir. 'The bombs fell like rain. You didn't know where they would fall. You could only pray.'

Shakir said his best friend, Madher Tayyara, 23, a civil engineering student and volunteer medic, had died in his home after being hit by shrapnel in his chest and head.

Several hospitals treating the dead and dying were raided by security forces, according to activists' reports gathered by Avaaz, a human rights group, which described the humanitarian situation as 'appalling'.

Small field hospitals set up to treat injured protesters were overwhelmed with hundreds of injured, according to activists. They accused security forces of preventing medical supplies from reaching the wounded and warned that many of up to 1,000 injured would die because there was no way to treat them.

Another witness, Waleed Fares, said that when the shelling began at around 10pm on Friday most residents stayed indoors. Then an enormous crashing sound prompted many to run outside where they saw the first two apartment blocks collapse.

Two further buildings, each with around 30 flats, had subsequently been devastated, with others partially destroyed.

As he tried to dig out the bodies of the dead and injured, Fares heard more shells exploding from the rooftops as the cry of 'God is great' rang out from minarets.

'There were children crying, women screaming, standing in their nightclothes because they had not had time to dress,' said Fares. 'We took the bodies and the injured to a nearby park. I counted around 40 bodies from the building collapse. The injuries were appalling: people missing limbs, people crushed so badly you couldn't recognise them, people pierced by metal.'

According to Fares, three bombs fell on the park, killing around 30 people, including his friend Omar Zarour, who left his home to help rescue those trapped.

Government sources said the army had reacted strongly to the kidnapping of its soldiers, in part because it has been losing increasing numbers of young men who do not want to fight their own people.

Residents described intolerable conditions in Homs. 'We're building a hospital in one of the houses but there's little medicine,' said one. 'We're afraid the army will come back.'

A 19-year-old boy who has spoken to *The Sunday Times* from Khalidiya over the past few weeks said residents had been living with little food, and heating oil had become prohibitively expensive.

'For much of the day, the electricity is cut,' he said. 'People are so poor that burglars broke into the local school and stole the windows.'

Sources in Homs and other predominantly Sunni cities warned that the regime appeared to be arming the minority Alawite community, to which the Assad family belongs.

There are growing fears of a civil war, with the FSA not only controlling parts of Homs, but also fighting in Damascus, the capital.

An FSA spokesman said it had lost 27 soldiers in the past four days and claimed the death toll from the shelling in Homs exceeded 350.

'We capture soldiers to show how weak the regime is,' said Abu Ali, an FSA commander. 'Their soldiers fight for one person: Bashar.'

A vet is only hope for Syrian wounded

HOMS

19 February 2012

Wounded civilians arriving at a makeshift clinic in the Syrian city of Homs are relying on a vet to save their lives because there is no doctor to treat them.

I found the vet struggling to treat patients who had been injured by shelling and sniper fire in the district of Baba Amr, a besieged enclave where 28,000 people are trapped by relentless bombardment. He was using his knowledge of sheep anatomy to treat life-threatening wounds in the sitting room of a house.

One of his patients, a 32-year-old mobile phone repairman named Mohammed Mohammed, had been shot in the back by a sniper. The bullet had come to rest in his chest. Fear filled Mohammed's eyes as the vet stuck a tube into his chest to siphon off blood and relieve pressure on his heart.

Another patient, Zaccharia Mutlaq, a carpenter aged 26, had a thigh wound and a broken foot from shell fire. The vet said his priority was to keep the man's wounds clean.

Neither the vet nor his location can be identified. Three so-called field clinics in Baba Amr, an opposition stronghold, have been destroyed by the Syrian army since the siege began 15 days ago.

Mohammed and Mutlaq were injured after going into a house that had exploded to find a mother decapitated, a father ripped apart by shrapnel and the couple's two daughters dead or dying.

The men's plight reflects the desperation of the civilians cowering in basements or scurrying from house to house to avoid shelling by the forces of President Bashar al-Assad as troops build up around Homs for a possible ground offensive.

Final dispatch from Homs, the battered city

19 February 2012

Marie Colvin was the only British journalist reporting from inside the besieged Syrian enclave of Baba Amr. This is her final report.

SYRIA, 2012

They call it the widows' basement. Crammed amid makeshift beds and scattered belongings are frightened women and children trapped in the horror of Homs, the Syrian city shaken by two weeks of relentless bombardment.

Among the 300 huddling in this wood factory cellar in the besieged district of Baba Amr is 20-year-old Noor, who lost her husband and her home to the shells and rockets.

'Our house was hit by a rocket so 17 of us were staying in one room,' she recalls as Mimi, her three-year-old daughter, and Mohamed, her five-year-old son, cling to her abaya.

'We had had nothing but sugar and water for two days and my husband went to try to find food.' It was the last time she saw Maziad, 30, who had worked in a mobile phone repair shop. 'He was torn to pieces by a mortar shell.'

For Noor, it was a double tragedy. Adnan, her 27-year-old brother, was killed at Maziad's side.

Everyone in the cellar has a similar story of hardship or death. The refuge was chosen because it is one of the few basements in Baba Amr. Foam mattresses are piled against the walls and the children have not seen the light of day since the siege began on 4 February. Most families fled their homes with only the clothes on their backs.

The city is running perilously short of supplies and the only food here is rice, tea and some tins of tuna delivered by a local sheikh who looted them from a bombed-out supermarket.

A baby born in the basement last week looked as shellshocked as her mother, Fatima, 19, who fled there when her family's single-storey house was obliterated. 'We survived by a miracle,' she whispers. Fatima is so traumatised that she cannot breast-feed, so the baby has been fed only sugar and water; there is no formula milk.

Fatima may or may not be a widow. Her husband, a shepherd, was in the countryside when the siege started with a ferocious barrage and she has heard no word of him since.

The widows' basement reflects the ordeal of 28,000 men, women and children clinging to existence in Baba Amr, a district of low concrete-block homes surrounded on all sides by Syrian forces. The army is launching Katyusha rockets, mortar shells and tank rounds at random.

Snipers on the rooftops of al-Ba'ath University and other high buildings surrounding Baba Amr shoot any civilian who comes into their sights. Residents were felled in droves in the first days of the siege but have now learnt where the snipers are and run across junctions where they know they can be seen. Few cars are left on the streets.

Almost every building is pock-marked after tank rounds punched through concrete walls or rockets blasted gaping holes in upper floors. The building I was staying in lost its upper floor to a rocket last Wednesday. On some streets whole buildings have collapsed – all there is to see are shredded clothes, broken pots and the shattered furniture of families destroyed.

It is a city of the cold and hungry, echoing to exploding shells and bursts of gunfire. There are no telephones and the electricity has been cut off. Few homes have diesel for the tin stoves they rely on for heat in the coldest winter that anyone can remember. Freezing rain fills potholes and snow drifts in through windows empty of glass. No shops are open, so families are sharing what they have with relatives and neighbours. Many of the dead and injured are those who risked foraging for food.

Fearing the snipers' merciless eyes, families resorted last week to throwing bread across rooftops, or breaking through communal walls to pass unseen.

The Syrians have dug a huge trench around most of the district, and let virtually nobody in or out. The army is pursuing a brutal campaign to quell the resistance of Homs, Hama and other cities that have risen up against Bashar al-Assad, the Syrian president, whose family has been in power for 42 years.

In Baba Amr, the Free Syrian Army (FSA), the armed face of opposition to Assad, have virtually unanimous support from civilians who see them as their defenders. It is an unequal battle: the tanks and heavy weaponry of Assad's troops against the Kalashnikovs of the FSA.

About 5,000 Syrian soldiers are believed to be on the outskirts of Baba Amr, and the FSA received reports yesterday that they were preparing a ground assault. The residents dread the outcome.

'We live in fear the FSA will leave the city,' said Hamida, 43, hiding with her children and her sister's family in an empty ground-floor apartment after their house was bombed. 'There will be a massacre.'

On the lips of everyone was the question: 'Why have we been abandoned by the world?'

Ban Ki-moon, the secretary-general of the United Nations, said last week: 'We see neighbourhoods shelled indiscriminately, hospitals used as torture centres, children as young as 10 years old killed and abused. We see almost certainly crimes against humanity.' Yet the international community has not come to the aid of the innocent caught in this hell.

Abdel Majid, 20, who was helping to rescue the wounded from bombed buildings, made a simple plea. 'Please tell the world they must help us,' he said, shaking, with haunted eyes. 'Just stop the bombing. Please, just stop the shelling.'

The journey across the countryside from the Lebanese border to Homs would be idyllic in better times. The villages are nondescript clusters of concrete buildings on dirt tracks but the lanes are lined with cypresses and poplar trees and wind through orchards of apricot and apple trees.

These days, however, there is an edge of fear on any journey through this area. Most of this land is essentially what its residents call 'Syria hurra', or free Syria, patrolled by the FSA.

Nevertheless, Assad's army has checkpoints on the main roads and troops stationed in schools, hospitals and factories. They are heavily armed and backed by tanks and artillery.

So a drive to Homs is a bone-rattling struggle down dirt roads, criss-crossing fields. Men cluster by fires at unofficial FSA check-points, eyeing any vehicle suspiciously. As night falls, flashlights waved by unseen figures signal that the way ahead is clear.

Each travelling FSA car has a local shepherd or farmer aboard to help navigate the countryside; the Syrian army may have the power, but the locals know every track of their fields.

I entered Homs on a smugglers' route, which I promised not to reveal, climbing over walls in the dark and slipping into muddy trenches. Arriving in the darkened city in the early hours, I was met by a welcoming party keen for foreign journalists to reveal the city's plight to the world. So desperate were they that they bundled me into an open truck and drove at speed with the headlights on, everyone standing in the back shouting 'Allahu akbar' – God is the greatest. Inevitably, the Syrian army opened fire.

When everyone had calmed down I was driven in a small car, its lights off, along dark empty streets, the danger palpable. As we passed an open stretch of road, a Syrian army unit fired on the car again with machineguns and launched a rocket-propelled grenade. We sped into a row of abandoned buildings for cover.

The scale of human tragedy in the city is immense. The inhabitants are living in terror. Almost every family seems to have suffered the death or injury of a loved one.

Khaled Abu Salah, an activist who took part in the first demonstrations against Assad in Homs last March, sat on the floor of an office, his hand broken and bandages covering shrapnel wounds to his leg and shoulder.

A 25-year-old university student, who risked his life filming videos of the slaughter of Baba Amr residents, he narrowly escaped when he tried to get two men wounded by mortar fire to a make-shift clinic.

He and three friends had just taken the wounded to the clinic, which was staffed by a doctor and a dentist, and stepped away from the door when 'a shell landed right at the entrance', he recalled last week.

'My three friends died immediately.' The two men they had helped were also killed.

Abu Ammar, 48, a taxi driver, went out to look for bread at 8am one day last week. He, his wife and their adopted daughter had taken refuge with two elderly sisters after their home was hit by shells.

'When I returned the house was obliterated,' he said, looking at all that remained of the one-storey building. Only a few pieces of wall still stood. In the ruins a woman's red blouse was visible; bottles of home-made pickled vegetables were somehow unscathed. 'Dr Ali', a dentist working as a doctor, said one of the women from the house had arrived at the clinic alive, but both legs had been amputated and she died.

The clinic is merely a first-floor apartment donated by the kindly owner. It still has out-of-place domestic touches: plasma pouches hang from a wooden coat hanger and above the patients a colourful children's mobile hangs from the ceiling.

The shelling last Friday was the most intense yet and the wounded were rushed to the clinic in the backs of cars by family members.

Ali the dentist was cutting the clothes off 24-year-old Ahmed al-Irini on one of the clinic's two operating tables. Shrapnel had gashed huge bloody chunks out of Irini's thighs. Blood poured out as Ali used tweezers to draw a piece of metal from beneath his left eye.

Irini's legs spasmed and he died on the table. His brother-in-law, who had brought him in, began weeping. 'We were playing cards when a missile hit our house,' he said through his tears. Irini was taken out to the makeshift mortuary in a former back bedroom, naked but for a black plastic bag covering his genitals.

There was no let-up. Khaled Abu Kamali died before the doctor could get his clothes off. He had been hit by shrapnel in the chest while at home.

Salah, 26, was peppered with shrapnel in his chest and the left of his back. There was no anaesthetic, but he talked as Ali inserted a metal pipe into his back to release the pressure of the blood building up in his chest.

Helping tend the wounded was Um Ammar, a 45-year-old mother of seven, who had offered to be a nurse after a neighbour's house was shelled. She wore filthy plastic gloves and was crying. 'I'm obliged to endure this, because all children brought here are my children,' she said. 'But it is so hard.'

Akhmed Mohammed, a military doctor who defected from Assad's army, shouted: 'Where are the human rights? Do we have none? Where are the United Nations?'

There were only two beds in the clinic for convalescing. One was taken by Akhmed Khaled, who had been injured, he said, when a shell hit a mosque as he was about to leave prayers. His right testicle had had to be removed with only paracetamol to dull the pain.

He denounced the Assad regime's claim that the rebels were Islamic extremists and said: 'We ask all people who believe in God – Christians, Jews, Muslims to help us!'

If the injured try to flee Baba Amr, they first have to be carried on foot. Then they are transferred to motorbikes and the lucky ones are smuggled to safety. The worst injured do not make it.

Though Syrian officials prohibit anyone from leaving, some escapees manage to bribe their way out. I met refugees in villages around Homs. Newlywed Miriam, 32, said she and her husband had decided to leave when they heard that three families had been killed and the women raped by the Shabiha militia, a brutal force led by Assad's younger brother, Maher.

'We were practically walking on body parts as we walked under shelling overhead,' she said. Somehow they made it unscathed. She had given an official her wedding ring in order to be smuggled out to safety.

Abdul Majid, a computer science student at university, was still shaking hours after arriving in a village outside Homs. He had stayed behind alone in Baba Amr. 'I had to help the old people because only the young can get out,' said Majid, 20, wearing a leather jacket and jeans. He left when his entire street fled after every house was hit.

'I went to an army checkpoint that I was told was not too bad. I gave them a packet of cigarettes, two bags of tea and 500 Syrian pounds. They told me to run.'

Blasts of Kalashnikov fire rang out above his head until he reached the tree line. He said the soldiers were only pretending to try to shoot him to protect themselves, but his haunted eyes showed he was not entirely sure.

If the Syrian military rolls into Baba Amr, the FSA will have little chance against its tanks, superior weaponry and numbers. They will, however, fight ferociously to defend their families because they know a massacre is likely to follow any failure, if the past actions of the Assad regime are anything to go by.

The FSA partly relies on defections from Assad's army because it does not accept civilians into its ranks, though they perform roles such as monitoring troop movements and transporting supplies. But it has become harder for soldiers to defect in the past month.

Abu Sayeed, 46, a major-general who defected six months ago, said every Syrian military unit was now assigned a member of the Mukhabarat, the feared intelligence service, who have orders to execute any soldier refusing an order to shoot or who tries to defect.

The army, like the country, may well be about to divide along sectarian lines. Most of the officers are members of the Alawite sect, the minority Shi'ite clan to which the Assad family belongs, while foot soldiers are Sunni.

The coming test for the army will be if its ranks hold if ordered to kill increasing numbers of their brethren.

The swathe of the country that stretches east from the Lebanon border and includes Homs is Sunni; in the villages there they say that officers ordering attacks are Alawites fighting for the Assad family, not their country.

The morale of Assad's army, despite its superiority, is said to be low as it is poorly paid and supplied, although this information comes mostly from defectors. 'The first thing we did when we attacked the house was race to the refrigerator,' said a defector.

Thousands of soldiers would be needed to retake the southern countryside. Hafez al-Assad, Bashar's father and former president, crushed his problems with Islamic fundamentalists in 1982 by shelling the city of Hama into ruins and killing at least 10,000 men, women and children. So far his son appears to have calculated that a similar act would be a step too far for his remaining allies of Russia, China and Iran.

For now it is a violent and deadly standoff. The FSA is not about to win and its supplies of ammunition are dwindling.

The only real hope of success for Assad's opponents is if the international community comes to their aid, as Nato did against Muammar Gadaffi in Libya. So far this seems unlikely to happen in Syria.

Observers see a negotiated solution as perhaps a long shot, but the best way out of this impasse. Though neither side appears ready to negotiate, there are serious efforts behind the scenes to persuade Russia to pull Assad into talks.

As international diplomats dither, the desperation in Baba Amr grows. The despair was expressed by Hamida, 30, hiding in a downstairs flat with her sister and their 13 children after two missiles hit their home. Three little girls, aged 16 months to six years, sleep on one thin, torn mattress on the floor; three others share a second. Ahmed, 16, her sister's eldest child, was killed by a missile when he went to try to find bread.

'The kids are screaming all the time,' Hamida said. 'I feel so helpless.' She began weeping. 'We feel so abandoned. They've given Bashar al-Assad the green light to kill us.'

LOYALTIES OF 'DESERT ROSE' TESTED

Asma, the British-born wife of President Bashar al-Assad, may well be feeling a sense of divided loyalty as the violence continues in the Syrian city of Homs. Her family are from the area, which has been a focal point for many of the recent protests against her husband's regime and the Syrian army's brutal response.

Despite growing up in Acton, west London, Asma visited her family's home in Homs every year throughout her childhood. She is also a Sunni Muslim, unlike her husband, who comes from the country's minority Shi'ite community.

Asma, 36, has been criticised for displaying an 'ostrich attitude', keeping a low profile as the conflict has intensified. She has refused to comment on the way her husband's regime has used tanks and other lethal means to crush protesters. In an email sent earlier this month, her office merely said: 'The first lady's very busy agenda is still focused on supporting the various charities she has long been involved with as well as rural development and supporting the President as needed.'

The daughter of a consultant cardiologist and a retired diplomat, Asma was born in London. She attended a Church of England state school in Acton and gained a BSc in computer science and a diploma in French literature from King's College London.

She went on to work for Deutsche Bank and married Assad in Syria in 2000. Now a mother of three, she was once described by *Vogue* as a 'rose in the desert'. In Homs, the beleaguered people may now take a different view.

MARIE COLVIN:
THE LAST ASSIGNMENT

26 February 2012

Jon Swain

She braved the dangers of Syria to tell the truth about its horrors. Jon Swain reveals the story of how his friend and colleague paid the ultimate price.

Inside the makeshift 'media centre' in Baba Amr, the journalists had retreated to the ground floor. It was an ordinary building, chosen because the narrow streets and surrounding structures offered some protection from the rockets and shells.

The top floor had been hit by the Syrian forces besieging the district, part of the city of Homs, but the others had largely escaped – so far.

On the ground floor Marie Colvin was asleep in a room on her own last Wednesday morning when the lethal rain of explosives resumed. An American who had worked as a foreign correspondent for *The Sunday Times* for 25 years, Marie was used to war zones and was expert in the ways of the Middle East.

The streets were littered with rubble, many houses wrecked, nowhere was safe. Yet the media centre was her temporary home and, true to local custom, Marie had left her shoes in the hall.

It was a gesture that would cost her life.

Also in the building were Paul Conroy, a *Sunday Times* photographer; Javier Espinosa, a Spanish journalist; Edith Bouvier and William Daniels, a French couple; and Rémi Ochlik, an award-winning French photographer. They were in the care of seven Syrian activists.

'Two rockets hit near the house,' said Abu Haneen, one of the activists reached last week. 'Then a third.' The explosion ripped through an upper room. Part of the floor caved in, crashing onto the journalists below. 'Dust was everywhere. Everyone was terrified.'

Believing the building was being targeted and more rockets were likely, Haneen shouted at the others to get out. Grabbing their belongings, the journalists gathered in the main room trying to formulate a plan.

It was the safest part of the building, towards the front side that had not been hit before. Earlier damage to the media centre had come from another direction, striking the back. This time the Syrians had changed their angle of fire.

Marie and the others knew they had to get to the safety of another building. But first she needed her shoes. She made a dash for the entrance hall. At that moment Hussein, another of the activists, heard a distant 'puff' – the sound of a rocket leaving its launcher.

It was early this month that Marie decided she had to go to Syria. The uprising against President Bashar Assad's regime was gathering force and the backlash was becoming more violent. The Syrian government was trying to hide its brutality by keeping journalists out. Marie felt the truth needed to be told.

When the Syrians obfuscated over a visa, she flew to Beirut, the capital of Lebanon, on 7 February, planning to find her own way across the border. She stayed one night at Le Bristol, but moved to the Gefinor Rotana hotel, which was more to her taste and where other contacts were based. Even as she prepared for the horrors of Homs, Marie, whose life flitted between combat kit and cocktail dresses, had certain standards.

In an email on Friday 10 February, she explained her hopes and motives to Sara Hashash, a friend and young journalist in Cairo. 'The overall picture I have been told about is that Homs is ringed by the army and tanks, and the army is stopping anyone from entering and leaving. I may have found a way in …

'The people inside, and the surrounding villages, fear they are about to be overrun … So, no pressure then.' She wanted to help before it was too late.

Other journalists had previously sneaked in to Syria across the border with Lebanon, but Marie had identified the area that seemed hardest hit as Assad's crackdown intensified. In an email the following day to Sean Ryan, foreign editor of *The Sunday Times*, she outlined the situation in Homs: 'Heavy shelling again … Trying to get more detail, seems it is mostly in Baba Amr and Ishaat neighbourhoods, the main strongholds of the FSA [Free Syrian Army]'.

Although parts of Syria are largely hostile to Assad, his forces still have checkpoints everywhere. Getting in would require the help of Syrian activists opposed to Assad.

Marie's years of covering the Middle East had brought her numerous contacts in the region, from high-ranking politicians to well connected fixers. The latter were what she needed now. Later that afternoon she sent another email: 'I am meeting Syrian "transporter" (read smuggler) tonight. The fixer came earlier today, and reading between the lines, it increasingly looks like tonight's meeting will not be actual transport but a discussion of logistics, inspection of gear (ie no flak jackets or helmets, can you fit three on a motorbike, yes, if it is that or walk).'

Her plans delayed, she had time to catch up with old friends in the field and swap the latest local intel. In Beirut she dined with with Neil MacFarquhar of *The New York Times*, revealing her concerns about the looming trip across the border. 'I cannot remember any story where the security situation was potentially this bad, except maybe Chechnya,' she told him.

She dined, too, with Lindsey Hilsum, international editor of Channel 4. Last week Hilsum recalled: 'I told Marie that I would

not sneak across the border into Homs because it was too dangerous. She said she was going to have a go anyway. She felt it was
important. "Anyway, it's what we do," she said.'

Days later Marie slipped over the border and was guided by
activists through back roads and fields into Homs. It was dark and
dangerous, cold and wet; the final leg of her journey into the
besieged neighbourhood of Baba Amr she promised to keep secret
to protect the smugglers.

Although she knew certain types of communication were risky,
late on Thursday 16 February, she contacted Ryan: 'This is a secure
line so I am taking advantage to send you a quick message to say I
have arrived safely at the heart of Baba Amr. The journey was
eventful to say the least. Pretty much every kind of danger, cold,
wet and muddy, but we made it! We are in what seems to be the
one place in the city that has electricity. There is a lot of shelling,
and snipers during the day.'

Conroy, a photographer who had worked extensively with Marie
in Libya last year, had also been smuggled in.

The only way to get communications out was via satellite. Marie
had decided to use a Thuraya satphone as little as possible because
its calls could easily be intercepted and its location identified.
Instead, she was mainly sending messages via Skype, which is
harder to track, on another system.

To do so, however, she was making use of equipment at the
makeshift media centre set up in Baba Amr where the activists had
been uploading videos to the internet. The centre had already
come under fire and internet security, Marie suspected, 'was out
the window'. Whether the Syrians were already targeting the site
deliberately or not, it was inevitably at risk as Assad's troops
bombarded the district.

Early on Friday 17 February, Marie sent another message to Ryan:
'Cupla [sic] technical things. Forget that number I sent you, it was
knocked out when the top floor of building I am in was hit yesterday.'

The top floor was badly damaged, but the activists kept operating from the other two. Marie continued: 'Heavy shelling this

morning. I counted 45 shells in 7 minutes nearby. When it lets up I will try to get out to the field clinic.'

That day she braved the snipers to interview locals huddled in houses and basements and to visit a makeshift clinic treating the wounded. The scenes she witnessed were grim.

In an email to a young friend, Lucy Fisher, she admitted her fears, writing: 'I did have a few moments when I thought, What am I doing?' Then she added: 'Story incredibly important though. Mx.'

That night she was smuggled out of Baba Amr and the next day, from a safer location, she filed a searing account of what she had seen. It appeared across two pages of *The Sunday Times* last weekend and could leave no one in any doubt of the indiscriminate violence being meted out by the Syrian army.

Marie, however, was never one to give up on a story. Last Sunday she spoke to Ryan and they discussed her next move. Should she go to another area, he asked. Hama, he suggested, another city about 30 miles north. Marie thought Baba Amr remained the epicentre. The residents were terrified they would be slaughtered if the Syrian army forced its way in.

Then last Tuesday another email dropped into Ryan's inbox. 'I am in Baba Amr, the shelling started at 6.30am.' She had gone back.

For all Marie's glamour and impressive connections, she remained down to earth, a defender of the oppressed and the wronged. The next part of her message to Ryan made clear why she was risking her life by returning to Baba Amr.

'It is sickening that the Syrian regime is allowed to keep doing this,' she wrote. 'There was a shocking scene at the apartment clinic today. A baby boy lay on a head scarf, naked, his little tummy heaving as he tried to breathe. The doctor said "we can do nothing for him". He had been hit by shrapnel in his left side. They had to just let him die as his mother wept.'

She knew that in a voraciously competitive media there was a risk that she might be regarded as repeating her earlier report.

Determined that the world should not ignore Syria, she added: 'I feel strongly that we have to include these stories of the suffering of civilians to get the point across.'

Supplies of water and electricity were short. The shelling was wreaking havoc. Two cars driven by activists had been hit that day, she had emailed, one destroyed.

Growing increasingly concerned for her safety, Ryan responded: 'I'm alarmed to read what happened to the two cars ... the first [question] is whether it's safe to move at all.'

The three of them, Marie, Conroy and Ryan, discussed the situation over Skype. Marie wanted to stay, arguing that it was an important story and she was the only British newspaper journalist there to tell it.

Shortly afterwards Conroy, unknown to Marie, sent a further email to Ryan, expressing his reservations. 'The situation here is extreme,' wrote Conroy, a former soldier who had served in the Royal Artillery. 'The shelling is only getting worse and expect it to continue ... I suspect that Marie's high profile due to this week's material in paper and TV interviews also compromises our safety.'

He added: 'As I am sure you are aware Marie can be tricky to convince once she has the bit between her teeth.'

Ryan responded with an email sent to both of them. They should all speak in the morning about getting out of Baba Amr at the first opportunity, he said.

Instead, Marie had a message to get out first, a message for the world about the truth of Baba Amr. In links to the BBC, Channel 4 News and to CNN, the US news network, she described the misery she was witnessing. She told the CNN presenter Anderson Cooper how she had watched the baby die. 'It is a complete and utter lie they're only going after terrorists. The Syrian army is simply shelling a city of cold, starving civilians,' she said.

David Remnick, editor of *The New Yorker*, saw her CNN broadcast and noted the next day: 'There was cool but profound rage in her voice.'

After her report in *The Sunday Times* a couple of days earlier, Marie's broadcasts rammed home the point: atrocities were being committed. Assad and his generals could no longer conceal the horrors of their three-week assault on Baba Amr.

A Facebook group of fellow journalists sent Marie a message applauding her courage for being in Homs. One of them thought she had already left the battered city and expressed relief that she was safe.

'I think the reports of my survival may be exaggerated,' Colvin responded. 'I'm in Baba Amr. Sickening, trying to understand how the world can stand by and I should be hardened by now.'

She told *The Sunday Times* that she wanted to stay one more day, saying in an email to Ryan sent at 10.36pm on Tuesday that she wanted to go back to the clinic the following morning. 'We would stay as long as possible; once inside we are pretty safe,' she said.

Her message included a wry afterthought: 'I have spent tonight gathering stories from some FSA guys from the front. Everyone I meet invites me to the front, what is it with me?'

Trouble and Marie had often gone together, but this time she had decided there was no point risking a visit to the front line: 'It is a line of destroyed buildings. I don't see the point in going, nor Paul, especially after the discussions you and I had [about the risk].'

Ryan messaged back: 'But I still think you should be ready to leave Wednesday night if conditions deteriorate and a ground offensive is coming.'

One more day and they would be out. That was the plan.

All the journalists were sleeping when, early the next morning, the shelling erupted again. After the broadcasts had Assad ordered the troublesome critics silenced? It was clear foreign journalists had got into Baba Amr – and the Syrians are known to be able to locate satellite transmissions. The means to target the journalists were there, but no one can be sure whether they were used.

For the first time the Syrian forces started firing at the media centre from a new direction. As explosions shook the building and the ceiling fell in, the journalists gathered their belongings.

Marie was not the only one who had left shoes in the hall. Espinosa, 47, a reporter with the Spanish daily *El Mundo*, grabbed his and raced back inside, crouching in a corridor on the far side of the living room wall with Daniels.

As Marie ran to the entrance to get her footwear, another rocket landed at the front of the building, a few yards away. The blast killed her and Ochlik instantly, rubble falling on their bodies in the hallway.

Espinosa and Daniels, sheltered by a wall inside, escaped almost unscathed. Conroy and Bouvier, in the living room near the hall, were hit by the blast and shrapnel.

Bouvier was the most seriously wounded, with multiple fractures to her leg. Conroy tried to stanch blood pouring from his leg. An activist tried to help him up. 'No, leave me here. Save yourself,' Conroy replied.

'They are words I will never forget,' the activist said later.

Espinosa helped up a wounded activist and fled the house through a haze of dust and smoke. Such was the chaos and confusion that he unwittingly stepped on the bodies as he went.

'This for me was the most horrible thing. I stepped on their bodies. I didn't know it was them,' he said.

As Williams stepped over them to leave, he slapped Ochlik's face to see if he was alive. There was no response and he moved on.

The journalists and activists struggled into a house opposite the media centre and the shelling continued. They managed, with the help of a car, to get the wounded to a field clinic.

For several hours no one dared to recover the bodies of the dead. Later, when the bombardment and gunfire eased, two of the activists ran back into the media centre where Marie and Ochlik lay and wrapped them in a shroud.

As soon as the deaths were confirmed, tributes poured in from politicians, friends and colleagues around the world. In Britain,

David Cameron said: 'This is a desperately sad reminder of the risks that journalists take to inform the world of what is happening and the dreadful events in Syria.'

In France, President Nicolas Sarkozy said the deaths of Colvin and Ochlik amounted to 'murder'. He urged that those responsible be found and held accountable.

For Peter Bouckaert, the emergencies director of Human Rights Watch, the killing of the journalists was a crime whether or not they had been deliberately targeted. 'There are two possibilities,' he said. 'Either it was a targeted attack on the building and it was a crime, or the journalists were the victims of the same kind of criminal attacks that have killed hundreds in Homs, which is also a crime.'

On Wednesday evening friends and journalists who had worked with Marie gathered at the Frontline club in London of which she was a founder member. There were tears but also much laughter as they celebrated her extraordinary life and listened to Jon Snow pay a closing tribute on Channel 4 News. 'She was a one-off and one of the most courageous of our age,' Snow said.

From New York, Marie's mother, Rosemarie, said: 'She was totally, totally committed to what she did and the importance of telling the story and writing it and getting it out to the world. That was her life.'

For Conroy and the other survivors the ordeal continued. Trapped inside Baba Amr, they were patched up by the activists as best they could. Bouvier needed urgent specialist treatment; Conroy, although suffering three large wounds to his leg, appeared calm in a video he posted to the internet, saying that 'any assistance would be welcome'.

Activists from a few miles away set out to smuggle medical supplies to them by crossing through an area controlled by the Syrian army. They never arrived. A search party later found seven of them shot dead, their hands tied behind their backs. Medical supplies were strewn in the street around them. There was no trace of two other members of the team, one a foreign paramedic.

When one opportunity for the walking wounded to escape did arise, Conroy refused to go. He did not wish to leave behind Bouvier or Marie's body.

From London to Beirut and Damascus, desperate talks went on to try to secure a ceasefire or any means of allowing in rescuers and medical help. When members of the Red Crescent aid service finally made their way to the wounded on Friday, Conroy again refused to accompany them, apparently fearing a trap and that he might be handed over to the forces of Assad.

Attempts to bring out the wounded and the bodies continued yesterday. Ambulances from the Red Crescent made their way through Homs, seeking to extract both civilians and the journalists.

Syria's conflict remains far from over. After diplomats and politicians from numerous countries failed to agree any firm action at a conference in Tunisia on Friday, there is little solution in sight to the clashes between Assad's regime and the popular opposition to it.

As the killing went on Haneen, who had pulled Marie's body from the rubble, expressed growing despair. 'We cannot count the ones that die in the shelling and are buried under rubble. No one knows of them,' he said.

'We are all waiting for our turn to die. Every evening we tell each other: thank God for your safety. Another day has passed and we have not been killed.'

But sadly, not for Marie.

'REPORTS OF MY SURVIVAL MAY BE EXAGGERATED'

(Marie Colvin, 20 February 2012)

The poet Alan Jenkins was a friend of Marie's and wrote this poem as a tribute to her.

> How can you be lying there?
>   Immodestly, among the rubble
> When we want you to be here
>   In some other kind of trouble –
>
> Luffing up, in irons, perhaps,
>   Just downstream from the Dove,
> Lost in South London, without maps,
>   Or capsized in love.
>
> What's keeping you? A kind of dare?
>   Come back and tell us how you stayed
> One step ahead, how you gave fear
>   The slip, how you were not afraid –
>
> As we are. Look – here's my idea.
>   Come back – this time, for good.
> Leave your flak jacket and your gear
>   In that burnt-out neighbourhood,

And fly home, via Paris. You'll be met.
    I'll buy a bottle from the corner store,
Like old times. You can have a cigarette.
    Marie, get up off that bloodstained floor!

                    *   *   *

    Tonight you threw your thin brown arm
Around my shoulders, and you said
    (There was this unearthly calm)
'Can't you take in that I am dead?

    Learn to expect the unexpected turn
Of the tide, the unmarked reef,
    The rock that should be off the stern
On which we come to grief?

    The lies, the ignorance and hate –
The bigger picture? No safe mooring there,
    In Chechnya or Chiswick Eyot.
Those nights I drank my way out of despair,

    And filling ashtrays filed the copy
You would read – or not read – with
    A brackish taste and your first coffee
Contending on your tongue; while Billy Smith,

    My street cat rescued from Jerusalem,
Barged in, shouting, from his wars. . . .
    As many lives as his – and now I've used them.
I wish I'd made it back to yours.'

                  Alan Jenkins

Marie photographed by Patrick Bishop.
This was her favourite photograph of herself.

Marie, sailing off the coast of Turkey on the
boat of Richard Flaye, her boyfriend.
Photograph by Maryam d'Abo.